D0449494

Children With A Star

The Pais children just before deportation, Harlingen, 1942.

Children With A Star

Jewish Youth
in Nazi Europe

Debórah Dwork

Yale University Press
New Haven and London 1991

Set in Sabon roman and italic by SX Composing Limited, Essex, England, and printed and bound in the United States of America by Vail-Ballou Press, Binghamton, N.Y.

Library of Congress Cataloging-in-Publication Data

Dwork, Debórah.
   Children with a star: Jewish youth in Nazi Europe / Debórah Dwork.
   p. cm.
   Includes bibliographical references and index.
   ISBN 0-300-05054-2
   1. Holocaust, Jewish (1939–1945) 2. World War. 1939–1945 —
Children. 3. Jewish children. I. Title.
D804.3.D86 1991
940.53′ 18 — dc20   90-23908
             CIP

The paper in this book meets the guidelines for permanence and durability of the Committee on Production Guidelines for Book Longevity of the Council on Library Resources.

10 9 8 7 6 5 4 3 2

To my mother, Shirley, and her sister, Sara,
from whom I learned about love and responsibility.

Contents

List of Illustrations

Photographs, like other sources pertaining to Jewish child life in Nazi-occupied Europe, survived miraculously and by accident. The most common repository was family members who had left Europe and were sent photographs by those who had remained. Within Nazi Europe, the circumstances for preservation were even more fortuitous. For example, Irene Butter-Hasenberg's family photographs were saved by her neighbors who, as they were photographers, felt that it was safe to keep them. Some organizations which hid children took photographs of the young people, either for identification purposes after the war or to send them to their parents in hiding elsewhere. Photographs taken by Jews in the ghettos of eastern Europe were smuggled out and hidden, in the hope of recovery later. Other photographs were taken by Germans, for propaganda purposes or by individual soldiers as mementos of sorts. Every picture has its own story.

The author would like to thank the following individuals and institutions for their generosity in supplying photographs:

Sarah Aletrino, 15; Amsterdam, Joods Historisch Museum, frontispiece, 8, 9 (Collection Ida Groenewegen), 11 (Collection Ida Groenewegen); Amsterdam, Netherlands State Institute for War Documentation, 5, 17, 18, 20, 21, 36; Berlin, Bildarchiv Preussischer Kulturbesitz, 24, 29, 32, 33, 39; Irene Butter-Hasenberg, 6, 19; Renée Fritz-Schwalb, 13; Hilma Geffen-Ludomer, 2; Sara Grossman-Weil, 1, 25, 34; Jerusalem, Yad Veshem, 21, 31, 35, 37; Jacqueline Kami-Cohen, 3, 12; Paris, Mémoires Juives – Patrimoine photographique: collection Henri Tziboulsky, 16; Prague, State Jewish Museum, 22.

Permissions

Acknowledgement is made to their publishers for permission to reprint extracts from the following books: Primo Levi, *Moments of Reprieve* (New York: Summit Books, 1986); Joseph Weill, *Contribution a l'histoire des camps d'internement dans l'Anti-France*, (Paris: Éditions du Centre, 1946); Saul Friedländer, *Kurt Gerstein: The Ambiguity of Good* (New York: Knopf, 1969).

Acknowledgements

One of the greatest pleasures of finishing a book is that it gives the author an opportunity to thank those who have helped to make the project a product. This is especially true in my case. I simply could not have garnered the information, collected the photographs, or even afforded the costs of this type of research without the assistance and aid of others.

This book is about the life experience of Jewish children in Nazi Europe. Perhaps it is well to remember that a mere 11 percent of European Jewish children alive in 1939 survived the war; one-and-a-half million were killed. The only way I could reconstruct the lives of those hundreds of thousands of children was through those who had lived. My first and greatest debt is to the hundreds of now-adult women and men who generously and with a full heart recounted their own personal histories and gave me complete access to whatever artifacts they had from that time: letters, diaries, photographs, drawings, ration coupons, identity cards. For the vast majority, this was the first time they had articulated their experiences in full. It required a lot of time, it took great care, and it was very painful. It was an enormous undertaking, and I am grateful to them for having accepted the burden, or as many of them called it, the "obligation and responsibility." To them I say with Rilke: "Golden thread, you are part of the weaving now."

The story of how I came to have contact with child survivors throughout Europe and the United States is a tale unto itself, but the single most important element was the role played by individuals and families in every city in which I worked. They took on the project with enthusiasm, and because they wished to see its successful conclusion, offered me hospitality, help finding accommodation, and aid with the practical problems of everyday life in a foreign location. Most important, these families provided me with the opportunity to meet those about whom I wished to learn. My acknowledgements to them are in alphabetical order by city.

I am delighted to thank Saskia Mazor-van Pelt and Eitan Mazor in Amsterdam for their unstinting hospitality and aid, and Max Arian and Judith Belinfante for their generous help with introductions and sources. Jacqueline Kami-Cohen in Baltimore actively supported this work, and I am grateful to her. I am deeply obliged to Mária Ember for her help in Budapest, which extended in every direction and included her services as a translator from Hungarian into English and from English into Hungarian. I am happily indebted to Esther Fine, a life-long resident of Cardiff, who welcomed me into her home and her community, and provided all the support I needed to get on with the project. Sylvia and Henry Starkman were of great help to me in Detroit. I turned out to be the guest who came to dinner in their home: I came one evening and did not leave for days. I thank Awraham Soetendorp in the Hague for his moral and practical support. I am deeply beholden to Chantal and Isabelle Brotherton-Ratcliffe in London, who took me on as their flatmate month after month, summer after summer, and to their parents, who made this possible. The entire Tolia Barsky-Odette Bérujeau family was involved with my research in Paris, and I thank them all – parents, grandparents, and children – for their energy and cheer. It is a special satisfaction to thank Susan Alice Fischer for her help in Rome. Through her I met the Fiorentino family, and to them also I am deeply obliged. They unreservedly committed themselves to this study. By the time of my research trip to Europe in 1989 I had a child of my own, and my gratitude to the Katz-Badian family in Vienna is happily colored by my appreciation for their recognition of, and help with, the difficulties of working and caring for a ten-month-old baby. My daughter is a member of their family, and I am the beneficiary. It would have been beyond the budget of any grant agency to cover the costs of the help that was given so generously and willingly by these friends. More important, I hope it is obvious that without their aid and support the work simply could not have been accomplished. Many of them had never met me before; they acted as they did because they wished to see the idea actualized. It was time for a history of Jewish child life in Nazi Europe to be written.

There are many other people to whom I am indebted. Tom Brown, Jeff Harris, Nina and Gary Wand, and Judith Wasserheit read the first chapters I wrote and encouraged me with relevant criticism and praise.

Susan Weingast, Leo Katz, and my working partner Robert Jan van Pelt persevered, and read each chapter hot off the printer.

In the professional life of every academic there are those who, by example, teach younger people very important aspects of scholarship. In this regard I am grateful to William F. Bynum (University College, London), Ron Walters (Johns Hopkins University), and Jay Winter (Cambridge University), whom I met through a professorial relationship. It is also my pleasure to thank my dearly loved colleague at the University of Michigan, Irene Butter, whom I met when I myself was an assistant professor. And it is especially gratifying to thank my father, Bernard Dwork, who all his life has shown by example the joys of deep engagement with research.

I have been particularly fortunate to have had the stimulation and support of colleagues at the three institutions at which I worked during the course of this project. With them I discussed my work in detail, and they, in complementary fields, provided perspectives and insights which were as helpful as they were exciting. I am delighted to acknowledge my obligations to Michael Geyer (with whom I began these discussions when we were both at the University of Michigan), Alexander Danchev, Elinor Murray Despalatovic, and Adrian M.S. Piper (fellow scholars at the Woodrow Wilson International Center for Scholars), and Paula Hyman and Rachel Wizner (whom I had the good fortune to meet on my arrival at Yale University).

A study such as *Children With A Star* requires a great deal of support services, and I am beholden to my research assistants for the help they provided. I am delighted to thank my mother, Shirley Dwork, for the work she did for me, particularly at the Centre de Documentation Juive Contemporaine in Paris. Her efforts made my own stay much more productive. It is a pleasure to thank my research assistants at the Woodrow Wilson Center, U. Gwyn Williams, Patrick Given, and Tracy Orcutt, and to my research assistant at Yale, Angelo Trujillo. It is also a great satisfaction to me to have the opportunity to thank those who transcribed the tapes of the recorded oral histories. Ann Cashion-Sharpe has been (and is still) responsible for the English-language tapes from the first to the ongoing current cassette; Gabriella Sommers transcribed the Italian tapes, Luc Chauvin and Elizabeth Shelton the French tapes, and Christel van der Eynden the Dutch tapes.

This study was very costly. I am deeply indebted to the Wellcome Trust (London), the American Philosophical Society, the American Council of Learned Societies, and the Woodrow Wilson Center for their generous support which helped to defray the cost of travel, tape transcription, research assistance, and salary support. Ken Warner dedicated secretarial services and special machinery for my use at the University of Michigan, and Stephen Waxman ensured that I had research funds to carry on this study at Yale University.

I am very appreciative of the many expert librarians and archivists who saved me much time by identifying useful sources. I am particularly obliged to the archivists in the Centre de Documentation Juive Contemporaine in Paris, Monsieur Jacobsen, Madame Mimoun, and Madame Halperyn, who took an interest in this project and helped in ways that went far beyond the archive walls.

I have been extraordinarily well treated by Yale University Press. I had the good fortune to see and speak with my editor, Robert Baldock, over a period of six years. With each year he became more supportive and more challenging. In addition to all the adjectives one usually uses for an editor (prescient, perspicacious, patient), I should like to add one: respectful. He was respectful of the children, respectful of my conceptual approach, and respectful of the manuscript; and I am grateful. I also thank Ann Geneva, the publicist in the London office of Yale University Press. Doing more in first gear than the rest of us do in fifth, Ann never left any doubt about her enthusiasm for this book. And I have been delighted with the time and attention the people of Yale University Press in New Haven have devoted to the production of *Children With A Star*.

Finally, I wish to express my loving thanks to Ann Smith, who was my daughter's "work Mom" from the time she was three months old, my working partner, Robert Jan van Pelt, who read every word I wrote the day it was produced on paper, to my husband, Ken Marek, who appreciated how compelling and absorbing I found this project, and to my daughters, Miriam and Hannah, who, *in utero* and out, kept me company every day.

New Haven
October 1990

Introduction

Search and Research

This book is about children. It is a history of those young people whose destiny began with their birth as Jews, whose fate was marked by their ill-luck to have been Europeans during the Nazi years, and, for the small number who survived, whose lot remained troubled after the war ended. Their history is their own personal story, but it is also the core of the Judeocide, the quintessence of the most profound catastrophe western civilization permitted and endured. That the oppression, persecution, and murder of children is the heart of this evil is stunningly symbolized in the Yad Vashem Memorial in Jerusalem. Yad Vashem is a complex consisting of an archive, a museum, and a number of memorials.[1] As the visitor leaves the museum and enters the memorial terrace, one final object is to be seen. It is the only shard from the past displayed in the exit hall, a single iconographical artifact which represents the horror and the loss. It is a child's high-topped shoe. And so this history of Jewish children in Nazi-occupied Europe can be seen as a kind of Cinderella story. We are in search of the children who fit that, and all the other lost, abandoned, and stolen shoes and boots.

Like the prince in the story, I too traveled from community to community in search of those who lost their shoes when time ran out. This book is a history of the lives of the children I found either in person or through diaries, letters, or archival records. It is about the unique complexity of their world. This chapter, however, is about my journey. It addresses the theoretical and methodological dilemmas of writing the history of Jewish youth in Nazi Europe. In the title and subtitle – *Children With A Star: Jewish Youth in Nazi Europe* – we face the first problems: sleights of pen and factual errors. We speak of "children with a star," but the correct translation of *mogen David* (from which the term comes) is shield of David, not star of David. The sign itself was transmuted by the Nazis and their allies from a symbol of honor to a badge of derision. And the object to which the emblem was attached was no longer a shield of armor to defend and protect, but an insignia of cloth which exposed and jeopardized. This was a cynical transformation; it is just one of the ways in which the Nazis severely damaged western culture through the subversion of its language and, as in this case, its symbols.[2] "Children With A Star" is a see-through mirror which both reflects the cynicism of the Nazis and simultaneously allows us to penetrate that cynicism to see the children as human beings. The cynical transformation of the past thus acquires a dimension of irony in the present.[3] The Nazis saw these children as objects to be purged from the community; in this book, we shall encounter them as subjects – as special children with whom we have community.

The phrase "Nazi Europe" is a linguistic shorthand. It denotes the countries of Europe which were brought under the whip of Nazism by invasion and occupation. While many countries suffered that fate (in chronological order: Austria, Bohemia and Moravia, Poland, Denmark, Norway, the Netherlands, Belgium, France, Yugoslavia, Greece, and the western portion of the Soviet Union), Berlin-inspired or dictated policies were adopted by Germany's European Axis allies (Rumania, Hungary, Italy, Slovakia, and Bulgaria) without or prior to invasion.[4] In Italy and Hungary the situation of course became infinitely more dangerous after German occupation; nevertheless it is important to remember that those countries passed antisemitic legislation which restricted and endangered Jewish life long before the Germans crossed their borders.

The second semantic trick is the phrase "Jewish youth." To adopt this construction is to accept Nazi definitions and terminology. It is nothing new, but well worth repeating, that the application of the various racial (and racist) laws passed or imposed throughout Europe identified many people as Jews who did not think of themselves as such. And is it appropriate to use the term to describe, for example, very young children who were hidden? They did not live with Jewish parents, they did not lead a Jewish life, they were ignorant of Jewish culture, history, religion, and tradition, and as they grew up in their adoptive surroundings they certainly did not recognize themselves as Jews. For the purposes of this book the term will be used self-consciously; here "Jewish youth" will mean those children whom the Nazis and their allies considered to be Jews. How, or what, they considered themselves was totally irrelevant. What is germane is that they were fatally at risk, and this book is about the lives of those whose very existence was threatened by the Nazi racist policy and program as it applied to Jews.

Finally, there is one factual error in the title. This book is called *Children With A Star*, yet a large percentage of Jewish children never wore a star at all. Young people who went into hiding did not wear the emblem, and children under the age of six or ten or twelve years (depending on the location) were not required to wear stars. Therefore, one may ask, why use this title at all? The answer is very simple: it is an icon. It is a symbolic image which embodies more than mere description; it transcends historical accuracy for the sake of historic truth.

The methodological difficulties of this research made the search for the children a veritable obstacle course. For a number of reasons documentation on child life is fragmentary for this period. To put it one way: as the children were not old enough to wear stars, they were not old enough to be explicit objects of policy, and therefore they never became part of recorded history. That is to say, in the period prior to the implementation of the "Final Solution" (i.e., until late 1941–early 1942) young people were not required to wear stars because the bureaucrats who administered the "Final Solution" to the Jewish "problem" did not perceive the children as persons or a "problem" in their own right. The Nazi edicts of this period were concerned with identification, segregation, and concentration of the Jews, and in these procedures children were appendages to their parents, especially their mothers. Thus the Nazi decrees of this period give us very little information about the special dimensions of child life.

After the Germans began to annihilate the Jews *en masse*, bureaucratic fastidiousness gave way to considerations of operational efficiency; if for the functionaries the children were irrelevant, for the butchers they were simply an irritant. Because young children were not so easily controlled as adults (they had difficulty understanding orders, they cried, they objected to the interruption of their normal routine), they were seen as an impediment to the efficiency of the murder system which depended on the maintenance of calm and the mirage of normality. Annette Monod was a Red Cross social worker who struggled heroically to ease the hardships children suffered at the French internment camp of Pithiviers. Her memories of the departure of a convoy of little children in September 1942 illustrate those – to the Nazis and their allies – irksome irritations intrinsic to dealing with very young people. It was early in the morning.

The kids were half asleep, and it was quite a job to get them down from their dormitories. Most of them sat on the ground, each with his little bundle next to him. . . . The gendarmes tried to get through the roll call, but it was impossible. The children did not respond to the names. Surnames like Rosenthal, Biegelmann, Radekski, etc., meant nothing to them. They didn't understand what was expected of them, and some even wandered off from the group. One tiny boy walked up to a gendarme and started to play with the whistle hanging from the man's belt; a little girl saw some flowers growing on a slope and went off to pick them and make a bouquet. The gendarmes did not know what to do. Finally they were ordered to take the children to the railway station nearby and not bother with the roll call, as long as the required number of children were put on the train.

We were standing only two hundred yards from the station, but that is a long way for small children hampered by clumsy bundles. . . . Once we were in the station, the children were loaded onto the trains in a sudden burst of speed. . . . It was at this point that the children felt frightened. They didn't want to go and started to cry. They would call to the social workers standing on the platform for help, and would sometimes even appeal to the soldiers. Jacquot, a little five-year-old of whom I was particularly fond, started shouting for me: "I want to get down, I want to stay with Mademoiselle. . . ." The door of the car was shut and bolted, but Jacquot pushed his hand through a gap between two planks and continued to call for me, moving his fingers. [An] adjutant . . . hit him on the hand.[5]

To obviate such hindrances, and to facilitate and expedite their factory line of death, the Nazis dispensed with the potential slave labor of the mothers and kept them with their children to maintain discipline and quiet. At this point the children were no longer mere appendages to their parents, they became their death sentence. As the Warsaw ghetto survivor Alexander Donat explained in his book, *The Holocaust Kingdom*, "[my wife] Lena met her brothers, Adek and Marek; their wives; and a schoolmate, Samek, with his wife and two-year-old daughter, Miriam. They were all young and healthy, . . . and their chances for survival would have been good – except for the presence of the child."[6] Later, Donat described what happened to Miriam and her parents. It was Monday, 7 September 1942, the second day of the penultimate great selection prior to the liquidation of the Warsaw ghetto.

When it came [their] turn . . . to march past the SS officer, Lena's brother Adek and his wife were in one row. With them was Samek and his wife, and they had given their two-year-old Miriam a sedative and put her in a knapsack slung over Samek's shoulder. The column advanced slowly while up ahead the SS officer grandly dispensed life and death, *left* and *right*, *links und rechts*. In the tense silence the wails of a baby suddenly rose. The SS officer froze and a thousand men and women held their breaths. A Ukrainian guard ran out, plunged his bayonet several times into the knapsack from which the criminal sounds had come. In seconds the knapsack was a blood-soaked rag. *"Du dreckiger Schweinehunde!"* the SS officer shouted indignantly, bringing his riding crop down on the ashen face of the father who had dared to try smuggling his child past. Mercifully the Ukrainian's bullet put an end to the father's ordeal then and there. Thereafter it became routine for guards to probe every bundle and knapsack with their bayonets.

Adek, Samek, and their wives were only three ranks away from the SS man at that point. All the blood drained from Samek's face, but his wife was stronger at that moment – or was it weaker? – or did she merely have presence of mind? "Take off the knapsack!" she hissed. As if in a trance, he did so and without losing his place in the ranks, he edged over to the end of the row of marchers and carefully deposited the knapsack on the curb. It took no more than a fraction of a minute.[7]

These selections for life and death were the welcoming ceremony at the major concentration camps. Women alone had a chance for a temporary stay of execution, but mothers and their children were sent to death immediately.[8] Sara Grossman-Weil, who was a young woman of twenty-five at the time (1944), recalled with overwhelming sorrow:

Our destination was Auschwitz. . . . We came out of the wagon with our bundles and were pushed to a side. Suddenly people were forming columns. We were wondering where are we, we did not know. But as the people who were working there were forming columns, we were standing waiting. I was with my mother-in-law and I loved her, and my sister-in-law Esther whom I do love, [Esther's young daughter, Mirka], and Regina, her adolescent daughter whom she had adopted in the ghetto. And the men were separated from us. . . . Men were put in a separate column and so were the women; and as they spilled the population out of the cattle cars, we were all formed in a line. I was standing there not knowing what's going on, overwhelmed with the amount of people around us, not believing that they threw us all out from these wagons in the manner they did. How they pushed and shoved and screamed. And these SS men with the dogs in front of us. I lost sight of what was going on. It's crazy. And I was standing with

1   Sara Grossman-Weil aged 18: Gymnasium photograph, 1937.

my mother-in-law and my sister-in-law with her little girl, when
someone approached us, and said, "Give the child to the grandmother." And my sister-in-law gave her child to my mother-in-law.
They went to the left, we went to the right. . . . My mother-in-law
took the little one and went to the left. Regina, Esther, and I went to
the right. To the left were all the people who were led into the gas
chambers, crematorium, however you call it. We again were placed in
columns of five.[9]

As far as the Nazis were concerned, children – and their mothers – were
simply fodder for the murder mills. They had absolutely no interest in
maintaining their lives for an extra moment. Their death was a matter of
automatic procedure. Clearly, then, there would be little Nazi archive
material directly relevant to child life.

On the other hand, those who attempted to protect children from the Nazi and other Fascist regimes by hiding them or helping them escape also had reasons for maintaining few records of the children's lives. First, they tried to obliterate their civic and religious registration forms to make them administratively invisible. Then too, clandestine activities were themselves poorly documented, as those involved in underground work did not keep records. It was too dangerous. Discovery by the Germans of such materials would have endangered the network and those involved in it, gentile and Jew alike. In an interview with three members of a Dutch underground group (the NV, or Naamloze Vennootschap) which managed to save 250 children, Ida Groenewegen van Wyck-Roose (IG), Cor Grootendorst (CG), and Truus Grootendorst-Vermeer (TV) remarked on the urgent need for such an organizational silence, but also on the difficulties it caused:

CG: We never kept statistics.
IG: We had no administration!
CG: At one stage we got so many children, and we had to work on so much of our memory (where which child was), because if you have . . . two hundred children – Let's say we were about ten people, that means twenty-five people [children] on average to look after. In fact it was more, because some of them in fact didn't visit the children in the end, but they went out for textiles [clothes] and shoes and things like that. You know, you got confused and perhaps didn't keep track of them. I remember we discussed, shouldn't we have some kind of card system with names and ages and addresses on them, just to be able to trace them?
TV: But we didn't. . . . Dangerous, dangerous thing to do.
CG: For some children, we didn't know any names, particularly the very young ones. Sometimes it happened that we were just given a child from the crèche [where children were taken in Amsterdam prior to deportation]: "Look, take it," and we didn't know what the child's name was or when it was born.[10]

It is one of the happier ironies of the war period that organizations such as the NV, which were dedicated to preserving and protecting Jewish child life, by their very nature were unable to maintain records about those children and their daily activities. Gratitude for the survival of the youths leaves no room for disappointment that there are no contemporary accounts of them.

A final reason for the lack of documentation on Jewish child life during the Nazi years is that, as with all histories of childhood, it is very difficult to recover the authentic young voice. Very young children do not have the requisite skills and therefore are unable to leave written records like diaries, letters, or journals. Older youths who are literate can (and did) do so, but under the shadow of Nazism such an undertaking was frequently physically impossible and, when feasible, an extremely hazardous business. To write requires instruments and paraphernalia, time, energy, and opportunity. Except in the "model ghetto camp" of Theresienstadt (Terezín), youths in camps rarely had access to such luxuries. In his book *Moments of Reprieve*, Primo Levi described one of his attempts to write to his family in Italy while he was in the slave labor camp of Buna-Monowitz of the Auschwitz complex. It should be noted that Levi was twenty-five years old at the time; already a young man and no longer a youth. People younger than he would have had fewer opportunities and greater difficulties.

I was alone in the cellar, anxious to carry through an important operation. I had gotten hold of a sheet of paper and a pencil stub, and for many days I had been waiting for an opportunity to write the draft of a letter (in Italian, of course) which I meant to entrust to an Italian "free" laborer so he could copy it, sign it as if it were his, and send it to my family in Italy. In fact we were strictly forbidden to write, but I was sure that if I could think about it for a moment, I would find a way to devise a message that would be sufficiently clear to the recipients but at the same time innocent enough not to attract the censor's attention. I could not risk being seen by anyone because the fact of writing alone was intrinsically suspect (for what reason and to whom should one of us be writing?), and the Camp and the workyard teemed with informers. After not quite an hour . . . I felt calm enough to begin writing the letter. . . .

I noticed [the Kapo, Eddy] only when he was already watching me. Instinctively – or, rather, stupidly – I opened my fingers. The pencil fell, but the sheet of paper descended slowly to the ground, swaying like a dead leaf. Eddy lunged to pick it up, then slammed me to the ground with a violent slap. . . . A slap inflicted in the Camp had a very different significance from what it might have here among us in today's here and now. . . . In that context it meant roughly, "Watch out, you've really made a big mistake this time, you're endangering your life, maybe without realizing it, and you're endangering mine as well." . . .

If he were to denounce me to the Political Section, I knew it was the gallows for me, but before the gallows an interrogation – and what an interrogation! – to find out who my accomplice was, and perhaps also

to obtain from me the address of the recipient in Italy. . . .
He made a speech to me that I find difficult to repeat. . . . That I
was crazy – there was no other explanation. Only a madman would
think of gambling in such a way with his life, that of the Italian
accomplice whom I certainly had, my relatives in Italy, and also his
career as Kapo. . . . But then Italians are all notoriously crazy, good
only for singing and getting into trouble.[11]

Strangely enough, children in hiding had difficulties similar in kind if
not at all in degree. Because the diary of Anne Frank is so well known,
there is a popular misconception that for young people like Anne who
were hidden away from the world in attics and cellars, keeping a diary
would have been a normal activity, dependent more on temperament
than circumstance. For many children, however, writing materials were
unobtainable, and sometimes they too were engaged in tasks which
afforded neither the leisure nor the vigor for other pursuits. But even if it
had been possible, creating written or pictorial accounts was extraordinarily dangerous – foolhardy in fact. In a raid, all such physical documentation could be found and, if discovered, used as evidence which
would lead to death or destruction. Levi's point that he took a desperately great risk, not only with his own life but with that of his friends,
family, and protectors (or accomplices), was expressed by child survivors who were in hiding during the war and who took similar chances.
Berthe Jeanne (Bertje) Bloch-van Rhijn, a Dutch girl who, like Anne
Frank, was in hiding with her entire family (but was not betrayed and
had the good fortune to survive) kept a diary throughout the Nazi occupation period. Her family had been offered refuge by an elderly lady
who lived alone in a large house with a garden, and they had more freedom of movement that did a family like the Franks who were in hiding
in an attic in Amsterdam. Bertje van Rhijn's parents recognized the
potential danger that their daughter's diary posed, and they buried it in
the garden for safekeeping. From time to time it was taken out, van
Rhijn wrote her entries, and then it was returned to its underground
home.[12] If it had been found, not only would they have been uncovered
as Jews but, from innocent remarks or unconscious clues, the network of
friends who had helped them inevitably would have been jeopardized.
The diary survives to this day, weather-beaten and water stained, but
legible.

Given this evident dearth of documents, how can the historian reconstruct and analyze the lives and experiences of Jewish youth in Nazi-
occupied Europe? Strange as it may seem, this want of contemporary
material is more apparent than real. While there is little documentation

in the archives on the organization of underground child rescue groups, few diaries and letters written by children, or German administrative files relevant to child life, much pertinent material does exist. It is there because, inevitably, people leave traces of their activities behind. Despite all the precautions taken by the oppressors, resisters, and victims to hide their activities (and each, of course, for his own reasons), they did not function in a vacuum. The Germans, for example, allowed social workers like Annette Monod to work in French camps, and so she became a witness. Resistance workers were, by the very nature of their activity, unable to maintain total silence or perfect secrecy. And the children actually existed; the act of living meant they would leave behind a few shards of childhood. It is this material which needs to be found, and it is by no means a simple or straightforward process. How, then, does one go about it? Where does one look?

Archive research in countries like France and Italy that had relief and aid organizations which managed to maintain a visible presence or above-ground existence (like the Oeuvre de Secours aux Enfants, or OSE, for instance) yields a wealth of social workers' descriptions of child life both in the internment camps and in special homes which were established for children who were orphaned because their parents had been deported. Then too, the women directors of these children's homes submitted accounts of the activities and educational programs run in their institutions with accompanying budgets to their respective central offices. This is, of course, in stark contrast to the situation in countries like the Netherlands or Poland where those involved in saving child life were underground workers, and all such activities were obscured in silence and secrecy. Even in those circumstances, however, utter reticence, perfect concealment, and absolute invisibility were impossible to achieve. It is in the nature of human activity to leave an imprint or mark. Thus, an organization like the NV, which consciously considered and decided not to keep some minimal documentation such as a register of the children in its care, allowed the children to write letters to family members, especially parents, in hiding elsewhere. This correspondence was read and censored by a member of the group, and hand-delivered through a chain of contacts. A number of those letters were saved by the recipients, and are part of ordinary family collections of memories and picture postcards today; they are considered by their owners to be of great sentimental value, but hardly worth offering to a library or archive.

The NV also photographed some of the children. As Cor Grootendorst explained, "That was very often done to satisfy the parents who were sometimes hiding in another place. They were not allowed to know where the children were because that would mean that they might try to visit them. . . . But we sometimes sent photographs to the parents to see that the child was in good health and happy."[13] This procedure was dangerous enough, but even more odd was the fact that the negatives were not destroyed and that group photos showing six to a dozen children hiking or singing were taken. Forty years after the war, when asked about the organization, one of the participants remembered that the photographs and negatives existed, and they were recovered. It would not be accurate to say that they had been forgotten, they simply were not important after the war – until someone asked.

Another source of information about child life is the records of refugee organizations (such as the Society of Friends, the Inter-Aid Committee, the Save the Children Fund, and the Movement for the Care of Children from Germany) which were based in neutral countries. Refugee workers in occupied Europe sent personal statements as well as official reports to their societies' headquarters which reveal much about the lives of those desperate to emigrate. A number of those children who did manage to escape were cared for, to varying degrees, by refugee children's aid societies in their new host countries. These associations' accounts and descriptions of the newly arrived youths tell as much about their past as their then current state. In a few of the host countries official government bodies became involved in the care of such children; thus, in the Ministry of Health records at the Public Record Office (London) there are reports on the welfare of Jewish German and Austrian boys in child refugee camps in England.

Within occupied Europe, adult chroniclers who undertook to write historical journals in order to record the tragic madness of their times included commentaries on and depictions of child life. By the very nature of their task these witnesses of the horror of the Nazi years were people immersed in the situation; they lived amongst Jews and not in hiding. The most extraordinary of these contemporary analytical journals are *The Chronicle of the Łódź Ghetto* and Emmanuel Ringelblum's *Notes from the Warsaw Ghetto*. The *Chronicle* was written surreptitiously by the Department of Archives, an official body in the Łódź ghetto. The Department of Archives was one of the five sections of the Department of Population Records established by the Elder of the Jews of Łódź, Mordechai Chaim Rumkowski. It was the task of the Department of Archives to preserve materials from the pre-war Łódź Jewish community, documents generated by the ghetto administration, and, as time went on, information for a history of the ghetto. As the department was part of the ghetto bureaucracy, it had access to and its activities were recognized by the other ghetto administrative offices; the German Ghetto Administration too was aware of its existence. Shortly after the archives were founded, the ten to fifteen department members began to compile the *Chronicle*. This was a clandestine activity although it was not formally underground. The Germans were unaware of its existence, and the authors sought to preserve that ignorance. Nevertheless, the *Chronicle* was written in a ghetto administration office, and its guarded style anticipates the possibility of German scrutiny, or that of the rest of the ghetto bureaucracy.[14]

References to and clues about child life are interspersed in the nearly daily *Chronicle* entries. At times such information was merely incidental to another subject. In a report of Sunday, 26 January 1941 on "The Dairy Product Situation," for example, the authors remarked that it was "worth noting that until now only children and sick people (with medical coupons) had been able to avail themselves of the butter allocation." Or again, on 16–22 June 1941, commenting on "Milk for the Sick" they explained that "until now only children up to the age of three, infants, and women lying-in have been receiving milk. Now the sale of milk for the sick, suspended since the beginning of the year, has been restored. . . . Milk will be sold to the sick after the children's needs have been satisfied."[15] In other entries, aspects of child life were themselves the central focus. Thus, the first of a new genre of report called "Sketches of Ghetto Life" which began on Saturday, 24 July 1943 and ran until almost the last entry of the *Chronicle* was entitled "The Ghetto Children's Toys."

The so-called Belgium cigarettes have been a disappointment to smokers in the ghetto, even to those who have smoked poor-quality tobacco all their lives. The countless packs with their gaudy colors and equally gaudy names could not alter the devastating judgment that has been passed on the quality of the cigarettes. . . . Since every object in the ghetto, no matter how worthless, acquires some value, even those boxes have come to be cherished. The smoker does not throw them out. He saves them, and makes sure that they do not go to waste. Children's eyes beg for those boxes, children's hands reach out for them.

Outside the ghetto, children receive beautiful and appropriate playthings as presents. . . . Our children collect empty cigarette boxes. They remove the colorful tops and stack them in a pile, until they have a whole deck of cards. Playing cards.

And they play. They count the cards and deal them out. They arrange them by color and name. Green, orange, yellow, brown, even black. They play games that they invent for themselves, they devise systems, they let their imaginations take over.[16]

Like *The Chronicle of the Łódź Ghetto*, Emmanuel Ringelblum's *Notes from the Warsaw Ghetto* also were culled from ghetto archive material. Ringelblum's entire operation, however, was an underground activity. A historian who, before the war, had written on various aspects of the history of the Jews in Poland, Ringelblum was particularly well suited to the task he set himself soon after the German invasion of Poland in September 1939: to record the current history of Polish Jewry. This intellectual undertaking was inspired by a sense of mission to inform the world about the situation of the Jews, and he managed to transmit documents through the Polish Resistance to the Polish Government in Exile in London. On Friday, 26 June 1942 he learned of his success. It "has been a great day for O.S." (Oneg Shabbat, or Joy of Sabbath, the code name for his archive organization), he wrote. "This morning the English radio broadcast about the fate of Polish Jewry. They told about everything we know so well: Slonim and Vilna, Lemberg and Chelmno, and so forth," he explained. "The O.S. group has fulfilled a great historical mission. It has alarmed the world to our fate. . . . I do not know who of our group will survive. . . . But one thing is clear to all of us. Our toils and tribulations, our devotion and constant terror have not been in vain."[17] It was Europe's tragic misfortune that neither the information nor its dissemination by radio broadcast stopped the slaughter of the Jews. Nevertheless, Ringelblum was correct; he and his group had fulfilled a great historical mission.

Within two months of the invasion Ringelblum began to take daily notes on what the Germans were doing to the Jews in Poland. Quickly realizing that the task was too great for one person, he started to recruit a team of people to report on different dimensions of the situation. By May 1940 the OS was in operation. With time, many people joined, and the archive grew rapidly. It remained a strictly underground activity, and many precautions were taken to protect the archives from the Gestapo. In contrast to the situation in Łódź, no one connected in any way with the Jewish Council was invited to participate; the OS felt the risk of betrayal was too great. Similarly, journalists were not included as they were considered to be professionally indiscreet, even if they personally were thought to be honorable. And all informants were investigated prior to being interviewed for the archives.

Concurrently with the organization and oversight of the OS, Ringelblum also wrote his own periodic summary accounts of the collected information. These are his *Notes from the Warsaw Ghetto*. As in the *Chronicle*, splinters of child life are intersown throughout the *Notes*.

The plight of children reduced to a state of beggary was of particular concern to Ringelblum, and he frequently lamented their condition. In some sense, these children seem to have epitomized the collective tragedy of the Jewish people for him; they represented a fatally impoverished future which would neither flourish nor flower, but would die of starvation, exposure, and neglect. "The abandonment of children in offices of institutions and Jewish police headquarters has become a mass phenomenon. The establishment of a home for 100 beggar children has not helped. Children are continuing to beg no less than before," Ringelblum observed on 18 March 1941.[18] Just five months later his description of the children's poverty clearly delineated their, and the community's, despair and desperation:

A special class of beggars consists of those who beg after nine o'clock at night. . . . They walk out right into the middle of the street, begging for bread. Most of them are children. In the surrounding silence of night, the cries of the beggar children are terribly insistent, and, however hard your heart, eventually you have to throw a piece of bread down to them – or else leave the house. These beggars are completely unconcerned about curfews, and you can hear their voices late at night, at eleven and even at twelve. They are afraid of nothing and of no one. . . . It's a common thing for beggar children like these to die on the sidewalk at night. . . . In front of 24 Muranowska Street . . . a six-year-old beggar boy lay gasping all night, too weak to roll over to the piece of bread that had been thrown down to him from the balcony.[19]

That the children represented, or symbolized, the whole community to Ringelblum became increasingly clear as the months passed. "Two beggar children sat in the street holding up a sign that read S.O.S. One is forced to concede that this is the simplest and truest statement of our predicament – and our only slogan," he remarked ruefully in October 1941. The sight and sound of the children were both the background to and the very substance of the horrendous calamity of existence in the ghetto. "The most fearful sight is that of the freezing children," he wrote in anguish in mid-November. "Little children with bare feet, bare knees, and torn clothing, stand dumbly in the street weeping. Tonight . . . I heard a tot of three or four yammering. The child will probably be found frozen to death tomorrow morning, a few hours off. . . . Frozen children are becoming a general phenomenon. . . . Children's bodies and crying serve as a persistent background for the Ghetto."[20]

Both the *Notes* and the *Chronicle* strove to be (as far as was possible under the circumstances) impersonal, objective, systematic compilations based on extensive archive materials and investigations conducted by numerous people. The fact that the *Notes* were written by one person and the *Chronicle* by a team is essentially irrelevant; the authors are important only in that they were competent to do their jobs. Both of these daily recorded accounts are histories of their respective ghettos; they tell the anguished story of an entire city of Jews, rather than the individual, personal tales of their authors.

Emmanuel Ringelblum and the OS, and the members of the Łódź Ghetto Department of Archives, were by no means the only people to have felt the urgent need to keep a historical record for future generations. Individuals unconnected with any larger archive project also sought to chronicle the contemporary communal history of the Jewish people. The events of the time were so momentous, so calamitous, and so bizarre that, despite the dangers they risked, many people sought the comfort of writing as a means of clarification, validation, and actualization. Perhaps in writing, in the process of transmitting the current situation to paper, transcribing the occurrences and atmosphere of the time into words, they would come to understand, grasp, and make real for themselves what they encountered and experienced each day. In any case, when life was so tenuous and fragile, and had so little political or economic worth, keeping a journal was a means of leaving a mark or legacy for the future. As the Warsaw educator Chaim Kaplan, the author of one such diary explained (5 September 1939), "I have made a rule for myself in these historic times not to let a single day go by without making an entry in my diary." It was not an easy task. September 9: "In my psychological state it is hard to hold a pen in my hand, and my pen is not the one to describe what befell us." Just five days later Kaplan described his dilemma in greater detail. "It is difficult to write, but I consider it an obligation and am determined to fulfill it with my last ounce of energy. I will write a scroll of agony in order to remember the past in the future." It was his unshakable faith in a collective if not personal future which sustained Kaplan in his efforts. "In our scroll of agony," he declared on 26 October, "not one small detail can be omitted. Even though we are now undergoing terrible tribulations and the sun has grown dark for us at noon, we have not lost our hope that the era of light will surely come. Our existence as a people will not be destroyed. Individuals will be destroyed, but the Jewish community will live on. Therefore, every entry is more precious than gold, so long as it is written down as it happens, without exaggerations and distortions." Three years later, on 4 August 1942, the last line he wrote was, "If my life ends – what will become of my diary?"[21]

Kaplan's journal falls into the first of two very broad genres of diary: the external, or relatively emotionally detached record of outside events, and the internal, or intensely personal, confessional diary. Both genres related the current catastrophic occurrences; the former understood those events as the collective history of the Jewish people, while the latter saw them through the mirror of the author's intimate life. Unfortunately, only a small percentage of the total number written survived the war. The vast majority were, ultimately, intentionally burned by their authors, accidentally destroyed in the general devastation of the Nazi years, or simply abandoned and lost in the cataclysmic frenzy of deportation (as Anne Frank's diary would have been had not Miep Gies [alias van Santen] chanced upon it). Of those which survive and were written by adults, it is journals of the external genre which are most illuminating for a history of Jewish youth as they included factual accounts of and analytical reflections on child life. Written by people with a range of pre-war experiences, these diaries were kept while they were inmates of ghettos or transit camps. There they had daily contact with what was happening in their immediate communities.

Chaim Kaplan, for example, was an educator in Warsaw before the war and he remained in the ghetto after the German occupation. In the west of Europe another diarist, Philip Mechanicus, was incarcerated in Westerbork, the main Dutch transit camp located in the province of Drente in the northeastern part of the country. In many ways these two men could not have been more different. Kaplan had received an extensive formal education and saw himself as a cultured central European. Both personally and professionally he lived within the Jewish community; he had married a Jewish woman, ran a Jewish school, and was very well informed about Jewish political affairs. His diary was written in Hebrew, and his imagery, allusions, and expressions reflect the classical Jewish tradition of the Bible and Talmud in addition to the cultural heritage of Jewish folklore. Mechanicus was, by contrast, an autodidact who became a well-known journalist with a west European perspective on current affairs as well as his own identity. In his private and professional life Mechanicus was a member of secular Dutch society. He married (and divorced) a Christian woman and, as literary editor of the highly respected *Algemeen Handelsblad*, he participated in the mainstream cultural life of the Netherlands. Yet both Kaplan and Mechanicus felt the same sense of mission Emmanuel Ringelblum described, and they experienced a corresponding relief in the process – and self-imposed duty – of writing. As Mechanicus reflected from his bed in Westerbork (the only place he had to work) on 29 May 1943, "I feel as if I am an official reporter giving an account of a shipwreck. We are all together in a cyclone and feel the holed ship slowly sinking . . . The idea is gradually forming in my mind that I have not been brought here by my *persecutors*, but that I have gone on the journey *voluntarily* in order to do my work. I am busy all day long and am never bored for a single minute; sometimes the days actually seem too short. Duty is duty and work is ennobling. I write during a great part of the day. Sometimes I begin at half past five in the morning and sometimes I am still busy in the evening after bedtime, gathering my impressions or experiences for the day."[22]

Kaplan and Mechanicus commented frequently on the lives of the children in Warsaw and Westerbork. Their brief, concise reports trace how the bizarre became the ordinary in children's lives; what had been unconscionable and unimaginable were daily occurrences. The most normal events in childhood, like going to school and playing outdoors, became abnormal activities. On 3 December 1939, two months after the Germans conquered Poland and prior to the establishment of the Warsaw Ghetto, Kaplan remarked that "permission has been granted to reopen the elementary schools for Polish children, but not for Jewish children." That meant, he went on to explain, that "thousands of them are out on the street because there are no schools for them. They remain untutored, uneducated, and above all unfed." Less than a year later, by November 1940, a partial ghetto had been instituted and edicts imposed which forbade entry to parks and other public places. The physical restraints these orders imposed had become part of everyday life. "The sidewalks are crowded beyond belief," Kaplan announced. "Most of all, mothers take up positions on the sidewalks with their children's cradles, and they lean against the sides of buildings all along the street. The conquerors have closed the city parks to us. Anywhere that a tree has been planted, or a bench has been placed, Jewish children are forbidden to derive enjoyment. It pains the heart to see the sorrow of our little children." But, he went on to observe, "there is nothing which does not become second nature through use. The Jewish mothers have already gotten used to their bad fortune, and in order not to deprive their babies of the sunlight, they take their stand with their cradles wherever there is a square or a vacant lot, or a sidewalk covered with sunlight."[23]

In Mechanicus's writing, as in Kaplan's, the extraordinary pathos of the situation was expressed in the mundane. The horrific circumstances of the camp regime simply had been incorporated into the prosaic details of daily life: "A mother sat at supper with her small daughter. The daughter pulled a nasty face at the pudding. Mother: 'Listen to me. If you don't eat up your pudding you'll go on the transport without mummy.'" Like other observers, Mechanicus also noted the phenomenal human capacity for habituation and adaptation. "Every morning the small children who have not been going to school for a long time because of the infectious diseases go for a walk under the supervision of women teachers," he reported on 24 October 1943.[24] "They play all kinds of games and sing all sorts of songs out in the open field." One of their songs was:

> We're having a lovely walk between the huts
> And go with the teacher nicely in a line,
> Past the great tall chimney
> And the little houses,
> Then along the railway and so back home.[25]

The quintessential symbol of the lethal rhythm of Westerbork – the weekly train transports of Jews from the Netherlands to the death camps of Poland – was merely a landmark of their outing: "'Then along the railway and so back home.'"

Thus far we have discussed the usefulness of archival records and the diaries, journals, and oral histories of adults who wrote about or worked with children. The most important sources, however, are the records left by the children themselves and oral histories taken from child survivors, now of mature age. From the adults much can be learned about the organization and operations of the resistance groups devoted to the rescue and aid of children, and about the circumstances of child life. But their view is, inevitably, that of the outsider. It is from the children that we learn what life was like for them: the specific and peculiar dimensions of their life under Nazi rule. The passage of each new discriminatory law oppressed both Jewish children and adults, but in some ways children were uniquely affected. Child life is a subculture of the dominant society, and that subculture was singularly stricken by the ever increasing burden of Nazi persecution. At a much younger age than their elders, and with far less maturity and a less developed sense of identity, children also had to cope with the Nazi (and their Fascist allies') process of differentiation (wearing a star), separation (segregation from their erstwhile "Aryan" companions), isolation (banishment from their former physical world of school, park, playground, library, cinema, ice cream parlor), and, finally, deportation and extermination. It is from the children, and only from them, that we can learn how they, without experience or perspective, understood and operated within this new and bizarre world with its new and bizarre rules.

The drawings, letters, diaries, journals, and oral histories of these children help us to understand their experience; they elucidate their daily lives. Rather than relating events or incidents in which children are seen collectively (the outings of children in Westerbork, the toys of Łódź Ghetto children), these sources describe or portray the personal, individual existence (my walk, my toys). The perspective of children was different from that of adults and, for the first few years of the war, until the final phase of deportation and extermination, their concerns were not those of their elders.

I began this chapter by announcing that this is a story of Jewish child life, and it may be well to reiterate that assertion. This book is about the world of the children and not that of their parents. It is about the children's concerns and their lives. It is not an analysis of the process of death, or the organization of the Nazi apparatus in each occupied or Axis country. Nor is it an analysis of how the Nazi system was brought to bear on, to crush and extinguish, child life. It is a history of the daily existence of children until their escape, liberation, or death. Thus, while the drawings, letters, diaries, and journals of children do not provide the overview supplied by the accounts of adults, they delineate and clarify the fabric of their lives. Each one recounts or depicts the thread of an individual child's life. Collectively they weave a tapestry of child experience; a composite picture of what life was like for children in a number of different settings: while still at home, in hiding, in short-term and long-term ghettos, and in transit and slave labor camps. Furthermore, the accounts surviving children have within them, their own personal memoirs and oral histories, complement and enrich the records left by adults about children and by children about themselves.

The use of oral history for a study such as this is not a simple or straightforward business.[26] It raises a number of issues to which there are no facile resolutions, and questions for which there are no answers proven to be correct. The most obvious problem is that, as only 11 percent of Jewish children alive at the beginning of the war survived to its conclusion,[27] can their oral histories or memoirs be considered as typical? The very fact that they survived at all makes them exceptions to the general rule of death. Furthermore, it is important to remember that *Children With A Star* is not a study of survivors or surviving, but of daily existence until death, or liberation, or escape. Is it justifiable to use the accounts of survivors to speak for the others? The answer is, unequivocally, yes. While the very fact that the child survived makes that child an exception to the general rule of death, that does not mean that the same child's life was itself atypical. There is absolutely no evidence to indicate that survival was due to anything more – or anything less – than luck and fortuitous circumstances. The notion that longevity was due to some "survival strategy" or a special "will to live" is not only arrant nonsense but a pernicious construct. The logical conclusion of such an insidious supposition is to blame the victims in a very subtle, but nevertheless absolutely vicious way. It suggests failure or stupidity on the part of those murdered. If those who survived did so because they were determined, staunch, and firm in their endeavour, the implication is that those who did not survive were undetermined, weak-willed, and irresolute; in short, inadequate to so great a task. Similarly, the neo-Darwinian proposal that those who survived did so because they employed a strategy to that end suggests that they, the survivors, were clever, fit, and adaptable, while their dead cohorts were foolish, deficient, and incompetent; in a word, inferior.

Allowing the living to speak for the dead implies the utter and complete rejection of the notion of a special will to live and the construct of the survival of the fittest. There are two essential reasons for this abjuration. The first is that these two concepts are wrong-headed inquiries. At best, they are red herrings, at worst they are malicious political manipulations; in either case their purpose is to divert attention from the enormity of the crimes committed against the victims to a scrutiny of the ability or inability of those victims to resist the system of murder in which they were trapped. The second reason for the repudiation of these proposals is that there is no evidence to support them. They are quite simply wrong. People survived who tried to commit suicide during their years of agony, while others were killed, or died of disease or starvation who, according to their companions, wished desperately to live. Then too, people made choices which happened to work out well for them, whilst others made the very same decisions – and their course ended in death. Within each of the patterns of life which shall be discussed, the daily lives of those whose existence ultimately would be extinguished and those who would have the good luck to survive were the same. The oral histories of child survivors are, therefore, legitimate testimonies for a history of Jewish youth in general, and not of survivors alone. They may justifiably bear witness for the others.

Another issue raised by the use of the oral histories of survivors for a study of this type is that, inevitably, this was an emotionally fraught period in the child's life. It was a time of great pain, sorrow, despair, and humiliation. It was an era during which they experienced human behavior they had never encountered before or after; behavior which certainly challenged and often destroyed their faith in a permanently stable and ordered society. It was the cataclysmic end of the world they had known, and it was a period during which they lived, as Primo Levi would have it, "outside the law." Child survivors who agreed to impart their personal histories faced the problem of how to describe that hell. "If I utter the words, they are just words," one woman exclaimed in despair. "And when I say them, I remember myself there, but we are here."[28] This quandary was complicated further by the fact that many of them had not spoken about their experiences, except in a very general way, since the war ended. For the first time in forty years these brave souls set themselves the task of remembering and recounting that about which they had remained silent; indeed, that which many of them had sought to repress and, if possible, forget. Because these now-adult children had not articulated their histories before, and because these experiences were so outside the realm of life as we know it, language, our medium of communication, failed us. Frequently these survivors asked, "Do you understand what I mean? Can you comprehend what I am saying?" This had nothing to do with technical tools; that is command of English, French, Italian, Dutch, Yiddish, etc. It was instead a manifestation of insecurity about the possibility of expressing the ineffable. How, as one survivor queried, with a mere combination of letters, and then of words, to explain what even the imagination cannot comprehend? How were they to describe what they perceived as a series of irrational and illogical events with no reasonable basis and no material motive? There was no way for these child survivors to fathom their experiences, no handle to make them intelligible or comprehensible. Indeed, their past was unintelligible, incomprehensible, inexplicable, inconceivable, unimaginable. For them it was a numinous experience. For the historian, however, the events the child survivors described are part of history; they are, and must be, subject to theoretical analysis and logical interpretation. No period of history, no events of our past, can be relegated to the realm of enigma, the recondite, or the metaphysical. They cannot be so easily dismissed or so conveniently ignored.

Given the fundamental, existential nature of these particular experiences, the discrepancy between the position of contemporary participant and *post facto* analyst creates a number of difficulties. Under ordinary circumstances unclear or possibly incorrect points in an oral history are subject to direct interrogation or challenge by the interviewer. In interviews with child survivors such queries must be broached within that individual's construct of reality, which raises the more important question of what is reality? Differentiating between the "objective" historical past (what "really" happened), the "subjective" psychological experience (that which the child believed, or the now-adult survivor believes to have occurred), and those fictional elements which are part of the retelling of any event (the way in which human beings structure the stories or histories they recount) is more complicated than might be presumed. In other words, historical truth, psychological truth, and narrative truth are not always separate and distinct entities.

A very common example will clarify one such difficulty. Many young women who were in concentration camps after the age of menarche have expressed their conviction that the Germans added a chemical to their food to prevent them from menstruating.[29] This is not a conjecture or supposition but a firmly held belief, and it is asserted so frequently and with so much assurance that the uninformed would be convinced of its veracity. Knowing that there is no evidence in the historical record of any such chemical having been mass produced and distributed, and that the conditions of camp life, like other situations of hard labor coupled with starvation, conduced to amenorrhea, I challenged these statements. "Do you think a chemical was added to your food," I asked, "or do you think that perhaps because your general health was so poor, your nutrition level so low, and your intake of calories so small your body ceased to menstruate?" While some women reiterated their belief in the poisonous additive, most were taken aback for a moment and then recalled that indeed, they had heard after the war that this was the reason for their temporary amenorrhea. Yet by the next session of the oral history interview they once again had forgotten. This led me to ask a different question to try to reach the "subjective" truth behind the "objective" falsehood. "Why do you think the Germans would have added such a chemical to your food?" The women's answers were clear and unequivocal, and nearly identical. Even if the Germans were to lose the war, the women said, and even if each individual speaking survived, the poison she had eaten would prevent her from ever conceiving children; thus the Jewish people would die out sooner or later. In other words, not only would these girls bear the scars of their imprisonment for the rest of their lives, not only would they never grow up to be women like other female human beings, but in a fundamental sense there would be no future for them. This construct rationalized their experiences: the Germans wanted to annihilate the Jewish people, and everything they did to their victims led to that end. Thus, if a girl ceased to menstruate she understood this phenomenon within that context, that was the truth. While this truth does not tell us about the components of the concentration camp diet, it illustrates one facet of the psychological state of these young adolescent women, a tiny fragment of the mental conditions under which they operated. Such an incident helps us to understand their fears and anxieties; the psychological circumstances of their daily lives. In this way oral histories help us to understand how the children experienced the events that befell them.

The verbal accounts of child survivors also relate the historical (or objective) "facts" of their lives. To use them for this purpose the historian must check the information obtained in a more or less standard way.

From contemporary documents, other historical analyses, or independent testimonies, is it likely that a child was where he now remembers to have been at any particular time? Was there a camp, resistance group, or escape network operating in such a place at such a time? Was there a transport of Jews from X location to Y camp, and when the now-adult child remembers it to have been? Were the diseases described prevalent or possible under the circumstances?

Perhaps another example concerning a bodily ailment will help to illustrate this sort of historical truth. Many child survivors recalled suffering from large painful abscesses which appeared especially in the most sensitive parts of the body; behind the ears, in the back of the neck, under the arms, between the legs. They were like "a pigeon egg," a man who was an older adolescent at the time explained, but they constantly "were growing and getting redder and eventually they burst." A number of children remembered that, when possible, the boils were treated with "a black sort of tar-like paste which was spread over" the abscess. The salve brought the abscess "to a head much faster and the thing broke open and the pus came out." Although extremely uncomfortable, these boils were not considered to be very important because they were not debilitating. "This was not something one was concerned about. . . . This was something you attended to. In the process of surviving, this is a minor matter. It is something which happens. It was probably connected with the food and with all the conditions of our life; with this whole misery we experienced. . . . In the nightmare within which we lived, we paid no more attention to this than I would if I today would develop a hangnail."[30] In concentration camps such as Birkenau, however, these boils were reason enough to be sent to death. If the inmates heard, or guessed, that a "selection" was imminent they attempted to have them lanced so that they would not be so obvious. Hanna Kent-Sztarkman, a child survivor who just prior to her fifteenth birthday in the autumn of 1944 had the good luck to find her older sister, Miriam, in Birkenau, lost her to the Nazi murder machinery because the latter was caught with these abscesses. Miriam "had problems with her boils," the younger sister recounted forty-one years later. "She complained to us [my mother and me] on Rosh Hashanah that she had boils and that she was very annoyed with the *Blockälteste* who was also the nurse for the block. She [the *Blockälteste*] was a religious Hungarian and she told my sister that she could not help her because it was Rosh Hashanah. Then we didn't see her anymore. I assume she didn't make it through the selection because of the boils."[31]

These skin ulcers were not immediately identifiable but the medical literature on starvation revealed that such abscesses are a result of severe malnutrition, and formerly were treated with a black, tar-like substance called ichthyol. Thus it is indeed probable that children who were in such diverse circumstances as camps, orphanages, and attics, and whose accounts include a memory of these sores, did suffer from them. They all were severely malnourished, and the tar salve was, as they remembered, a common remedy. These examples – amenorrhea and boils – clarify the difference between psychological truth and historical truth, between the children's subjective experience of the world in which they lived and the objective circumstances of their lives.

The issue of narrative truth is the most obvious, but in some ways the most subtle. This does not refer to the problem of whether an account is both reliable and accurate, but the more complicated question of what is remembered. How does anyone reduce her experiences in a historical period that lasted, for that individual, from a few to a dozen years to a few to a dozen hours of recorded oral interview; and how is that account structured? Unfortunately, this cannot be assessed precisely. We are not omniscient; we do not know all the things that happened to that child and so we cannot note what was remembered and what forgotten, what told and what left unsaid. But we should be aware of this problem, and we can make educated guesses. For example, although by and large people try valiantly to recount their lives chronologically, they remember by subject association. Then too, major disruptions of or movement in their lives are recalled with special attention, while the daily drudgery and misery, or monotony and boredom are sparsely described. It is as if in relating their personal lives during that particular period of history they are answering the question, "What happened to me?" rather than, "What did I do?" This makes perfect sense; it reflects the reality of the Nazi years. These now-adult children were caught in the cataclysmic horror of a genocidal machinery primed and ready to devour them. The calamitous events that befell them are what was crucial, and remain so in their accounts. Their scope for independent action was, by contrast, insignificant and therefore is now recalled as of little importance. This does not mean that these adults have forgotten their daily lives at that time. Such recollections are easily elicited by direct questioning ("What did you do whilst . . . ?" "How did you feel?"), but they are not the landmarks by which they spontaneously plot the story line of their recollections of their lives during those years.

In the historiographical literature much attention has been devoted in recent years to the idea of explanation by emplotment.[32] As Hayden White, one of the leading participants in this discussion, has explained, "Providing the 'meaning' of a story by identifying the *kind of story* that has been told is called explanation by emplotment. . . . Emplotment is the way by which a sequence of events fashioned into a story is gradually revealed to be a story of a particular kind." What is interesting for our purposes is that, just as the historian structures her account of the past in particular ways, so do people who recount their personal histories. Child suvivors, and the adults who helped children during the war years, are the historians of their own lives, and they too use classical story structures which "explain" the events that befell them. White has focused on four different modes of emplotment: romance, tragedy, comedy, and satire.[33] The use of these archetypal story modes is one of the facets in the very complex issue of narrative truth. Three of the four modes of emplotment discussed by White are used by child survivors: romance, satire, and tragedy. While the world view expressed in comedy simply is not consonant with their experiences, the perspective of resistance workers who were dedicated to the rescue and aid of children is very different from that of the youths themselves, and very occasionally their oral histories follow the comedy pattern (the story of their underground activities is recounted as if it were a boys' adventure tale[34]). The great majority of the child survivors interviewed for this book were hopeful about the future. Despite the anguish and tragedies of their earlier years, and the pervasive effects of those experiences on their current lives, the despair and desolation of satire were not often expressed. The most frequently used story modes were those of the romance and tragedy. In other words, either evil was overcome, or at least these now-adult children feel that they have achieved a more profound understanding of the good and evil in their fellow human beings. Recognizing these story forms and realizing that, by employing one or another of them, the "participant/historian" (i.e. child survivor or resistance worker) has explained, or given meaning to, her life in a specific way provides the listening historian with a handy tool to use to investigate that particular oral history. It also reveals additional information about the participant's world view. The listening historian has an advantage over the reader of a printed history because she can ask questions of the participant/historian to challenge or question that explanation of history expressed by the story mode employed.

In short, the issue of narrative truth is not a question of veracity versus mendacity, or candor versus deceit. It is a methodological problem of analyzing and assessing an oral history account so as to understand better how the content has been selected and structured to provide meaning or explanation. Like the problem of psychological truth and historical truth, narrative truth is simply another dimension to the use of oral history, of which both the historian and the reader should be aware.

The final point which must be considered with regard to the use of oral history for a study of Jewish children in Nazi Europe is that of reliability and accuracy, or, as some historians have called it, validity. According to the oral historian Alice Hoffman, "Reliability can be defined as the consistency with which an individual will tell the same story about the same events on a number of different occasions. Validity refers to the degree of conformity between the reports of the event and the event itself as recorded by other primary source material such as documents, photographs, diaries and letters."[35] The question of reliability and validity would be an issue for any oral history, but child survivors lived through extraordinary events. Given the emotionally fraught nature of their experiences, are the accounts of these children more suspect or less accurate? My own research flatly contradicts any such supposition. First, in the course of my work I had reason to reinterview a small number of child survivors two to three years after the first history was recorded; their accounts were entirely consistent. Then too, a few of the people with whom I spoke had given interviews previously or, more often, having begun to talk about their experiences, they subsequently agreed to be interviewed by other historians or oral archive organizations. I was able to compare the two interviews and found that when the survivor discussed the same event it was described in very similar language. Emplotment may help to explain how it is that the story line of an individual's life is told similarly over time (because it structures or solidifies the narrative), but it is not sufficient reason for the remarkable constancy of the details of the account. I would contend that the extraordinary nature of their experiences does not in any way interfere with the reliability of child survivors' accounts. Indeed, perhaps precisely because they were so painful, oppressive, and catastrophic they were etched in the memory in one particular way and thus are remembered similarly over time.

This may also help to explain the exceptional degree of accuracy or validity in the great majority of the oral histories of child survivors. It is a commonplace of psychology that traumatic events are remembered with great clarity while peaceful periods in one's life are more easily forgotten or confused. To reiterate Hoffman's definition, the "conformity between the [now-adult children's] reports of the event and the event itself as recorded by other primary material" is so remarkable as to be in itself eloquent of the anguish endured. The only caveat that need be noted is that child survivors' accounts tend to use more restrained language than do contemporary reports. This is due, perhaps, to the shared, fundamental skepticism about the efficacy of words, language, to convey or express the sights, scenes, smells, and sounds they remember.

Survivors themselves frequently comment on the clarity of their recollections. In his book *Moments of Reprieve*, Primo Levi remarked rue-fully that his memories did not dissipate with time. "It has been observed by psychologists that the survivors of traumatic events are divided into two well-defined groups: those who repress their past *en bloc*, and those whose memory of the offense persists, as though carved in stone, prevailing over all previous or subsequent experiences," Levi noted. "Now, not by choice but by nature, I belong to the second group. Of my two years of life outside the law I have not forgotten a single thing. Without any deliberate effort, memory continues to restore to me events, faces, words, sensations, as if at that time my mind had gone through a period of exalted receptivity, during which not a detail was lost."[36]

Younger people attested to the same phenomenon. Halina Biren-baum, for instance, was a ten-year-old Warsaw schoolgirl when the Germans declared war on Poland and fifteen when she was liberated from Neustadt-Glewe, the fourth concentration camp to which she had been shipped. In the conclusion to her book about her experiences (*Hope Is the Last to Die*), written twenty years after the war's end, she too confessed her inability to forget. "Everything, down to the most minute details, remained unerased and fresh in my memory, as though it had happened yesterday," Birenbaum averred. "When my first son was born . . . I, with pride and emotion, like all young mothers, looked at the mouth of my child, wide-open, greedily seeking nourishment, [and] I recalled with horror the thousands of unfortunate mothers in the ghetto who had nothing with which to feed their starving infants." The past was always present. "So it is that always, involuntarily, at almost every step, scenes, memories and comparisons with those other days are mixed with my present life."[37] Many child survivors echoed Birenbaum's assertion; their pervasive and persistent associations between the past and the present attest to the durability of their war-time memories. As Isabella Leitner affirmed with anguish thirty-four years after she had been deported as a young girl from Kisvárda, her native town in Hungary, "I am condemned to walk the earth for all my days with the stench of burning flesh in my nostrils." And when she, like Halina Birenbaum, fed her first child, she too was possessed by the past. "When I gently ease the bottle between his tender lips and he is satisfied, drinking life, I too am drunk with life. But I cannot help it. . . . I remember the two longest nine months of my life – the nine months while I was counting the seconds to see the life within me, and the nine months while I was dazed, half-crazed, wondering whether the liberators would come in time to save a single heartbeat." Leitner, like so many other child survivors, desperately would like to be released from those memories. "Help me," she pleads at the end. "Help me to see only life. Don't let me see the mad-man anymore."[38]

The purpose of this discussion of the use of oral history was not to defend the technique, but to review critically the questions its application raises for this particular study. We have seen, in summary, that it is indeed legitimate to use the recorded recollections of the fortunate few who survived to elucidate the past of Jewish children in general during the Nazi years. Furthermore, we have noted a number of hazards and examined several nuances of interpretation and analysis: the perceived inadequacy of language to convey what was for the children an existential or numinous experience; the subtleties of historical truth, psychological truth, and narrative truth; and finally, given the emotional weight of the experiences, the passage of time, and the fact that while children lived the remembered events adults now describe them, the issues of reliability and accuracy. Awareness of these problems helps historian and reader alike to be both more sensitive to and critical about the intricacies and complexities of the oral histories of child survivors and the adults who helped them. They are, in the final analysis, a very fertile and absolutely unique resource. It is for this reason that oral histories are the main source of survivor testimony used in this book. There is a rich and very wonderful survivor memoir literature, and some examples have been cited in this chapter. In the following pages, however, it is the recorded children's voices that will be heard. They are but a fraction of those who shared their histories for this study.

The purpose of *Children With A Star* is to identify and analyze a number of general life patterns Jewish children experienced during the war, and to investigate critically the role and function of such factors as culture, class, age, gender, degree of religious observance, and parental political affiliation in their lives. This book is not a statistical study. The people interviewed for this work were not, and could not be, chosen according to accepted sampling techniques. Furthermore, while it is true that oral histories were an invaluable source, the arguments in this book are by no means based on them alone. As I noted earlier, there is a plethora of relevant material in libraries, archives, and private collections. My goal was to obtain information about the daily lives of Jewish children in Nazi Europe from those who were in a position to know about this – primarily children who were newly born to sixteen years old when Nazism or Fascism first affected their lives, and the adults who helped such young people. Indeed, even if it had been desirable the figures are not available to conduct a standard statistical inquiry on this subject. The approximate number of Jewish children alive before and after the war in each country individually and in Europe generally is known. Less precise figures are also available on age distribution. However, it is not known how many children experienced any particular pattern of life. During the course of the war most children experienced more than one; for example, a child may have lived in a ghetto, been smuggled to a hiding place, and then betrayed and deported to a death camp. Finally, how long each child endured each pattern of war life until death or liberation, the number of weeks, months, or years, is also not known. Thus in this study statistical analyses are irrelevant; they simply do not help us to draw general conclusions.

Let us then return to the purpose of this book. *Children With A Star* is a social history of the daily lives of Jewish children in Nazi-occupied Europe; it is a book about the texture of quotidian existence. It is concerned with the ordinary, the extraordinary nature of the ordinary, which is explicated by and elucidated through the details of the children's life stories themselves, those shards of human existence which disappear in such general statements as, "they starved to death; they froze to death; they died of a number of common infectious diseases." There was much more than that to their lives, and in this book we shall examine the substance and structure of the general patterns of existence Jewish children experienced during the war. As we have discussed in some detail, there are two equally important ways to reconstruct the daily lives of these children: through them and through those adults who helped them. The records left by the children and by the officially sanctioned and underground relief and rescue organizations, as well as the current testimonies of child survivors and resistance workers, are the primary materials for this study.

What different types of living experiences did Jewish children have in Nazi Europe? They lived under the direct rule of the Germans in ghettos, forced labor camps, and death camps. They eked out a marginal existence in hiding and hidden (concealed in an attic, closet, or closed convent), or in hiding and visible (openly obscured: adopted by non-Jews, in religious orders, Christian orphanages, on the run without papers, or passing as Christians with false papers). *Children With A Star* is organized on the basis of these general patterns of existence. Thus, the chapters are entitled "At Home," "In Secret," "Transit Camps," and so on. The aim of all the chapters is to clarify and analyze the ordinary details of everyday life: the children's education and occupations, how clothes, food, and fuel were obtained, who their companions were, whether they were with or separated from their siblings and parents, and who (if anyone) assumed responsibility for them. The remembered feelings and impressions during those years by people now of adult age, as well as perceptions recorded in diaries and drawings will be considered and, for those who survived, the influence they believe the war had on their lives assessed. Writing in the shadow of the catastrophe perhaps it is well to reiterate once again that although the vast majority (nearly 90 percent) of the people who are the subject of this study were killed, we shall deal not with the machinery of their murder but with the circumstances and conditions of their lives.

Careful reconstruction and close examination of these general life patterns will allow for the critical investigation of a number of factors which helped to determine the children's perceptions of their changed lives during the war and, in some measure, helped to shape their destinies in the Nazi era: degree of religious observance, familial political affiliation, gender, age, culture, and class. It is obvious, for example, that the experience of a child of six was different from that of a young person of sixteen – whether in hiding, adopted, or in a transit camp. It may be less obvious that, as we shall see, it was not economic status but the number of contacts a family had outside the Jewish community which was primarily involved in securing a hiding place. Then too, according to members of the underground organizations which helped children, it was rather easy to find places for three-year-old girls; the situation for boys over the age of twelve was, by contrast, extremely difficult. In slave labor camps, of course, the situation was reversed. Youth was a death warrant. The older the child, the more mature and robust in appearance, the more likely he was to be assigned a position on a work detail.

It is impossible to work on children in isolation from the adults who accepted responsibility for them. The study of child victims of the Nazi genocide policy has led also to the elucidation of those underground and "legal" groups which were organized specifically to protect their lives. In each European country there were people who acted individually or as part of an organized network to save Jewish children. Their history is an integral, albeit secondary, concern of this book. It is interesting to observe that while much is known about the armed resistance, the history of the groups that helped children has not been part of the recognized, legitimate public past. Many of these resisters were women; after the war they disappeared from public life. They did not seek publicity and they had left few records of their activities. Research on these rescue and relief organizations is as long overdue as is recognition of the participants' courage and cleverness, and a second purpose of this book is to address those issues.

Children With A Star is a social history of the stuff and substance, the bizarre and tragic dimensions, of Jewish child life under Nazi rule. Our aim is to try to understand what life, in a number of different circumstances, was like for these children. What, precisely, happened to them? What did they do all day? What were their hopes and fears, thoughts and observations, dreams and nightmares? How did they cope with, and how did they comprehend and perceive, the reality they lived?

Why is such a study important? If this history were to improve or refine our understanding of childhood in a situation of politically engendered trauma or to add to the general discourse of the history of childhood it would be sufficient justification for this book. The examination of the history of Jewish youth in Nazi-occupied Europe does more than that, however. First of all, by looking at the most vulnerable members of the community, those without power, resources, or connections, it elucidates how European society functioned during the war years: precisely how the German noose tightened, and how the Jewish victims and their gentile neighbors responded. The passage of each new discriminating law or decree oppressed both Jewish children and adults, but in some ways the former were uniquely affected. Child life is a subculture of the dominant society, and that subculture was singularly stricken by the ever-increasing burden of Nazi persecution. Understanding that process provides another and perhaps more sensitive perspective on European history during the Hitler years. It uniquely clarifies and crystallizes the horror and the evil of the Nazi genocide of Europe's Jews. Our unwillingness to accept the murder of children is emotionally different from our incomprehension of the genocide of adults. When one deals with the massacre of the innocents, questions like "Why did you allow this to happen to you?" are understood for what they are: inconsequent and irrelevant. Adults are never seen as totally helpless; it is a contradiction of our understanding, our archetypal image of what an adult is. But in the case of children no such defense exists. Children are, and are expected to be, helpless and dependent. In their case it is no longer possible to be angry with and to blame the victim.[39]

Similarly, a number of stereotyped statements which are commonly adduced in connection with the Judeocide are laid bare of their illusory validity and are revealed for the convenient deceptions they are. Assertions like "The Jews kept to themselves," "The Jews did not assimilate into the general culture," "The Jews were an obvious leftist presence," "The Jews were ostentatious about their wealth," "The Jews were disproportionately involved in banking, the professions, the arts" are used as veiled excuses for or somehow explanations of the genocide. The study of the persecution of children obviates all such nonsense. Even if such pronouncements meant anything – and they do not – they are simply irrelevant or inapplicable to the maltreatment of children. In the case of a child, someone who saw his neighbor carted away by the SS, or French police, or Hungarian gendarmes, could no longer say to himself to rationalize what he witnessed, "I wonder what he did to provoke the authorities," because an infant or three-year-old or six-year-old could not possibly have done anything.

When all such justifications, rationalizations, and stereotyped assertions are jettisoned we are left with the quintessential essence of the genocide: the ideology of the stranger. Examining the experience of the children dissects the process of persecution to lay bare the universal substance of this ideology of the perceived alien. It is an ideology applicable not only to Europe between 1933 and 1945 but in general to a particular way in which human beings torment and mistreat each other. The history of Jewish children in Nazi Europe tells us, from the perspective of those young people, how they became strangers in their own countries, how they were denied respect, lost their rights, and, finally, were designated to be killed. How were they, who were once part of the fabric of society, the body politic, ripped asunder, extirpated? *Children With A Star* investigates that process through the experience of the young people themselves.

Part One

The Recognizable World

Chapter One

At Home

The story begins with Jewish children at home with their families.

"My father was an accountant," Hilma Geffen-Ludomer recalled, "and evidently he did all right as far as his clients were concerned . . . because in 1931 he had built a home in a suburb of Berlin called Rangsdorf. . . . It was a very nice house for 1931. It had every modern convenience. . . . We had a nice garden around the house, fruit trees, flowers, . . . we had a very, very comfortable life." "We were observant," Ludomer continued, "but certainly not orthodox. We didn't keep a kosher home. But I remember we never had pork in the house. I remember my mother baking *challah* [a braided white bread] for every Friday night; she did that every Friday. We always had Friday Shabbat dinner, and lit the candles for Shabbat. I stayed home for the high holy days. We went into Berlin for the service and we went to synagogue."[1]

"My grandfather had a fruit shop in the Muiderstraat and the other grandfather had a fruit shop on the Hoogte Kadijk, which was a little outside the ghetto" of Amsterdam, Philip Gerrit Mok recounted.[2]

Then my father set up his own fruit shop in the Retiefstraat which is in the eastern part of the city. [It] was a predominantly Jewish neighborhood; a new outlet for Amsterdam. It was kind of a promised land for the very socialistic-oriented Jewish community.

My family, to begin with that point, is from Holland, at least from my father's side, for more than four hundred, five hundred years. . . . It was a very tight family. . . . Each son of my [paternal] great-grandmother had to come to visit his mother once a day. If he didn't, hell

2   Hilma Geffen-Ludomer with her friend Gerhard on an outlawed outing on the
Wannsee, near Berlin, in the summer of 1942. All Jews over the age of six were required
to wear a star by that time, but Ludomer ignored the injunction: after she had left her
flat she whipped off her star.

broke out. So that's the kind of family we were in. It was a very large
family, hundreds of people.

From my mother's side as well many people lived in the same
neighborhood. When I was a little child it meant that I could walk in
the street and each two minutes meet an uncle and aunt, or anything
that was related to me from either side. . . . I am talking about a
period that I profoundly remember. . . . I mean, I had to cross the
street and there was a sister of my grandfather's living opposite our
house. I used to go up there and get cookies and God knows what. . . .

We lived in a Jewish neighborhood. . . . We lived in our own
ghetto, in our own surroundings, in our own atmosphere. . . . The
normal Jews were orthodox. But the majority didn't do a darn thing
about it. Except, of course, they kept the holidays and well, it's not
whether you kept a kosher kitchen or not so much. We didn't eat a lot
of things that you weren't allowed to eat. I mean you didn't think of
doing that. [We] had Passover, we had the *seder* [Passover ritual
meal] table. I learned the prayers, we spoke Amsterdam Yiddish.[3]

"I was born sometime in November, either of 1929 or 1930, but I'm
not sure and neither is my mother," Moishe Kobylanski reflected. "She
knows it was Chanukkah but it could be a month off or it could be two
months off." Kobylanski was born in the city of Rovno in the Ukraine.
Some time in the early 1930s his family returned to the village where his

mother had been born, Gruszwica, about 14 kilometers from Rovno. When Kobylanski lived there it was a village of about 6,000 with no electricity, no radio, no pavement, no running water. "Just a little mud road." [4]

My father had a little store, basic things like a little general store, the food items were added on later . . . tobacco, sugar, nails, soap, spices . . . a little dinky store. But I guess he got somehow a living. I do know that the house we lived in was nice, relatively speaking. Compared to the others', the neighbors', it was a substantial house, nice house. [We] had a nice garden in the back, but you could not support a family on the garden itself. . . . One room of the house, with a separate entrance and exit, was the store. And there was one bedroom finished. We had a dining room, a nice kitchen. Behind the store was a storage room and a hallway, and one bedroom was never finished.

We had wooden floors which was up, you know, that was prestigious already. We didn't have the wooden floor all the time. We used to have a dirt floor, and every Friday it would get whitewashed with red paint. It was swept up and it would be painted. You waited until it dried and you could use it, every Friday. But eventually, I remember, they put in wooden floors. Oh, very nice! Not parquet, but they were smooth, there were no cracks or anything. Nice floors. So that was in the kitchen and the dining room, which was dining room, living room, meeting room, the whole works. . . .

The town was 6,000 total and that included the Jews and the Ukrainians, Czechs, and Polish people. There were eight Jewish families comprising about forty-eight persons in the Jewish community. Forty-eight souls, Jewish. . . .

There was no official synagogue. . . . I don't think we were that religious, our little eight-family community. We observed, I mean, we didn't do any work on Saturday, on the Sabbath. The store was closed. But, you know, if it was a good deal, you sneaked it into the back door! You had to make a living. We went to *shul* [synagogue] every Saturday. On high holidays, definitely; even the minor holidays were observed. Kashruth was observed, but I don't know to what degree. I know we did not eat any unkosher meats at home. . . .

My father was an easy-going man, gregarious; he liked to have company in the house. I don't think that my mother enjoyed it that much. I mean, my father had an open house, let's put it that way. And my mother, I think, complied. True, she did most of the work. . . . I remember that I used to go to bed and they [the guests] still argued on. . . . There used to be a lot of shouting and screaming and hollering, and drinking of tea. . . . It was like background music to me.[5]

"I was born in Radom, Poland, in February 1924," Mania Salinger-Tenenbaum began. "I was the second child, of parents [who] were rather affluent; we were an upper middle-class family. My father had a shoe factory; Radom was the leather capital of Poland. . . . I also had a younger brother who perished during the war."[6]

> I was a terror in the house. I had friends and I always had noise and music. . . . I took after my mother very much – in looks and in temperament, and in every other way. And my mother therefore favored me; I didn't realize that, but I was really a spoiled little girl. . . .
>
> My father went every Friday night to services, and we had a kosher home. All Polish Jews had kosher homes as far as I was concerned. But we weren't very religious. . . . My parents observed Shabbat in a way that on Shabbat, my father stayed home and did not go to work, and took his children for a walk, and brought Friday night, goodies for the children. And we had a Shabbat dinner; my mother lit candles. . . .
>
> In elementary school I remember very little. I had girlfriends, and I was a kid. . . . And I remember my mother checking my books. Do I have everything I needed for that day? She was very involved. . . .
>
> I then attended high school, and I joined [the Zionist youth organization] Masada. . . . Masada was a very large coeducational group of Jewish high school and college students. Our main purpose was to raise interest in and money for the resettlement of Palestine as a Jewish state. . . . But Masada was much more than that. It was my second home. It was something unbelievable. It was the warmth and continuation of a home life on a social level, because of the people who were there. It was a fantastic group of people. . . . Masada was my second home. In Masada I made friendships which last to this day. In Masada I learned about dedication and fighting for what one believes in.[7]

Like Mania Salinger-Tenenbaum, Frieda Menco-Brommet also lived the life of a bright, sociable young girl in a major European city. Born in 1925 in Amsterdam, Brommet had, as she herself declared, "a very good youth." She was an only child and, she explained, "I had a very close relationship with my father. I had a less close relationship with my mother. . . . When I was a child, she was the one who cooked the meals and who was never in a lousy mood, and my father and I were the ones who went for walks and talked about every subject including, at that time, sexuality and homosexuality, which was in those years I think very exceptional. My father was a window dresser himself, and he was a teacher of window dressing. . . . I was very proud when I was still a young child of about ten years old that he allowed me to help him."[8]

We were not wealthy; we didn't have a car, we had bicycles. . . . I thought, myself, that I had lots of dresses which my father took home for me, or he brought home fabrics and somebody came in and he just, with pins, made it on my body and showed the one who was there how to make it. I always said to my parents that I am sure there is not a princess in the world who has more beautiful clothes than I have. . . .

I wasn't very much aware that I was Jewish. My father came from a family – they were Jews but they weren't aware of it at all that they were Jewish. (My grandfather had a very non-Jewish profession: he was a jail director.) My mother was more Jewish, not in the sense of Judaism, but in the sense of a white tablecloth on Friday evening and even more sweets than on other evenings. . . . I remember I was a few times in my life in synagogue.[9]

In short, she concluded, "We had a family life. I had four grandparents. Family. So, I should say, kind of a middle-class life. . . . I knew I would study. Some day I would be able to study. That was what we thought. And so my father had insurance for me and put away money for me to study. So there were a lot of certainties. But the certainties ended when I was fourteen years old. They never came back again, of course."[10]

The children lived in suburban dwellings, *shtetl* [village] hovels, modernist apartments, stately city mansions, tenement blocks, back-street mews, farmhouses, village houses, shop-houses: homes. Their households differed in nearly every way: orthodox and secular, politically engaged and uninterested, educated and unschooled, prosperous and impoverished, contented and depressed. But these were their homes. They were the last places these children lived as ordinary citizens, members of families and integral parts of their communities. For Brommet the dependable stability of the future ended in 1940 when the Germans invaded the Netherlands, but in other areas of Europe the normal structure of Jewish life had begun to be destroyed seven years earlier, with the German elections in 1933 and the appointment of Hitler as Chancellor.

The first children to be singed by the great conflagration to come were those who, like Ludomer, lived in Germany; they were followed by children in countries and areas annexed by the Reich, then Germany's allies and, finally, by the children (such as Mok, Kobylanski, Salinger, and Brommet) who lived in occupied nations. This chronology is not, in itself, of great interest to us. We are engaged with another problem: the pattern of dispossession from and destruction of their place in society that all the children suffered. This was the first stage in the Nazi genocide machinery which would proceed incrementally but inexorably towards the total isolation of the Jewish community from their neighbors, the aggregation of the Jewish population in ghettos and transit camps, and, ultimately, to deportation to slave labor and extermination camps.[11]

During the late 1930s, as the European nations moved towards increasingly belligerent positions, both gentile and Jewish children were subjected to the restrictions engendered by this preparatory state, and by the war that ensued. Obviously, all children were affected by these conditions: the very concept of a real, human, tangible enemy, the loss of adult male family members to the armed services and female members to war-effort work, ration coupons, bombardment, the actual presence of enemy troops, anxiety, evacuation, destruction, death. Jewish children, like their gentile neighbors, suffered these disruptions and terrors. But apart from that, and absolutely distinct from it, the former began to experience a nightmare all their own. It is the beginnings of that nightmare, the first flashes of the future fire, which is our present concern. What were the early rumbles and tremors? How were the initial steps of this special war against the Jews manifested with regard to child life whilst the children were still at home, and how did the children themselves experience these signs?

The siege of the Jews began with a legal definition. The Nazis defined Jews on the basis of a concept of race rather than religion. According to National Socialist ideology, Judaism was inherited from parents and grandparents. The precise requirements for someone to be defined as a Jew differed slightly from country to country, but the principle of passage through the blood remained constant. In Germany itself, for example, Jews were defined in the First Ordinance to the Reich Citizenship Law of 14 November 1935. Its main provisions in this regard were:

ARTICLE 2

2. Partly Jewish is anyone who is descended from one or two grandparents who are fully Jewish by race, in so far as he is not to be considered as Jewish under Article 5 Section 2. A grandparent is to be

considered as fully Jewish if he belonged to the Jewish religious community.

ARTICLE 5

1. Jew is he who is descended from at least three grandparents who are fully Jewish by race. Article 2, paragraph 2, sentence 2 applies.
2. Also to be considered a Jew is a partly Jewish national who is descended from two fully Jewish grandparents and
a) who belonged to the Jewish religious community, upon adoption of the [Reich Citizenship] Law, or is received into the community thereafter, or
b) who was married to a Jewish person upon adoption of the law, or marries one thereafter, or
c) who is the offspring of a marriage concluded by a Jew (as defined in paragraph 1) after the entry into force of the Law for the Protection of German Blood and Honor of September 15, 1935, or
d) who is the offspring of an extramarital relationship involving a Jew (as defined in paragraph 1) and who is born out of wedlock after July 31, 1936.[12]

Italy, Germany's first ally, adopted similar legislation in its Provisions for the Defense of the Italian Race dated 17 November 1938–XVII (i.e.; the seventeenth year of Fascism under Mussolini). The second part, "Pertaining to the Jewish Race," of this rather long and inclusive antisemitic legal decree began with Article 8, "Those affected by the laws":

a) He is of the Jewish race who is born of two parents of the Jewish race, even if he belongs to a religion other than the Jewish faith.
b) He is considered to be Jewish who is born of one parent of the Jewish race and the other of a foreign nationality.
c) He is considered to be Jewish who is born of a mother of the Jewish race whenever the father is unknown.
d) He is considered to be of the Jewish race who, although born of parents of Italian nationality of whom only one is of the Jewish race, belongs to the Jewish religion, or is inscribed in a Jewish community, or has in any other way manifested Judaism.
Not to be considered of the Jewish race are those who are born of parents of Italian nationality of whom only one is of the Jewish race, who as of the first of October 1938–XVI belonged to a religion other than Judaism.[13]

Poland was the first country to be occupied by Germany, and the "Official Definition of the Term 'Jew'" in the Government-General was dated 24 July 1940.

ARTICLE 2

1) A Jew is a person descended from at least three fully Jewish grandparents by race.

2) A person is considered a Jew if he is descended from two grandparents who are full Jews by race and

a) if he was a member of the Jewish Religious Community on September 1, 1939, or joined such a community subsequently;

b) if he was married to a Jew on the date on which this Regulation came into force, or married a Jew subsequently;

c) if he is the product of extra-marital intercourse with a Jew in accordance with para.1 and was born after May 31, 1941.

3) A grandparent is automatically considered a full Jew if he was a member of a Jewish community.[14]

These legal definitions were indeed ominous; they reflected a perception of Jews as the other, the stranger who, because of her or his birth, never could become part of the "Aryan" community. But the definitions as such did not in themselves affect the daily lives of those children deemed to be Jews. Only when the definition was used to frame legislation which differentiated between the newly defined "Aryans" and "Jews," and when these laws became operational for legal discriminatory action did they affect the normal activities of Jews. The first action with immediate consequences was the many laws and edicts designed to remove Jews from positions of public influence and to impoverish Jews by appropriating their businesses, and forbidding them to work in a number of capacities in gentile enterprises. German Jewish civil servants, for instance, lost their jobs as a consequence of the 7 April 1933 Law for the Reestablishment of the Professional Civil Service. Between 1933 and 1938 Nazi Party propaganda and pressure were (very effectively) brought to bear on German Jewish business enterprises to liquidate entirely or to sell out to a German "Aryan" company. After 1938 this expropriation was no longer "voluntary" but compulsory.[15] The Reich's allies followed suit. Hungary, for example, passed a Bill for the More Effective Protection of Social and Economic Life in May 1938 which defined Jews and reduced the scope of their economic opportunities. A second anti-Jewish law, the Bill to Restrict Jewish Penetration in the Public Affairs and Economic Life of the Country, was introduced in December and passed in May 1939. It barred Jews from civil service and fixed a quota system to regulate Jewish participation in the professions and in commerce: 6 percent in trade and the professions, and 12 percent of the labor force in individual industrial, commercial, and banking concerns.[16] Similar economic restrictions were passed or promulgated in the occupied or puppet government countries. The first *Statut des Juifs* passed by the French Government at Vichy on 3 October 1940 excluded Jews from the upper echelons of the civil service, the officer corps, and the ranks of non-commissioned officers and "from professions that influence public opinion: teaching, the press, radio, film, and theater." It also included a provision for a future quota system to restrict the number of Jews practicing the liberal professions.[17]

These edicts were directed against adults. They were faced with the daunting prospect of trying to continue to earn a living, to carry on within the restrictions. A small group of Jewish children, who were themselves employed, were also affected by these antisemitic economic decrees. Jacqueline Kamiéniarz and her brother were professional child entertainers in Paris. She had just turned fourteen in the spring of 1942, and she and her brother were engaged to perform a song-and-dance act in a nightclub. Then the management sent all their employees a questionnaire which asked that religion be specified. That was the end of their engagement. "We were out of that club. We stopped working there. We could have put 'Catholic,' 'Christian,' but we didn't. We didn't want to. We put 'Jews.' And they told us: 'Sorry.'"[18]

Most children were not employed, of course, so to have been fired from a job was decidedly unusual. The changes in the financial situation of their families caused by the economic sanctions had other reverberations in their lives. If a few lost their jobs, it was much more common for the opposite to occur, that is, for young people to begin to work to supplement the declining family income, or to help out in the now reduced family business. Rudolf Rosenberg was eleven years old and living in Berlin when the Nuremberg Laws (comprehensive antisemitic legislation passed by the Reichstag in September 1935) came into effect. His father was a wholesale tobacconist in a small way; he also had a retail shop. His mother "helped with the business quite actively." His father, Rosenberg recollected, maintained the shop until 1935. The pressure to close or sell the business mounted continuously, and his father decided to relinquish the retail end and transfer the wholesale trade to the family flat, which was located on the first floor of a Berlin tenement building. This meant that the family members slept in one room, used a second room for living purposes, and devoted the third to the business. Loyal customers who wanted to continue to deal with the Rosenbergs came after hours rather than during the work day.[19]

As I said, the one room was turned into a business. People used to come and collect their orders of cigarettes and cigars and tobacco, or we went to deliver. I was the delivery boy, actually. . . . Shortly after my father transferred the wholesale part of the business up to the flat

3 Jacqueline (aged 10) and Marc (aged 12) Kamiéniarz, juvenile entertainers, circa 1938.

... I started regularly delivering parcels of cigarettes and so on by bike to all over the place in Berlin. I had a big rucksack and a sort of carrier on the back of the bike. ... Not only did I have to deliver parcels of cigarettes, but I also collected money. And I came home with hundreds of marks in my pocket. ... I went round on my bike every afternoon after I'd done my homework, [from about] four o'clock ... to, say six o'clock in the evening.[20]

Rosenberg delivered parcels for the family business six afternoons a week, including Saturdays. On Shabbat mornings he went to synagogue, which his parents encouraged very much. This situation continued for a year. Then, when he was twelve years old, "suddenly – and it must have hurt them very much – they turned around and said, 'Look, we need your help.' I was old enough at the time to realize this. And that was the end of synagogue going. I had to help in the business on Saturday as well. Because Saturdays (I don't know why) turned out to be one of the busiest days. On Saturday, of course, I didn't go to school and therefore I worked full-time." Despite the family's united efforts to maintain their small business, by the winter of 1937–8 "things had become so difficult – the business was going downhill, people weren't allowed to trade with [us] – that [our] source of income was swept away from under [our] feet."[21]

While some children were fired from their jobs as a result of the anti-semitic economic measures, and others began to work, the great majority were only tangentially affected by these laws and edicts. Their impact on the children's world was filtered through their parents. Sometimes this meant that questions were raised about the future. Thus, for example, Alexander Ehrmann remembers that in 1936, when he was a ten-year-old living in southeastern Czechoslovakia (an area that was to be annexed to Hungary two years later), his parents heard reports of the appropriation of the property of German Jews and that, coupled with "the uncertainty of the [Czech] republic itself" engendered "uncertainty and anxiety about what was going to happen to us." As a child, he said, he "picked up these threads and wondered a lot what was going to happen. I saw my parents concerned; there were discussions between [the adults] as to what would be a good thing to do, how to plan ahead, what kinds of safeguards to take." For him, this translated into a feeling of in-stability and impending change: "talking about learning trades instead of continuing education for us children; the decision for my elder sister to learn the trade of corset-making; my sister next in line learning how to sew, to knit . . . plans that she would go into that business."[22] Indeed, vocational training rather than an academic education became a com-mon occupation for young people. The resolve to abandon former ex-pectations to accommodate to the new political realities often was taken on a community level, as well as on a personal basis. The statement of the Reichsvertretung der Juden in Deutschland (the National Organiza-tion of German Jews) in response to the Nuremberg Laws announced this decision explicitly. "The Jewish schools must also serve in the systematic preparation for future occupations," the RJD announced. "Emphasis will be placed on guidance toward manual work. . . . The *in-creased need* for emigration will be served by large-scale planning, firstly with regard to *Palestine*, but also to all other available countries, with particular attention to young people. This includes . . . *training* in pro-fessions suited for emigrants, particularly agriculture and technical skills."[23]

Most children, however, noted the changes in family circumstances, but were neither bothered nor personally concerned. Mirjam Levi, for

4   Adolf Zirker, a master cabinet maker from Cologne, with his students. Faced with
antisemitic quotas and restrictions, and the threat of war, many Jewish children learned
trades and Jewish master craftsmen became teachers in vocational schools.

instance, was eleven when her father's medical practice in The Hague
was restricted by the 1 May 1941 prohibition against the employment of
Jewish professionals by gentile clients. She remembers that for days after
the edict came into effect her father's office was "full of flowers [sent by
gentile patients]; I never saw so many flowers," and that shortly thereafter the family took in a boarder because "there was less money," but
she, like most Jewish children at the time, was not particularly worried
by these signs and changes.[24] In a very real sense, the punitive economic
regulations belonged to the world of adults; they did not touch the children's daily lives. Their families were intact, they neither took on jobs
nor were fired from them, they continued to eat and be dressed, and
their own immediate activities and future plans were not threatened in
any way they could feel.

The complacency and unconsciousness of childhood was shattered by
the restrictions on normal social life that came with the second wave of
antisemitic legislation which was designed to ensure the social segregation of the Jewish population. The subculture of child life was deeply
affected by these edicts and regulations; their reverberations resounded
and ricocheted against the parameters of the children's daily activities.
The first, and at least initially for many, most tremendous of these
shocks was the expulsion of Jewish children from the state and state-

supported schools. (Again, although the dates of institution differ, the basic pattern of antisemitic legislation was essentially the same throughout Nazi and Axis Europe.) Nearly all schools were included in this legislation as schools of religious denomination in Europe were supported by the state. In many ways, this was the equivalent within the realm of childhood to the economic and employment prohibitions which adults suffered: children go to school, adults go to work. To go to school was the absolute social norm of childhood, a fixed activity of their lives, of the world they inhabited. This is what they were told they would do when they came of age, this is what they saw older children doing, and this is what they themselves began to do.

This violent separation from the community they shared with their gentile friends raised two distinct but obviously related sets of issues, and engendered a two-part reaction. The immediate response was related to the trauma of ostracism and expulsion. Suddenly, from one week to the next, a basic structure of their experience collapsed – and collapsed for them alone. Their subsequent reaction centered on the question of Jewish identity. For the first time in many of these children's lives, they were forced to confront the concept of what being a Jew meant to them and to the society in which they lived. They had no choice but to understand that they were thrown out of school solely because they were Jews. It was a legal and societally accepted sign that they were marked as different. No longer members of the community, they were strangers.

Given the implications and impact of this legislation, it is not surprising that its effects figure so prominently in the oral histories, memoirs, and diaries of Jewish children in Fascist and Nazi Europe. As Mariella Milano-Piperno, a well-to-do Jewish girl at the time explained, her parents tried to "sweeten the pill" of Mussolini's Fascism for her, but after the passage in November 1938 of the racial laws which excluded her from school, she felt "marginalized." That was, she said, the heart of the matter for her. She was simply excluded and discarded. "The day that we could not return to school, I remember that I was ashamed before my companions, to tell them: I cannot come because I am a Jewish girl." And then the questions came. "Why? What did I do not to be allowed to go to school?"[25]

At that point her family (like other Italian Jewish families) had two choices for their older children: to send them to a Catholic or to a non-denominational private school. The former was problematic in that there the children had to follow the entire Catholic rite, and the latter was designed for students who had to repeat a year because they had failed in the public schools, i.e. for remedial education. In Rome, as in many other cities in Italy, a Jewish primary school (grades one through five for children aged six to ten) was already in existence, but there was little in the way of Jewish secondary education for girls and boys the age of Mariella Piperno. To meet that need, a number of Jewish communities established schools for their young people.[26] They were taught by the schoolteachers and university professors who had lost their jobs as a result of the same racial laws of November 1938. For the adults the problem was resolved: their children would receive a good education; they were in school. For the young people themselves the solution was not so simple or so easily accepted. Their perspective was entirely different; this issue was fundamental to their daily lives and raised questions of community and identity.

Mariella Piperno's family considered the matter carefully. They were anxious for their daughters to live as normal a life as possible and to continue to go to school with Catholic Italian children. Furthermore, her grandmother, who was rather elderly at the time, "remembered all that the Jews had suffered in the ghetto [of Rome] when it was closed [until 1870], and she remembered with terror that fact of being enclosed all together." She urged her granddaughters, " 'Now that we have obtained liberty, why don't you profit by it, revel in it! Why must you enclose yourselves once again?' "[27] For two months Piperno attended a nondenominational private school, but the education she received was too poor to be acceptable and she enrolled in the Jewish high school.

By all accounts La Scuola Ebraica di Roma, like its counterparts elsewhere, was an extraordinary institution. The school in Rome provided three separate courses: gymnasium/lyceum (or academic high school), a technical institute, and a teachers' training school. It functioned for five academic years, from 1938 through 1943, and according to Italian law it was accredited by the state. (The principal was a state employee and an "Aryan.") The broad range of education offered was only one aspect of this phenomenal high school. The reason it is remembered with such affection and esteem is because the teachers and professors provided a forum for, and encouraged participation in, discussion of the questions which were central to their being at that school at all. When we went to the Jewish School, Piperno explained, "we asked: 'Who are we? What does it mean to be Jews?' " They, who had been very assimilated before and lived among Catholics all their lives, faced these questions when they were together. And they learned that Judaism was not a religion alone. "This was the great discovery of the Jewish School: when we began to understand that to be Jewish was not only to be of the Jewish religion. A Jewish culture existed, a Jewish civilization existed, that, in other words, all that is meant by Judaism existed. And this was very important. In my opinion, the Jewish School was like the opening of a book for us, and we began to read in this book which had been completely closed to us before." Furthermore, according to Piperno and her ex-schoolmates, their professors were quite simply excellent, and they received an incomparable education. This was true not only for the technical subjects like mathematics (which was taught by the well-known mathematician Emma Castelnuovo), but also for history and philosophy (taught by Monferrini) which, they said, they had to relearn completely, as they previously had been taught according to Fascist ideology. The intellectual openness and the depth of inquiry fostered by the professors were appreciated by the students. The intense personal interaction between the young people, in that particular atmosphere and special situation, led to the development of close friendships which are still dear to them today.[28]

Many of the elements of the experience of the Roman Jewish children were similar to those of young Jews from Amsterdam in the Netherlands to Kolozsvár in Hungary. A school system was established everywhere that there was a sufficient hiatus between the introduction of antisemitic legislation affecting social life and the operation of the actual machinery of deportation. In the Netherlands, for example, the edict prohibiting Jewish children from attending schools was published in August 1941. As in Italy, the Jewish education apparatus was not extensive, and the Jewish Council (which had been appointed in February 1941, nine months after the invasion of the Netherlands) faced the problem of constructing an entire school system. Primary schools were established in several cities and towns, and high schools were set up by the Council in Amsterdam and The Hague. All Jewish children were compelled to attend these schools, and the onus of compliance was on the parent or guardian. (Many Catholic and Protestant schools would have been willing to continue to educate converted children, but it was the parents and not the school authorities who were threatened in consequence.)[29]

Like their Italian counterparts, Jewish children in the Netherlands were forced to confront their expulsion from school and, as a result, the issues of Judaism and Jewish identity. Again, the first reactions of shame and shock were followed by the sense of something new and interesting, and of being at ease. Salvador Bloemgarten, for instance, was sixteen when he began to attend the Jewish Lyceum (where Anne and Margot Frank also were students) in September 1941. He, like many other pupils, was there for only one academic year (although the Lyceum continued to function into 1943) because deportations from the Netherlands began in earnest in July 1942 and so children were picked up or went into hiding.[30] Indeed, those who began the second academic year in

5   A class in a Jewish school in the Netherlands during the academic year 1941-42.

the Jewish schools remember it as a bizarre experience because each day
new seats were empty; their companions had disappeared and the children who remained wondered when their inevitable turn would come.[31]

But that first year, from 1941 to 1942, was for many students, as Salvador Bloemgarten affirmed, "a wonderful year." The schools for Jewish students were set up like other educational institutions, with the
usual classes, a headmaster, senior master, janitor, and so on. The education the Jewish pupils received was equal to that of gentile children;
after the war the Dutch government recognized the graduation certificates the schools had issued. It is important to note, however, that while
equal, the training was not precisely the same. First of all, the schools for
Jewish students were closed on Saturdays and Jewish holidays, as well as
Sundays. Then too, as the teachers recognized that their students would
not either attend or finish school in the normal way, they deviated from
the standard curriculum to offer programs they found interesting or en-
riching. Thus, at the Jewish Lyceum eight Friday afternoons in early
1943 were devoted to a series of lectures on the Romantic movement.
Not only was this unorthodox, it also had its complications. At one session a group of musicians played a Schumann quintet for the students,
but as the composer was a good "Aryan" the Jewish musicians were forbidden to play his work. They ignored the injunction.[32] On a more

personal level, students who survived the war remember their school experiences with warmth, and with the sense that they felt comfortable in that environment. "It was a strange thing; all the assimilated Jews [now in a completely Jewish environment] felt very comfortable with each other, there was a good atmosphere, and we also had good teachers [including] Dr Michman, who is now in Israel, and Presser as history teacher," Bloemgarten recalled.[33] Or as Mirjam Levi, who as a ten-year-old transferred to the newly created Jewish Montessori school in The Hague explained, "I remember a very amazing thing. . . . I remember when I was with these Jewish children in this Jewish school, very suddenly I felt very much at ease, and I felt that it was that we came from the same origin. I felt very good." She no longer had to be so careful about what she said and to whom. She felt that the children shared the same fate, had the same sort of family lives and, in that "intimate surrounding" she felt "free."[34]

The pattern for Jewish children in Kolozsvár was very much the same. Between the two world wars Kolozsvár, or Cluj as it was then (and is now) called, belonged to Rumania. Then, in 1940, the northern part of Transylvania (which included Cluj) was returned to Hungary, and its inhabitants became Hungarian. With the new citizenship came subjugation to the Hungarian racial laws, the Bill for the More Effective Protection of Social and Economic Life (May 1938) which defined who was a Jew and trammeled Jewish economic activity, and the Bill to Restrict Jewish Penetration in the Public Affairs and Economic Life of the Country (May 1939) which, among other measures, restored the Numerus Clausus Law of 1920 that had limited the admission of Jews to institutions of higher education to 6 percent.[35] This meant that a quota on Jewish students in the education system after the first four classes of elementary school was once again operant. As Sherry Weiss-Rosenfeld, who was eleven at the time, put it, "As soon as the Hungarians came, our life . . . changed. . . . We became, as children, totally segregated." She was supposed to start the first year of gymnasium and, like the great majority of Jewish children in Kolozsvár, she was denied admittance. "We didn't have any place to go. . . . We were left on the street with nothing to do." Jewish primary education already existed in the city, but a secondary school (which in Hungary began with the fifth grade at age ten) had to be organized immediately. As in the Netherlands and Italy, the students of this school remember their teachers, who had lost their state jobs through the same discriminatory legislation, as having been "excellent, excellent."[36] And again, these young people who had been legally separated from and rejected by the society in which they lived, were comfortable and at ease in the Jewish school. Gabor Czitrom was one of the few Jewish students to attend a non-Jewish school under the quota system the first year Kolozsvár became part of Hungary. It was a Calvinist institution, which he described as "a tolerant and excellent school. Nevertheless," he reflected, "we were two Jewish boys in a class of thirty. There we felt, and we were made to feel by a certain part of the class, that we were Jews – and stinky Jews too." This was his first encounter with this sort of abuse "as an institutional behavior." The following year Czitrom enrolled in the Jewish school: "I somehow went home. I was made to feel, quite distinctly, that I was out of place in this Calvinist school. . . . So going to the Jewish school, I definitely felt that I was going home. It was quite a natural move to go to a Jewish school with all the Jewish youth of my home town." At school, the students discussed politics and the war and, as in Rome, they were exposed to a dimension of Jewish culture other than religious observance. "What I found interesting," Czitrom observed, "was our religion teacher, a rabbi, who explained Biblical texts more on a literary and historical level than with its religious implication." That was something new; it was exciting and engaging at the time, and still worthy of note forty-five years later.[37]

In most countries except Germany itself, the institution of legal definitions to determine Jewish identity and the imposition of antisemitic economic measures were followed by the first step of a three-stage social isolation process. Expulsion from school, the sudden and shocking introduction of segregation in education, was the first of the legalized social abuses Jewish children suffered. Unfortunately, in the end, it was neither the last nor the worst. The next two components of this tripartite process, the innumerable prohibitions on normal daily activities designed to harass, terrorize, and subjugate the Jews (and to separate them from their gentile neighbors by forcing them to conduct their lives according to a distinct set of rules and regulations), and of course, the visible brand of the Star of David were imposed nearly everywhere, but not in one specific order. Thus, in Austria, Belgium, Germany, the Netherlands, Rumania, and Slovakia restrictions on social life preceded the star, while in most of Bulgaria, occupied France, Hungary, and Poland the star was introduced first (Vichy France and Italy never adopted the external star mark at all).[38] In either order, these antisemitic measures affected all Jews, including children. They narrowed, circumscribed, and made extremely perilous the world they as children inhabited.

In the interim period between the first step of this tripartite process (exclusion from school) and the last (either the star itself or the edicts which made it impossible to operate normally), Jewish children experienced a more or less gradual process of social segregation.[39] The public policy of antisemitism was played out in the private arena of their own daily lives in the form of personal discrimination on the part of their erstwhile friends and companions. Jewish children who had had amicable relations with, or even had been close to or intimate with, their gentile neighbors found themselves scorned and disdained. This was not, for them, a political measure; a law passed by others, an edict published in the papers. This was personal. For Lydia Gasman-Csato, who was fifteen when she was expelled from her school in Rumania, the essence of this process of segregation was humiliation and she, like many other children, made the obvious association and identification between that mortification and being Jewish. As a young child she had not been very "keenly aware of being Jewish or not being Jewish." She lived in a neighborhood of *Volksdeutsche* [ethnic Germans] and gentile Rumanians, and she was close friends with their children. "Until I was thrown out of high school I was [only] subliminally aware of being Jewish. The actual circumstances of my childhood, being among Germans and Rumanians, just made it irrelevant." That changed radically. "I, who was always the first in my class, was just thrown out of high school." It was then that her debasement began, and her personal sense of identity as a Jew started to be formed. "My best-loved friends were not Jewish," Csato explained. "One of them was, and remained, wonderful even during the war. . . . She came to visit me during the war; she brought me presents. She never changed. The other one, the third of this trio [we formed], Aurora Pavel . . . changed immediately. When I was thrown out of school she sent me a letter saying that she couldn't be friends with me because I came from a cursed race. So she wouldn't be friends with me anymore." Csato did not suffer physically during the war but, she asserted, "I suffered in one thing, and that is as bad as dying. Humiliation. Lack of dignity. . . . I consider human dignity to be as important as food and as breathing, and that is what I was deprived of." This was manifested in many ways: expulsion from school, loss of friendships, subjection to taunts, laughter, and ridicule, being barred from the cinema, and finally, for a short while, wearing the star. But it was the theoretical ideology and not the "different facts which supported this abstract situation of humiliation [which] mattered to [her]." There was only one reason for this lack of dignity: the concept of Jewish identity legally and commonly accepted by the society in which she lived. Therefore, she declared, "when I say I'm Jewish, I'm Jewish because I participated in the humiliation and slaughter of the Jews for 2,000 years." Or, to put it another way, "When I became aware" of being Jewish, it meant to be "committed, obligatorily committed for moral reasons, to a community which was slaughtered and humiliated for 2,000 years." It meant to be "committed to the destiny of the Jews."[40]

The text and sub-text of this process, segregation and concomitant humiliation, public policy and private abuse, political agenda and personal relations, was expressed by other children living elsewhere, albeit in more concrete terms. Alexander Ehrmann, for example, remembered that "when the Hungarians came in [to occupy the area of Czechoslovakia in which he lived] and we witnessed beatings for no apparent reason, that started the process which ultimately resulted in fear, and feeling terrorized and helpless. . . . I couldn't understand why. That was the constant question. Why? Why do they impose this kind of authority on us? Why do they have a right to beat us?" Within two months, the local boys "who were so friendly to me before, who called me by my Jewish name [which indicated the degree to which they had accepted him, as a human being and as a Jew] suddenly started to turn their backs on me. . . . Ultimately they too started beating us and pulling on our *peyes* [earlocks], and calling us 'dirty Jew.'"[41] Or, as Frieda Menco-Brommet explained, "At a certain moment my non-Jewish friends were not allowed to come anymore together with me." Suddenly, she said, she realized that "some of my friends were Jewish and some were not. And some of these non-Jewish friends were very loyal and others less loyal."[42]

German Jewish children had a long period in which to experience the inevitable exclusion and ostracism, as a 1.5 percent admission quota was introduced in April 1933 with the Law Against the Overcrowding of German Schools, and the star was not introduced until 1941. For Hilma Geffen-Ludomer, the only Jewish child in her neighborhood in the Berlin suburb of Rangsdorf, the transition was brusque. The "nice, neighborly atmosphere" ended "abruptly" in 1933. "Suddenly I didn't have any friends. I had no more girlfriends, and many neighbors were afraid to talk to us. Some of the neighbors that we visited told me, 'Don't come anymore because I'm scared. We should not have any contact with Jews.'"[43] Lore Gang-Saalheimer, who was eleven and living in Nuremberg, was exempt from the public school quota because her father had fought at Verdun in the First World War. Nevertheless, she said, it "began to happen that non-Jewish children would say, 'No, I can't walk home from school with you anymore. I can't be seen with you anymore.'" By 1935 she had had enough. Her reaction was similar to that related by other children. "Somehow, that seems to have been the year when the consciousness of my Jewishness and the differences, and the fact that I was disadvantaged came home to me." Saalheimer transferred to the Jewish secondary school and joined the Zionist organization Habonim, as well as a Jewish sports club. She, like many others, then began to live a two-layered existence. Externally, things "got worse. . . . Children in the streets used to shout out to me 'Jewish cow.' Or I'd have tickets to Jerusalem thrust in my hand." On another level, however, she was "extremely happy in my Jewish school in Germany. . . . I wallowed in it. I just loved it. . . . Whatever deprivation there was didn't seem to touch me all that much, . . . I accepted it as part of life."[44] Saalheimer was by no means unique in her appreciation and enjoyment of the cultural life she found in Habonim and the school for Jewish children. It was her personal experience, an individual manifestation, of a larger Jewish cultural renaissance which occurred in Germany between 1933 and 1938.[45] It ended with *Kristallnacht*, the Night of the Broken Glass, when the Nazis engaged in a planned pogrom of devastation of public and private Jewish property, for which the Jews were then forced to pay.[46] Saalheimer was living in Berlin at the time; she was attending a special school to acquire skills which would be useful after emigration from Germany. "My parents rang [the next evening] and said 'come home.'"

> I travelled home [to Nuremberg on an] express train. . . . I knew enough, I wasn't that stupid that I didn't know something had happened. I don't think I realized how bad things were until I got home. My parents were on the platform. My mother was in a sweater and skirt, no make-up, no jewelry, no anything. My father looked awful. . . .
>
> We went home. [There] was an atmosphere of complete gloom and no ornaments, no anything anywhere; the house was in mourning. . . . My parents had had a huge sideboard full of the best china, and [the Nazis] had taken an axe and smashed it, smashed the china. They had had a glass display cabinet with a lot of pretty things in it, and also glasses and so on. [The Nazis] had just taken it and thrown it over. I mean every little tiny last bit of it was broken. . . .
>
> Getting food was difficult. No shops were allowed to serve Jews in Nuremberg at that time, immediately after the ninth of November. . . . I remember my father trying to ring [his toy] factory, and trying to go there, but they wouldn't let him in. He had been dispossessed. [It was like] being struck on the head. The general feeling was one of huddles and talks and whispers, all quietly. The feeling of oppression. It was the first time I think I really felt a feeling of oppression and persecution. . . . This was a quantum step. This was the real thing.[47]

Given this process of segregation and separation, ostracism and humiliation, the introduction of the star was neither so sudden nor so traumatic for young people as it may appear in retrospect, or as it may have been at the time for adults. Indeed, for many children wearing the star itself had no awful symbolic meaning. They did not have the sophistication to comprehend that to be marked in this fashion transformed them from members of the community into strangers. A number of factors figured in this lack of consciousness. In part it was a question of personal nature, maturity, or political awareness, but in part it was also a result of context, or proximity to violence. Thus, both Peter Levi, a six-year-old child living in Budapest, and Gerry Mok, who had just turned five in Amsterdam, thought the star was marvelous. "I thought it was wonderful; I considered it a decoration," Peter Levi declared. "I remember my mother not buying one (you could buy them in the shop professionally made), but she found some yellow fabric and vaguely made one herself. My friends and my mother's friends sported nice, shiny shop-bought yellow stars which I thought were far more interesting. No way at six did I consider the stars as branding; I just thought they were something interesting to wear." [48] From the moment adults began to wear the star, "I envied them," Mok affirmed. "I wanted to have one as well and I wasn't allowed; I was too young. By the time I went into hiding it was likely that I wouldn't get it, so I missed it. After the war, when everybody had an orange kind of thing on his dress – because orange is also the color of our Queen – then I said, 'Now everybody has a star and I should have one too!' I really made a point of it after the war." [49] Gabor Czitrom was not, like the young children, excited by the prospect of wearing a star, but as a seventeen-year-old he did not fear it either. "I think it was not as upsetting at that time as I feel it now in retrospect. . . . It was very far from being a natural and normal thing, but it wasn't as revolting as I think it ought to have felt." It did not intimidate him because, he said, "we had no contact with any violence at that time." Furthermore, "for me it was quite obvious that in town people knew that I was a Jew, so the star did not add something new to all this." [50]

There is no question but that both the anticipated and actual response to the star made a tremendous difference to children. It was not the fact of being marked, but the potential physical harm which might result that caused them concern. In her diary entry of 1 May 1942, Bertje Bloch-van Rhijn delineated her fears and anxieties. The previous Wednesday she had returned home from an afternoon of physical exercise and went upstairs to her room to prepare for a geography exam.

> I saw the paper lying on the stairs and glanced at it for a moment and saw ANNOUNCEMENT and the word JEWS and started to read, totally

interested. Well now, all who are Jews, according to the umpteenth article, . . . had to wear a Jewish star (hexagonal), with JEW in the center. I didn't realize at first what it was, but I began to detest it gradually. All those NSB [Dutch Nazi Party] people! . . . And only then I started to think about it. That a lot of people would be very nice and that the NSB people would yell after me Yid, dirty Yid!

May 8
I have recovered from the anxiety about the star. Last week I thought about the NSB people, but nothing of that. The people are very nice, some even say good-day to you. Thus, yesterday I passed that boy of Jansen who said, "Hello Sister." Instead of [saying] something nice to me, he used to insult me deeply. Schoolboys scream, "Oranje Boven" [long live the Dutch Royal House of Orange] (because the star is orange) and some say "Yes, Orange triumphs over Germany," or "Jews survive the demise of Germany." [Others joke:] You know what it is when three Jews walk on the street? Night! And what is the name of the Joodebreestraat and the Waterlooplein? The Milky Way and Place de l'Etoile! And when you see a Jew fall you may make a wish.[51]

Soon after the introduction of the star, Peter Levi, Gerry Mok, and Bertje van Rhijn went into hiding. Gabor Czitrom was deported. For better and for incomparably worse, their experience with the star and its sequelae was rather short. Children who lived with it for some time endured its consequences. While initially similar, their perceptions changed with the passing months. Irene Butter-Hasenberg, for instance, lived in Amsterdam for over a year after the star edict came into effect. She was eleven years old in May 1942 when the badge was introduced in the Netherlands, and was deported to Westerbork in June of the following year.

The way the Dutch people responded to this edict that all the Jews had to wear stars was that large numbers of gentile people wore the star in the beginning. They felt that if everybody wore the star, it would defeat the purpose. Then, of course, measures were taken against that. So, because the Dutch people reacted that way, they said that wearing the star is a sign of pride; there was a positive association. I don't remember being upset or afraid of the consequences of having to wear the star. But then, after a while, things started happening. The Nazis started, or the NSBers started abusing that policy. For example, they stopped people on the street and then said, 'Take off

6   Irene Butter-Hasenberg (aged 4 or 5) and her father John Hasenberg at home in
Berlin, 1934 or 1935.

your coat' and if you didn't have a star on your jacket or your shirt
under your coat, they would prosecute you or punish you or beat you
for that. Or if one of the prongs of the star was not carefully sewn on
– I mean, they started doing some horrible tricks so that it became
very dangerous because it might never be right. It might just not be
right. Or sometimes people forgot, or it was summertime and they'd
take off their jackets and they didn't realize they didn't have the star
on; . . . really crazy things. As time went on, of course, there were
more and more incidents of brutality and of beating, shooting, arrest-
ing. So every day was fearful. You never knew what could happen.
     I didn't think it was a punishment. I didn't feel bad about my being
Jewish. I never hid my being Jewish. I wasn't taught to hide it and I
never had a bad experience or I never did hide it. It was only the consequences of having to wear the star as they emerged that became
troublesome.[52]

It was precisely these consequences which made the Parisian child professional singer Jaqueline Kamiéniarz feel "an outcast, different, and frightened. . . . I remember going to school and holding my books in such a way that they would not see my star. Why? Because I was afraid of: number one, being an outcast; number two, we were targets with that yellow star of pranks, and just nasty things – by the French themselves, *by the French themselves.*"[53]

The plethora of edicts and regulations to harass and mortify the Jewish population by regulating its movements in every facet of ordinary social life affected children too. Little by little, their normal activities were curtailed and the parameters of their physical world reduced. Unlike the star, which was feared for its consequences, these prohibitions meant *ab initio* that the children could no longer go to the park or the zoo, an ice-cream parlor or cinema, a museum or library. They were not welcomed as sports fans – it was prohibited to attend sports events – nor could they use public athletic facilities like swimming pools or tennis courts. Transportation, for fun or as a means of conveyance to a permitted activity, became increasingly problematic. Bicycles were appropriated, only the last car of the metro or trolley could be used, travel was allowed only at certain hours of the day, and then it was prohibited entirely. Their world continued to shrink. Curfews were introduced. Visits between Jews and gentiles were forbidden. Jewish friends were deported or disappeared. Children could go nowhere and could do nothing in the outside world. They were restricted to their own homes, gardens, courtyards.

But they had those homes, gardens, and courtyards. For a time, at the beginning of the war against the Jews, Jewish children had their homes and their families, their loyal gentile friends and their Jewish friends. And then came the moment of departure: to go into hiding, to escape as a refugee, to go to the ghetto, to be deported. "I came out [of Frankfurt am Main] in July 1939 with the children's transport," Hilda Cohen-Rosenthal recounted. "I remember going to the [central] station with my parents and my brother and this large trunk. . . . We were not a very kissing family . . . and I remember how odd that they all kissed me. . . . I thought I was going on holiday. [The] things I brought were *khumeshim* [the Five Books of Moses] and *sidurim* [prayer books]. This was the sort of thing my parents gave. What else could they give? [That was] the sort of people they were: the trunk was loaded with . . . special *khumeshim* and special *makhzoyrim* [holiday prayer books], for sending this child of ten out with what they thought was the most important thing in life. . . . There certainly wasn't a scene. Although I wasn't aware that I was going away probably for ever, they must have been aware that there was a very strong possibility that they would never see me again. And there was no question; there was no scene and there were no tears."[54] Mária Ezner, who was from Abádszalók, a small town on the great Hungarian plain, remembered the day her family was forced to leave home. "On the sixteenth of May [1944] we had to go out from our house, but we could hire a peasant cart, and on those peasant carts we could go. We had to pay ourselves. And we could bring [to the ghetto] for every person a bed, for every person a chair, and one table for the family."[55] Isabelle Silberg-Riff's mother was very house-proud. In 1937 the family moved into a new flat in Antwerp "with central heating and modern furniture." When her "father would come home on a Shabbat afternoon and he wanted to put his feet on the *new* chairs [my mother] ran quickly to get a paper to put under his shoes, it shouldn't spoil the new chair. That was 1937; 1940, the war broke out, and we left everything: the new chairs, the new chandeliers, whatever was new in 1937, what was fashionable in those days – we left it."[56]

Hasenberg was deported from Amsterdam to Westerbork in June 1943.

> I think it was a Sunday. . . . We heard either the night before or that morning that there was going to be a big *razzia* [round-up] and it was going to include our part of town. . . . This kind of news was always known and travelled very quickly. So what could you do? . . . Sooner or later the NSB started marching and they came with all their wagons and they blocked off the streets. They had these loudspeakers and they yelled out things. The Dutch people weren't allowed to go out, nobody was supposed to be out on the street, nobody could leave any house. Then they [the NSBers] started just going door to door; ringing bells and knocking and screaming, and getting people. You could stand at the window and just watch when they would be at your house.
>
> My father asked [the lover of our upstairs neighbor to go] somewhere to some person, to somebody's house to see if they could do something for us. . . . Since he was German he thought he could take the chance to go out even though there was really a curfew. . . . And he went to wherever it was that my father wanted him to go, but, you know, nothing was possible. . . . So, anyway, he came back. . . . But there was this discussion at some point . . . about whether he should take us somewhere, or whether we should hide somewhere, or whether we should hide in the attic – this was my brother and me, because my father thought that that could be arranged.
>
> So there was all this commotion going on and then in the meantime

we were getting ready. It was a very hot day. I remember we put on lots of layers of clothes, like three or four layers of clothes. And we had these rucksacks packed. Then at a certain point, they came and we went.[57]

At that moment, they left their homes. That was the end of life as they knew it. Few returned.

Chapter Two

Into Hiding

Ivan Buchwald was five years old, separated from his parents, and about to be deported to Auschwitz from his home town of Novi Sad in Yugoslavia. "We marched in a long line, row upon row of people, going to the station. We were walking along right next to a wood and an aunt, Etel Scleer, who lived in Vrbas, twenty miles from Novi Sad, and who was quite a character, suddenly ran out of the wood and picked me up in her arms, and ran into the wood again. . . . I went with my aunt to live with her for the rest of the war. Her house was in the country. I was hidden for the rest of the war, and I survived. Well, I wasn't *hidden*. They kept me at home as much as they could and it was drummed into me that on no account must I say that I was Jewish, although even at the age of five I knew I was Jewish. My parents must have been somewhat observant. Luckily her home was in the middle of the country, and all the neighbors who knew kept quiet."[1]

Ivan Buchwald's rescue was extremely dramatic and, a hastily devised maneuver, very different from the planned and orderly departure of Anne Frank and her family (who have come to be seen as paradigmatic of Jews in hiding during the war) from their home to their hiding place. Anne Frank's parents, Otto and Edith, made financial and practical arrangements for the hiding period well in advance of the actual move. Ivan Buchwald's parents were deported before they could formulate such plans. The Frank family hid as a unit. Buchwald was alone. The Franks remained in the city totally obscured from the world's vision (in hiding and hidden). Buchwald was taken into the country where he was in hiding but visible. The Franks lived in the attic for twenty-five months and ultimately were betrayed. Buchwald's clandestine existence lasted less than a year, and he survived. In other particulars also the two children could not have differed more: one was female, the other male; Anne was an adolescent, Ivan a young child; she was a relatively sophisticated urbanite who had some sense of national, cultural, and religious identity, while he was still unformed – he knew he was Jewish in the same way as he knew his own name. In short, in terms of culture, class, age, gender, degree of religious identification, and experience they shared little. Yet both were marked as Jews, as the other, the stranger, and at the behest of their elders both went into hiding for some period of the war in an effort to survive the German machinery of death.[2]

In this and the following chapter we shall examine precisely how this was done, how arrangements were made and contacts organized. We shall investigate the various sorts of networks that arose spontaneously to save and protect Jewish children: who volunteered to do this kind of work, how did they carry out their projects, what sorts of families took in the young people, and how did they manage to provide food and clothing in war-ridden Europe? We shall differentiate between, and investigate the difficulties of being in hiding and hidden as compared with in hiding and visible. And we shall try to come to understand the parameters of these experiences both in terms of daily life, and in terms of their effect – what did the children do all day, how did they live, and what did it mean to them to live clandestinely?

Arrangements for hiding were made in one of two ways: informally through a family and friend network, or with the help of some type of organization. In other words, the problem of an individual child was resolved through a personalized solution, while those who were concerned with the plight of all Jewish children tried to devise a generalized, or universally applicable solution. There was also a rare third pattern. Sometimes no arrangements were made, but the child, operating independently, nevertheless went into hiding. All of these plans were precarious at best – there were no guarantees – but to hide oneself, to function alone, was in many ways the most insecure of all. To do so meant that the young person spent the war years on the run, moving from place to place constantly maintaining an existence outside the law or, alternatively, by obtaining false papers and simply living and working illegally, "passing" as a gentile. In either case the child had to be of an age to be able to care for himself, and the majority of those who undertook to hide themselves in this way were older than the young people who are the subject of our study. There were children who did do so, however, and Jerzy Kosinski and Jack Kuper were amongst them. Kosinski's poetic memoir, *The Painted Bird*, and Kuper's fictionalized *Child of the*

Holocaust depict their extraordinary ordeals. Kosinski was six and Kuper eight years old when they were left on their own to wander from village to village in rural Poland, hiding their Jewish identity and past history, and scrambling to survive by doing odd jobs for peasant farmers in exchange for food and a place to sleep.[3]

By their very nature children were too young to operate independently, and arrangements were made for them. The most common situation was that of informal contacts. Thus, for example, Margaret Ascher-Frydman, who came from a prominent and assimilated family, was helped through her parents' acquaintanceships. In the summer of 1942 she, her mother, and her younger sister were living in the Warsaw ghetto. Frydman's mother sought a refuge for her daughters, then aged twelve and six. "My mother learned that there were some children in [The Family of Mary] convent, and asked a woman, a friend, a wife of a lawyer whom my father knew and who was very religious, whether she could ask the sisters to take me. And they took us [the two girls] on the ninth of September. . . . We came to the convent, the sisters were there, and the Sister Superior said yes; she accepted us."[4] In Rome, the eighteen-year-old Roberto Milano and his friends were helped in very much the same way; that is, through his father's gentile business associates. On 8 September 1943 the Italian government asked the allies for an armistice and it became clear that Germany would occupy Italy. The situation for Italy's Jews who, until then, had been spared the worst, became urgent. A few of Milano's friends' fathers met in his parents' home to discuss the current state of affairs, and they decided that the boys had to hide. The following day Milano and three of his companions went into the Abruzzi mountains. "We went to this area because it was the birthplace of a delivery man for my father's stores. He was a trustworthy person who had worked for my father for thirty years, and he himself suggested that we be sent to that tiny village where there were not even streets, and which could be reached only by climbing through the woods and up the mountains."[5] The physical circumstances of Milano and Frydman could not have been farther removed, but both were menaced by the threat of deportation, and in both cases arrangements for their flight to safety were made informally, through the family's own network of contacts.

"Informal" contacts meant that the parents would ask a friend, or a friend of a friend, or the relative of a gentile relative-by-marriage whether she would hide, or help to hide, their family. Families usually separated when they went into hiding (unlike the well-known example of Anne Frank's household). Some did so to reduce the risk of total annihilation. Most, however, found that for purely logistical reasons it was impossible to remain together as a single unit. To hide one person was an enormous undertaking; it required space and food as well as constant vigilance and luck. The more people hidden in one place, the greater the risk and the more onerous the task. Furthermore, families separated because there were more opportunities for children to be hidden than for their parents. It was easier to hide a child; if they were young enough they did not need papers, and even older children simply were not the subject of official curiosity. Often they could be passed off as relatives come to stay or war orphans from a bombed city or evacuated area. The net result of these practical and sensible considerations was that the child found herself alone, separated from her family. Eline Veldhuyzen-Heimans, for instance, was just under three years old when she went from Amsterdam, where she lived with her parents, to Zuilen, where she was hidden from 1942 to 1944. According to Heimans, extensive arrangements had not been made. The family with whom she was hidden were relatives of neighbors who lived around the corner from her parents. From what she was told after the war, she understood that the whole matter was settled very simply. "In a conversation [between her parents and their neighbors] it was once mentioned that they had family who lived in such and such a place, and were prepared to take a child." Heimans called her foster parents "aunt" and "uncle," and they introduced her as their niece to their neighbors and friends.[6]

Georges Waysand, who at fourteen months of age was even younger than Eline Heimans, was explained to neighbors as an evacuee. Waysand's parents were communists and Jews, and deeply involved in the Resistance. As they both were very active "there was naturally the question of who will take care of me." According to Waysand, it was through the communist network that his parents located a family to look after him. He was not well treated there "so [my parents] took me back. And they asked friends whether they didn't know of another place. Finally they selected the village where I was going to be, [and] they brought me to a house where I was just supposed to stay for a few days, because it was a house used by the Resistance movement." In the end, Waysand remained with this family in La Bassée, in the north of France. "In the street they said that I was a 'child of the coast,' which means that when there was the bombing of Dunkirk, all the children were taken out of that zone, which was not so far away, and were housed with families all over the country. They said, 'He's one.' The only problem was that I was also a little bit dark, and I didn't look like the children of Dunkirk! But they managed to say that to the people in the street, and apparently everybody made believe that. They didn't ask any questions."[7]

Waysand's parents' contacts were, as we have seen, through an organization (the communist apparatus), but as they themselves were members, the people with whom the arrangements were made were simply their friends or comrades; the actual contact was an informal one. In other instances, however, such networks operated as an organization to hide children. The term "organization" may be misleading. Within the context of the war and the resistance work of hiding children, all that it is meant to imply is the creation of a network or system to save children, rather than individual, informal family and friend arrangements. Such an "organization" could have been started by just one person, or a family like the Boogaards which developed their own network and hid hundreds of Jews (as well as others) on their and their neighbors' farms in the Haarlemmermeer area of Holland.[8] It could have been a group formed by a number of disparate people whose common cause was their concern about the Jews, like Żegota (the Council for Aid to Jews) in Warsaw, or the Naamloze Venootschap (or NV, the Dutch equivalent to Ltd, i.e. limited company) in the Netherlands. And finally, extant institutions, such as the Protestant and Catholic churches, self-help associations like the Oeuvre de Secours aux Enfants (OSE), youth groups from the scouts to university student clubs, or as in the case of Georges Waysand, the apparatus of political parties, undertook to hide children as part of their resistance work.

For all three genres of organizational arrangement the pertinent questions are the same: how was contact made between those who needed help and those willing to offer it, and how did the system function? Antoinette Sara Spier, a fifteen-year-old girl living in Arnhem in 1942, remembered that "a brother of my mother was living quite near the Haarlemmermeer, and it was his idea that we had to hide there. He thought it would be safe and he had the address of the farmer Boogaard, that famous farmer who always came to save the Jewish people." Sara Spier and her cousin Joop Mogendorff were the first of the family in Arnhem to be hidden. "We were very fond of each other, and our parents decided to send us together so it wouldn't be too bad for us. It was a good idea, I think. We went together with Johannis Boogaard. And when we arrived the brother of my mother was already there with his wife and two children. They were very cheerful when we came, they made jokes, so it made it a bit easy for us and well, we sulked just for a few minutes. Still, I found it very difficult to leave home. Yes, it was difficult – with that strange looking man. He was wearing a frock coat and it was very strange. But I felt safe because my cousin was with me, and when I came there I saw family."[9]

Joop's younger brother, Paul Mogendorff, was almost ten years old in late August 1942 when Johannis Boogaard returned to Arnhem to bring

7 Metje Boogaard with a younger sister and a Jewish boy, said to be a cousin, in hiding with them.

the boy to his farm in the Haarlemmermeer. His memories of that day express his sense of the normality and inevitability of his transition from family life in the morning to a clandestine existence in the afternoon. "A man came to our house. He was Oom [uncle] Hannis, Hannis Boogaard. He was helping Jewish people because he was convinced that Jewish people should be saved. He was a very religious man . . . and he helped many people," Mogendorff explained. "He collected me that day; he was wearing a tuxedo with long tails. Yes, he was wearing tails which was very funny, of course. That was his best suit; he was a farmer." Paul Mogendorff had been to school that morning. "I just came home at lunch time, and I went off two hours later to my hide-out. . . . I remember that I didn't wear a star when I went off, of course not. [My parents] told me to be quiet in the train. Actually, I don't remember many extraordinary things. Nothing special. I just went with this man and he told me he would be good to me, so I accepted this. And I understood why. I really understood why. I was then almost ten years old, so I was old enough to understand what was happening."[10]

The Boogaard family had come to hide Jewish children more or less by happenstance. The elderly farmer, Johannis Boogaard, his adult daughter Aagje and four sons, Antheunis, Willem, Hannis, and Piet, their cousin Metje and their families were known anti-Nazis in Nieuw Vennep. During the first two years of the German occupation the Boogaards manifested their political sentiments through individual acts of economic sabotage. Then, early in 1942, they took in Jan de Beer, a young gentile man who had been called up for forced labor service in Germany and had refused to go. Among the labor conscripts who subsequently took refuge on the Boogaards' farm was a Jewish fellow. When he asked if his parents also could hide on the farm as they too were in danger, the Boogaards saw a need to be met and a responsibility to accept. From then on, Hannis Boogaard traveled throughout the country to find Jews, especially children, and bring them to the Haarlemmermeer. As in the case of Sara Spier and her Mogendorff cousins, contact usually was made through family connections between the Boogaards and those who wished to hide.[11]

The Boogaards also found a way to help children who did not have the advantage of familial networks to make either informal or organizational arrangements. Aided by two women collaborators in Amsterdam, Truus de Swaan-Willems and Lies de Jong, Hannis Boogaard had children abducted from the Jewish orphanage in Amsterdam and brought to his farm. Lies de Jong had been a resident of the orphanage in her youth; she knew the habits of the institution and its personnel. It was her task to pick up children as they walked in a queue to school and on outings. She passed them on to de Swaan-Willems who, in turn, handed them over to Hannis Boogaard. It was in this way that Maurits Cohen came to the Boogaard family. In 1942 Cohen was eight years old and living in a Jewish children's home in Amsterdam. "On a certain day, we small children walked along the streets in Amsterdam. The underground came and took me out of the line of children into a urinal and they cut off the star – back on the street – and I was sent to [the] farmer [Boogaard]. I was not told in advance; it just happened."[12] Maurits Cohen, Sara Spier, and Paul Mogendorff did not remain on the Boogaard farm long. It was their point of depature for the next three years of hiding; their access to the network which evolved out of the Boogaards' initial efforts.

The Boogaard family took on the work of hiding Jews and other people who had to disappear out of a deep religious conviction and strong anti-German sentiment. Their network began with a familial nucleus. As their operations became increasingly complex, other people joined them in their efforts. Other groups did not begin with such an organic core. People who were unrelated to each other, and indeed shared nothing except their common cause, came together to establish organizations to accomplish the same ends. Their motivations varied. Animated by political ideology, humanitarian beliefs, and religious principles, they formed alliances to aid and assist Jews through the Nazi years.[13] Thus, for example, in Poland late in September of 1942 people as different as Zofia Kossak-Szczucka, a well-known novelist and one of the founders as well as President of the conservative Catholic social organization, the Front for Reborn Poland, and the democrat Wanda Krahelska-Filipowiczowa worked together to found the (clandestine) Temporary Committee to Help Jews. The Committee's activities were centered in Warsaw, but branches were opened and contacts maintained in Cracow and Lwów also. In the first two months of operation the Committee aided 180 Jews, primarily children. At the same time, the Committee submitted a proposal to establish a permanent and national version of itself to the Delegatura (the representative body on Polish soil of the Government in Exile in London). The Delegatura accepted the proposal in November and early the next month they established the Council for Aid to Jews (Rada Pomocy Żydom, or RPZ), which was known by the cryptonym Żegota. Representatives of the political parties of the Delegatura participated in the work of the Council, including the Front for Reborn Poland, Democratic Party, Polish Socialist Party 'Liberty-Equality-Independence,' Bund, Jewish National Committee, Union of Polish Syndicalists, and Peasants' Party; in other words, the entire political spectrum was committed to this endeavor.

The purpose of Żegota was to help Jews by securing hiding places for them, and by providing financial assistance and false documents to those leading a clandestine existence. Like its predecessor, Żegota's activities were concentrated in Warsaw, but it too functioned to some degree in a number of areas in Poland (Cracow, Lwów, Radom, Kielce, and Piotrków, among others). Furthermore, saving and caring for children remained a central focus of the Council's efforts: in July 1943 a Children's Bureau was established under the direction of Irena Sendlerowa. She was well chosen for the task. When the Germans invaded Poland in 1939, Sendlerowa was working in the Social Welfare Department of the Municipal Administration of Warsaw. From the beginning, she created a network to provide financial and material assistance. "I decided to take advantage of my job to assist the Jews," she explained. "The Social Welfare Department of the Municipal Administration had a wide network of centres in various districts at that time. I managed to recruit trustworthy people to cooperate with me, at least one in each of ten centres. We were compelled to issue hundreds of false documents and to forge signatures. Jewish names could not figure among those of people getting assistance." She continued these activities even after the ghetto was instituted. By that time, Sendlerowa and her collaborators "had about 3,000 people in our care, of which 90 percent found themselves behind the ghetto walls from the very first day. With the setting up of the ghetto our whole system of assistance, built up with such great effort, was destroyed. The situation became even more complicated when the gates of the ghetto were closed. We then had to solve the problem of how to legally get into the ghetto." Sendlerowa obtained documents for herself and her close colleague Irena Schultz which allowed them to enter the ghetto legally, and she established contact with Eva Rechtman who, on the other side of the wall, organized a secret network of women employed by the Jewish charitable organization CENTOS. In this way, Sendlerowa and Schultz were able to bring money, food, medicine, and clothing (which they obtained by presenting false documentation to the Social Welfare Department) into the ghetto, where it was distributed by Rechtman and her associates.[14]

The creation of Żegota provided an additional impetus to this undertaking. Sendlerowa and Schultz began to work under its aegis; their activities gained a more secure financial basis and their network of contacts expanded. It was none too soon. Mass expulsions of the Jews from Warsaw had begun in 1942, and Sendlerowa and Schultz were determined to smuggle children out of the ghetto to hide them on the "Aryan" side. They had addresses of families in the city who were willing to take the children; their problem was to spirit them out of the ghetto. According to Irena Sendlerowa, Schultz specialized in this. In her account of their activities she explained that "the children were usually brought out of the ghetto through the underground corridors of the public courts building and through the tram depot in Muranów district." The children were placed with families or in orphanages and convents; the former received a maximum of 500 zlotys a month from the Council, in addition to clothing, food parcels, and milk coupons as needed. By the end of 1943, in addition to those in private homes the Children's Bureau had found berths for 600 youngsters in public and ecclesiastical (over 550 children), and relief organization (at least 22 young people), institutions. In total, some 2,500 children were registered by the Warsaw branch of the Council.[15]

The Council for Aid to Jews was one branch of Poland's official underground work; as we have seen, it was formed with the consent of the Delegatura, and representatives of the political parties of which that organization was composed participated in the Council's efforts. Other underground groups equally devoted to saving Jews – and Jewish chil-

dren in particular – were organized far less formally. Unaffiliated with
any established association or political party, they were formed by
people who, very simply, felt the need to act. It is important to note that
many of these groups, which were organized specifically to protect
human lives, did not receive either honor or attention after the war. Indeed, while much is known about the armed resistance, the history of
the organizations which helped children has only recently become part
of the legitimate public past. There are a number of reasons for this:
practical, political, and social. First, as the majority of these underground networks (like the NV or Piet Meerburg Group) did not apply
for or receive financial assistance from their respective national central
councils of resistance organizations, their work was never on public
record. But there were also ideological reasons for the marginalization
of underground activity dedicated to the rescue and relief of children.
For many years after the war, each country's "Resistance Movement"
was defined in terms of those groups which undertook activities of a
more public nature: armed defiance, underground newspapers, lightning
attacks to destroy records or steal documents, tactical maneuvers, sabotage. These more "heroic" operations were clearly patriotic and nationalistic, and they became part of the history of the honor of each country.
Saving children was, by contrast, neither a public deed at the time nor
the stuff of glory afterwards. In short, celebrating or commemorating
such work did little to foster the ideology of the suffering of the nation
under Nazism, and of the illustrious deeds which were undertaken to
throw off the yoke of oppression. Less obviously nationalistic and mani-
festly humanitarian, the business of saving lives during the war was not
politically useful in reconstructing a national consciousness and
patriotic pride when the hostilities ended.

     Finally, the majority of the resistance workers who undertook to save
and sustain life were women, and the people for whom they cared were
children – Jewish children. In other words, the disparity between this
and other resistance work is the difference between the nursery and the
battlefield; one is private the other public, the former is seen as personal,
family history, while the latter is national in scope and character; the
realm of women and children in contrast to the domain of men. These
divisions were enhanced by the fact that the rescuers' perception of the
work they had done, their view of their achievements, was rather different from that of the militant resisters. After the war these women
underground workers disappeared from public life. They did not seek
publicity and they had left few records. Unlike the men who had joined
the official resistance and who assemble each year at the national monuments of remembrance to mourn their fallen comrades, these women to

this day speak unceremoniously of their activities as just another job that had to be done, and they insist that they are not remarkable for having undertaken it. As Rebecca van Delft, one of the couriers of the Dutch NV group put it, the question was "would I be ready to accompany Jewish children by train from Amsterdam to Heerlen (in the province of Limburg, in the south of Holland) where better could be found homes for them to hide, in order to save them out of the hands of the Germans. Of course I was willing to do such a thing: it was just a natural thing to do." Van Delft was eighteen or nineteen years old at the time, and living at home with her family in Amstelveen, just south of Amsterdam. She did not discuss her decision with her parents; "I don't remember [asking them] for their permission: it was evident that I should do such a thing, being asked for." In fact, van Delft explained, the work only could have been done by women. "For young men it was very dangerous to do such a thing by train, because the German soldiers always asked young men to show their identification cards: young men should be working in factories in Germany. But young women they would not so easily suspect – and indeed, during the time I did the job I was never stopped by a German soldier."[16] Jooske Koppen-de Neve, who was brought into the NV network both by Rebecca van Delft and through her friendship with the first people the group hid, the Braun family, echoed van Delft's assessment of her role in the operation. "To praise [me] would be the worst thing that ever could be for me. Everything I did during those days was just normal. Any other person in my place would have taken that on, I'm sure of that. . . . When it comes so real to you in person, in a living person then, yes, you get involved. You can't get on with your ordinary things."[17] As another woman who was central to the passage of children out of Amsterdam to hiding places in the provinces commented, "Yes, we did it, of course we did it. It's nothing special that we did it. We were in the circumstances to do that. The circumstances were that I was there. . . . We met Christian people who wanted to help Jewish children, and therefore we did it. I always say it was nothing special."[18]

One last factor needs to be mentioned to explain why organizations dedicated to the rescue of children only recently have become the focus of public attention. The children themselves, the very people who were saved, either were not or were not perceived to be articulate witnesses after the war. Individuals and organizations concerned with saving adults were honored much sooner, as those they helped were able to demand this recognition for their benefactors. It took forty years for the children who were hidden and helped to come of age. And it was only when these former children took on the responsibility of adults in public life that they were able to call attention to those who had saved them, the ignored women and men of cleverness and courage during the war.

Let us return to the question of how informally established underground groups which were organized to save Jewish child life functioned. Unlike, for example, the Council for Aid to Jews, these networks were not officially established or recognized by a national central council of resistance organizations. How were they created, how did they operate, and how were contacts made between them and those they wished to help? The history of the NV group is essentially typical of the development and operation of the marvelous, but tragically too few, underground networks which sprang up spontaneously throughout Europe to rescue Jewish children from Nazi persecution. The organization which became the NV began with an encounter between two young men, Gerard and Jacob Musch, who refused to accept the German invaders' deprivation of human liberty, and Marianne Marco-Braun and her family, who were in danger. The Brauns had come to Amsterdam from Vienna in 1938. Marianne was then fifteen years old. In Amsterdam, the family took the unusual step of conversion to the Dutch Reformed Church; "there we made new friends," Braun explained. "So when things, after the invasion, got worse as they did slowly and gradually, there was a lot of concern for us in the church where every Sunday we used to go for service." In May 1942 "we had to wear the star," she recalled. "And with the star, of course, on Sundays we went to church. So then [the situation] was even more obvious, and people used to come and commiserate and think how terrible it was." Soon thereafter, Marianne and her brother Leo "were called up to go to Germany for work. That's when really all people, all the friends, were very concerned. . . . This is when the brothers Jacob and Gerard Musch came to us. We knew them, but not all that well. They came up one day and they said to us, 'Are you going? What's happening?' I said, 'Well, what can we do?' They said, 'We could possibly find you some addresses to hide.'" This was "a totally new idea" for Braun and her family, and initially her parents opposed it. "I remember my father said, 'This won't be possible; they can hide you, but for how long? They [the Germans] will find you in the end. It's not possible to be hidden; the Germans are far too clever and sophisticated. And where can you be hidden? Eventually, they'll find you.'"

So we sat and we didn't know what to do; we didn't know what to do. [Gerard and Jacob] came back the next day and they said they had an address for us, for my brother and for me. I said, "But we can't go without our parents. What about our parents?" They felt it was more important to take us, being young. I couldn't take that. I said, "No, we can't go unless you find something also for my parents." So they went away again and a couple of days later they came back and said they had found an address for my parents, too.

By that time it was near the date when we were called up . . . and we had to decide. One moment we said, yes, we'll go, and the next moment we said (as a family it was), we can't do it. We'd better go to the labor camps. [We] finally decided, yes, we must go. But then it had to be very quick. I remember some school friends of mine came and arranged everything. You see, it was already quite dangerous. . . .

Gerard and Jaap came and said everything is arranged. There was a curfew already at night when people were not allowed to walk the streets after a certain hour. So we quickly had to go with them. We said goodbye to our parents and of course one didn't know if one would see them again or when. They would come back for the parents a few days later. . . . We spent the night at the Musch house. The next morning they took us up to Friesland where they had found addresses for us. I stayed with a schoolteacher, my brother with a farmer.[19]

It is important to note that Jacob (or Jaap) and Gerard Musch, the original two central figures of the organization that eventually was known as the NV, came to create an underground network to save Jewish children's lives more or less by happenstance. In the spring of 1942 they had no such formed concept. Like so many others who became involved in this work, they did not have numerous Jewish friends. But when they realized that the Brauns were in danger and needed help, they were ready to organize that assistance. Gerard Musch co-opted his friend Dick Groenewegen van Wyck and, after resolving the immediate problem of placing the Braun family, the three young men began to plan a way to rescue Jewish children from the Germans. They concentrated their energies on children because they themselves were young and they felt they would not be able to deal so effectively or authoritatively with older people, and also because they believed they would have greater success in hiding children. They faced two major practical problems: finding homes for the children, and establishing contacts with those who needed to be hidden. They did not have an easy start. They went to the northern province of Friesland in the hope of securing addresses but, perhaps because they did not have sufficient connections or the right introductions, they were unsuccessful. Undaunted by their failure, they decided to try the southern province of Limburg. There, in the fairly large mining town of Heerlen, they made contact with a Protestant mini-

8　Marianne Marco-Braun.

ster named Gerard Pontier. As the population of Limburg was over-whelmingly Catholic, the Protestant community was tightly knit. Dominee Pontier knew his congregants personally, and the church members were well acquainted with each other, and each other's business. It was through this chain of contact that the Musches and Groenewegen came to the Vermeer family in nearby Brunssum, which became the secure core of the network in the area. Truus Grootendorst-Vermeer still remembers when Jaap Musch came to the door to speak with her parents. And suddenly half her family was involved – her mother and father, her brother Piet, and very soon Truus herself, who gave up her job to do this work full time. "My parents couldn't afford to do without my salary then. (I gave them everything and got pocket money!) So for them and for me it was a big step. . . . I thought, here these bloody Germans are doing something against innocent people, and that put my back up. They were so arrogant. I can still see them coming in. We first heard the planes going over, that was for Rotterdam. But then, not an hour later, the German soldiers came through the streets. We were all hanging out of the windows. If looks could have killed, they all would have been dead! . . . I'll never forget that hate feeling. Yes, I liked my office job, but I liked the people more."[20]

At that time, Truus Vermeer had a friend (whom she married after the war), Cor Grootendorst, and she sent a message to him telling him to come to Limburg. There was work to do. "And that's how I became number six!" Cor recalled.

CG: Our work was in the first place finding addresses. Going to families (and you almost felt like a salesman), knocking on doors through introductions. We didn't go blindly from house to house. We had to know that the people were safe, and there was a reasonable chance that they might be willing to help. [The introductions came] mostly through the clergy.

TV: My mother, because of her big family, was very well known to and had a good name with a Catholic priest. So we also went to a priest and we got addresses from him as well.

CG: It worked like a snowball virtually. You get one address and even if it's a yes or no, there always would be a person against the Germans. Whether the answer was, "I don't dare to," or for some reason "I can't," the stock question was, "Do you know anyone else who might be willing?" And they gave you two or three addresses. It's like a chain. So it was not too difficult to find potential addresses of people who might help you.[21]

Leaving the local people (the Vermeer family and Truus's friend Cor) to identify potential hiding addresses, Jaap and Gerard Musch and Dick Groenewegen returned to Amsterdam to get children. By this time (the summer of 1942) the situation for the Jews in the Netherlands had become desperate. During the first half of 1942 the Germans had forced the Jewish population to leave their homes throughout the Netherlands and relocate in Amsterdam. As they were permitted to lodge only in Jewish quarters or to live with Jewish families, a ghetto without walls was created. This physical concentration of the Jews facilitated the process of wholesale deportation, which began in July 1942. Initially, Jews (like Marianne Braun and her family) were sent letters commanding them to report for "labor service," but by the late summer the Germans decided that too few were complying with these written orders. The *razzias* began. Arrested Jews were marched or driven to a central deportation point, first the Central Office for Jewish Emigration, and then from mid-October, to a theater, the Hollandsche Schouwburg. There the Germans processed the captive Jews for removal from Amsterdam to the transit camp of Westerbork.

The Germans interned enormous crowds in the theater; often more

9   Jewish and host children in the Vermeer family's garden at the end of the summer of 1943. Left to right: Lea Winnik (in hiding), Ronnie de Jong (in hiding), Greetje Kloots (in hiding), Lien Vermeer (not Jewish) and Miep Vermeer (not Jewish).

than 1,500 people plus their allowed luggage were packed into the building. People were held there for days, sometimes for weeks. There was no room to sleep, the hygienic conditions were abominable, and the noise was unbearable – even for the jailers. To reduce their own discomfort, the Germans decided to send children under the age of twelve across the street to a child-care center. This crèche had been a well-established neighborhood institution used by working-class families. In 1942 it was taken over as an annex to the Schouwburg. The director, Henriette Rodriquez-Pimentel, and the young Jewish women who assisted her, had no illusions as to the fate awaiting the children. They were determined to smuggle the children out of the crèche and pass them on to others who would take them to safe addresses. As every person, adult or child, who entered the Schouwburg was registered by an employee of the Jewish Council (which was controlled by the Germans of course),

Pimentel needed help from an insider to destroy the children's records. This task was undertaken by Walter Süskind and Felix Halverstad. Their positions with the Council did not give them access to the registration cards, but they too were resolute and concocted all sorts of ruses to rifle the records. Thus a number of children disappeared from the files of the bureaucracy, and this meant that neither their parents nor the crèche personnel would be held responsible for them. Officially they did not exist. It was now up to Pimentel and her assistants to get the children out of the crèche and to pass them to resistance workers to be hidden.[22]

Jaap and Gerard Musch and Dick Groenewegen knew about the crèche but not about its underground traffic, and they had no connections with Jews who had not yet been arrested. Probably through Piet Meerburg, a leader of an Amsterdam student operation devoted to the same cause,[23] they were given the name of Joop Woortman, alias Theo de Bruin. De Bruin was the sort of person who knew almost everybody in the city ("a real Amsterdammer"), and he was a serious and dedicated resister. Because of his huge social network, which included many Amsterdam Jews, de Bruin had been approached early in the occupation for help in obtaining false identity cards, ration coupons, and, finally, hiding places. This work became increasingly consuming, and by the time he met the Musch brothers he and his wife, Semmy, were constantly involved with it.

Semmy Woortman-Glasoog's recollection of the initial meeting was that "the boys came to our house. We had a meeting, we talked, but the boys didn't know too much because they were very young. But Jaap was a serious man and Theo was, on this point, also very serious. And we talked about what we could do and how it would take shape. I listened and I told them, 'You have to realize that if you are going to do what you are talking about, then your life after this is a gift. If you don't want that, you shouldn't go on.' And they all said, yes, they wanted to do it. I think the younger boys didn't realize exactly what they did. But Jaap, he knew what he did, he knew; and Theo knew very well, and I knew."[24]

In the plan they evolved, each small group of people was responsible for one link of the network. To delimit danger in case of arrest they did not tell each other how they proceeded or with whom they had contact. Theo de Bruin (and to some extent Semmy also) made the connections with the crèche and with the Jewish families who had not yet been taken to the Schouwburg. According to Rebecca van Delft, who had worked with him, de Bruin was a man of "almost improbable courage and boldness" who did things others considered impossible, including "simply picking up [children] during a *razzia* in the street."[25] Sometimes he sent

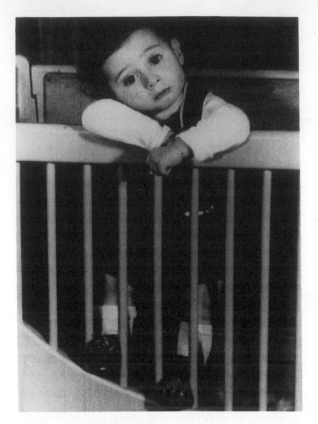

10 Remy, a foundling, just before deportation, 1942 or 1943. The Germans declared all foundlings to be Jews to prevent unknown parentage from protecting possibly Jewish children.

one of the younger men to collect crèche children from the agreed delivery point, or he gave them the address of a Jewish family with a child to be hidden. But in general it was he who undertook that part of the rescue work. Gerard, Jaap, and Dick got the children from Theo and Semmy and, with a few young women who had joined the organization, brought them to Limburg.

Marianne Braun had been the connecting link between the original women couriers, Rebecca van Delft and Jooske Koppen-de Neve, and the Musch brothers. Van Delft, de Neve, and Braun had been good friends at school, and remained close after Braun was forced to leave the Amsterdam Lyceum to attend a Jewish school. When Braun and her family went into hiding, Marianne told the Musches about her friends. It was Gerard who went to visit Rebecca to ask her if she would accompany Jewish children from Amsterdam to Heerlen. "One day in summertime (as I remember, July 1942) at our door came Gerard Musch – an unknown young person, who told me that he came as a friend of Marianne Braun, and if he could have a personal talk with me. It all seemed mysterious to me."[26] Van Delft agreed and soon thereafter told her friend Jooske de Neve about the underground network and put her in touch with Gerard and Jaap. De Neve was more than happy to become involved. She had been vexed by the Germans' abuse of the Jews since the first measures had been instituted, and especially so when she experienced the ostracism of her friend Marianne. After Braun had been barred from the Amsterdam Lyceum, de Neve went to visit her in her home in the Jewish quarter. "I don't remember exactly where or how that looked. I only remember that I entered that ghetto and then things hit me. I was very confused. It was so horrible that I was very determined to do something about that, as far as for me it could be possible. I was completely *boulversée*, absolutely turned around. It made me sick, physically sick: the realization of driving together human beings, like cattle; the humiliating facet of it, and being oneself human as well. To be, yes, to be witness of such a thing – that I couldn't digest."[27]

The introduction of the star made it impossible for de Neve to remain inactive. When she saw Braun with a star the nature of her feelings metamorphosed. It was not simply that the situation made her sick, "from that moment on I felt *responsible* for her. . . . Things changed that horrible day when I saw Marianne and her brother Leo with a star on their clothes. That was a *horrible* experience. . . . We had heard of it by then, of course. But then you saw, suddenly, the dividing of people; how malicious it was. Yes, I can still feel that now – the fury that such things are possible."[28]

By midsummer 1942, Theo de Bruin found children who were then passed to Gerard, Jaap, Dick, Rebecca, and Jooske. The women traveled alone with the children, or in the company of one of the men, passing as a married couple. The children were brought to foster homes in Heerlen which had been arranged for them by the Vermeer family and Cor Grootendorst. In the autumn, de Bruin began to get children from the crèche as well. With the permission of the parents, Süskind and Halverstad destroyed the children's registration records, and Pimentel and her assistants smuggled the youths out of the child-care center. There were two nearly impossible aspects of this system. The first was practical: how to get the children out of the crèche? After all, they may not have existed on paper, but they were real children and the crèche was guarded by the Germans. Many stratagems were devised to elude their control. For instance, as the young women who worked in the crèche were not under arrest, they were free to go in and out of the building. They took advantage of this mobility and, in their backpacks, carried out infants with pacifiers or bottles in their mouths, praying that the babies would not start to cry. Articles commonly in use in the crèche and therefore not

11   Semmy Woortman-Glasoog; alias Semmy de Bruin.

likely to arouse suspicion were used for the same purpose: potato sacks, food crates, valises. Older children had to be smuggled out in other ways. Accompanied by one or two of the staff, toddlers and older children were allowed to go on walks. Sometimes on such occasions a few of the unregistered children were included in the outing and, at a previously specified point, whisked away from the rest of the group by an underground worker. Finally, Pimentel obtained the cooperation of a neighboring institution. At one side of the crèche was a small teachers' training college, the Hervormde Kweekschool. Seen from the street the two buildings were not connected, as there was an alley between them. Contrary to appearances, however, their back gardens adjoined. "The head of the school, Professor van Hulst, saw in the garden that there were a lot of Jewish children and, well, he was good (we call it good or not good) so he tried to help. . . . We could bring the children from the garden of the crèche to the garden of the Kweekschool and the students and other 'illegal' people came to the Kweekschool and took them out [by the two side streets,] the Plantage Parklaan and the Plantage Kerklaan."[29] As the entrances to the college were not guarded, the controls could be avoided completely.

The first of the two almost insuperable problems – smuggling the children out of the crèche – was practical. The second was emotional: to obtain the parents' permission to hide their child. Who would be willing to give up a child? Who could imagine that life in the "labor camps" was not life but death? The parents did not know the young men and women who asked to hide their children; they were total strangers. They had no reason to trust them. Surely it was better to remain together as a family than to give up one's child to an unknown young person. Ida Groenewegen-van Wyck-Roose, who came into the NV through her friendship with Dick (they married later) related one such tragic encounter. "Dick had a very sad experience with a Jewish couple who lived in Amsterdam with a very small boy. They didn't know Dick, but Dick had their address, and he said, 'We have a good address for your child in Limburg, so please give me your child.' And they said, 'No, we cannot. We must think it over.' Dick sat there for hours to talk and talk and, well, they couldn't make up their minds. It was very difficult for them. Finally, they said, 'Leave him here one last night and come back tomorrow morning.'" There was a *razzia* that night and when Dick returned the following day "they were all gone."[30]

This conscious act of separation of parents and children was so painful that many of the resistance workers who were involved with rescuing children came to believe as they grew older that they were able to do this work precisely because they themselves did not have children. At that time they simply did not understand or comprehend the intensity of the parent-child relationship. "We were still very young," Cor Grootendorst reflected. "We were all aged between twenty and twenty-five. Now as parents and grandparents you start thinking. What would your reaction be if a youngster, twenty years old, comes and knocks on your door? Would you so willingly trust them enough to give your child away?"[31] Piet Meerburg, another Dutch student devoted to saving Jewish children during the Nazi occupation, has given this problem some thought over the past near half-century.

There must be a reason why most of the people working with the children were so young. My explanation is that we were not fathers ourselves, we were not mothers ourselves. You don't realize if you're twenty or twenty-one. Of course it makes an impression on you if you see it – if you go to the parents and they give their child away, and they don't know if they'll ever see the child again. But as a boy of twenty-one you don't realize what it means. You think it's very unpleasant; you can cry about it, but you don't realize. And I think that's good; that's why we could do it. And that's the reason so many young people did it and not older people. For older people I think it was very difficult to do that; they realized much more clearly what it did to the parents. . . .

I now realize I understood only half of it. It's a very difficult decision the parents had to make. I think only the very intelligent and wise people came to the conclusion that they had to get rid of the children, because it's so unnatural to give your child to a complete stranger whom you've never seen before, knowing, well, the chances that you will see your child again is what percent – I don't know. The parents cried tremendously most of the time, which was very depressing. But I think the people who did it had a lot of courage. It took very much courage – and you know how Jewish mothers are. For a Jewish mother to give away her son or her daughter to a strange *goy*, that's something. It took a lot of courage in my opinion, and foresight.[32]

Nevertheless, parents driven to desperation by the situation were willing to give away their children to a "strange goy [gentile]"; the NV had 252 young people under its care and Piet Meerburg's group between 300 and 400.[33]

The development of Piet Meerburg's network was remarkably similar to that of the NV. Early in 1942 Meerburg was at the University of Amsterdam.

One day I was sitting at the students' club and I was studying with a friend, a Jewish boy. We were sitting together in the club and he was called to the telephone. He came back, and he said to me, "I have to go home, there's something wrong with my family – the Germans." I said to be careful. I never saw him again. . . . Well, if you experience something like that you say, "Why am I studying? . . . Then (that was about mid '42) things got really bad. You live within the city, you see what happens, you see the *razzias*. You see the Jewish people picked up, the whole blocks of houses. . . . At that time I said, "I stop my studies." There was only one thing: that you resist these absolutely inhuman and impossible actions of the Germans.[34]

Meerburg began to set up a network to save Jewish children from deportation by the Germans because, he said, "it presented itself. . . . Children were completely helpless. You had to take care of them from the beginning to the end. . . . And if something went wrong, you had to take them away. If a grown-up is in trouble, he can go on the street, but a child is much more dependent on your help."[35]

Like the Musch brothers, Piet Meerburg went to Friesland to obtain hiding addresses, and he also approached ministers and priests: "people that you could trust a little bit more." Meerburg was successful in his attempts and, through the religious leaders, set up small bases of operation. The other center for Meerburg's organization, like that of the NV, was in the south where Nico Dohmen, a student hiding from the Germans' compulsory labor service, and Hanna van der Voorst, the daughter of the family with whom Dohmen was staying, organized an extensive network in the small North Limburg town of Tienray. Van der Voorst was a maternity nurse; she knew everyone in the area and was trusted by them. It was not difficult for her to find hiding addresses. Tienray was a farming community and overwhelmingly Catholic. Families were large and they took in another child without much fuss. According to Dohmen, a typical response was, "Well, okay, we have five [children] at the table, six at the table is also possible." In this way 132 children were hidden.[36]

The basic operating procedures of the Meerburg group and the NV were very much the same. Both got children from the crèche as well as from families that had not yet been arrested.[37] In both networks women couriers and local workers were not only an essential component of the operation, they constituted a majority of the members. Meerburg estimated that 90 percent of his co-workers were women, and he cited the same reason for this overwhelmingly female involvement as did Rebecca van Delft. "It was much more suspicious for a boy of twenty to travel with a child than for a girl. It was absolutely a big difference. We went to fetch the children from the crèche together, but then the woman student accompanied them on the train to Friesland and Limburg."[38] In many other respects the two networks had similar experiences. One of the interesting and unexpected problems the underground workers from both groups faced was that the foster parents had preferences as to the age and gender of the child they wished to have, and that the vast majority of requests was for "a girl of four years old. For a girl of four or five years old you could get as many places as you wanted."[39] This prejudice in favor of girls may have been due to the fact that Jewish boys were circumcised while the rest of the Dutch male population was not,[40] but both Iet Groenewegen and Nico Dohmen believed it had more to do with the foster parents' ideas about boys and girls. Groenewegen thought it was because "a lot of mothers loved little girls. They could make nice little dresses and play with them like a doll." Dohmen's feeling was that it had more to do with the behavioral concomitants of being "a little doll" rather than the dressing up itself. The foster parents, he explained, felt "more confident to have a girl; boys were a bit more strange for them. . . . Boys are more naughty and not as easy to handle as girls."[41] In any case, this was not a fundamental problem for the foster parents; preferences were largely irrelevant; they took whatever child the organizations could smuggle out of Amsterdam. For example, of the 132 children for whom van der Voorst and Dohmen took responsibility, only about 30 were girls.[42]

Monetary considerations were not a factor in the decision to take a child. Despite the financial strain supporting an extra person put on their family budgets, few of the foster families would accept money from the resistance organizations. (According to Nico Dohmen, "no more than 70 guilders [a month] were paid for 132 children.") Indeed both networks were run on very little money. Train travel cards for the workers and ration coupons for the children were supplied by other underground groups. Clothes were pooled and handed around. Shoes were the biggest problem – as they were for everyone in the Netherlands – and many children learned to wear wooden clogs.[43]

The great majority of children did not remain with one family for the entire period of the war. Some lived with as few as two or three families, while others were at as many as thirty addresses. These changes were made for practical and emotional reasons. Foster parents began to suspect that their neighbors guessed the child was Jewish, and not a Rotterdam evacuee, which was the standard explanation. The children themselves sometimes betrayed their identity by singing Jewish songs, or talking about their past lives. Then too, resistance workers found that the children were enormously adaptable but not infinitely so, and sometimes it happened that the cultural difference between the foster parents and children was too great, or the family interaction patterns too different. The relationship simply did not work and the child had to move on.

This meant that the local workers were constantly preoccupied with visiting the children and foster families, and with finding new addresses. The NV was centered in a mining district and the van der Voorst-Dohmen branch of the Meerburg group in a farming community. In addition to the (working-class) miners and farmers, the two communities also had their share of middle-class people. The resistance workers were not selective with regard to income or education level as to whom they approached. Those who were recommended, who were considered safe, were asked if they would be willing to take in a child. Both networks found that "people with more money and better positions felt more exposed. They were more afraid, more attached to their possessions and status." In other words, they felt "they had more to lose."[44] The miners and small farmers were, by contrast, far more willing to open their homes. The underground workers had a number of explanations for this disparity. Their experience was that the poorer people were "closer to needs and suffering; . . . they were used to helping each other more than perhaps the wealthier people [did]."[45] Thus, those who agreed to be foster parents focused on the fact that "the child had no parents" and they were concerned with "the difficulties of getting food in the big cities in Holland." They were not so interested in the Jewish identity of the children. Living so far from the major cities, and especially from Amsterdam, they did not "one hundred percent realize the danger they had in hiding such a child."[46] Many had never known a Jew before, none of their neighbors was radically afflicted by the German regime, they did not see the *razzias*. Just 200 kilometers away from the street scenes of Nazi violence and murder, people could not imagine it; it was so totally foreign to their daily lives, so removed from the social order they knew. Their self-help systems, community structures, and strict adherence to religious tenets were not destroyed by the German invasion.[47] In other words, their very isolation made them less fearful and, less blinded by fear, they were better able to see the child in need as a human being to be helped.

We have considered how children came to be hidden through informal family and friend contacts, and with the help of two types of organizational network: family groups like that begun by the Boogaards in the Haarlemmermeer, and groups that were run by a disparate group of people who came together because of a common dedication to saving children. Some of these were formally structured, like Żegota; others like the NV and Piet Meerburg networks far less so. The third genre of organizational arrangement involved the transformation of an extant structure from legal to illegal work.

The charitable preventive health care organization, OSE (Obsczestvo Sdravochraneniya Eryeyev, or Society for the Health of the Jewish Population), was founded by Jewish physicians in Russia in 1912. After the revolution its headquarters were moved to Berlin and, following the election of Hitler in 1933, to Paris. It was there that the society took the name "Oeuvre de Secours aux Enfants et de Protection de la Santé des Populations Juives." Like the Russian and German branches, the French division of OSE focused on medical prophylaxis in general and child welfare in particular. The OSE leadership in France was responsive to the deteriorating situation in Europe, and in 1937 began to concentrate on the protection of Jewish children. This work was done legally at first; later, when France was occupied and the Jews were besieged, the organization and its operations went underground.[48]

When the war began in 1939, OSE was supporting 300 refugee children, primarily from Germany and Austria, in special homes created for the purpose (*maisons d'enfants*). The organization also provided extra-institutional help, and subsidized many young people who lived in poverty with their parents. The fall of France in June 1940 and the subsequent division of the country into the northern "occupied" zone and the southern "free" zone under the collaborationist government of Marshal Pétain in Vichy forced OSE to move quickly. In the midst of the occupation of Paris and the mass exodus to the south, OSE emptied its *maisons d'enfants* in the Parisian suburbs. The children and most of the OSE staff fled to the southern zone, and for purely practical reasons the organizational apparatus split along the geographic lines. "OSE-Sud" became responsible for the activities carried out in the unoccupied zone and two officers, Falk Walk and Eugène Minkovski, continued with their work in Paris. Due to their efforts the OSE office on the Champs-Elysées remained open throughout the war.[49]

As it became increasingly clear that, at least initially, foreign Jews were at greater risk than their French-born co-religionists, the first task of OSE-Nord was to smuggle central and eastern European children across the demarcation line into the free zone. OSE-Sud, in its turn, immediately began to develop its network of services. Medical and social assistance were made available to the great number of refugees arriving in Vichy France, and more homes were opened to accommodate children sent to the south by their parents, as well as those who were orphaned and abandoned. The most important centers for these activities were in Marseille, Lyon, Grenoble, Montpellier, Périgueux, Toulouse, Limoges, Nice, and Chambéry, but services were also provided in a more modest way in other cities and towns.

In addition to the medical and social aid offered to adults and children living more or less normally and the support of the children in the *maisons d'enfants*, OSE refused to abandon the Jews enclosed in internment camps.[50] The French internment or concentration camps (*camps d'internement*, or *camps de concentration*) had been built in the spring of 1939 at the insistence of the ultra-conservative right to minimize the perceived security problem posed by the flood of refugees from the Spanish Civil War. By the time war was declared in September many of these refugees had returned to Spain. The camps were ready for the incarceration of all enemy aliens but specifically for foreign Jews. Stateless, impoverished, decontextualized, and unable to speak French well, foreign-born Jews were particularly vulnerable to administrative harassment and maltreatment. A year later (after the fall of France in 1940) there were thirty-one camps in the southern zone and perhaps half as many in the occupied north.[51]

The antisemitic decrees in the north and the passage of similarly oppressive legislation in Vichy ensured that all Jews, but especially those who were neither French nor financially well off, were at special risk of imprisonment, and when the round-ups began in 1941 it was to those camps that the Jews were sent. The most urgent task of OSE was to find ways to liberate the internees and to provide emotional and material support to those who remained. Like a number of other philanthropic organizations,[52] OSE sent social workers to live in the camps as voluntary interns (*internes volontaires*) "to share the daily life of the internees, to know their real needs, to provide whatever assistance was possible, and to defend their meager rights," as OSE workers reflecting in 1946 on their experiences explained.[53] Or, as Vivette Samuel-Hermann, who, during what should have been her student years, was an OSE *internée volontaire* in Rivesaltes put it, her role was quite simply "to be present." Just to be there was significant. In the camps at that time "to be present could still mean something. That was why there were representatives of international philanthropic foundations. If someone was there, the guards and the people who represented Vichy could not give full vent to their evil side."[54] It was a job that required commitment and engendered despair. "I do not really know how to depict or to make you understand, uncle, what goes on and the entirely exceptional nature of the events we live," an anonymous social worker wrote on 17 November 1941. "My only hope is that the people who come from here and have seen with their own eyes the walking cadavers of Drancy will find, perhaps, the words and expressions needed to make you feel the depth of the tragedy and the moral importance of our work."[55]

The Oeuvre specialized in health care. To combat disease and alleviate malnutrition and its concomitants, OSE started medical services and opened clinics, infirmaries, pharmacies, and food distribution centers. OSE concentrated specifically on child welfare and instituted a crèche and children's program in a number of the larger camps. The primary concern of the organization, however, and its most essential business was not to ameliorate life in the camps but to extricate those sequestered in them. In a September 1941 report on their activities, especially on behalf of young people, they stressed "the liberation of children. As always that question is the essence of our main preoccupation. . . . The prolonged stay in a camp constitutes a permanent danger for a child and we must strive to free as many as possible."[56] While OSE pressed the interests of individual adults who had reason to be administratively exempt according to the particulars of each case, it presented the problem of child internees to the government as an issue of general principle. Following prolonged and intensive negotiations, Vichy for a short time allowed young people under the age of fifteen to leave the camps on the condition that they were placed in OSE homes and that they were granted a residence certificate by the prefect of the department to which they were to go. Montpellier, which is the Hérault departmental seat, quickly became the center for efforts to liberate the children through legal channels. The préfect of Hérault (Benedetti) and his associates (Ernest, the general secretary of the Préfecture de l'Hérault and Frédérici, the chef de service) were willing to provide the necessary permits. A number of OSE vacation camps were set up in the area and the children were passed from them to other departments as at their age no other legal formalities were required. In this way more than a thousand children were freed from the Vichy concentration camps.[57]

While OSE-Sud worked to protect children by legal means, OSE-Nord, operating under the conditions of occupation, engaged in clandestine activities from the moment the Germans marched into Paris. Initially OSE-Nord concentrated on the secret transfer to the south of refugee children. After the ferocious manhunt in Paris of 16–17 July 1942 (the round-up of the Vélodrome d'Hiver, or Vél d'Hiv, as it was known), OSE-Nord engaged in a plethora of underground activities. Named for the indoor sports arena in which the arrested Jews were incarcerated, the rafle [or round-up] of the Vél d'Hiv was the result of the so-called Spring Wind operation to arrest 28,000 foreign and stateless Jews in the Greater Paris region. Ordered by the Germans but conducted entirely by French police and their auxiliaries, the razzia trapped 12,884 people in two days. A total of 6,900 people, of whom 4,051 were children, were forced into the Vél d'Hiv. Single men and women, and families without children (5,984 souls), were sent to Drancy. There the deportation trains were filled and began to roll.[58] For OSE-Nord there could be no more delusions about the ultimate fate of Jews caught in the occupied zone, and their main objective was to hide as many people as possible. In January 1943 one of the two OSE-Nord directors, Falk Walk, was arrested, sent to Drancy and deported. The other, Eugène Minkovski, remained in Paris and, together with five women collaborators (Hélène Matorine, Simone Kahn, Jeanine Lévy, Céline Vallée, and Madame Averbouh), organized a child camouflage service. Using a youth club as a cover for their activities, they passed Jewish children to gentile families, who hid them. The OSE workers maintained contact with the foster families throughout the war to ensure that the children were well treated and to provide maintenance funds, ration coupons, and false identity papers as needed. This network helped 700 children to survive the German occupation in the north.[59]

Clandestine activities to save Jewish children were undertaken later in the south than in the north. Until the wave of *razzias* that began in the occupied zone swept over the demarcation line, washing away pretense and stripping bare the antisemitic collusion of Vichy, the OSE staff in the "free" zone (like everyone else) operated under the illusion that a French government would deal more kindly with its Jewish citizens and refugees than would the German invaders. In the wake of the August 1942 dragnets which ravaged several cities in the south, OSE decided more or less officially to begin underground operations. The legal structure of children's homes and health care centers remained intact, but they also served as a screen for the organization of secret border crossings, for laboratories to produce false identity papers, and to hide those in imminent danger of arrest. The German occupation of the free zone in November 1942 meant that fewer resources could be wasted on legal work; more energy had to be channeled towards clandestine activities. At a meeting in Lyon on 16 January 1943 the OSE directorate decided on "the systematic camouflage of children sheltered in the various children's homes." The young people in the OSE residences had become too obvious and too vulnerable a target. They had to be hidden.[60]

An extensive network was developed to move, screen, and save the children in OSE's care. The architect of *le réseau Garel* or Garel network, as it came to be called, was a young man named Georges Garel, who had gained the great respect of the OSE leadership through his devoted efforts to liberate the children caught in the brutal *rafle* in Lyon and subsequently incarcerated in the concentration camp of Vénissieux.[61] "Some months later," Garel recalled, "Dr Joseph Weill (of the central governing board of l'Union OSE) proposed to me that I organize a clandestine network in the southern zone of France for children of trapped Jewish families."[62] Garel was well chosen for the job. He was not an official leader of any Jewish organization so was unknown to the authorities, he was involved in resistance activities and thus had useful contacts, and he was dedicated.

With an introduction from his contemporary (and later brother-in-law) Charles Lederman (a member of OSE whom Garel knew through other resistance activities and with whom he had worked in Vénissieux), Garel met with Monsignor Jules-Gérard Saliège, the elderly, partly paralyzed, and very popular archbishop of Toulouse. From the beginning of the occupation Saliège had publicly decried antisemitism and con-

12   Simone Kamiéniarz (aged 10) at the O.S.E. home in Chabannes in 1941.

demned racism and racial programs. He had also been among the first Catholic prelates in France to denounce the deportation of the Jews in a pastoral letter read in all the parishes of his diocese on 23 August 1942.[63] And he was ready to help Georges Garel. "Monsignor Saliège advised me not to create a new philanthropic organization but to work within the framework of the Catholic or other charitable organizations which already existed. He had the great kindness to give me a short note of recommendation worded thus: 'I enjoin your good will for the bearer and his plans.'" Furnished with this reference, Garel made contact with public, private, religious, and non-sectarian organizations. The network grew rapidly until it covered nearly the entire southern zone. In each department or diocese a philanthropic society or institution took in children. Among many others these included Catholic (such as the Conférences de St Vincent de Paul) and Protestant (Comité Inter-Mouvements auprès des Evacués or the Conseil Protestant de la Jeunesse) charities, and official (le Secours National, for instance) and private (Mouvement Populaire des Familles) groups.[64]

Garel and his associates divided the children into two groups: those who could "pass" as gentiles, and those who for cultural, religious, or linguistic reasons could not do so. The former, with false identity cards or birth certificates and doctored food and clothing ration cards, were dispersed in "Aryan" milieus where they were not known. This group remained under the direct surveillance of Georges Garel. The other children, more than a thousand young people, were cared for by a *réseau* [network] run by a young woman named Andrée Salomon (the "Circuit B"); they lived at home with their own families or, using their own names, with other families. Andrée Salomon's Circuit B looked after these children openly until OSE went underground in February 1944. When OSE was forced into an entirely clandestine existence the children were smuggled over the French border, primarily into Switzerland but occasionally also into Spain.[65]

The children of the *réseau* Garel remained in France. His system was extensive but uncomplicated. He and his OSE collaborators found organizations and institutions willing to help save the children, and they prepared the young people for their new lives, teaching them their new names and family histories and providing them with the appropriate (false) documentation and ration coupons. The children were then passed to the receiver agencies which, in turn, either kept them under their own aegis (in group homes, orphanages, convents, or boarding schools) or matched them with foster families. Thus, two circles were created. The first, composed of Jews, was responsible for running the *réseau* and maintained contact with the parents if they were in France. The second, made up of individual gentile organizations, was directly responsible for the children in their new surroundings. These receiver institutions remained independent of each other throughout the war. They did not communicate amongst themselves about the OSE children; all contact was through Garel alone. This structure ensured a greater degree of safety. If a child were betrayed, only one atomized part of the network would be uncovered. Then too, if the children were in an entirely gentile environment the camouflage was more secure and it was less likely that they would reveal their true identity inadvertently. Finally, the two-circle division also helped to avoid direct communication between parents remaining in France and their hidden children. Such contact was fraught with difficulties and could lead to disclosure all too easily. (Letters, for example, were passed through Garel from the personnel of one circle to that of the other.) However excellent the idea of separate Jewish and gentile circles may have been in theory, Garel found that in practice "often the non-Jews were incapable of resolving questions [that arose] because the environment was strange and things escaped them."

Jewish *résistants* with false identity cards were put on the personnel lists of the institutions and organizations which had taken Jewish children into their care. As members of the staff they were able to have contact with the hidden young people and to ease some of their difficulties.

With more than 1,500 children to look after by the summer of 1943, the network had become so extensive that Garel divided it into four separate geographic sections. Garel was the central coordinator, and a regional director with an assistant or two ran each area. The *réseau* had become comprehensive too; it was supported by an infrastructure of services. The clothing department saw to outfitting the children either by purchasing ready-made items or by finding the material and having garments made. The documents staff dealt with identity and ration cards, birth and baptismal certificates. They obtained false papers in a number of ways. Initially they altered authentic, used papers. Later on they cajoled legitimate forms out of sympathetic mayors' offices or bought them on the black market. As the need for such papers increased, counterfeit documents were printed on the underground presses. Finally, a transport division was responsible for moving children quickly and at short notice when it was necessary to do so.[66]

The *réseau* Garel and Salomon's Circuit B differed from the networks run by Żegota, the Boogaards, or the NV in that the former were developed within an already extant organization (OSE), depended on pre-existing institutions, and were run by Jews for the benefit of their co-religionists.[67] In other respects, however, the OSE rescue and protection operations had much in common with the underground groups. It is obvious, but bears repeating, that all were dedicated to maintaining Jewish child life in the face of ruthless persecution and despite the risks such work posed. These networks were run by young people who refused to be daunted. Unlike so many others, they were not incapacitated by intimidation. Then too, a great majority of OSE couriers, like their counterparts in the clandestine organizations, were women. Women assistants worked in the OSE *maisons d'enfants*, and when these were closed and the children dispersed, the women carried on with the responsibility of safeguarding the children's lives. At times they, like Irena Sendlerowa and Andrée Salomon, were the architects of the systems. But they were always integral, intrinsic, and essential to their operation. They worked on the ground, finding homes for the children, escorting them from endangered locations to hiding places, obtaining false papers, food, shoes, clothes. What they undertook was perilous and terribly exhausting. Finally, the OSE *réseau* in practice functioned very much like the other networks. It too depended on courageous and sympathetic gentiles to shelter children for the duration of the war. Like the foster families who collaborated with formally founded organizations such as Żegota, family-based operatives such as the Boogaard network, or spontaneous almost fortuitous enterprises such as the NV, the gentiles who joined effort with OSE were, by and large, unsophisticated and far from wealthy. They, like their cohorts elsewhere, were paid minimal sums (a maximum of 500 francs a month) to defray the costs of caring for the children, who came equipped with ration cards, a set of clothes, and little else. Like those who cooperated in similar aid and rescue operations, the OSE foster families preferred to "adopt" children who spoke without a foreign accent and who could blend in physically and culturally with the rest of the population. They too requested young girls rather than older boys. The same cover stories of bombardment or city famine were told. And, as the *résistante* Madeleine Dreyfus recalled, in the end the OSE foster families retracted their requests and dismissed the adduced pretexts. They took in the children simply and solely because they were youngsters in need.

Dreyfus was officially the chief OSE administrator in Lyon and, unofficially, the *assistante-chef* for the Lyon-based section of the Garel network. Arrested for her underground work on 27 November 1943, she was deported to Bergen-Belsen via Le Fort Montluc and Drancy, and was one of the few to return after the war, in May 1945. Prior to her arrest Dreyfus and another *résistante*, Marthe Sternheim, were in charge of finding places for children to hide and they scoured the countryside in search of sympathetic homes. In her account of her clandestine activities Dreyfus emphasized the part played by these foster families.

> I was specially responsible for the area of Chambon-sur-Lignon. The first contact obviously was with the Pastor Trocmé and his wife who received us as they know how to do and gave us advice and valuable information. It was in this way that I came to make the acquaintance of Madame Deléage (she was widowed) and her daughter Eva (now Eva Phillit who lives in St Etienne). They lived in the hamlet of Tavas and they immediately devoted themselves to our cause. [Mme Deléage] was our devoted friend, she herself contacted those families most likely to help us, to help us hide those little Jewish children hunted by the Gestapo, very aware of what she risked, she herself hiding numerous children at her place and insisting that the small farmers with whom she took contact accepted those children "from Lyon and St Étienne so poorly fed and who needed to build themselves up in the fresh air of the Haute Loire." Those people knew very well what sort of children these were, but everyone pretended "as if"

one believed that tale. . . .

Here is how things were organized: Many times each month I would take the train to Lyon with about ten children. Sometimes these children were entrusted to us by their parents, sometimes they were children who managed to escape from the hands of the Nazis at the moment of their parents' arrest. We would go to St Etienne to take the small local rail line from Tence that brought us to Chambon.

Often, Dreyfus was met at the station by Eva Deléage. They deposited the children at the Hotel May and then made the rounds of farmers who might consider taking one child, or even two children if they were siblings who did not want to be separated.

In general these small farmers "prepared" by their pastor and Madame Deléage responded to our demands rather quickly. If it was a question of boys over twelve years old it was rather difficult, however. "They talk back," we were told. I remember one day when a "case" of two fourteen-year-old boys remained – a difficult task. I went from farm to farm throughout the whole area surrounding Chambon . . . no one wanted my two boys. Finally I arrived at the house of an older couple, the Courtials, and I recited my tale to them: these were children from the city who were hungry, of course they had their ration coupons, and the air of Chambon, etc. . . . etc. . . . The Courtials answered amiably but firmly that it really was not possible for them to take the two. Then I played all to win all and I told them the truth: "These were two Jewish boys whose parents had been arrested and whom the Germans pursued so as to imprison them along with their parents." Not a single hesitation remained: "But you should have said so sooner, certainly you must bring your two boys to us."[68]

We have discussed at such great length the networks that preserved and maintained Jewish child life that a word of caution may be helpful. Commenting on the situation of Jews in France and Belgium, the historian Lucien Steinberg rightly observed that "the majority of Jews who survived either did not need the help of the Jewish and non-Jewish rescue organizations, or turned to them very infrequently. It is obvious that these organizations could not save the entire Jewish population. Most of the Jews who survived did so thanks to their own initiative. The majority supported themselves illegally, but on an individual level, they received help from the local population."[69] Although precise figures are not available, the picture that emerges indicates that this pattern prevailed throughout Europe. By and large, the better part of Jewish children were not helped by organized networks but through personal, familial contacts. This point often is obscured because it is easier to write the history of institutions or organizations, even if they were informally established and loosely coordinated, than of private relations, the dull grey of everyday that at that time was neither dull nor everyday, but both momentous and essential. Indeed, first and foremost the children were saved by their parents. The act of giving up one's child, of surrendering one's own daughter or son, of recognizing that one no longer could protect and shelter that small person to whom one had given life, was the first and most radical step in the chain of rescue. It was a paradox: to save one's child one had to accept that one was unable to protect and defend the child.[70] Whether one relinquished that son or daughter to a personal friend or a stranger, a resister, that initial act of abdication was the fundamental beginning. The work of the organizations which dedicated themselves to safeguarding Jewish children and the devotion of the great majority of families who took them in should not be underestimated. The women and men who undertook this task for the most part were steadfast and loyal. They did what they believed to be correct and nearly half a century later still do not feel that it is extraordinary that they behaved as they did or that they should be specially honored for their actions. In fact, of course, their stance was exceptional. Their wonderful deeds and remarkable feats should be admired and their probity and rectitude are to be esteemed. Nevertheless, it would be a mistake to say that these people alone, however estimable, just, kind, considerate, or accommodating they may have been, saved the children. It was the parents who took the first and most terrifying step of all.

Chapter Three

In Secret

In the last chapter we examined the role of the adults (the parents, foster parents, and resisters) who took decisions for and acted on behalf of the children. It was one thing to save a young person, however, and quite another to be the child who was saved. To hide children was an extremely complicated business, but to be hidden was even more so. For the resisters and foster parents the difficulties were practical. Their beliefs, tenets, and creed were not challenged. They acted as they did because they thought it correct; they took responsibility for the young people with an easy conscience and a glad heart. The children who needed their help were there, the actual physical existence of the youngsters justified and made real what they did. And they had customs and archetypes to validate and reinforce their resolutions and choices. The decisions and actions of the underground workers and those who sheltered the children fitted into a western Christian tradition of charity and heroism. Those who undertook to preserve child life were a wonderful (and, for a change, philosemitic) variant of the knights of yore who in their chivalric oaths swore to safeguard widows and protect children.

Jewish children, however, had no valid models to explain their situation. Their tradition and heritage did not help them to understand their position as victims. The persecution of the Jews had never gone so far. The closest parallel they had from history was the Egyptian plan to kill all the male children. This was the story of Moses, and he, through the ruse of his sister, Miriam, lived with his own family. The children in Nazi-occupied Europe did not have that option. And so they faced their future without guidance or direction.

In this chapter we shall discuss the experience of these young people themselves. What was it like to be in hiding and hidden, like Anne Frank, or in hiding and visible, like Ivan Buchwald? What did these children do all day? With whom did they play? What were their hopes and fears, chores and tasks, occupations and preoccupations?

Each genre of experience, to have been in hiding (in hiding and hidden) and to have been "in hiding" (in hiding and visible) was problematic in its own way, but the former was more obviously, more bluntly and brutally so. To go into hiding meant that all, or nearly all, ties with society were severed. Whether in an attic in the city or a warren in the forest, the child literally was hidden from the mortal danger the rest of the world represented. Even the restricted sphere their lives had become was denied to them. They had been segregated from their former gentile playmates, banished from the world they used to inhabit of school, cinema, and parks, and identified and isolated with the star of David as the "other," the "stranger." Finally forced to flee their very own homes, to separate from the few friends who remained to them and, very often, from their families too, these children began a new ever more estranged existence. Completely cut off from any community, without mobility or access to either goods or services (food, clothes, shoes, medicines, books, medical care, dentistry), their lives became straitened and circumscribed. "Now, at fifty-one years of age," Marco Anav, a Roman Jew, reflected about his period in hiding in 1944 with his family in a Catholic friend's apartment, "I can tell you that the most important thing about being in hiding was the lack of freedom; the fact of being confined, the fact of being enclosed in a room smaller than the one in which I am sitting now: the fact that when one knocked – you had to knock, one two three, because if you heard one, two, it was something else – 'Silence children, be still!' "[1] Indeed, the most primitive of human needs, to wash and to go to the toilet, were practiced only with care and by plan. Moishe Kobylanski and his family hid in the countryside surrounding Gruszwica, their village in the Ukraine. From the end of 1942 until May or June 1943 they lived burrowed in a straw loft in a pigsty. "Bathroom facilities were excellent. You just went over there in the other end and you bundled everything up in straw. And when I went after food I took it with me and I went crazy to find a place to dump it." It was Kobylanski's job to forage for food and, at the same time, to remove the family's excrement. "The urine was easy. It was in a bottle and as soon as I walked out I dumped it. That was no problem. The faecal matter was a problem. I went where they had cattle manure, I found a place, and I tried to hide it there. But how does human excrement fit in with cattle manure? No good either. It was always a problem because I might leave evidence after myself."[2] In short, to be in hiding meant to be committed to an extraordinarily punitive prison cell, not because the child had committed a crime but because everyone else was acting criminally.

Each child's experience was unique, but certain aspects of life in hiding were almost universally shared. The first of these was a fundamental lack of comprehension of why events transpired as they did, and a concomitant, ever-present fear and tension. Their previous lives had not prepared them for this new existence. The children understood that the Germans and their allies were dangerous, but precisely what that danger signified was beyond their grasp. This was especially true for younger children who were more likely to perceive the peril as an inchoate insecurity rather than a specific and comprehensible calamity. "Why must I hide?" was the fundamental question. With no good answer (indeed, there was no rational, comprehensible answer), and only a dim (or clear) understanding that to do so meant to be safe, came great anxiety and trepidation. They did not understand why they were forced to leave their homes, their families, their friends, and they did not know what was safe and what dangerous. Precisely that which previously had represented security was now lost and abandoned. What was stable, where was shelter?

Judith Ehrmann-Denes was not yet four years old when her mother, eighteen-month-old brother, and she went into hiding in Budapest. One Sunday in the early spring of 1944 they went out, as was their custom, to visit relatives in the afternoon. When they returned they found their concierge, "who was a very, very nice lady," waiting for them in the courtyard. "She said, 'Don't come in, don't come in! The Nazis were here.' The *Hungarian* Nazis . . . the Arrow Cross. . . . They were there and they took all the Jews away [who were] living in the house. So we went that evening to my father's gentile friend. . . . We lived with them, and I couldn't understand why we were not going home. We were staying there. . . . I remember being there and not understanding. I remember anxiety all the time, which seeped over from my mother, who obviously had anxiety twenty-four hours a day. . . . That's all I remember is anxiety. And I thought life was like that. What does a three-year-old know? This is the way life is. You just have anxiety all the time, and fear."[3]

It was both physically and psychologically difficult to go into hiding. To be so completely removed from ordinary existence, to sever all normal activities, was a great shock which required radical adjustments. As one man who was then a teenager explained, "It was all of a sudden a way of life without life [without living]."[4] Every act of daily life had to be considered consciously and adapted to fit the situation; the obstacles

13   Renée Fritz-Schwalb (aged 5), with her mother and cousin in the garden of Mrs Degelas, with whom they were in hiding: Brussels, 1942.

to surmount or circumvent were never-ending. To maximize her family's protection, Judith Ehrmann-Denes's mother obtained the original legal papers of a young gentile woman her own age who, like her, also had two children. Mrs Denes felt that this was insufficient, and she decided to transform her eighteen-month-old boy into a girl. "My brother was dressed as a little girl, because boys could be checked to see if they were circumcised or not." The Deneses hid with a number of Christian families in Budapest. They avoided contact with the outside world, but were not absolutely sequestered. "Nobody really knew us, and being that we were both 'girls' there was no way to check. People would just take the word. If somebody reported us and the Arrow Cross came by to check, there was not much they could do with two little girls. My brother had blond curly hair with a red bow so it just wouldn't even occur to them to think, 'That's a boy.'" The deception posed its own problems. "My brother, who by then had learned to stand up to pee, had to sit down again. And remember, there were no toilets. . . . So my brother had to learn to sit on the chamber pot again. Luckily he spoke real late, so he couldn't really talk. He put up a fuss about it, but nobody knew why, because my mother had to make sure that nobody knew it was a boy. And there were a lot of problems and anxieties that, God forbid, this kid should unzip or pull down his pants."[5]

While it was safer to be female than male because of the physical identification of Jewish identity by circumcision, older girls had their own biological difficulties. Herta Montrose-Heymans was fifteen when she went into hiding. Her family had moved from Germany to the Netherlands to escape persecution, but the Nazis caught up with them and in 1942 they were forced to go underground. In the winter of 1943 Heymans moved to an address where she spent the rest of the war years. She, her grandfather, and another elderly man lived with an older couple in a "tiny little working-class house" in Enschede, in the east of the Netherlands. "Menstruating was absolutely harrowing," Heymans re-called. "In those days, you had little pads that had to be washed. The landlady couldn't hang them on the line, could she? The neighbors knew there was no young person living there."[6]

The essential problem was to leave no evidence or sign of one's pre-sence, to live without trace or vestige of existence. This was accom-plished through concealment and dissimulation. In Heymans's case, for example, not only was it impossible to dry her menstrual pads on the outside clothes line, it was also out of the question to hang out her grandfather's shirts. "Nobody was supposed to know that we were there," Heymans emphasized. "We couldn't hang two shirts out when there was only one man living there." They moved about the back rooms of the house quite freely, but "we whispered, we never spoke up really. It became second nature." What was not hidden was masked in one way or another. For instance, the host couple "had a harmonium which they played on Sundays especially. As I had started to learn to play the piano before I went to live underground, I learned to play the harmonium for them which gave them great pleasure." They of course pretended that one of them was playing. "There was a lot of pretense going on all the time."[7]

To obfuscate the actual situation became a way of life for both host and guest. Various stratagems were employed, ranging from obvious tactics to subtle maneuvers. As the guest children were not supposed to exist, they could not be seen. They were forbidden to go near the win-dows so as to prevent detection from the outside, and when visitors came they were restricted to a confined space and had to maintain com-plete silence. Often this meant that the children could not move. Hidden in a cupboard or behind a curtain, any change of position would have meant disclosure. Just as the children were not to be visible, they were not to be heard. Like Heymans, they learned to speak in whispers, or not at all. They could not laugh aloud or, forgetting themselves, cry out from a sudden pain. Nor could they do anything which by its noise would reveal their presence. Thus, if a child was alone she could not flush the toilet; if the host was in the front room, she could not wash up in the kitchen. Activities and sound had to be attributable to those who were known to be present in the house (or barn, like Moishe Kobylanski, or warehouse, like Anne Frank).

Obtaining goods and services for the children in hiding required thoughtful planning. If a child did not have ration coupons, food had to be purchased on the black market, which was very expensive. With ration cards (provided by the Resistance) the prices were controlled, but how could a housewife present coupons for three when her baker knew perfectly well that only two people had lived in her household for years? Women who had children hiding in their homes spent hours in queues in numerous shops in the effort to acquire the maximum their ration cards would allow without arousing suspicion. Bertje Bloch-van Rhijn and her family were hidden in the home of an elderly lady just outside Kampen in the east of the Netherlands. This woman "lived there alone, and it was very difficult to bring in food. Naturally, one could not come into the house with bags full of shopping. . . . The mistress of the house had a maid and a housekeeper, and the housekeeper was really too dumb to dance for the devil [as they say in Dutch]. The important point about Marietje [the housekeeper] is that she held her tongue in all the stores where she went to do the shopping. She always bought with a ration card and she had to go to many grocers to buy with the different ration cards she had got from the underground. She could not present more than one card in each shop since she had to maintain the pretense that she was shopping for [the mistress of the house]. So," van Rhijn concluded, "it's not nice of me to say that she was stupid."[8] Food was an essential and constant problem, but the contours of the dilemma and its solution remained constant for other goods as well. Books, for instance, were very important to many young people in hiding; reading was a way to pass the time and to escape the confines of their harshly delimited existence. Philip Maas and his parents were hidden by a working-class family who had used the public libraries long before their guests came to live with them. With the Maas family's arrival their needs increased. "They were members of two libraries and they very cleverly sometimes only took one or two books from one library while at the same time taking many books from the other."[9]

In short, both the children and those who hid them strove to conduct themselves in such a way that the young people's presence would not be disclosed by their behavior either in the house or in dealings with the outside world. In these domains the children and their hosts had some measure of control. The operations of the Germans and their allies, however, could not be checked. A *razzia* or search had nothing to do with unwitting self-betrayal; it was an expected but unpredictable calamity. That it would occur was anticipated, but when was unknown. Very often, special hiding places were constructed to be used in such emergencies, and the children were drilled to ensure that they would disappear within seconds. Tiny hidden spaces within a wardrobe or closet, under the stairs or floor, in the attic or cellar were constructed with false walls and floors. The children remember rehearsing to get into them, as well as the terrifying times when they were necessary. When Herta Montrose-Heymans first went into hiding in 1942 she was with a cousin who was spastic. "How long we stayed in our first address I really can't remember. But as a child it was a terrific responsibility to look after this spastic child as well. As you must appreciate, we had regular exercises in hiding in certain hiding places which had to be done very, very quickly from the time the bell would go. You were given, say, a minute to hide either in the cupboard or . . . . In our first place, I remember we had to go under the floorboards which was all right for me because I was healthy, but my cousin couldn't walk very well. So it was all very harassing and complicated, and a terrific burden on a young girl of fifteen."[10] Like Heymans, Selma Goldstein was a German Jewish girl whose family fled to the Netherlands after *Kristallnacht*. She was ten years old when her family went into hiding in a small worker's house in Enschede.

The room in which we stayed was not so small. It was a bedroom with two beds and a rather big wardrobe. In the wardrobe a second cupboard was made where we could hide. It was about 25 centimeters wide; a very tiny space. It was built into a little niche in the wall, but you could see it if you looked carefully because you could see that the space inside the wardrobe was not so large as that of the external wardrobe. Also, when you knocked on it, you could hear that there was a space behind it. So it was not really a safe place to hide.

Once it was used. Somebody was running away from the Germans and decided to come through our house. He jumped into the back garden and went through the back door, through the hall, through the front door, and left at the other street. The Germans were behind him, but the man with whom we were staying wanted to give this man a chance so he locked the front door so that in any case the Germans would have needed to open the front door and would waste time. But that did not happen. The Germans came into the house . . .

and one of the girls of the family kept them busy talking while we got into our cupboard. We were in the cupboard and then the Germans thought that because the door was locked the man could not have left. They started to look very carefully to see if the man was there. I was so frightened I started to hyperventilate and my mother put a sock in my mouth.[11]

Despite the hosts' and the guests' precautions and care, situations constantly arose that made clear how compromised their lives were and how tenuous and fragile their arrangements. For example, the family with whom Philip Maas hid had two children, a girl of thirteen and a boy of eleven. The young boy had a friend who lived next door. "I slept in the little boy's room," Maas explained, "and the boy next door would knock on the wall to make contact with his friend and then also sometimes he would climb across the gutter from his room to mine. So then I had to close the window very quickly to prevent him from getting into my room – because I was sleeping there, and not his little friend as he thought. There were problems with that, because the neighbor boy did not know there was somebody hiding there – the little boy never told – and he expected to play as they normally did."[12] This predicament was comic, almost farcical, although of course it could have had literally fatal consequences. Other such unanticipated incidents were absolutely tragic. One year after Selma Goldstein and her parents went into hiding, her father died. "The problem was how to get him out of the house," Goldstein recalled. The people next door and the family across the road were Dutch Nazis. "So my father was sewn into a bed and the neighbors were told that the bed had to be cleaned. The bed was carried out of the house with my father in it. Then it was brought to a country estate out of town where a good policeman stood guard while my father was buried."[13] For Goldstein, the normal process of mourning the death of her father was replaced by the horrible dilemma of how to get rid of his body.

Given the practical problems of being in hiding and the physical constraints on their activities, what did the children do all day? Or, to put it more appropriately, how did they pass the time? "Our major activity was to think about food," Philip Maas reported. "From the moment we got to that hiding place food was a big problem and we talked about it all the time."[14] Several thousand kilometers away, in a pigsty in the Ukraine, Moishe Kobylanski and his family had the same concern.

We used to sit all day and debate where to go [to ask for food.] We sat there; we sat there every day and followed the ritual. First, there wasn't much to eat. .... So we just sat, counted the hours and killed lice. Just sat around. Didn't do anything. What can you do? You were dreaming, talking about this and talking about that. Making plans [to forage for food], maybe tomorrow if it's quiet, if it's dark. My parents weren't peasants in the term of knowing the seasons, the moon schedule. .... Is this the month there's going to be a full moon, or is it going to be a quarter-moon, half-moon? So you waited . . . I think this is going to be a quarter-moon so I'll be able to go because it doesn't shine so bright. The weather doesn't look too good; if it's a storm it's a good night to go hunting for food. That's how the day was taken up.[15]

In addition to dreaming and scheming about food, many children who were old enough took up hobbies. If they were able to obtain the materials, and were permitted to do so, children turned their energies to all genres of writing, art, and handicrafts. Anne Frank, for instance, wrote short stories as well as her diary, which she rewrote in three versions. Philip Maas specialized in woodwork. Wood was brought to his hiding address and with it he constructed model windmills and fashioned pictures of marquetry. His pieces were very fine and intricate, and like Anne Frank's diary reworked several times. Sara Spier crocheted. "I made little things to put on the table and I gave them away. I made them from very thin thread because there was not much in the war. It was quite nice, like lace."[16] Frieda Menco-Brommet also crocheted. "I made curtains, and I made tablecloths too. And I never did those things again after the war."[17]

As might be expected, reading and studying were common activities for children of school age. With a paucity of alternatives and a plethora of time, intellectual pursuits were a natural choice. Furthermore, children expected to go to school. To continue with their education signified in a very basic and fundamental way that they meant to return to society, that they believed they would resume a normal life. "I took my schoolbooks with me, and my mathematics [exercises]," Spier remembered. "Every day I did again the last mathematics problems I had at school, just not to forget them, because I couldn't go on." She kept on studying, "but I missed my school very much because I loved to go to school. I was in a lyceum and you could choose at the end of the second year if you wanted to do *gymnasium* [university-track high school]. I had chosen classical languages which I always wanted to learn. And there was nobody to teach me. So I had my books and, well, I couldn't go on further because nobody could see what I did right or wrong. I just read, and read again what was written in the books."[18] Frieda Menco-

Brommet was with her parents and so the educational process was more interactive. "During our two years in hiding my father and I spent our days together teaching each other. His English was much better than mine, so he taught me English. My French was better than his, I taught him French. We read the same books and we discussed them."[19]

One of the most important factors in determining what a child did all day was the culture of the host with whom she hid. Quite often, the people who took in children had their own ideas of what they considered appropriate activities. Thus, for example, Bertje Bloch-van Rhijn and her family were hidden with the mother of a university friend of Bertje's mother. The university friend had been well educated in her youth and her mother believed in the importance of schooling for young people. She had saved her children's books and toys, which proved a treasure for van Rhijn and her sister. "The lady of the house had a whole lot of books – she'd had three children – and she had schoolbooks, big history atlases, a complete set of Dickens, and lots of biographies." Indeed, the hostess's dedication to the van Rhijn girls' education led her to reveal the girls' existence to the directress of the local public library, fortunately without harmful consequences. "The lady of the house was a very well-read woman; she knew a great deal. She had a membership at the library, of course, and she went for us, naturally also for school-books. She had to ask for them in one way or another and so the directress of the library knew."[20] Sara Spier's experience could not have differed more. While the van Rhijn girls were hidden at only a few addresses throughout the war, Spier was moved thirty-two times. And where the van Rhijn family was united in May 1943 and lived together until the end of the war, Spier was separated from her sister, brother, and parents, and the latter three were betrayed and deported. She mourned the loss of her family long before she knew of their death and, not knowing of their deportation, she missed their home life. She was hidden by people who had very different ideas about how to occupy oneself; they came from another culture and had their own mores.

> The people who hid me were farm laborers, very simple, very nice, very sweet. But they didn't know anything about [high] culture or languages. Their life was very simple and they were Christian. So I came into a totally different milieu where there was no education and a different religion. I felt the difference very forcefully but of course I didn't say anything. I realized they were people who hid me and I couldn't say I didn't like their way of life. For example, they didn't read books. They were always knitting, or doing some embroidery, or busy in the kitchen, or busy in the garden, or doing something. But

reading was something luxurious. They accepted that I had my schoolbooks, but when I would ask for some book to read, they said you can do something more useful.[21]

Once Spier and a distant cousin were hidden by a miller who maintained himself as a farmer during the war. He and his wife worked very hard, getting up at five in the morning and laboring in the fields all day. The two girls arose "not so early because we had nothing to do."

> We were not allowed to do anything in the house. From time to time we could peel potatoes, but we were not allowed to help in the house. So what we did was, we had some knitting work and we were *schmoozing* [chatting]. The miller's wife let us put on the radio [when she was in the house]. We could sit with our knitting work and chat, but we were not allowed to read, because to read all those books and novels was sin. The only thing we were allowed to read was the Bible. . . . I read the Bible, New and Old Testaments. And I remember after weeks and weeks the miller came once from the village and he just said, "Here, that's for you." He took a book from the library, a book about farmers' life. . . . We didn't do very much because we were not allowed to, just a bit knitting and chattering and reading the Bible.[22]

The differences between the host culture and that of the children not infrequently proved to be emotionally oppressive for the young people. It is easy to wonder (with the benefit of hindsight) what these children found so harrowing. After all, one might say, they were hidden, they were safe, they were not deported; their lives were luxurious compared to those in the ghettos and camps. While this certainly is true, it is also facile, lacks historical perspective, and, most important, it is beside the point. Children in hiding did not have a concrete concept of the misery they were fortunate enough to escape; they had no experience of it. They feared deportation and concentration camps, they lived in dread of betrayal, but the horror of "resettlement" was more rumor than real. Furthermore, tragedy and hardship are absolute, not comparative. Who dances at the funeral of one parent because both have not died? Children in hiding, like everyone else, lived within the parameters of their own experience, and that was unpleasant enough. The appropriate comparison is not with those who suffered more, but with those who suffered less, not with life within the machinery of death, but with life as it should have been, in "normal" times. To lose that perspective is to accept the Nazis' ideas of what those children had a right to expect. As it was, they were literally minimized (belittled to the point where they had to vanish)

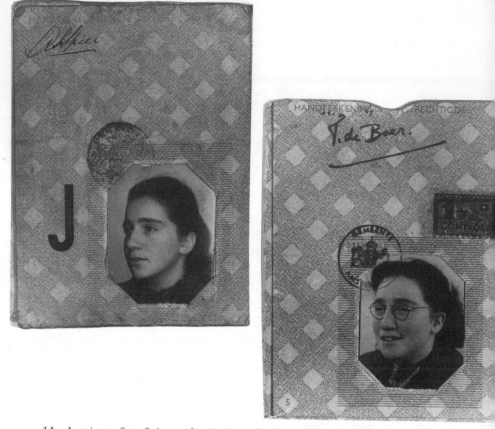

14   Antoinette Sara Spier, authentic (note the 'J') and false identity cards.

and marginalized (pushed so far to the perimeter that they disappeared). Their old lives had ceased to exist. They were decontextualized and lonely. And however righteous and charitable, their hosts also had their own expectations that the children would conform to their way of life and their rules – and would be grateful to boot.

The children were caught in a complicated situation. They were vulnerable and they had no rights. They had no choice but to adapt to the customs and manners of the family that hid them. They recognized that their hosts risked a great deal on their behalf. They felt they ought to be grateful, and tried to please. "My attitude was that of a mixture of gratitude and . . . I wanted to show I was a good Jew," Salvador Bloemgarten recalled. "I didn't want to give people reasons to complain." Friends of his hosts, who also were sheltering a Jew, visited and once "they were complaining about their Jew who was so difficult and then [my hosts] talked about me, 'Our Jew' – I felt ill to my stomach – 'Our Jew is a nice Jew.'"[23]

The children's discomfort in the host environment was due primarily and most obviously to the situation. The mortal danger posed by the Germans and their allies had forced the gentile hosts to offer shelter just as it had forced the children to seek refuge. It was neither a love match nor a true adoption; Nazism, altruism (mostly), greed (sometimes), and need brought them together. As Jews, the children were despised and hunted at large. In their hiding homes, they were debtors. It was their burden to adapt. Sometimes the discord arose from the practical consequences of different social milieus. Thus, for example, Sara Spier, who was from a bourgeois educated family and hidden with people who did not value intellectual growth, was deprived of the life of the mind. She was housed and she was fed but, with a few exceptions, in thirty-two homes in three years she was not nurtured emotionally or intellectually. It is not surprising that as time went on she became increasingly subdued, despondent, and remote. Children from working-class families who were hidden in middle-class homes were acutely aware of their hosts' disapproval of their washing habits, table manners, speech patterns, and so on. On the outside, in society, they were considered unfit to live. In their hiding homes they certainly were allowed to live, but they were made to feel inadequate and not only unaccepted but unacceptable. It was not a situation in which self-worth flourished.

Many of the difficulties the children experienced stemmed from nothing more than their hosts' lack of affection or empathy. Whether they wished it or not, these adults were in fact foster parents. From the child's perspective the relationship was involved and close; they were not chairs to be stored in the attic for the duration. And yet many felt totally estranged from the very people who were so intimately committed to their well-being. As Max Gosschalk, who had been hidden in his youth, explained, "When the war was over, I didn't want to see any of [the people who had hidden me] again because somehow no one ever understood what they were doing."

> I came from a safe home. I had to understand so many things which I could not understand. You had left all your safety, all your security. You had to grow up in a week; it's not possible. But you felt so insecure. If you took something with you it was always fear; fear of being caught, fear of being tortured, fear of betraying other people. Those are three of the worst. You never got any love from anyone. As a young person, I've been in the houses of wonderful people. And I never could trust them because today I was there – how long? One

week, two weeks, nobody ever said anything. Then suddenly, something new. Never a chance of getting attached to someone.

If I had been in the position of the people who hid me, I would do it differently or I would not do it. They were hiding not a Jew, but a human being, a child at that time, [and that they did not] recognize. You never were welcomed; you were tolerated.[24]

Children were sent to people who were willing to take them and who were trusted not to betray them; considerations of "a happy family" or "a stable home" were superfluous. For some children the problem was not only that their hosts were indifferent to them, they were none too fond of each other either. One girl who went into hiding when she was eleven was shocked by the brutality of her foster father towards her foster mother. Her own parents had had a happy marriage, and now she saw her host lock his wife out of the house. During the day he refused to speak to his wife, but when evening came and visitors arrived, he sat next to her and stroked her hair. Upset by the behavior she witnessed, the child began to question her own parents' relationship. Other children found themselves the focus of their hosts' avarice, frustration, and aggression. Young people were taken on as cheap maids or farm-hands and then summarily dismissed if their work failed to please. How were they to find another place? Perhaps inevitably in such a situation of control and dependency, aggression was manifested sexually. One woman who was hidden as an adolescent remembered the insidious way in which she was made to feel awkward, uncomfortable, and guilty. She was in the home of a woman and her husband who was in the coal business.

Once he changed coal for a very nice velvet dress for me. I was very happy with it. I remember I had it on and I was upstairs and he came to me and I said, "I'm so happy with my dress," and he embraced me and took me close and close and close and I was suddenly afraid. I thought, "What's he doing?" It happened two more times that he came and said, "I'm so glad because we have no children and you are a bit like my daughter." He put his arms around me and he put me against him and I didn't feel safe. . . . I started to hate to be there because he always came upstairs, and he never did it when his wife was there.[25]

It was not easy to be in hiding and hidden. As time went on and the months plodded into a year, and the year into two, three, and even four, many children became depressed and apathetic. They were hard pressed: safe for the moment, but also in the trap of gratitude and self-abnegation. They lived with people whom they felt obliged to please and towards whom they were beholden because they, the gentile adults, allowed the children to live, because they risked their lives also, because they too lived outside the law. Not only did this unnatural situation preclude a healthy relationship between hider and hidden, it also reinforced the prevailing ethos that to be a Jew was despicable and dangerous. What kind of pride or dignity, self-esteem or self-respect was possible when one was forced to feel grateful for what should have been one's right? Children who were in hiding and hidden were denied a normal childhood, and they were robbed of all that would have ensued from such a youth: education, development of abilities, models for familial relationships, a normal socialization process. Instead they suffered deprivation and a persistent psychological dilemma between the (usually silent) assertion of their right to live and a (too often manifest) gratitude towards those who protected them.

For many children, life in hiding and visible posed problems similar to those which young people in hiding and hidden experienced. To be in hiding and visible ("hiding") was in many ways parallel to being in hiding and hidden (hiding). Children who "hid" lived openly, indeed sometimes they were fortunate enough to lead the normal life of a child but, especially if old enough to understand (however dimly) the dangers of the situation, they also feared inadvertent exposure or denunciation. It was not their physical existence that children who "hid" had to conceal, but their Jewish identity. Eugenie (Jenny) Lee-Poretzky was born in the Free City of Danzig in 1934. By 1938 her family felt the German threat louring and they moved to Paris. With the invasion of the capital imminent in 1940 the Poretzkys, like so many others, fled the city. After their own *tour de France* which took them from Alvignac to Nice to Cahors, they ultimately went in 1943 to the tiny village of Lestrade in the Auvergne where Jenny was sent to the local convent school. By that time she was nine years old.

That convent episode was the worst for me. [My parents] said I was getting older and I ought to learn something, but that was the most awful experience because I couldn't say I was Jewish. I had to participate in all the goings-on of this convent place. I had to go and take communion. I had to go and take confession. I didn't know all these rites, and I thought I would be found out any minute if I did something wrong. And I thought not only that, but God would kill me dead for taking this communion when I was not supposed to; I hadn't been confirmed – whatever that meant. I used to invent all kinds of sins when I went to confession. I said I'd done terrible things; in fact, as a little girl I'd done nothing. Thank goodness I lost my wooden clog one day and stayed in church and went in the snow and got pneumonia. So back I went to my parents in Lestrade.[26]

The six-year-old Peter Levi did not worry, as did Jenny Poretzky, that he would betray himself, but that he could was a fact of life and he was carefully instructed what to say and what not to do to avoid arousing suspicions. "My mother's acquaintances down in the country, about twenty miles from Budapest on a farm, kept us for the whole of the summer of 1944." They went to a "not so little village, about fifteen to twenty miles south of Budapest called Erd. . . . At the end of August when I had to start school in Erd, my mother *re*-emphasized that my name is not Peter Levi but Amon Reszö, and that I mustn't go to the toilet at the same time as other kids. . . . My mother never told me about circumcision, so I genuinely felt that was evidence that we *are* different."[27] It was essential to their safety that he should not forget his new identity and that he should not urinate in the presence of the other boys.

The fragility of the situation was a constant in their lives. As Jacqueline Kamiéniarz, who at fourteen lived openly with her mother and sisters in the south of France, explained, "Always at night I was afraid to go to sleep, always saying, 'Are we going to wake up all right?'" During the day Kamiéniarz went about her business, working when she could, looking after her niece, and foraging for food. But "at night I was afraid. Is there going to be a knock on the door in the middle of the night? That's what I was afraid of, and they were not unfounded fears."[28] Fear was always there. "A lot of fear, really a lot," Romano Dell'Ariccia remembered about his time "in hiding" as a boy in Rome. Dell'Ariccia was from a very poor family without resources or powerful connections. When the *razzias* began one month after the Germans occupied Rome, the Dell'Ariccias, like all Jews who had remained in the city, understood that it was dangerous to stay in their own apartment. For one month the family managed to sleep in a warehouse owned by a relative married to a Catholic, and in a camp in the country run by communists. But they were too indigent to maintain this itinerant life. They returned to their own apartment at Via Marmorata 169 and hoped for the best. Dell'Ariccia was nine years old.

At the very end we stayed at home because we had no opportunity to hide. Where were we to go? We were, without my brother whom the Germans had taken, five children, a family of seven, and no one wanted us. No one took the responsibility to hide us.

We went out, and we were afraid. . . . We were always on guard if a truck of Fascists passed and stopped not to get too close, to act as if we were indifferent. . . .

I was very much afraid, because I realized. I remember the times when I went out alone in the street. . . . Every now and then I saw German trucks going to a nearby doorway and with submachine guns they took away Jewish families. I remember this. Then I began to understand my mother's worries even better. She would say, "That which has happened will happen to us too," "They will come to take us too."[29]

As Jacqueline Kamiéniarz pointed out, these fears were not irrational. It was all too easy for neighbors or playmates to become suspicious and to report their conjectures to the authorities. Romano Dell'Ariccia's case was extreme because the neighbors knew the family was Jewish; sheer good will, and perhaps solidarity, motivated them to keep silent. Most children who "hid" did not remain in their own homes. But how far could they go? They always faced the possibility of encountering someone who knew their true identity. A chance occurrence, an unreflected step, a careless decision could expose the child. The six-year-old Peter Levi gave himself away. In the spring of 1944 he and his mother obtained false papers and he took on a new identity. "I had to swot up laboriously, not only my new name . . . but a new birth date, new name for my mother, new name for my father, had to swot up things like 'Hail Mary' and the Lord's Prayer. All of this was drummed into me relentlessly for reasons I didn't quite understand." Mrs Levi rented rooms in an area of Budapest where Jews were forbidden to live, and she and her son went "to lodge with a family in our own room with false papers. She had sewn the yellow star on (I remember it very, very clearly) with just a few threads, hers and mine, . . . and suitcase and all [we] walked out of the house with the yellow star. We started to walk down the boulevard and whoosh! My mother whipped off the two yellow stars." They lived in the room Mrs Levi had taken for a day or two until "stupidly, I said to my mother as she put my overcoat on, 'Where is my star?' I immediately realized what I had said, and I just said, 'Sta-.'" Unluckily, however, "there was a big, fat boy there of age twelve or thirteen who heard that and immediately reported it to his mother. And the mother immediately told us to leave."[30] Even less obvious missteps could betray a child's identity. Zippora Soetendorp-van Yssel was six weeks old when she was sent late in June of 1943 to "hide" with a family in the province of North Brabant. It seemed an ideal situation. She was a tiny baby, she had been moved from one end of the Netherlands to the other, and not even her foster parents knew her real name. What could go wrong? "The woman who took me in had a daughter, and as far as she knew, I was the child of a mother who was in a sanitarium and my father was fighting in France. But when she started receiving parcels from Amsterdam in the first few months, she started to be very suspicious and she didn't want me anymore."[31] Van Yssel was "handed over" and moved to the province of Limburg where she lived with seven different families in the following two years. In short, whether in hiding and hidden or in hiding and visible, it was enormously difficult to maintain the pretense, the status quo, and very easy to blunder or be betrayed. For children of an age to comprehend this, fear was a constant concomitant of their lives.

Risk of disclosure and its accompanying anxiety was an aspect of life "in hiding" which paralleled that of children whose existence was concealed. The most important similarity in their experiences, however, was the key role played by the host or foster families. Like those in hiding and hidden, the lives of children in hiding and visible were very much determined by the character and culture of the host family. That this was so is dramatically illustrated by Mirjam Levi, who went from "hiding" to hiding to "hiding." Mirjam Levi had recently turned twelve when she went to live with a bourgeois childless couple in The Hague early in 1943. At first the neighbors were told that she was her hostess's cousin from Zeeland. "In Zeeland there are people of Spanish origin, so I was her cousin from Zeeland. I went outside the home in the evening sometimes, and it was freely told that I was there. But after half a year perhaps it became very clear that some people had suspicions about it, and that I was Jewish, and then I didn't go out anymore. In fact, I wasn't there anymore. I had left. Only one single neighbor who lived upstairs knew. From then on I was completely hidden." This adverse turn did not radically alter Mirjam's life. Her "aunt" and "uncle" had agreed to hide her, and they continued to do so, but they were a "very religious dogmatic couple . . . very strict . . . very formal." They were not affectionate people, and they left Mirjam completely alone. Her life became more restricted after she "disappeared," but its tone and tenor did not change. Her occupations (studying; she was not allowed to dust or wash dishes because she broke too many things) and relationships (practically nonexistent) remained the same; only the parameters of her existence narrowed. It was not until she left that family that her situation improved. In the late winter of 1944, about sixteen months after she had arrived, "somebody came and had to see me. Then my uncle said, 'Tomorrow you are going in the evening with this man because your aunt is not feeling well. She has a stomach [ailment].' (She was very nervous and had pains in her stomach very many times.) 'She is nervous and she can't cope with this situation, so you have to go.'" Mirjam went to a tiny village in Friesland where she lived with a primary school teacher, his wife, and their two small children. "I was so happy as – I don't know what." She was delighted because, as she said, "I was completely free there! I could go out and go to school and play in the garden." But she was also glad of the change because, "well, I felt very well in this family. They were *very*, very nice to me." Her foster mother, or new "aunt" as Mirjam Levi called her, was "a very simple but emotionally wise woman. She has told me later that she saw this girl [me] without a mother and thought, 'Gosh, this girl must be so lonely; I have to be nice to her and be a mother to her.' She liked having an older girl. She could teach me how to do the household, how to knit. (I knitted a lot of things there.) She talked with me and . . . she loved me. And I felt very good there. . . . It was like coming from hell to heaven."[32]

The culture and social habits of Mirjam's foster family in Friesland were very different from her own family's customs. Her new family lived in a small village of 500 people while Mirjam had been brought up in The Hague. Her parents had been busy, professional people. In the village Mirjam experienced another genre of community life, which included a lot of gossiping and interest in each other's affairs. Her aunt and uncle's home was not so luxurious as her parents' apartment had been, and they ate only with a fork while she had been taught to use a knife as well. But she embraced, and was embraced by, her foster family. They loved her and accepted her for who she was: an urban Jewish girl who had come to live with them until the war ended and her parents returned.

Children who for one reason or another fitted into their foster families, as did Mirjam Levi with her family in Friesland, had a happy time in hiding and visible.* Their experiences most closely resembled normal youth. Newborn or very young chidren sent alone to a childless couple who wished for a small person in the house seemed to have had a good chance of integrating into the household. Thus, for example, Georges Waysand "fit well" into his foster "family story." His foster parents were involved in underground work, and because of the risks that entailed they were supposed to send him on to another couple. "But when they saw me (I was quite a pretty [fourteen-month-old] boy), they decided to keep me." Georges's foster mother, a young widow with an eight-year-old daughter, had remarried a man who was sterile. "There was no hope for them to have children in common, so because of that

---

* A number of these children suffered later, either tragically, because they were betrayed and deported or, if they were fortunate enough to survive the war, because of their removal from their foster families.

15   Rita Judith Aletrino (left, aged 6 or 7) in hiding, with host children: Drachten, the Netherlands, 1943 or 1944.

they kept me. . . . It was just as if I were their child."³³ Dolly Hamery-Przybysz was nine-and-a-half months old when her mother, brother, and sister were deported in September 1943 (her father had been caught in July 1942, prior to her birth). She was saved by a neighbor who simply took the infant at that moment and miraculously was permitted to keep her. Like Waysand, Przybysz's adoptive parents had no other children of their own, and she became their daughter.³⁴

Being childless, however, did not guarantee that the foster couple would be affectionate parents. As we have seen, the first people with whom Mirjam Levi "hid" had no children, and they did not have a clue how to treat appropriately the young person who had come to them. At the opposite end of the foster family size spectrum, very young children who were sent to live in families with many children also seem to have had a good chance of being well looked after and fondly treated. Indeed, some underground groups that hid children strongly preferred to place their wards in such families. According to Nico Dohmen of the Piet Meerburg group, he and Hanna van de Voorst "never brought a Jewish child to a family who did not have children at all." This policy posed no problem in the area of Limburg in which they operated because "it was so normal [in Tienray] for families to have between five and ten children." There were two reasons for their decision. First, they feared that childless couples would find it more difficult to return a foster child to his or her parents after the war than would a family with children. And second, "when couples have children, they are much easier. . . . When the couple does not have children, they are much more anxious: 'how do we handle that? And what's that? And what's this?' "[35] Alfred van der Poorten experienced the advantages of joining a large family. When he was about six months old he was sent to the sister of a friend of a patient of his father's medical practice. This woman's husband was the managing director of one of the big biscuit factories in the Netherlands and "they lived in quite a substantial home, a very nice spot in Amersfoort." The family had four children and "I was, in effect, the fifth. . . . I simply was brought up there as the fifth child. . . . This was my family."[36]

In the end, foster family size was not particularly relevant to the reception the child received. Max Arian went to a miner's family with two children, a boy of fourteen and a girl of twelve. "It was my foster brother who brought all this up because he wanted [my stepmother] to have a little child, and she said, 'Oh, no.' . . . Then my foster brother came with little clothes for a baby. . . . So they decided to take a Jewish child. . . . They asked for a little Jewish baby girl and they got a little boy of two-and-a-half years with a drippy nose and with a doll of rags, [a] cowboy doll." It worked out well. "I think they loved me from the first moment. And I had a beautiful time. . . . I was so much a member of the family. They loved me so much; I felt so warm and safe."[37] Judith Belinfante also had a happy foster family experience "in hiding" and she was in a completely atypical household of seven grown-up children and their two elderly parents. She was born while her parents were already in hiding, and she came to her foster family in an ingenious fashion:

A lawyer in The Hague had a very simple and bright idea: when Jewish children were born to try to give them an official non-Jewish identity and then the whole persecution part would be no problem. My parents tried to do that, but it was difficult because you needed someone who had courage enough to say "I'm the mother." And as those days were still fairly old-fashioned from the point of view of unmarried women having children, or babies suddenly popping up in an existing family, it was hard to find someone who could cope with the social complications. In the end, the maid who had worked for my parents before the war (and who was then twenty years old) was willing to go to the Registrar's office and say that she had a daughter named Willie Oosthoek. She herself was called Oosthoek – and no father. The purpose was to get the food rations necessary for survival and a non-Jewish identity card.

Everyone forgot that Lien was only twenty, meaning that legally she was an unwed mother. There were people who took care of "fallen girls," kind of unpleasant, decent, elderly, unkind persons – ladies usually. And suddenly, one of them showed up at Lien's house; her family was living in the Schildersbuurt in The Hague . . . a workers' area. And they lived with seven grown-up children and two parents in a tiny house. When we were all at the table, you couldn't open the door any more. So this lady came along and said, "Where's the baby?" Lien said, "Baby?" (I was never meant to be with her, [but to remain with my parents in hiding].) Then she had to go and visit this lady every month to show that the baby was all right and healthy and well taken care of, and that she [Lien] was behaving well. So suddenly, she had to tell her family that she had done this, and had to find a way to live with me.[38]

In the meantime Belinfante, who had been born at 6.5 pounds, had lost weight until, at six weeks old, she weighed 2 pounds. When Lien took Belinfante home, "the first thing her father said was, 'I thought you were bringing a baby here, not a corpse.'" The whole family took part in resuscitating the infant. Belinfante was very comfortable in her foster home. "It was filled to the brim with people and noise and things happening. And it was warm. And there was always someone taking care of cooking something."[39]

While infants and toddlers appear to have had a better chance than older children of integrating happily into their foster families, extreme youth did not ensure success, nor did age prevent it. The infant van Yssel, for instance, was passed to eight families during her two years "in hiding," and she did not form deep attachments with any of them. By contrast, as we have seen, the by then fourteen-year-old Mirjam Levi was delighted with her foster home in Friesland. In short, neither the age nor the sex of the Jewish child to be taken, nor the recipient foster family size was a major determinant of the sort of life the child would lead "in hiding." As with children in hiding and hidden, both the emotional well-being and the physical activities of children in hiding and visible were determined by the physical situation in which they lived, and by the nature and culture of the host family. Children who were loved by their foster families and accepted as integral members of the household lived more or less normal lives, in so far as any child's life was normal in war-torn Europe. This was especially true for those (like Georges Waysand, Dolly Przybysz, Ivan Buchwald, Max Arian, Judith Belinfante, and Alfred van der Poorten) who were below school age. Older children, even those in warm and affectionate homes, had more difficulties. First, they were of an age to remember, miss, and mourn the loss of their families and home life. Then too, that most mundane and universal of childhood rites, going to school, posed a problem. Children who lived openly were not always in such a secure situation as to risk school attendance. Children had to register for school; birth certificates or other identification papers had to be presented to the education authorities which were part of the civil service. Many children did not have any papers at all, others were forged or falsified and would not pass detailed scrutiny. Furthermore, school attendance requires a certain measure of stability. No one could guarantee how long a child would be safe at any given address. If a child had to be moved, the consequent removal from school could raise uncomfortable questions.

Most children were not so fortunate as to have been accepted into their foster families and their new communities as children like all the other children, to have had so stable and secure a life "in hiding" that they could go on as if theirs were a normal childhood in a country at war. They did not have the luxury of leading such a life. The question is: what were their activities, tasks, and hobbies? Or, as Gerry Mok, who was not quite five years old when he went into hiding, asked himself over forty years later, "What did I do during the day?" His immediate response was, "It depended on the address." Mok was taken from his parents' house in Amsterdam to "hide" in Hoorn in February 1942. Subsequently he was moved about fifteen times; he never went to school and only sometimes was it possible for him to play with other children. At a number of homes his foster parents "started to teach me reading and writing . . . I was very eager to read, I wanted to read. . . . So they gave me lessons. I didn't go to school, first of all because I was too young and, second of all, by the time I was six years old there was no way to put me in school." As he could not attend school, a major factor in his life was "whether at [each] new address, yes or no I could play outside, yes or no children were to know I was there. . . . If I could play outside it meant that I had contact with others, it meant that I had my occupation, because what was my occupation? If you are a child, you play. So the main thing I did was playing. If I could not play, I could read. . . . I read a lot of books that I didn't understand a bloody thing of, but I read them. Anything that was readable, I read."[40]

"There was a lot of fantasy," Mok remembered. "I think, in this respect, I lived partly in a dream world because you had to tell yourself constantly what it would be [like] later. When liberation day came, it could never live up to my expectations, because I had lived through that day a million days before, all those days before that I was in hiding."[41] Daydreams, a world of fantasy, a magic domain, in other words, another reality, was very important to many children in "hiding." The eight-year-old Jenny Lee-Poretzky from Danzig was, unlike Gerry Mok, in "hiding" with her family, and she was in the country while he was mostly in towns, but she too created a realm of fancy and imagination. Poretzky and her family fled from Paris to the village of Alvignac. "That part of France is quite deserted. It's a wild and chalky area, so there are lots of caves, famous caves there." Accompanied by the local baker's daughter, Jenny Poretzky roamed the countryside "and being a town child, this was magic. . . . There is a very famous place of worship called Rocamadour where, from about the twelfth century in France, pilgrims have been coming to worship this black madonna. . . . It's quite an extraordinary place. So *that* was amazing. And the countryside was amazing for me, the walks and all these things that a child in a town would not have known about." Poretzky did not attend school regularly, but she roved the countryside each day. "I remember the walks, and I remember – most wonderful – a spring, [a] cleansing spring. . . . It seemed magical. I used to go with this girl for walks, and there would be hares coming very close, or we would go into a cave of stalactites and stalagmites. . . . There was nothing else to do, and this is one thing I *could* do."[42]

The magical world Poretzky found in nature filled her daily life, and gave her joy and solace in an otherwise tense situation. In Alvignac her family was denounced, arrested, transported by truck to a small local transit camp (a collection point for Jews in the area), and from there taken to the train station to be shipped across the border. Through the intervention of a woman with whom her mother had become friendly, the Poretzky family was rescued; they were permitted to disembark from the train. The family immediately left the area and ended in the Auvergne, but the denunciation and her family's narrow escape from disaster affected Poretzky deeply. "After that I was scared much more than before." Her sense of "something menacing, . . . the impending menace" was more vivid, "but why or how I did not formulate at all." Her consolation was the world of nature. "The contact with nature, and all the natural things, was wonderful, and I have the most wonderful, small memories about going to look for birds' eggs in nests, and tickling a trout with my hand, in the river . . . actually feeling the fish in my hand. [It was] wonderful, magical."[43]

While Gerry Mok imagined liberation day and the life he would resume with his parents, and Jenny Poretzky was enchanted by the world of nature, Giacometta Cantatore-Limentani dreamed of Fred Astaire. Limentani was sixteen and hiding with her parents and sister during the occupation of Rome. They took shelter wherever they found it; it was, as she said, her "odyssey within Rome." "We slept a few nights in the public morgue, then in the house of some friends, always hungry and always afraid." Finally, her father found a place with other friends who were hiding, while she, her mother, and sister were taken into a convent. "What I desired most of all in the world [was] to go and study dance with Fred Astaire," Limentani recalled. "I think the only real moral help I had in all those years, and right after the war, to keep my mind in place, was Fred Astaire and his stupid films. They were so serene, so far from the darkness of this world, and the dancing was so perfect. During the occupation I went on thinking about him. Yes, the real help I had was from Fred Astaire."[44]

This sort of fantasy was different from that of most children in hiding and hidden. Completely cut off from the world, carrying on in a sphere of minimal stimulation, children in hiding tended (as we have seen) to become rather depressed and subdued over time. Children in hiding and visible had many more contacts and experiences, which may have helped them to retain a fresh and vivid imagination.[45] Living in uncertainty and danger in their physical world, they found comfort in another realm, a world of reverie, fantasy, and the magic of nature.

Not all children "in hiding" had the inclination or the leisure for such pursuits, of course. Many, even young children, were forced to work, physically, very hard for their hiding places and they were, perhaps, too preoccupied and exhausted to daydream. This was the case for Jana Levi. She and her cousin Gabbie were taken out of the ghetto in Cracow to a hiding place on a farm through a contact of Gabbie's father. It was the summer of 1942 and Levi was eight years old. "[My uncle] had a connection, a contact with a friend of his who was a professor at the University in Cracow and who was also a friend of the professor in Kleza Dolna on the farm. And this professor, the middleman, Professor Michałkiewicz his name was, came to the warehouse," where Levi and her cousin were hidden.[46] The children were supposed to be gentile Poles, brother and sister, whose parents had gone to work one day and had not returned. Distantly related to Professor Plisiewicz in Kleza Dolna, they were to go to live with him.

> I was wearing a white dress and white gloves. And Gabbie was wearing grey flannel pants, short pants, with a blouse that had buttons around [the waist] and the pants were buttoned [to the blouse]. [My] white dress, I think it was piqué, had a yoke and pleats in front. I was wearing black patent leather shoes. [We had] two little cases, very small little cases.
>
> Professor Michałkiewicz came and he said, "We're going now." I remember one thing. I remember that I did not want to cry. I remember that I knew – I did not question or anything.
>
> They explained about going on papers. In Polish it was *iść na papi-*

ery, which meant that you had false papers and you were going to go out and live normally, not hide. If you had papers, you would live normally, so that you wouldn't be suspected. Some people lived without papers, hidden in a room or something like that, like Anne Frank in the attic. But if you went on papers, it meant that you had to assume the personality and the name that was given to you, that you had this history and that you had to know who you were. My uncle explained to me that the papers were made and when they came they would tell us all about the history and that we would be somebody else. . . .

The papers were made a year younger, both of us were a year younger, so I was seven. My name was Janina Lesiak . . . and Gabbie was Gabriele Lesiak. We had come from Lwów and our parents were called Aniela and Jan Lesiak. . . .

Professor Michałkiewicz got us [and] we left my uncle, and I remember only this part: after he hugged and kissed us, I was walking down the stairs for the first time, these wooden stairs, and out the door. I remember not being able to see the stairs because I had tears in my eyes which I did not want to show. I remember coming outside and this brilliant light of sun hitting me, and I was wiping my eyes and saying to Professor Michałkiewicz "I'm not crying, it's just the light, the sun is too strong."[47]

Levi and her cousin went to the train station with Professor Michałkiewicz. The journey to Wadowice took "a couple of hours" and "it was an exorcism: 'You are no longer Jana Levi; forget that name,'" Professor Michałkiewicz told her. "'You were not born in Cracow. You do not understand German; you do not understand German at all. When you hear German, look the other way so that there is no recognition in your eyes that you understand. You were born in so-and-so, on this-and-this date and your parents were this and that.' This went on for the whole time of the ride. . . . 'Particularly make sure that Gabbie doesn't pee in front of anybody, that nobody sees. Make sure that you don't speak about your home. Make sure you don't talk.'" It was an "obliteration" and "it was frightening, but at the same time" it was also acting, which Levi loved to do as a young girl. "It titillated me, the idea that I was someone else. I think that, aside from the basic information, I made up the character I was going to be."[48]

The two children joined the family of Professor Plisiewicz, his wife, and three daughters, Haneczka, Maryla, and Krysia, who were then about sixteen, eighteen, and twenty years old. Professor Plisiewicz was crippled and walked, dragging his legs, with a cane in each hand. Levi was useful to him. "I started working with the Professor. He was grafting trees; he taught me how to do that. I used to carry the saplings and the string and things. . . . Gabbie became the brother that the three sisters never had."[49] The arrangement Gabbie's father had made, and for which he paid at least $55,000 in gold before he himself was deported, was that the children would live on the farm as relatives of the Professor, and that they would be educated and raised like other children of the same social class.[50]

Slowly, I don't even know how it happened, . . . but ultimately and eventually, I became sort of a Cinderella. In other words, I was working from four o'clock in the morning when I would get up to say my prayers and do whatever, and then prepare the feed for the horses who were going out into the fields about six. I had to feed them early so that they would eat for a couple of hours before they went out. I had to clean them down. I remember when we got there, there was a groom who worked in the stables, but later on, there was no more money or food or whatever, so there was no groom. . . . And we took care of the pigs and the cows, and we started working in the fields, planting. All of this was a gradual sort of thing. . . . There was work that was being done during the winter and there was work that was being done in the spring. And as time went, it became more and more work. [It was] really heavy work: baking bread, making the dough, polishing the floors, etc. . . .

Aside from the harshness which life eventually became, there was little food. For everyone. But, you know how it is, if you are the power you find ways to hide bread. . . . Very quickly I found out that nobody was going to look after me but me. And Gabbie was very hungry. So [I was] looking after him. [And I worked.] I worked with the Professor, with the bees, grafting trees, transplanting seedlings. I worked in the kitchen. I worked a lot. I worked in the fields and I worked in the stables and I shoveled out manure. I milked the cows and [sometimes] I took the cows into the pasture. But if there was other work to be done, I did it. I polished floors. Everybody worked. But it was like I was more capable.[51]

Hilma Geffen-Ludomer, like Jana Levi, had to work, physically, very hard in her hiding home, but she was older and therefore better able to manage the tasks and to maintain her sense of self. Nevertheless, she too became completely absorbed by her daily labor. Geffen-Ludomer and her parents had moved from their home in the town of Rangsdorf to nearby Berlin in August 1939. In October 1942 the Gestapo came to arrest and deport the family. "My mother was at home. I was not at home. But when I came back from work I opened the door, the outside door of the apartment, and my mother met me and she said, 'Run away. They came to pick us up.' It was in the late afternoon. And without anything I turned around and left."[52]

At the age of seventeen Ludomer became a "U-boat," a Jew who lived underground. For six months she had no fixed address, shuttling back and forth between friends, acquaintances, and short-term employers. One friend, a boy her own age named Gerhard, remained steadfast and loyal. With his help she obtained a valid post office identity card and made contact with an older couple, the Körbers, who were willing to take her in. Mr Körber was a letter-carrier and had been a very active Social Democrat. After the election of Hitler in 1933, he had been arrested and sent to a concentration camp for six months. By the time Ludomer went to live with them in March 1943 they had moved out of the city to their weekend house in the Berlin suburb of Falkensee and Mr Körber had been drafted. Mrs Körber wanted someone to help with the garden and Ludomer, under the alias of Marga Gebhardt, went to live with her as her niece. Mrs Körber knew that she was Jewish, but was never told her real name. "I lived there and I worked. I worked very hard. I worked in the garden. I cleaned the house. . . . We raised chickens, rabbits . . . we had vegetables from the garden."[53]

Ludomer had her bicycle from Rangsdorf and once a week she went to Berlin to collect potato peelings to feed the rabbits; she got them from a friend of Frau Körber who owned a restaurant. The rest of the time she worked. "One thing I must say for this woman [Frau Körber]: she made me work. She was a slave-driver. I really had to work. She made everybody work. Not in an unpleasant way, but she was that kind of person, that you had to work. She also worked. She worked from morning until night."[54] Ludomer's whole life revolved around this all-encompassing work.

> How did I feel during all this? . . . I had never thought, "How do I feel?" . . . It's just lately that I finally came to the conclusion what I thought: I didn't think. And I didn't feel. . . . I certainly did not cry when my parents were taken, because I was so busy getting myself into a place, into a safe place for survival. I don't think I cried one tear during those entire years. From the day my parents were taken until liberation, I don't think I cried one tear. I don't remember ever mourning; I had absolutely no feeling of mourning. . . . I did not cry, I did not mourn. I just survived. . . . I know I did not cry. I know I did not mourn my parents. I just didn't have time, I didn't have energy.

All my energy went into planning to survive and to day-to-day: we did one day, let's see about the next day. And there was no time, no room for any other emotion.[55]

Jana Levi and Hilma Ludomer worked for their keep. It was one of the adjustments they had to make to integrate into their new environment. Unlike those children who were taken in simply to be cheap servants or farm-hands, in their particular cases their host families probably would not have turned them away had they refused to work, or in any case to work so hard. Nevertheless, they felt it incumbent upon them to acquiesce to their foster parents' demands; it was their task, responsibility, and burden to accommodate. This business of accommodation, the concern to fit in, to conform to the situation, was pervasive and ubiquitous. It also took a lot of time and energy, and was a major occupation of children in hiding. As Gerry Mok explained, "The fact that I was in hiding kept me busy. I was dealing with people who were constantly different people. There was always a new experience and a new experience does not let you stop to think about what happened." It is only later that one has the luxury to reflect, "'Oh, God, this I did, and this I did; what an impossible this, and how terrible that.' When the terrible things actually happened, then they're just terrible, but they happened. And when they happen, it means an active occupation, and then it's not frustrating, not as frustrating as later on."[56]

Even children who were as happy in their foster homes as was Max Arian were busy with the task of accommodation. For Arian, it began when he was not yet three years old and at a temporary address prior to being taken to the family with whom he remained for the rest of the war. "I think I learned a lot there that has to do with the whole building of your character. I learned to be silent, not to sit in the window, be sweet and be a nice little child." Shortly thereafter Arian moved to the Micheels family, where he was very much loved. Even there, however, Arian molded himself into a boy who would be little trouble or bother, and therefore be allowed to remain. "I think I acted. I don't know. After the war I found out that I liked many things that were crazy. [For example,] I'm the only person I know who likes a little skin in his milk. Nobody ever likes it. I reconstructed it. Perhaps at that time already I got used to wanting the milk with the skin." To like what his foster brother and sister detested was a way of fitting into an empty space in the family. "Also, my foster mother would tell me that I liked so much home-fried potatoes. Now here in Holland, it's kind of a left-over [food]. You first cook the potatoes and then the next day you fry them. I still love them. It's very nice to eat. She [my foster mother] was ashamed when the neighbors would come and I would be eating fried potatoes and they would eat bread because it would look like she would give me something worse. But I still liked it! And I still like it. So that's an adaptation you do being hidden." By transfiguring his own desires, Arian transformed himself from the stranger, the outsider, the little Jewish boy, into a child his foster family not only would but could treasure and cherish.[57]

This sort of obvious and insidious pressure to adjust, adapt, and conform was not healthy either for the foster parents or for the children. Inevitably it occasionally led to the psychological and sexual abuse of the children. Ineluctably, for young children it was an obstacle to building up an integrated sense of self. And inexorably, in the case of older children, it led to a certain disintegration of their former identity. Children in "hiding" were in a very complicated and fragile situation. Like children in hiding and hidden, they too wished to please. The assertion of their own likes, dislikes, desires, former habits, and customs was out of the question. As Gerry Mok put it, "I always had the feeling that I was not behaving as if I were myself, but as if I were somebody else. I took my new identity and tried to live in that new identity."[58] Children in hiding and hidden were burdened with terrible isolation and deprivation. Their lot was to live as if they were not living, to exist without trace. Children in hiding and visible did not have those difficulties. Their oppression was packaged differently; it was their burden to live another identity.

To live as a gentile among gentiles, to give up the past and adopt a new history, to renounce who they were and become another person created its own problems. The designation itself, "to live as a gentile," encompasses a spectrum of experience. There were those who, like Andrew Nagy in a Swedish home in Budapest, or Naomi Levi in a Swiss children's home in France, or Emma Fiorentino-Alatri in a Catholic convent in Rome, found refuge in an institution protected by a neutral power. These sites were not, strictly speaking, juridically extra-territorial, but in practice they functioned as if they were. So long as Germany needed the neutral powers (for raw materials, to conduct financial business, to preserve the allegiance of Catholics) the Nazis were (reluctantly) willing to tolerate the claims to neutral protection. Children who were fortunate enough to be in such places did not have easy lives, but as they were often with other Jews, and sometimes even with their own families, they did not suffer the decontextualization and isolation that children who were passing as gentiles endured.

Andrew Nagy, for instance, was not quite twelve years old when the Germans marched into Hungary on 19 March 1944. His father was arrested, beaten, and sent to a concentration camp. Nagy and his mother did not fare too badly until Horthy's call to the Hungarians to lay down arms and the Arrow Cross coup that autumn. The tempo of deportation then accelerated abruptly and, like the other Jews of Budapest, Nagy and his mother sought a way to escape the dragnets. Jews in Budapest initially were not concentrated into a ghetto but were forced to move into specifically designated buildings. The apartment house in which the Nagys lived in the fifth district was one of those buildings, and they understood that their fate was signed and sealed. It would be only a matter of time before they were delivered to the depot. Through her husband's brother-in-law, Nagy's mother obtained a Swiss *Schutzpass*, or protection pass. "I, who was barely over twelve, forged my name on to my mother's Swiss pass. I took an old, beaten-up typewriter from my father's office and typed 'und Sohn' [and son] on to the pass. Clearly it was a different type, it wasn't very sophisticated, but at least the 'und Sohn' appeared so now I also was protected with the Swiss pass." Shortly thereafter protected houses began to appear, apartment buildings in which people who had Schutzpasses from a neutral power lived with some degree of security. "In other words, the Wallenberg Swedish houses, the Swiss houses, even some Vatican houses started [to operate]. Since we had Swiss passes . . . we went to a Swiss house. . . . I vaguely re member that the Swiss house we moved into had something like twenty people to a room. We stayed there for about a day, a day and a half. My mother realized that our apartment house was declared Swedish and . . . we could just as well live in our own apartment. So we went back to the Swedish house. . . . We moved back to our own apartment and spent the rest of the war, the other two and a half months, in our apartment." Nagy was cognizant of the peril in which he lived, that he was constantly at risk, but he was with his mother and they were living in their own home (with about twenty other people of course), which had come to be protected by Sweden. So, while "I was certainly aware that being Jewish was dangerous," it was not something that had to be denied or forgotten.[59]

Like Andrew Nagy, Naomi Levi did not give up her pre-war identity while "in hiding" in a Swiss children's home in Le Chambon-sur-Lignon. A small village in southern France, Le Chambon is one of the few extraordinary exceptions in the sad story of civilian complicity and collaboration in the Judeocide. Le Chambon, or more precisely the Chambonnais, offered refuge to the persecuted, and resistance groups throughout France brought Jews, and especially Jewish children, to the village. For example, as we saw earlier, Le Chambon was central to the work of Madeleine Dreyfus, the *assistante-chef* of the Lyon-based sec-

16   Group photo of children and instructors at a U.G.I.F. children's home at
Montreuil-sous-Bois in 1943.

tion of the Garel network. The few thousand Jewish adults and children
who came to Le Chambon stayed for the duration of the war or were
passed over the border to Switzerland. Many people were harbored by
individual families, others lived in seven group homes supported by philanthropic organizations (such as the Society of Friends, the American
Congregationalists, the Comité Inter-Mouvements auprès des Evacués
[CIMADE], etc.) and national governments (most notably Switzerland
and Sweden). Naomi Levi lived in "Abric," one of the homes run by Le
Secours Suisse aux Enfants (Swiss Relief for Children).[60]

Levi had been born in Belgium in 1929 to Polish parents. Her mother
and father subsequently divorced and by 1932 Naomi and her mother
were living in Paris with her mother's second husband, a naturalized
Frenchman. With this second marriage her mother also obtained French
nationality and therefore, when the war came to France in 1940, Naomi
was the only one in the family who still had a Polish passport. As foreign
Jews were, in the first instance, at greater risk than Jews with French
citizenship, Levi's parents sent her away hoping that it was a dispatch to
safety.

One day I was accompanied to the train station, a tag was put on me, and I left with other children. It was a very long trip, very complicated. One moment that little train and then you arrive at Chambon. Officially, I left for two months, in reality I stayed for three years. . . .

The Secours Suisse had opened three children's homes in the village. . . . Those three houses were Swiss territory, not French territory. On the door there was a sign to that effect. One part of the three houses was truly a holiday camp. The children really came for two or three months and then returned to their families. One part unofficially was not a vacation camp. The endangered children remained, and therefore it was confusing to understand why this one or that one was still there a year later. . . . The French youngsters who were not touched by the war served as a camouflage, without knowing it, for the children who were so, or for whom it was best not to return to their own homes.[61]

According to Levi, the Swiss homes were relatively poor. The children received food from Switzerland and therefore were well nourished, but otherwise their lives were very simple. At l'Abric there were few adults: the director (who was also a nurse so as to be able to care for sick children), a cook, a housekeeper. The children, who were between six and sixteen years old, were divided into teams responsible for a variety of tasks: cleaning, kitchen work, or errands. "It was three homes with girls and boys. It was a boarding house where all the children had their own lives, their own problems." Like the others, Levi attended one of the local schools, in her case the Cévenol School, which she enjoyed very much. "In this story I was one of the lucky ones because I had parents, which was not true for all my friends. I saw the results of war before understanding war. That village of Chambon is a truly, truly extraordinary village. . . . I arrived thinking it was for vacation and I realized that I was not returning. I was called 'Nanie,' and I was told, 'You, Nanie, we will keep.' But I did not know why. It was only by degrees that I learned that to be a Jew was a special case, only slowly, from the accounts of the others."[62] Or, as Cirlène Liberman-Zinger, who was just eight when she began to live at l'Abric put it, "I have nothing but happy memories of Chambon." And she went on to explain, "For me, Chambon was not the war; I did not have to hide there. . . . It was not something gloomy for me. There were painful times in Marseille, in Paris, but once I arrived in Chambon it was over. I was no longer afraid."[63] In fact, Levi and Zinger and the other children were "hiding." They were, as Levi pointed out, camouflaged by the vacationing children. They went to the local Protestant church and learned to sing hymns. But they did not feel as if they were hiding and they were not compelled to do these things. They were enjoyable activities, and the children participated in them for community and pleasure, not to maintain their cover. In short, they were Jewish children living in a Protestant environment, but they were not compelled to live as Protestants, to take on a Protestant identity, however temporarily.

Many Jewish children "in hiding" in convents and monasteries in Italy after the fall of Mussolini (25 July 1943), the surrender of Badoglio (8 September), and the subsequent German occupation were in a situation similar to that of young people of Le Chambon. Like the youngsters in Le Chambon, by and large they too were in the company of other Jews or even their own families. They were in hiding, they lived in a Catholic sphere, but they did not have to adopt a Catholic identity.[64]

Few Roman Jews went into hiding immediately after German troops marched into the city on 10 September 1943. For five weeks the situation appeared if not calm, at least stable. This illusion was shattered, violently, with the sudden round-up of the Jews in Rome's ancient ghetto area on 16 October, *il sabato nero* (the Black Sabbath). Over a quarter (1,259) of the neighborhood inhabitants were caught; ultimately 1,007 were deported. Those who escaped the dragnet, both in the immediate vicinity and throughout Rome, were shocked into action. "The morning of October 16, at dawn, the lawyer Pasquali Lasagni, who was a dear friend of my father ... telephoned us," Emma Fiorentino-Alatri recalled. He lived in Largo Argentina, adjacent to the ghetto, and he said, "Alatri, Alatri! Flee! Flee! They are entering all the Jews' houses and taking them away!" The Alatri family left the house; the mother and two daughters went one way and the father another. "That day we went out, it was raining, and we left just like that, dressed as we were, without stockings, in sandals, in the rain all day long. We approached all the convents on Via Nomentana, but as we did not have a letter of recommendation, all of them answered, 'It is not possible.' ... I remember as if it were a nightmare that long Via Nomentana that never ends, full of convents, full of gates, full of doorbells that rang." They did not find a place that day; later, Alatri's aunts gave up their positions at Notre Dame de Sion for the two girls and their mother. "We entered the convent towards the end of October and left at the end of January. During that period my aunts returned, they joined us there. There were many Jews there. (To be truthful, they said they had been accepted without a letter of recommendation – while we had not been so successful.) We stayed until the end of January, the beginning of February, and then we could not manage it anymore. It cost too much, and no one knew how long the situation would continue. So we left and went to family friends, two sisters on the Via Po. . . . We stayed there until the fourth of June, Liberation Day."[65]

For the Jews of Rome, as for Jews throughout Europe, the first and greatest problem was to find a hiding place. Economics were a factor, of course, as those who could pay found refuge more easily while those who, like the Alatri family, could not afford the constant expense had to leave. But it was not so simple a calculation. There were convents and monasteries which asked only basic maintenance costs, or did not charge at all. Here, as in the case of the gentile families which kept children without reimbursement, the problem was not that of money but opportunity. As Sergio Tagliacozzo, who was nine when he and his two older brothers entered the Collegio Nazareno in the autumn of 1943 explained, "the problem was not financial or economic, the problem was simply to find a hiding place." Tagliacozzo and his brothers lived in the Nazarene school for seven months. "The priests knew that we were Jews, but they did not say anything about it to us, they treated us normally, like the other boarding school students. We did not have any problems of any kind. There was us, another one of our cousins who was with us, and two or three other Jewish boys whom we knew were Jews but they did not say anything to us about that."[66]

Life in the *de facto* extraterritorial places like the Swedish houses in Budapest, children's homes in Le Chambon, or monasteries and convents in Rome, had its problems. The Jewish children who found refuge there were among the hunted. They may have been fortunate in the place they had found (or had been found for them), but the fact remains that they had to seek shelter at all. Uprooted from their homes, separated from a part if not all of their family, they lived in often crowded, usually primitive conditions. Cold and hunger were constant companions and familial love and affection all too often missing. And there were anxieties: trepidation that they would have to leave, disquiet about their loved ones. These were rational fears. Zinger's father was deported and did not return. Both of Tagliacozzo's parents were caught and shipped east; only his mother survived. These children were "in hiding." They were prey because of their Jewish identity, and they lived a camouflaged existence: with marginally valid Swedish papers, among gentile children on recuperative holidays, amidst the other inmates of Catholic institutions. In this way they passed through the nets as gentiles without adopting a Christian identity.

Living in a home or institution protected by a neutral power was not the only way in which children were camouflaged without actually taking on a Christian identity. Other young people simply lived in their own homes or those of others; their neighbors knew perfectly well that they were Jews and they could have been denounced at any time. An unspoken alliance of silence was their sole protection. This was the case, for example, both for Judith Belinfante in The Hague and Romano Dell' Ariccia in Rome. The cover story for Belinfante, who, as we have seen, was taken into the home of her parents' pre-war twenty-year-old maid, Lien, when she was six weeks old, was unconvincing and implausible. Although Lien had claimed at the Registrar's office that she had given birth to the infant, she could not rely on that fiction in her own neighborhood. "That would have been a miracle! No, the story was that she had a friend, and that the friend had delivered, but had tuberculosis or something like that, a kind of illness people were scared stiff of. So no one dared to talk about it and everyone knew what it was really about. The funny thing is that in the same street there was one member of the NSB [Dutch Fascist party], but he never talked about it to anyone. Everyone knew; it was silly."[67]

Romano Dell'Ariccia had no cover story at all. After hiding for a month in a warehouse in the city and, through the Communist party, in a barracks in the country, the family returned to their own apartment. The Dell'Ariccias had lived there for years and everyone knew them. "Except my brother whom, tragically, they took away [earlier], thank God we were spared. Maybe because they wished us well in the neighborhood nobody informed on us. It would have been enough for a neighbor simply to go to tell the Fascists that we were there and they would have come to get us. They took everyone, just everyone, all the families." The Dell'Ariccias did not practice their Judaism during that time. They lived quietly and at the margins amidst their Catholic neighbors. But they themselves did not have Catholic papers, nor did they participate in the rites of that religion.[68]

For children in the protected homes and in situations like that of Dell' Ariccia (who, at the age of nine, knew he was a Jew), there was little conflict between the life they led "in hiding" and their understanding of their own identity. Children who "hid" and in so doing had to assume a Christian faith were in a more complicated position. This applied to the great majority of children "in hiding." Like so many of the children we have met in these pages (Max Arian, Mirjam Levi, Georges Waysand, Jana Levi, Judith Belinfante, Peter Levi, and so on), they had false names and fictive histories. By and large, the foster families who hid these children knew they were Jews, but as they were meant to be Christians they were discouraged from clandestinely practicing their religion or discussing their past lives. For everyone's safety it was imperative that the child present a smooth gentile facade to the outside world. Any crack, a single slip of gesture or tongue, could betray the child, the foster family, and the network of contacts that had brought the two together. Very young children who had no concept or memory of Jewish life simply grew up as Christians. Slightly older children, those from about four or five years old, remembered their families and former customs. They had to be constantly vigilant to avoid disclosure. For years they lived a dual reality as internal Jews and external Christians. To live as a gentile among gentiles created a disjuncture between their former idea of themselves and their current reality. It engendered distance and divisions: no one outside the foster family was to know who they really were, no one was to be trusted.

For some children this situation also caused confusion about the value of their Jewish identity. With time, questions and doubts arose; the passing years, the constant barrage of antisemitic propaganda current in Nazi-occupied Europe, and the persistent strain of living life as someone else did their work. Everyday incidents, such as hearing a common antisemitic remark and not being able to reply to it as a Jew, gave rise to shame – shame for failing to respond, shame at one's own impotence, and, ultimately, shame about being a Jew. It would be so much easier, so much more comfortable, simply to live the lie as truth, to be like the others, to be a Christian in fact, not fiction. Isabelle Silberg Riff was in hiding for only a few days. Her family had fled from Antwerp to the south of France. After the sudden round-up in August 1942 of the Jews in Puisserguier where she and her sister were staying with an aunt, the two girls were sent to Switzerland. A Spanish woman, a friend of an uncle who was studying at the University of Montpellier, was to be their guide part of the way; the seven-and-a-half-year-old Isabelle and her four-year-old sister were supposed to be her daughters.

This person came then, and she took us to Béziers [where my parents were], and she gave me instructions: I shouldn't talk, I should only answer questions, and as short as possible.

She took us . . . to the block of flats where my parents were hiding. We climbed five or six flights of stairs; they were in the attic. And my mother had prepared a meal; I remember it very clearly. She had some new clothes for us. Where she had found the clothes I don't know, but she had a new dress for each of us. She had new shoes for us. And I remember her giving me a comb in my hand, and she said to me from now on I must comb my sister's hair. (She was only four and she had long, curly hair.) I must wash her, I must clean her, I must look after her. And that we were going to Switzerland, and I had another uncle who lived in Switzerland then, and that he will be there to receive us.

How we would get to Switzerland, or who would take us, she didn't know. I remember we had a meal together, and then they kissed us goodbye. . . .

It was two o'clock in the afternoon, hot, and we walked through the town, and then I remember instinctively thinking, "I wish I was like a French girl, like the other French children, so that I shouldn't have to hide." Because I knew that I couldn't be myself, I had to hide. I was walking with that strange woman. She was protecting me. I had to hide. I wasn't the same as the others who could run free. I knew that my life was in danger. And she said to me, "You mustn't say that you are Jewish. You don't look Jewish so don't say that you are Jewish. You can say even that you are Protestant or Catholic, anything but that you are Jewish."

And that feeling, that because you are Jewish you should feel guilty about it. This is a terrible feeling, to be aware that what you are is a reason that you have to hide it. There are no words for it. This is to feel ashamed for what you are.[69]

These conflicts were exacerbated in the case of children who had to maintain the fiction within their foster homes, to keep their identity entirely to themselves. Vivette Samuel-Hermann was one of the OSE workers who cared for Jewish children during the war. She supported the principle that to save the children physically was the most urgent priority of the underground network, but she was sensitive to the emotional contradictions this could raise. After the war, in 1948, she interviewed the OSE children about their experiences of life in hiding. Later, in an unpublished paper, Madame Samuel (who by then had become director of OSE) discussed the difficulties chidren encountered at various degrees of hiding: the simple Gallicization of a foreign name, the temporary adoption of false papers as a means to pass the frontier, and the assumption of a gentile identity for the duration of the war.[70] The Garel network, unlike other child rescue groups (such as the NV, for example) had the firm policy of keeping the child's Jewish identity secret from the foster family (except possibly the foster mother) for the protection of the child, the family, and the network. The practical concomitant of this for the child was that she or he was forced to dissemble within the host family. The result was "perpetual tension." The suffering living that lie caused was worse for the children than the fear of the actual danger they risked.[71]

It was easier and it was safer for the children to forget the past and remember only their new histories. To give up who they had been and to become who they were supposed to be; to hide their Jewish identity not just from the Germans and their allies, or their new friends and neighbors, or even their host families, but from themselves was a wonderfully direct way to resolve their anxieties, conflicts, and tensions. There was just one problem with this sublimely simple solution. If they forgot their names and who they had been, and the war ended and someone of the family returned, how would he know how to find them? They would have ceased to exist and it would be impossible to trace them. "The most prevalent, horrendous fear" Jana Levi had, she said, was that

> I didn't remember anymore what my real name was. I only dreamt about it at night. When I woke up in the morning, I wouldn't remember again. I knew that I had a different name, but it was so important for me to forget it that I actually did completely forget it. I knew that if [my parents] didn't know my name they couldn't find me. They wouldn't know, nobody would know who I was. I had completely become someone else and the real person, no one would know who it was, and that they didn't know who I was either. I mean, that *nobody* knew. It was such a secret that nobody knew.[72]

The ultimate adaptation to living as a gentile among gentiles was in fact to become a gentile, either through simple attrition or by formal conversion. The adoption of a Christian faith was not rare. Several factors were influential in determining a child's receptivity to the influences and atmosphere which surrounded him. Age and religious practice prior to the hiding period were important in that older children simply had had more time to build up their character and self-concept than younger children had had, and those who had come from observant homes had a stronger feeling for their own tradition, which was more firmly integrated into their sense of self than was the case of children who were not Jewishly educated or identified. The circumstances of the hiding environment also played an important role in directing a child's interest in Christianity. Children who hid alone were more inclined to adapt to their surroundings than were those who were supported in their Jewishness by the company of other family members or friends. Similarly, young people who had found refuge in religious institutions or pious Christian families had greater opportunities to become absorbed than children who hid in secular establishments or unobservant homes. And of course, the duration of the hiding period was also a factor: the longer a child lived as a gentile among gentiles, the easier it was to become incorporated into that way of life.

This radical adjustment took many forms, and the degree to which the children sincerely embraced Christianity as a religious faith varied greatly. The most common instance of this (it must be stressed) in-frequent occurrence was the case of very young children who lived in pious homes or religious institutions. As these children were in hiding it would have been foolish for their foster parents or teachers to tell them that they were Jews. They were cared for as if they were of the same background as the other children; to have reinforced or inculcated a Jewish identity would have been tantamount to inviting the child to betray herself. Those children who developed a Christian identity in this way did not have a conversion experience as such. They did not turn away from or renounce their own culture. They simply grew up as Christians. It was a natural part of the life they led. Most foster parents, and many of the church organizations involved in protecting child life, did not have a great desire to proselytize. They were interested in and they were devoted to safeguarding the children. These were not words nor mere sentiment; they risked their lives for it. To that end, they camouflaged the children as best they could, and in the case of two-, three-, four-, and even five-year-olds this well could have meant keeping their Jewish heritage a secret from them until after the war. If there is any quarrel with the behavior of the Christian community in this regard, it must be confined to their actions after and not during the war.[73]

Older children were in a different, but similar, situation. As they were not so young, they had the concept of going from one culture to another. But they too were in hiding and they also had to participate in the daily life of their private or institutional homes. If they were in a religious environment, they could observe and feel the beauty and the significance of these rites and beliefs to those who cared for them. For fanciful or emotional reasons, to share, to join, to be part of that community was very attractive. Jana Levi "hiding" in Poland, and Max Arian "hiding" in the Netherlands were drawn to the Roman Catholic Church in this way. And Cirlène Liberman-Zinger "hiding" in France felt similarly about the Protestant Church. "If I had stayed very long at Chambon," she declared, "I certainly would have become Protestant."[74] (As it turned out there was only one conversion at Le Chambon: a Chambonnais boy became a Jew.) "I fell in love with church," Levi confessed.

> Very shortly after we got there, I got in the swing of things and I loved church. I absolutely loved church. The theater of it was absolutely [entrancing]. I envied the altar boys because they were dressed up and they were coming and going at the altar and bowing and kissing and doing. I loved going. I mean, the whole ceremony of Sunday mass was just absolutely wonderful. Eventually, after my first communion

(which was a great event in my life, I wore a white dress with flounces on the bottom. I thought I looked like a princess! And a garland of flowers on my head and a big white candle and all of that), after my first communion, I became a procession flower girl. So that meant that I had a little basket with flower petals hung on my neck and that I walked in front of the procession that went around the church perimeter. And the boy with the incense and I would throw petals in front of the procession and kneel, and then go backwards and throw petals and kneel. I mean, it was tremendous, it was like being on stage.[75]

In the end, neither Zinger, nor Arian, nor Levi converted.

In happy foster placements that worked well there was real affection between the children and their parents. Some of the older children admired their foster parents. They were positive role models. The children perceived that if their parents' faith meant so much to them, it might be something to accept. This was the case for Sara Spier. Spier was in over thirty households during her nearly three years in hiding, but one couple, Cor and Trijntje van Stam, were steadfast and loyal to her. As they were deepy involved in underground work she could not stay with them for long periods (the risks would be too great), but they found addresses for her and she was always welcome in their house. The van Stams were very convinced Calvinists.

They were Christians and very good Christians. It was something natural. They told me that they could never do this resistance work which was so dangerous if they didn't have their belief. I was very impressed by this because I had the feeling that it was something true, something that's no game. Well, my parents had been betrayed [in 1943]. They [Cor and Trijntje] told me what had happened and they also told me, "We always pray and it gives us a lot of strength. We just want to tell you that." Every time I saw them (and this was also due to the fact that my parents were away) I thought of them as a kind of parents. I think I became Christian because I had the feeling, well, I'd like to be one of them. I've been a Christian I think nine years [1943–52], a long time. *Gereformeerd* [Calvinist]. Well, anyhow, I had quite a belief in the war and it gave me some rest. It also gave me the feeling, as most of the people I came to were *Gereformeerd*, it gave me a bit of a feeling of assimilation, I think.[76]

Clearly Spier would not have been so deeply impressed by Calvinism without the example of the van Stams, but her reasons for becoming a Protestant were complicated. Living in thirty-two homes in thirty-four months, an average of a new family every thirty-five days, and most of them Calvinist, Spier felt that to be of their religion would help her to adjust, to cope with the difficulties she faced.

There were less positive reasons for adopting a Christian faith, of course. Some church institutions brought a lot of pressure to bear on the children they helped. They were in the business of saving souls as well as lives. And a small minority of foster parents shared that ideology. The couple with whom Mirjam Levi lived in The Hague were "very religious, dogmatic." They felt it was "their duty to help" and they wanted to convert her "to save a child because of the saving." They were temporarily successful. "I was Christian too, in my thoughts, and I hoped my parents would be saved by Christianity because that was their opinion, the opinion of my foster parents. I was converted. I had not so much religion at home and this was a time when this happened because I had to adjust to the situation. I couldn't make a difference between them and me anymore."[77]

The onus of the acceptance of Christianity, the ultimate adaptation of the Jewish child to the gentile world, lies with the Nazis and their allies, and not the foster families and religious institutions which participated in protecting and defending these young people's lives. The political situation in which the children functioned was responsible for their enforced lives as gentiles and for the harsh lesson they took to heart: their problems arose because they were different, because they were the strangers. The immediate post-war sequel for those fortunate enough to survive the years in hiding was not conversion but, not infrequently, an intense desire to be like everyone else. In this chapter we have discussed and analyzed the experience of children in hiding and hidden and in hiding and visible, those who had to conceal their physical existence and those who had to conceal their Jewish identity. In *The Destruction of the European Jews* Raul Hilberg summarized the past 2,000 years of Jewish history in a few sentences. First, he said, Jews were told, "You have no right to live among us as Jews." Then they were told, "You have no right to live among us." Finally, in Germany's Third Reich, Jews were told, "You have no right to live."[78] Jewish children who went into hiding began life with a different fourth message from the gentile world. "You *may*, you are entitled, to live among us as Jews," they believed. Within a very short time, sometimes even a month or week, they experienced the three stages Hilberg had identified. "You have no right to live among us as Jews," and they went into "hiding," they began a camouflaged life. But for many that ruse did not suffice. "You have no right to live among us," and they went into hiding, they lived but left no trace of their existence. Again that did not satisfy. "You have no right to live." Like Anne Frank, they were betrayed and deported.

Part Two

A World With Precedent and Without Parallel

Chapter Four

Transit Camps

•

On 1 July 1944, Frieda Menco-Brommet and her parents, her maternal uncle and his family, were arrested by the Gestapo. They had been hiding with a Catholic family in Warmond (the Netherlands) for two years. The Brommets had paid for the privilege. They even had paid their hosts for black market ration coupons which, unknown to them at the time, had been obtained free from the local underground. Their situation deteriorated and, as it became increasingly awkward and unhappy, the hosts "came with the proposition that they knew somebody who could bring us to Switzerland. My father decided we would do that," Brommet recalled. Her family's final payment for that passage to Switzerland turned out to be their fare to jail in Amsterdam. "When they had all the money . . . the Germans came to pick us up." Their host was taken too, "but he could go home immediately, so we knew he had betrayed us." The family spent three nights in jail and then were sent to Westerbork, the Dutch transit camp in the province of Drente in the northeast of the Netherlands.[1]

"Three days in jail and then we went to Westerbork, and Westerbork was wonderful for us. Somehow, when we were caught, there was less stress because we couldn't get caught anymore, because we *were* caught." The Brommets were sent to the punishment barracks for their crime of hiding. "We were dressed there in overalls, dark blue, with a red kerchief." Brommet had been fourteen when the Germans invaded the Netherlands in 1940. By the time she was deported to Westerbork she was eighteen. "I had long, black hair and that overall looked great on me," she remembered. "And there were a lot of men and there was enough food, so it was *wonderful* for us."[2]

17   Children in transit between Amsterdam and Westerbork.

18   A woman plays with a child in transit from Amsterdam to Westerbork.

At nine years old, Esther Levi was half the age of Frieda Menco-Brommet when she and her family were deported to Westerbork in 1943. In many respects their family lives and backgrounds could not have differed more, and yet for Levi too the immediate experience of life in transit camp was edifying and exciting. Esther Levi had been born in Frankfurt am Main in 1934. Her father dealt in diamonds, gold, and silver, and her mother was an old-fashioned housewife. Their family life was very loving and very traditional. "In Germany we lived in an extremely big three-story house. My grandparents lived on the ground floor. There were five children, two of whom were married, and each married couple lived in one of the upper floors. [In my memory, and also what I understand from an older cousin] there were very good family ties; they did everything together. I come from a very religious, observant, Orthodox Jewish family. . . . My mother wore a *shaytel* [wig] and even [after we moved to] Amsterdam we had a *Sefer Torah* [Torah Scroll] in the house. The whole family was really very pious."[3]

The entire extended family moved to Amsterdam in 1937–8 and Levi's life continued as before. Her brother Alfred was born in 1936, her sister Bertie in 1938, and the youngest, Fanny, in 1942. Then in 1943 this family of six was deported to Westerbork. For Esther it was, unexpectedly, a revelation to live in a community of Jews.

In the camp I saw for the first time that there were other types of people. When I was a child of about four or six I walked around with blinders on. I just followed that narrow path of going with my father to *shul* every morning, always learning the Torah, I had Jewish lessons, and so on. That is what I did as a child. Then I went to school in Amsterdam, the Palach school which was also a Jewishly observant school, and so again along that same straight and narrow path: pious. Not that I objected to it. At that time it was like that, you simply went along, . . . and all our friends and acquaintances followed the same path, so I was in a kind of ghetto. The moment you leave that, it is different, but so long as you follow that route you have your blinders on.

I did not know anything else. And I only saw that there were other sorts of people, people who did Jewish things differently, when I came in the camp. Then I thought, "Hey, those people do not do this, or that. They don't keep *Shabbat* [for instance]." I only learned that there. I knew that there were other types of people in this world, of course. But what they did, and how they did those things I only learned in the camp.

That was actually something that I thought, "Hey, does something like that exist?" I had come into a totally different world, really in a totally different world, because I also had to deal with other children whom I encountered daily and who were very different. For me that was a great revelation.

That was really the most impressive experience, I can easily say that, that I realized that there were other [ways of life].[4]

For Frieda Menco-Brommet, who had been in hiding and hidden for two years, and Esther Levi, who had led a very sheltered existence, life in Westerbork was, at least initially, an expansion of their previously confined worlds. Neither was unhappy or despondent to be there. Both were with their families and, with that structure intact, they could appreciate the very little that was to be enjoyed: the freedom to meet new people. For most children, however, life in transit camps was a much more ambiguous experience. It was the beginning of a process of adaptation to a world without precedent or parallel. It was there that children began to live a split, dissociated life. They carried on with the external, normal forms of childhood and at the same time let go of the dependable, rationally structured world they had known. It was a schizophrenic existence of participating in the mirage of stability and absorbing the dissolution of the principles on which that order had been based.

"When we came to Westerbork it was dark," Irene Butter-Hasenberg recalled. "I remember we had to go through various procedures. They examined our heads for delousing and everyone had to take off all their clothes and they were checked by a doctor. I remember being very frightened because it was the first time in my life I had seen naked bodies and there were all these, just large numbers of naked people. It was very strange to me." Hasenberg was twelve and a half years old, and she found the institutionalized system of sorting, sifting, and screening abhorrent. "It was late at night and it had been a miserable day, and there were people of all ages, and sick people. Men and women were separated. That took a long time, standing in line." Nothing in her previous experience had prepared her for this regimentation and depersonalization. Suddenly, she had become an anonymous naked body, probed and prodded, and pushed from one queue to the next. "They shaved off all the hair of the people who had lice. That was something I was always scared of: that they would find lice on me and I'd lose all my hair. It was so degrading and humiliating not to have hair on your head. They did shave people, and that was a very scary thing. You can't recognize people without their hair."[5]

From one day to the next, Hasenberg had lost the structure and context of her daily life. Her life at home had been annihilated, eradicated; she and her family were forced into the institutional life of the transit camp. "Eventually we were marched into a barrack and were assigned beds and settled down to sleep. The four of us [my mother, father, brother, and I] were in the same barrack, half was male and half was female. The barracks were very depressing, very gloomy, mostly beds, three beds on top of each other, sort of metal frames like bunk beds, but metal and a mattress. . . . That's all you had."[6]

Ivan Buchwald, like Frieda Menco-Brommet, had been in hiding and was betrayed. But he was five years old and all alone, and he found life in transit camp a horror. Buchwald had been hidden in his home town of Novi Sad in Yugoslavia with an aunt, Esi Kellner, who was married to a non-Jew. Someone "told the authorities that I was there, that there was a little Jewish boy hidden."

I was picked up, and I remember being taken to what seemed to be a prison. I remember a high window at the top, with bars, and yelling my head off because I couldn't get out. I was alone, and I didn't know what was happening. And I remember being absolutely terrified. . . .

I was then taken to a transit camp with a lot of other Jews from the town. We stayed in this camp for about ten days, and there were people who knew me. In fact one of my uncles, one of my father's brothers [was there], so he looked after me. Again, I was a little boy of five, I was frightened. I was without my parents and I didn't know what was happening. [I remember] the bewilderment, without any idea what was happening and why it was happening. And probably there was a sense of abandonment.

[In the transit camp] there were no sanitation facilities and toilets. I seem to remember I didn't have any clothes some days. . . . I was actually walking around bare. [I was] ashamed because I had been brought up as a child to cover myself up when I was with other people. . . .

The food was diabolical. All I can remember is baked beans, baked beans, baked beans and nothing. Or what seemed to be baked beans. And then it was sort of liquidy, almost like a soup. It was awful. I think I was sick [nauseated], but I was so hungry in the end that I had to eat something. I had a revulsion about it, but at the same time I wanted to eat it because I was so hungry.

We were in the transit camp for about ten days, and then we were marched to the [train] station to go to Auschwitz.[7]

Transit camps were, quite literally, holding pens or repositories for Jews in transit to the east. Frieda Brommet and her family were sent to Auschwitz, the Levi and Hasenberg families went on to a second transit

19   Irene Butter-Hasenberg (aged 12), passport photo, 1942. Mr Hasenberg sent this photo to someone in Sweden who obtained passports from a neutral country for the Hasenberg family.

camp, Bergen-Belsen, and Ivan Buchwald was rescued by another one of his aunts (Etel Scleer) on the march to the train depot. The vast majority of Jews, however, were shipped directly to the extermination centers, and the transit camps facilitated that process in a number of ways. First of all, as Raul Hilberg has discussed in great detail in *The Destruction of the European Jews*, and Claude Lanzmann illustrated very clearly in his documentary film, *Shoah*, the German bureaucracy of death was carried out by a number of disparate and often competing administrative offices. It was an all too efficient *ad hoc* agglomeration of Nazi party organizations (such as the SS and the Office of Race), German military commands, German and local bureaucracies (including police forces), and collaborating militias which functioned differently in each European country involved in the war. They were committed to a common policy of Judeocide, but the actual mechanism for it varied from place to place according to regional conditions. All of these agencies and departments, however, depended on transportation to effect their goal, and the train lines became the physical, practical, unifying network, the sole systematic connection between them and the extermination centers. Each bureau and operation, including the transportation office, had its own agenda, priorities, obligations, and schedule. A *razzia* in Paris, for example, was not perfectly coordinated with the maximum "legal" dispossession of Jewish property, the contemporary demand on the railways for military purposes, or the current extermination capacity in the death camps. Thus Jews were held in way-stations or depositories until the gas chambers of Birkenau or Sobibor could accommodate them and the railway cars and train lines were available to move them.

The transit camps, then, helped the murder machinery to be more efficient; they prevented inexpedient strains on the system and at the same time provided an additional screen or camouflage for the ultimate goal of the Third Reich's Final Solution. For both these reasons transit camps were primarily a phenomenon of the operation in the west and not the east of Europe. The logistical difficulties of moving people through a greater number of individual bureaus and to a more distant destination engendered more problems and, therefore, a greater need to have human warehouses. This was rather different from the situation in the occupied Soviet Union, where *Einsatzgruppen* (special detachments detailed to carry out the Final Solution) killed Jews on the spot (so there was no need to collect and ship people to extermination sites), or in Poland where the ghettos served as storage pens and, as the distances to the camps were short, the authorities could coordinate their activities more closely. In the west there were no closed ghettos; the position of Jews in the major cities was much more ambiguous. To avoid alienating the local population unnecessarily, to circumvent the scene of cattle cars for human beings in the cities' central stations, it was useful to send the Jews by third-class rail to a removed location within the country and from thence east. There was no direct connection either in space or time between the capital cities of western Europe and the new necropoli in the east. That route was not direct; it went via the transit camps. Finally, there was another, possibly unanticipated, advantage to the transit camp stage in the journey to death. It gave the Germans an additional opportunity to plunder, extort, and depredate. Money and property that had not been appropriated earlier was exacted as payment for the privilege of remaining in the camp. Jews who had marginally valid passports from neutral countries were identified and separated, as perhaps they would have some future political value as hostages. From time to time, people with highly specialized skills (like diamond cutting) which were needed for particular German projects were set aside. And finally, the transit camps provided the Germans with the occasion and subterfuge to dissemble and deceive. Publicly reinterpreting their intentions, they broadcast a chimera. These were not transit camps, but permanent settlements. "The Führer Gives the Jews a Town," the propaganda film about Terezín proclaimed.

The Germans' prevarications and perversions notwithstanding, the transit camps were not stable, merry communities but temporary wretched stopovers on the trip east. Indeed, many of the people photographed by the Germans in Terezín had been deported and exterminated by the time the film was shown. These way-stations were the children's introduction to institutional life under German rule. It was there that they began to learn how to live on two levels simultaneously, to adapt to the abnormal, indeed to the bizarre, while at the same time to function normally. This is implicit in both Ivan Buchwald's and Irene Hasenberg's accounts. "The food was diabolical," and yet Buchwald ate. Hasenberg found that quintessential sign of institutional and not familial life, the barracks, "gloomy," "depressing"; it signified the end of living together as a family (Hasenberg and her mother were in the women's section, and her father and brother in the men's), and yet she "settled down and went to sleep." Life went on and the children evolved a new way to live it.

In transit camps, as elsewhere, education was of great importance to children; it was a symbol of normal life and a sign of hope for the future. "There are about 250 children between the ages of 6–15 years," an anonymous social worker reported about Gurs, a Vichy French camp in the foothills of the Pyrenees. Like many of the camps in France, Gurs had been built as an internment center for refugees of the Spanish Civil War; from September 1939 German Jews who had fled to France were sent there. A year later, in the autumn of 1940, the Germans deported thousands of Jews from the upper Rhineland (Baden and the Palatinate) to France and insisted that Vichy accept them. Eventually they were driven into Gurs. The population of the camp swelled to about 13,200, of whom only 400 were children.[8] Of those of school age (250), "200 are divided amongst the four women's blocks,* I, K, L, and M. The rest are in the men's blocks, D, E, G. The I, K, L, and M blocks have their own individual schools. The communal school of the three others

* Barracks were grouped together into "ilots" or blocks. Each block was surrounded by barbed wire. At Gurs one such block contained 22 to 24 barracks, or 1,200 to 1,500 people. Men and women were separated. (Joseph Weill, *Contribution à l'histoire des camps d'internement dans l'anti-France* [Paris: Éditions du Centre, 1946], p.30.) This arrangement was basically the same in concentration camps throughout Europe; only the terminology differed. A number of barracks made up a "block" or "camp," and each of these administrative units was surrounded by barbed wire. (In Auschwitz, for example, a barrack was called a "block" and a number of blocks made up a "camp.")

will begin one day soon." The curriculum was very much like that of a normal school. "The main subjects taught are: French, English, arithmetic, geography, religion, (grammar), the natural sciences, gymnastics and the manual skills." Students were divided into three groups according to their age. "In general, it is the teachers who came with them from Baden who run the courses; in this way they continue – to a certain degree – the studies which have been interrupted by internment." The classes were very basic "because in fact there is still a lack of tables, chairs, large blackboards, and teaching materials. The camp authorities have promised to obtain them for us, but the problem of school furniture is now too acute to hope for an early solution. We are wanting, in effect: *10 large blackboards, 12 tables, 25–30 benches.* But above all, it is a question of the nearly absolute lack of teaching materials. We need:

French	250	books	for	elementary teaching	
English	45	"	"	the elementary level	
	72	"	"	" middle	"
	77	"	"	" upper	"
Arithmetic	79	"	"	" elementary	"
	73	"	"	" middle	"
	72	"	"	" upper	" [9]

In the camps in the occupied north too, education was considered essential. A report on a visit of 19 June (1941?) to "the headquarters of the social workers at Pithiviers" noted that the diet was execrable, but that the lack of books was equally serious. "The social workers believe that the books are as necessary as bread."[10] Pithiviers had begun to house Jews in May 1941; just over a year later, in late July and early August 1942, it was to be a depot for the damned.

As we have seen, the situation in France was unique in that social work teams from various philanthropic organizations (such as OSE, the American Friends' Service Committee, Unitarian Service, CIMADE, YMCA, Service Social d'Aide aux Émigrants, and Secours Suisse aux Enfants) were permitted to live in the camps on a voluntary basis. Their function was to ameliorate camp life by providing additional food, medicaments, and clothing, and by organizing medical and dental clinics, kindergartens, and schools. They were a link to the outside world, a sign that the prisoners were not forgotten. With regard to children their primary goal was to work towards liberation. Until that could be accomplished, the voluntary interns tried to normalize the young people's lives and to that end they established educational facilities. In other words, they attempted to recreate the normal structure of child

life. In camps in the other occupied and Axis countries, where the phenomenon of voluntary intern social work teams was unknown, education for children was just as central an issue. There, as in France, there
was a great discrepancy between what was supposed, and even reported,
to exist and the actual situation. Westerbork, for example, was meant to
have an extensive child welfare service which was to include a crèche for
pre-schoolers and classes for the older children. In *The Destruction of
the Dutch Jews*, Presser mentioned the "regular schooling" and, referring to Camp Order No. 40 of July 1943 he noted wryly, "we might
ask ourselves if children under fourteen lacked anything at all. The Child
Care Department looked after those between one and six throughout the
day; all children from six to fourteen attended classes and there were
even special inspectors whose task it was to apprehend truant pupils."[11]
Clearly no such system was operant. As in the French camps, a school
did exist administratively, one was meant to function, but given the lack
of teaching materials and the constantly changing camp population,
classes were in session only rarely. Thus, Esther Levi remembered that in
Westerbork "as a child I was kept busy, [there was] a little school, a
small little class, but beyond that they really did not have too much to do
with us [children]."[12] Other children, however, had no memory of a
formally organized class. Simon Philip (Flip) Frenkel was not quite
eleven years old when he and his family were deported to Westerbork.
He recalled that "we [children] had a kind of lessons there, a kind of
school in Westerbork in the barrack." It was not, he clarified, "a special
or local school, or anything like that. In the barrack, the people who
didn't work gave us a kind of lesson."[13] Evidently, Irene Butter-Hasenberg was not so lucky in her barrack-mates. According to her "there was
no school" of any kind.[14] Undoubtedly, all three children are correct. A
school did exist in principle, but in fact lessons were held intermittently
at best. There were numerous reasons for the lack of continuity: neither
teachers nor children were exempt from the weekly deportation trains
which left Westerbork every Tuesday, the barracks in which the school
was housed often were needed for other purposes, and for long periods
classes were suspended because of "infectious diseases."[15]

   The more privileged or protected the transit camp, the more regular
the schooling and conversely, the more fragile or chaotic the situation
the less organized the education for children. Thus, for example, in Terezín or Barneveld young people had more structured classes than their
counterparts who, belonging to one or another of the special status
groups reserved by the Germans for possible exchange for German prisoners or nationals, were sent in transit to Bergen-Belsen.[16] The latter
had no systematic teaching. Céline Joosten-Mogendorff, who was just

four years old when she and her family were deported to Bergen-Belsen in February 1944, remembered that her mother and another woman with a young son taught the children. "My brother was with me and . . . we learned together a little bit. There was also another small boy and my mother and another lady tried to teach us just a little. My brother was five years older and had to go to school. So they taught some small children a little bit." Mogendorff enjoyed it. "I liked to learn, to write." It was a way to pass the time. "Just to come through the time they, the different parents, wanted to teach us, so we had something to do."[17] In Bergen-Belsen, as elsewhere, there was a great dearth of teaching and reading materials. As Gabor Czitrom explained, "There was *one* copy of (among other books) Thomas Mann's *Zauberberg* [*The Magic Mountain*]. I had the right [to read it] from six to seven, let us say. It was one of the highlights of the day, when somebody passed it to me. I went into a corner to be at peace and then I had an hour to read it."[18]

The situation in Barneveld, a privileged camp in the Netherlands, was very different. The community was composed primarily of members of the middle-class intelligentsia. Flip Frenkel's family, for example, was deported from Rotterdam to Vught in April 1943. After a horrendous fortnight, they were transferred to Westerbork and from thence to Barneveld. Frenkel's father was a physician and his mother a dentist. Life at Barneveld was very comfortable compared to Vught and Westerbork. "It was heaven on earth in that time for us," Frenkel recalled. "It was a very luxurious society there." Barneveld "was a little community with school and very good teaching, because some people there were professors." Unlike in the other transit camps, instruction was a regular activity. "We had normal lessons, with books and so on. [I studied] arithmetic and French, I remember." Frenkel was, even then, very well aware of just how special Barneveld was. "I always thought at that time that there were so many worse things, so I was happy at that time. I could compare it [Barneveld] with Westerbork and Vught, and they were so much worse that [my attitude was:] be happy with what you have now."[19]

One of the main reasons why life at Barneveld was so comfortable was that the population was stable. Deportation trains did not leave from Barneveld; the entire community was spared the Westerbork ordeal of the weekly transport trains to the east. As Frenkel put it, "Westerbork was a place from which you could be sent to Poland, Germany, work camps. And Barneveld was more in the country; it was far from Westerbork and farther away from Germany." Unfortunately the idyll did not last long. On 29 September 1943 the Germans staged "a kind of *razzia*" at Barneveld. Suddenly, with no warning and a lot of

20   Children on a walk in Westerbork.

yelling and shouting, people were ordered to pack their belongings. "The German officers shouted, 'Pack! You have to move to Westerbork in two hours.'" Within a few hours the entire Barneveld community was transferred to Westerbork, where they continued to be kept together as a group. A year later, in September 1944, they were sent to Theresienstadt.[20]

Unlike in the transit camps in the west, formal education for children was forbidden in Terezín. Nevertheless, there too they carried on and, because of the cultural ethos of the camp, many intellectual and creative pursuits were encouraged as in no other transit center. Terezín, or as the Germans called it, Theresienstadt, had been built as a fortified garrison town by the Austrian Emperor Joseph II and named in honor of his mother, Maria Theresa. Over a century and a half later Reinhard Heydrich transformed it into a transit camp. By his order (February 1942), the small walled city not far from Prague was evacuated and a "Jewish settlement" or "old people's ghetto" officially was established.

Originally intended as a place for elderly Jews unfit for the "hard labor" demanded of those who according to Nazi propaganda were deported to the east to work, Terezín helped to perpetuate the myth of Jewish resettlement in Poland, and obviated embarrassing questions. To the same end, highly decorated or severely disabled war veterans also were eligible for Theresienstadt, as were a certain number of very well-known Jews.[21] Terezín, however, was hardly a settlement or a ghetto; as the statistics show all too clearly, it was simply another transit center. Between November 1941, when the first Jews to be deported to Terezín arrived, and the liberation of the camp in May 1945, 141,162 Jews were sent there; 88,162 subsequently were deported, 33,456 died, 1,623 were released to neutral countries (1,200 to Switzerland and 423 to Sweden) in 1945; and 16,832 remained.[22]

Oddly enough, the (purely theoretical) construction of Terezín as a stable community had an effect on the inmates too. Despite the constant threat of the deportation trains, the famine, lack of hygiene, and disease, the Jewish inhabitants created an intellectual and cultural life for both adults and children. Ellen Levi remembered that a few days after she and her parents arrived in Theresienstadt they happened to meet "Max, the brother of my future aunt's [whom they already knew] before. He was from Würzburg. He said, 'Even in Würzburg I didn't see such a good performance of *Tosca*.' I said, this man is mad! I think this man must be mad!" Ellen Levi was fifteen years old at the time. Born in Düsseldorf, she and her family had emigrated illegally to the Netherlands and had lived in Amsterdam, Haarlem, and Arnhem. In December 1942 the family was deported to Westerbork where they remained until September 1943 when they were shipped to Bergen-Belsen and from thence in January 1944 to Theresienstadt. As she said, by the time she came to Terezín she "already had the experience of Bergen-Belsen, and he [Max] was talking about an opera performance! . . . He said it seriously. He was a cultured man, I realized that. Yet I hadn't had any experience with opera by that time. I thought he must be mad!" For her what was bizarre was that he was not insane, that "operas *were* performed in Theresienstadt." While the transport trains continued to be filled with a thousand souls each time, "there was some culture, the possibility of culture. But later on, all those people, all those cultured people were taken to Auschwitz anyhow."[23]

This pursuit of creative or intellectual endeavors took many forms. For example, because proper scholastic classes were strictly prohibited, teaching became an underground activity. When Flip Frenkel and his family arrived in Theresienstadt with the Barneveld group, he and the rest of the children were put into a young people's barrack or *Kinder-*

heim, children's home. "I was there in the children's home and there, too, unbelievable, but we were at school. . . . We had our lessons." Naturally "it was not a regular organization," but those who for one reason or another were exempt from the usual ten-hour work day taught the children.[24] Frenkel's experience was not unique. Child welfare was taken seriously by the adult inmates of Terezín. The first Elder of the Jews (appointed by the Germans), Jacob Edelstein, in particular, and indeed the entire Council of Elders in general, believed that this task was central to their mission. Children accounted for about 10 percent of the population of Theresienstadt; the Germans (happily) took little notice of them, leaving their governance to Edelstein and his Council. The latter were glad of the opportunity to do what they could, and established a Youth Welfare Department (*Jugendfürsorge*). The purpose of the department was to safeguard the children's health and to continue their education despite the Germans' draconian prohibitions. To that end, the Jewish administrators supported the policy of instituting separate children's homes. Beginning in early 1942, children under the age of four lived with their mothers, after that age the majority were placed in a *Kinderheim*. At that time many of the Jewish leaders were Zionists, and they believed that this collective life would help to instill the values of Zionism while at the same time to protect the children from the worst of the brutality of life at Terezín. In more prosaic ways too, the Youth Welfare Department sought to improve conditions for children in the transit center. Their living quarters were less crowded than those of the adults. Late in the summer of 1942 the Department prevailed on the Germans to allow the children to use the courtyards and gardens, and they even were permitted to play on the fortifications of the city. (Adults did not have that privilege for another two years.) Within a few months a children's kitchen which provided more and better-quality food was started, and early in 1943 a children's hospital was opened.[25]

The most outstanding work of the Department, however, was its support of clandestine classes. Secret study circles were established, and many of the *Betreuerinnen* or *Betreueren* (child care workers) in the homes were devoted to the cause of education. For them, as for the children, it was an act of faith in the future. Helga Kinsky-Pollack had great admiration for the *Betreuerinnen* and the life they fostered in her room in the Czech home for girls aged ten to sixteen. Born in Vienna in 1930, Pollack's parents had sent her to her father's family in Kyjov, over the border in Czechoslovakia, after the Anschluss in 1938. In the spring of 1939 her mother went to England as a domestic worker. Her plan was to arrange the emigration of her daughter. Without family, friends, or resources in England, Mrs Pollack-Meisels felt that some preparations should be made prior to her daughter's arrival. The plan was good, but the timing poor. The German army marched into Czechoslovakia and mother and daughter were separated. Pollack's father managed to reach her in Kyjov in 1942 and in January 1943 they were deported to Theresienstadt. They were amongst those who remained in the transit center; 2,000 people from the same transport were sent on to the east immediately.[26] Pollack was assigned to room 28 of L410 (house number ten on the fourth lengthwise street), the Czech children's home for girls. Her father, who had been severely wounded and highly decorated in the First World War, went to the home for war invalids of which he eventually became the Ältester, or head. The children's home was an extraordinary and singularly positive experience for Pollack. As she understood it, the purpose of the home "was to take the children away from their parents [so that] the children shouldn't see all the suffering and trouble of the grown-ups. The children were organized to lead a child's life. The moment you lead this child's life, especially supported as such wonderful people supported us, the rest goes into the background."[27]

The particular group to which Pollack had been assigned was special. "We were a quite well-organized room, and maybe also a well-known room, the room 28 in this home. It was a very active room." There were, Pollack explained, a number of possible reasons for the success of her group. First of all, it was probable that most of the girls were well educated. "Not everybody could stay on in Theresienstadt. The parents had to have some sort of qualification which fit into the organization of Theresienstadt." Thus, for example, the head pediatrician of the children's home was the father of one of the girls, and it would be reasonable to assume that "she had learned a lot already, had had the opportunity to learn a lot." Then too, "maybe our *Betreuerinnen* were better than the others." And finally, "maybe our age was just the right age to do something with us, because the smaller children you couldn't do much with them, and the older children maybe already had different interests and couldn't be kept so much together." Whatever the cause, this room of approximately thirty girls (the population fluctuated with the transports, although less dramatically than elsewhere because their parents or older siblings were able to protect them) and three *Betreuerinnen* was "a very close community."[28]

The *Betreuerinnen* promoted an intellectually, culturally, and emotionally nurturing environment. "They taught us a lot about Zionism and other things. We also had secret teaching, not all the subjects I was taught at school but many; those which they could teach without using books or writing materials."[29] The range of activities that these *Betreuerinnen* managed to organize on either a daily or a regular basis is astonishing:

> We were woken up in the morning [by] one of the women [who] slept
> with us. It was always another one which had duty. We slept in bunk
> beds three stories high. [After] we were woken up in the morning, we
> had to air our bedding. We had our duties which always changed.
> Some had the duty to fetch the coffee, some had to clean, others to
> sweep the room.
>   Then the tuition [lessons] started in the morning. There was always
> tuition and it was always illegal. Then, again a group fetched lunch
> and after lunch . . . we usually had some activities. Theresienstadt was
> an old fort. On one of the bastions was a green and we all would go
> there together and play some games. Or we were allowed to go into
> the courtyard and play a little bit.
>   We had a choir because our chief *Betreuerin* [Ella Pollack, whom
> the girls called "Tella"] was a piano teacher and a concert pianist. She
> gave us tuition in choir, usually in Ivrit [Hebrew] or in Czech. We
> were playing theater and celebrating Jewish holidays. Those were
> the biggest festivities to which we children looked forward. Our
> *Betreuerin* even managed to get food for us, special food which we
> never had otherwise, sandwiches and puddings, things like that. How
> she managed it, I don't know.[30]

In addition to educating the girls in academic subjects, music, and art,
the *Betreuerinnen* encouraged the ideals of Zionism, the spirit of democracy, and an affectionate atmosphere. As in many other children's
homes in Theresienstadt, "everything which had to do with Israel
[Palestine] was looked upon as something fantastic, and something
everybody wanted to do was to go to Israel and be in a kibbutz." Unique
to room 28, however, was that "we had a parliament, we had an
emblem, we had a hymn which we sang, and we had a uniform which
we only had on at festivities." All the girls chose a sign for their beds;
Helga Pollack's was a lighthouse because "in the dark sea when everything is dark, only one place shines and helps the people drowning in the
water. That is a lighthouse, and I thought it was an emblem of somehow
to survive." And finally, and perhaps most important, the girls were supportive of each other and "very close."[31]
   Life in room 28 provided a rich education for Helga Pollack and her
companions. Clearly, formal education was not the only way to teach
children, and in different periods in the history of Theresienstadt cultural and scholarly activities were not only tolerated but actually encouraged. This policy suited the Germans' propaganda program. To

perpetuate the myth that Terezín was a functioning, unexceptional city with a stable population and a normal civic life, starting in the summer of 1943 a coffee house, bank, post office, and even a petty crimes court were opened, as were stores which sold goods robbed from the newly arriving inmates. (Sometimes people purchased their own possessions.)[32]

A cultural department was established, and music, art, and theater became part of the life of Terezín. The artistic activity in this antechamber to Auschwitz was quite wonderful. Art and music in particular flourished. There were, for example, five cabaret groups and several small orchestras, in addition to a "municipal" orchestra of thirty-five musicians. As we have seen, a number of operas were produced, including Smetana's *Bartered Bride*. A jazz band and solo concerts by singers and virtuosi were also popular. Children attended these performances as well as those put on specially for them. One man began a puppet theater, two dramatists, Gustav Schorsch and Josef Taussig, entertained young people with lectures, poetry recitations, and literature readings, and Mozart's opera *Bastien and Bastienne* was produced for the children's enjoyment. The young people themselves participated in these ventures. The composer Karel Reiner worked with children, Karafiat's *Fire-Flies* was interpreted as a dance-play for children by the dancer-choreographer Kamila Rosenbaum prior to her deportation (it was shown nearly thirty times), and best known of all, the conductor Rafael Schächter trained a children's choir and produced Hans Krasa's children's opera *Brundibar*.[33] Helga Pollack remembered these activities very well. "Some chidren were in choirs singing from Smetana or *Brundibár*, and some were playing theater and some were dancing, because there was a choreographer from the National Opera House (a *Betreuerin* as well). ... One of my best friends of those days was Ella [Weisberger] who was in *Brundibár*."[34] This sort of cultural activity was undertaken in the homes also, and the children put on their own plays, made music together, fashioned collages and drew pictures and wrote poems and stories on the packing paper from parcels (which the inmates were permitted to receive).

While Theresienstadt may well have had the richest cultural life, a variety of educational activities in which children participated were undertaken in other transit camps too. According to Elisabeth Hirsch, who was one of the voluntary intern social workers at Gurs, the camp "was very well organized, from the social [i.e. cultural] point of view, by the inmates themselves. That was in '41. [There were] physicians, musicians, nurses; really very competent people who organized lectures and concerts. There was the rabbi who did commentaries on the Torah – really remarkable things."[35] Ruth Lambert, the OSE resident social

21   Children playing in Theresienstadt.

worker at Gurs, agreed. In a letter of 29 September 1944 to Father
Gross, who had been the representative of Caritas Suisse at Gurs, Lambert reviewed the situation at the camp; the information was to help him
with his lectures and conferences. Fritz "Brunner [the violinist, and his
accompanist, the pianist] Leval and their concerts, every Sunday from
10:30 AM until noon for fifteen months. Painting exhibits, handicrafts.
Plays, the famous revues of Nathan-Leval, numerous artists of all sorts
and marvelous caricaturists!"[36] Children were brought to the concerts
and were encouraged to attend the lectures. Special performances for
them were organized. A program for a Christmas concert for "big and
little children" at three o'clock in the afternoon on Wednesday 25
December 1940 featured Gounod's "Ave Maria," the overture from *The
Marriage of Figaro* by Mozart, Puccini's duo from *La Bohème* and
"Frère Jacques," "Daughter of Zion," and a children's chorus.[37]
     Music and lectures were the most common cultural and educational
activities in which children engaged in the transit camps. They were
easily organized and needed little special equipment. When instruments
were unobtainable, the children could make music themselves by singing. "I know that we sang songs all the time there," in Westerbork,

Esther Levi recalled.[38] Irene Butter-Hasenberg also remembered singing with others. "I have memories of in the summertime [in Bergen-Belsen in 1944] that there was a group of young people; on a Friday night there would be *Oneg Shabbat* and we would sit together between two barracks and sing songs. A couple of times there were lectures, and we listened to the lectures. . . . It must have been allowed because we were sitting outside. There were watch posts [in the camp], so it couldn't have been hidden. Maybe it became disallowed and therefore discontinued. I don't remember it happening very many times, but I have the image of sitting out there in the evening in the summertime for *Oneg Shabbat* and singing Hebrew songs. Hebrew songs and other songs, but I particularly remember that we sang Hebrew songs."[39]

These were, after all, transit camps for Jewish people; it is not surprising that the activities of the children were influenced by their religious identity. Gabor Czitrom and his family were in a Hungarian group of several hundred people for whom Rudolf Kastner and Joel Brand had managed to negotiate a deal with the Germans. Kastner and Brand were two of the four main officials in an assistance and rescue committee which had been organized by a group of Hungarian Zionists in January 1943. Their original purpose was to aid Jews who had fled to Hungary, but by the end of the year they realized that Hungarian Jews were at great risk, and they concentrated their efforts on negotiations with the Germans to prevent deportations. One such plan involved the purchase of 1,600 Jews for 6.5 million pengös, which at that time amounted to 4 million Reichsmarks or $1.6 million. These Jews were to be allowed to emigrate to Palestine. Children were to be the beneficiaries of this deal, but the Germans objected, and a complicated list was drawn up composed of various categories: Zionists, orphans, Orthodox Jews, and so on. It was the Czitrom family's good fortune that Kastner's father-in-law came from Kolozsvár; nearly one quarter of the people included on the list came from that city.[40] The group of which the Czitrom family were members was deported from Budapest to Bergen-Belsen in July 1944. They were held in the transit camp while negotiations continued. It was there that Czitrom read *The Magic Mountain* and it was there too that he was exposed to the charm of biblical scholarship. "There was quite a series of [lectures by] young rabbis. These young rabbis were rabbis because of the simple fact that there was a *numerus clausus*, of course, in Hungary at university. But if you were a rabbi you could follow university courses in any other topic, like literature, philosophy, and so on." The result of this was that "young Jewish instructors were inscribed in Jewish theology which enabled them to go to university." A number of these students were in Czitrom's group and from them,

22   Clandestine education: drawing by Helga Hosková-Weiss (aged 12),
Theresienstadt, 1942.

"there [in Bergen-Belsen], I had a glimpse of how highly interesting
biblical exegesis could be. There was a fascinating series of lectures by
these young rabbis on various chapters of the Bible, putting it into historical context. I do not recall facts, but I do exactly recall the huge interest of it, and that I discovered quite a new perspective."[41]

The educational and cultural activities we have discussed so far were exceptional events in the ordinarily dreary and dismal days in a transit
camp. Most of a normal day's events were dictated by the conditions of
camp life, and they were paltry and petty indeed. There were tasks that
were imposed by the camp administration. Older girls, like Ellen Levi,
who was fourteen when she was deported to Westerbork, were assigned
menial work. "We had to have some occupation. I was ordered to the
Nähestube [sewing barrack]. I had to mend socks almost all day. I hated

it." Later on, in Theresienstadt, "I worked in a *Kinderheim*, a children's home with a group of boys. I went with them to play football [soccer], as well as scrubbing the floors. The lady who was in charge liked me very much because I was quite diligent."[42] Frieda Menco-Brommet, who was by then an older adolescent of eighteen, "had to do something with batteries. We just got dirty, that was all."[43] Younger children, like the nine-year-old Esther Levi and her small siblings, were also detailed to monotonous chores. "I remember that what they often made us do [in Bergen-Belsen] was to pick up pebbles. There was a mountain of pebbles and then it was said, 'You have to move those pebbles one hundred meters from here, and then you must make another mountain.' We were kept busy that way."[44]

Many of a typical day's activities simply revolved around the exigencies of the institution itself. To live in a transit camp was very demanding in terms of time, and even more so with regard to vitality, energy, and health. As Irene Hasenberg put it, "it was just quite a task to do what you needed to do to keep going." Theft, for example, was extremely common in transit camps, and Hasenberg remembered that "what I did most of my time was to protect our belongings; just sit there and watch them! Because theft was just awful." Other than that, in Westerbork "the kids did nothing. There was no school, no organized activities to speak of. A few times we harvested potatoes from the ground, maybe twice. . . . The rest of the time there was nothing. I asked my cousin [also a Westerbork inmate] who telephoned the other day what did she remember. And she said there was absolutely nothing to do."[45]

If daily life at Westerbork was characterized by mind-numbing tedium and such niggardly occupations as standing watch over one's possessions, the situation in other transit camps was infinitely worse. The normal habits of everyday existence – to eat, drink, relieve oneself, wash one's clothes and clean oneself – became complicated and enervating undertakings. Marie Claus-Grindel, for instance, was seven and a half years old when she was deported in September 1940 with her mother and two younger sisters (aged five and four) to the transit camp of Agde. Earlier that year they had fled to the small town of La Châtre in the south of France from their home in Strasbourg, and it was the mayor of La Châtre who ordered all the refugee Jews to be sent away to a camp. Agde had been built a few years earlier as a camp for refugees from Spain. According to a report by the Secours Suisse dated 20 November 1940, the camp population was 3,060, of whom 70 were children.[46] Marie Grindel and her sisters were amongst them. "It was a camp with no water. Only once a day water trucks came to bring water

23   Children celebrating Chanukkah in Westerbork.

and we had to queue for hours to have a little bit of water." To go to the toilet was hazardous and frightening. It was a type of trench latrine with a platform a meter high which was reached with a ladder. There were no walls around the pit and the excrement was fully visible. "One thing which shocked me a lot at the time: it was the toilets. I had [to mount with] a ladder; it was very high, about a meter, with big holes [in the platform], and I could see all the feces below. I was so afraid to fall into it. This is one of the most horrible things, the fear of falling into that shit."[47] In the very temporary transit camp to which Ivan Buchwald was taken there were no toilets at all. "Suddenly, I couldn't be clean. I had to go through what I considered some animal motions to relieve myself. And I felt ashamed."[48]

    Washing oneself also posed a problem, less menacing perhaps than the terrors of going to the toilet, but certainly as important in maintaining health. When Ruth Lambert, the OSE voluntary intern, arrived at Gurs in January 1941 she asked another social worker who had come a few weeks before, "How does one wash here?" To which Ninon Hait replied, "Torso nude under the pump!"[49] According to a report on the conditions in the camps in France in May 1941, Rivesaltes had showers, "but too few for such a large population." Furthermore, "the wash basins are too small, the wash houses cannot be cleaned, and, at Rivesaltes they are not always provided with drainage pipes." The net result of this was filth, of course, and "infection with lice was endemic everywhere."[50] Children spent their time queuing to get water, queuing to go to the toilet, queuing to wash, and then they idled away an hour searching for and destroying the lice on their bodies and in their clothes. Indeed, keeping one's clothes clean was another daunting and time-consuming challenge. Even if one were fortunate enough to wash them, they could not be left to dry or they would be stolen. "One of the things I remember doing in Bergen-Belsen," Hasenberg recalled, "was to take care of the laundry for the family. There was no place to dry things, we had to hang them out on a wash line. There was a lot of theft, so usually when I hung out our clothes I sat right there until they dried, to watch them. So that took a bit of time."[51]

Many older girls were called upon to take care of young children. In some transit camps both men and women had to work, which meant that small children were left in the barracks with no one to look after them. Then too, there were a number of children who had no parents; they already had been killed, or deported, or were still in hiding, ignorant of the fate of their little ones. Adolescent girls occupied themselves with these youngsters. Sometimes this was taken on voluntarily, as a response to the immediate situation the girls faced. This was the case for Hasenberg. "In Westerbork, women who had children didn't have to work. But in Belsen everybody had to work, so I remember for a good part of the time helping to take care of children in the barracks during the day when the mothers were gone." As Hasenberg pointed out, older sisters quite naturally looked after younger siblings: "In Bergen-Belsen one of my close friends was Hannelie Goslar, who was also one of the close friends of Anne Frank." The two girls lived in the same barrack. "Hannelie was there with her father and she had a little sister [about] three years old. Her mother had died before they were in the camp. Hannelie had full responsibility for this little sister, and for her father to a certain extent. So I helped her take care of this little girl, Gigi, who was a very cute little girl."[52] In other instances, the task of looking after young children was allocated formally. "During the summer [1944] I got a [new] assignment for work, and it is very painful for me," Ellen Levi admitted. She was in Terezín at the time.

I think I liked to do that work. I worked with babies who were separated from their mothers. I think they had to work. Some girls took care of the babies. We *shlept* [hauled] with warm water to bathe them and to do everything possible to make life as comfortable as possible. All those babies later went to Auschwitz. But, of course, yes, while you were doing that you did not think of it, you just did your duty, you took care of the children as well as possible.[53]

Ellen did not know then about Auschwitz; she only knew that these little babies were taken away. "Later, when I came to Auschwitz, I realized. I had got a special apron, a kind of an apron; my mother took the apron home [after the war]. The apron I wore was still there, but not the babies."[54]

Two other activities were dictated by the Germans' harsh and despotic rule: the ritual of *Appell* (or roll call) and the queues for food, which in any case was insufficient to maintain health. There were children who because of age or circumstance did not go to school, wash themselves or their clothes, or bother about the toilet. But they all had to wait for food, they all were hungry, and in many transit camps, they all were counted. Seen from the Germans' perspective, the phenomenon of *Appell* was emblematic of transit camp existence. The children (indeed all the inmates) were there simply as bodies, units to be counted. They were brought into the camp, registered, and deported, and all that mattered to the German camp administrators was for their figures to tally. "*Appell* – that was something which gave them [the Germans] great pleasure, apparently, because they made us stand there for hours. A lot of time was wasted on that," Esther Levi reported.[55] The reason it took so long was because the figures had to be accurate. "There was the interminable ritual of *Zahlappell* [roll call]," Gabor Czitrom remarked. "Well, you know of course what it is, and it [the total] was never right. I don't know why, but it was not right so we were [left] standing."[56] "We were counted a lot. A lot of our time in Belsen was spent on what they call *Appell*, when you had to be out in a big square and it has taken as much as nine or ten or twelve hours of standing in the square because they couldn't come up with the right number. And the right number was derived," Hasenberg explained,

from counting all the sick people in the barracks, and in the hospital. When people went to work, they left the camp and they always were counted when they went through the gate. And so they counted the people who left for work, and then everyone on the square, and it had to add up to a certain number.

Sometimes it took eight or nine or whatever hours before they could get the right number. For whatever reasons, we were standing there and it just took a tremendous amount of time. In the winter the weather was cold, [in summer] very hot, and you still might end up standing that long.

We never got new clothes, we just had what we had. Our [the children's] feet grew and the shoes got too small. In the winter in particular I remember standing in the cold and having shoes that didn't fit properly. That's what I remember the most: these terribly painful feet, and the poor [quality] shoes, and being forced to stand up that long, and to stand still.[57]

There were many reasons why the number did not tally to the Germans' satisfaction, but for a child prisoner the worst was when she herself was to blame; she knew the agony everyone felt. Ellen Levi, for example, was mortified when she was the cause of the delay. "One evening I missed the *Appell*. That was a terrible experience! I missed *Appell*. I was asleep. People were standing outside for quite a long time and one was missing and that was me – in bed. All of a sudden, this SS came into the barrack and found me in bed. That was awful! I had the feeling that it was my fault that all the tired people had to stand outside because of me. This was absolutely awful."[58] Of course she was punished; she was ordered to work in the shoe tent, taking apart old shoes by cutting the stitches so as to salvage usable leather. It was hard labor for the crime of falling asleep.

If the ritual of *Appell* reflected the Germans' concept of the position of the Jews in the transit camps, for the children, waiting on queue for their meager portions of miserable food was the quintessence of their experience. It represented the two major determinants of their life: waiting and want. The children stood on line three times a day, and the rations for which they waited were insufficient to keep them alive. Hunger was ubiquitous. In a report of May 1941 on the conditions in the French internment camps this was explicated in some detail.

Famine rages in the camps, its sinister precursory symptoms already have marked the inmates by the dozens; for six months a considerable part of the population . . . has suffered cruelly from a malnutrition which is only imperfectly explained by the figure of 800 calories (instead of the essential 1,500 calories – while normal life demands 2,000 to 2,500 calories) and has paid a heavy toll in disease and death. . . .

The months have passed and their [the inmates'] energy reserves have dissipated and, implacably, day by day, the defenses [to fight in-

fection] have had to give up ground step-by-step. The children that
one sees jumping and playing, full of life, upon examination show
pale mucous [membranes], scrofulous ganglia, deformed limbs,
crooked spinal columns, and one fine day their resistance suddenly
will give up. We fear that day is approaching.

We assert, after an exhaustive investigation, that the daily ration
that contains ever smaller quantities of fat, sugar, and albumen does
not reach 500 calories per person per day. We contend that, if this
situation continues (and in all likelihood it will become worse), the
number of survivors will be but a small percentage. . . .

It is a question of life or death. . . .

A typical daily ration:
Bread, per day: 180 to 200 grams
Fat: ?
Sugar: 2 to 3 grams
Meat: 60 gr. (?) 2 times per week
Vegetables: Rutabagas and turnips in the form of soup
Quart of coffee

. . . Children have the benefit of one legal ration of milk. . . .

For the rest they share the same meals as their parents. . . .

Hunger oedema has been seen in a number of camps. . . . This
symptom will become more prevalent. . . . Vitamin deficiencies . . .
scorbutus [etc.].[59]

By the time this report was written, the Secours Suisse aux Enfants
and the American Friends' Service already had begun, most notably in
Gurs and Argelès, to distribute supplementary food rations (provided by
their own and other private organizations) to children. Unfortunately,
however, the largest number of young people was in Rivesaltes. The
urgency and the dimensions of the problem were the major issues discussed at a meeting on 22 May 1941 of the Committee on Children,
which was composed of representatives of the American Friends' Service
Committee, the Secours Suisse, and OSE, all of whom maintained voluntary interns in the transit camps. While there were only 59 children at
Gurs and about 300 in Argeles, there were 3,200 in Rivesaltes. The
newly built Rivesaltes had become a kind of dump site for children in
transit; a few months earlier, in the winter of 1941, most of the youngsters from Agde, Bren, and Gurs had been sent there. This state of affairs
was exacerbated by the fact that until about June of that year the camp
authorities would not allow social workers to live within the boundaries

of the camp nor, in that initial period, were they permitted to run the sorts of social services they had developed elsewhere: canteens, kindergartens, medical clinics, food distribution depots, and so on. When the Committee on Children met in Nîmes on 22 May their central concern was "the nutritional condition" of the children in Rivesaltes, as there were "no supplementary rations there as in Gurs and Argelès." Malnutrition was rampant, and they felt that the adolescents suffered especially severely.[60] The predicament of children in transit camps in the Occupied Zone was if anything even more desperate. According to the testimonies of inmates who had been liberated from Drancy, the problem of hunger was overwhelming. A physician who had gained his freedom emphasized, "one more time, and to conclude, Drancy is a long, alarming chapter about hunger. All the other miseries would be bearable if there were not that hunger which saps the life of the inmates."[61] After the great *rafle* of 16–17 July (the round-up of the Vél d'Hiv in Paris) and the influx of thousands of people into the camps, conditions became even more dire. Some 3–4,000 children were held in Pithiviers and Beaune-la-Rolande where it was impossible to wash, change, or feed them. Everyone suffered from the lack of food, but children had the greatest problems because they had neither milk nor food they could digest.[62]

With the help of the voluntary interns and the support of the philanthropic organizations, the situation in the south began to improve a little. When Marie Claus-Grindel was deported to Agde in September 1940 "it was a camp where people were dying from hunger, with no water."[63] A year later, it had been closed. By November 1941 the approximately one hundred children still in Gurs received from OSE "with the collaboration of the Secours Suisse: fruit, vegetables, porridge, rice pudding, chocolate, gingerbread, sweets, etc." The 2,500 children (700 of whom were Jews) in Rivesaltes received similar supplementary foods.[64] However auspicious and encouraging that may have appeared on paper, and indeed however great an improvement it was in reality, the children still suffered from hunger. In an article based on the diary she had kept while a voluntary intern at Rivesaltes, Vivette Samuel-Hermann described the children on their way to get the snack provided by the Secours Suisse. It was the day of her arrival, 4 November 1941. "The paths are nearly empty. Yet here come some groups of children towards us. Dirty and in rags, they advance painfully on the rocky ground, holding in one hand the edge of the grey blankets in which they are covered from head-to-toe, and in the other an old tin can, generally rusty, which serves them as a mess tin: it is snack time at the Secours

Suisse where they will get a hot drink."[65] Even after the children who were fortunate enough to leave the camp had been liberated, they did not forget the hunger they had endured. In an entry of 25 February 1942 Hermann mentioned that she had visited the OSE homes in Limoges and she noted that "the children there are undoubtedly happy, but they cannot forget the camp. To tell the truth, it is only now that they realize what their stay there was. Everywhere [in all the homes] the observations [of the teachers] are the same. The children suffer from a true hunger phobia. Their physiological unbalance and their insecurity is such that they have not come to rely on 'the daily bread,' and they must be prevented from devouring unbelievable quantities of food at the table, and from stuffing their pockets."[66]

With very few exceptions, children in transit camps queued for food and felt the pain of hunger. When Flip Frenkel was deported to Vught in 1943 he learned "the importance of eating. Before that it was a normal thing. From that time, in Vught, it became an important thing every day. I know there was no hunger problem in that camp at that time. What was a problem was just to have to eat, to take it from the kitchen, to stand in queues. It was the first time in my life I saw a queue, and took part." In Westerbork too Frenkel queued for food. It was only in Barneveld that he was not forced to do so, and one of the reasons why he perceived life there as "luxurious" was precisely because eating "was not a daily problem, like it was in Westerbork and Vught." For Frenkel, the return to Westerbork meant the resumption of "the food struggle every day, queuing, and the need to be there at the right time" which continued in Theresienstadt.[67]

Hunger and malnutrition were as common in Terezín as elsewhere. During the first three and a half months Helga Kinsky-Pollack was there she lost 4 kilograms.[68] Remarks about food and famine are scattered throughout the diary she kept during her years in Terezín and reflect her own depression and that of others. "Tuesday 16 March 1943. . . . I went to see my uncle in the Sudeten barracks and there I saw them throw out potato peelings and ten people threw themselves on the little pile and fought for them."[69] Two years older than Pollack, Charlotte Veresova was fourteen when she was deported to Terezín from Prague. She also kept a diary and, given the importance of food in the children's lives, it is not surprising that she too discussed the subject at some length. "The food here stinks. I wonder that anyone can eat it. [I'm told] that in no time I'll be eating it too. . . . [The food] is impossibly cooked and the soups are the same every day. They look like water from washing the floors." A little later she wrote:

We . . . get only one kilogram of bread every three days. . . . Sometimes we get mouldy bread and that's bad. We cut off the mouldy part and then we must slice the rest in very thin slices to make it stretch, and it doesn't matter at all that we have to eat dry bread. If only we got enough. Sometimes I'd cut off another slice but I mustn't. . . . I'd just gobble it all down and then the third day I wouldn't have any. Now I've begun to think too much about food. I even eat the disgusting soup sometimes, and only a little while ago I couldn't have imagined it.[70]

As with children who had been in the French transit camps, the very small percentage of those young people who passed through Theresienstadt and survived were unable to forget the food-related misery they had experienced. In Inge Auerbacher's autobiographical memoir, *I Am A Star*, she described the wretchedness of the whole eating ordeal.

Most of the kitchens were located in the open courtyards of the huge barracks. The lines were always very long. It was especially hard in the winter, waiting in the bitter cold. Breakfast consisted of coffee, a muddy-looking liquid, which always had a horrible taste. Lunch was a watery soup, a potato, and a small portion of turnips or so-called meat sauce; and dinner was soup. By the time the people reached the barrels from which the food was ladled out, they were so hungry and exhausted that they immediately gulped their portion down.

I remember Mama marking off each day on our rationed loaf of bread to make certain that we would have enough left to last us a week. This was often difficult. When the hunger pains became too strong, she regretfully cut slightly into the next day's portion of bread.[71]

The bread in Gabor Czitrom's group in Bergen-Belsen was cut by one person for everyone in his room in the barrack. They got "one loaf of bread for so many people" which was "German military bread; it's like a brick more or less." In Czitrom's room, where "people were fundamentally decent," the inmates felt it was important that it be distributed equitably.

In our room we had a civil engineer who had his slide rule, and he was supposed to slice the bread, so he measured it very exactly, surrounded by so many people who checked him. Everyone was focused on food, so he measured it exactly. He sliced it up and it was

distributed, and the right to sweep up the crumbs was a right that was
going around among the young people under eighteen. There was an
age limit under which people were considered as hungrier than
grown-up people. To lick out the [soup] caldron was equally a right.
We took turns among the young to lick it out.[72]

Czitrom's group was extremely privileged compared to others in Bergen-
Belsen. They "were hungry," but it was "not real hunger in the sense of
being starved; we were far from being starved."[73]

Marion Stokvis-Krieg and her parents were not so fortunate. They
were amongst those with "Palestina Papieren"; people who had been
able to obtain Palestine papers, and were held by the Germans for possible exchange with German nationals living in Palestine. Krieg was
born in Amsterdam in 1936 to German Jewish parents who had emigrated a few years before. Deported to Westerbork in the spring of
1943, they were shipped to Bergen-Belsen in October of the same year.
She had not yet turned seven. Krieg's parents had to work, and she was
left alone in the barrack. "My parents went [to work.] Nobody told us
what they were going to do, nothing, we didn't know anything. And in
the concentration camp, there was no one . . . who could comfort me a
little bit or tell me what was going on. . . . Anyhow, nobody was speaking to me. I had a little doll and that was all I had. I was very, very afraid
of course. I was walking around and crying." Luckily, like many others
who came into the camps, she soon found people she knew. "Suddenly,
[and the camp] was big, I saw two children walking together, and they
were my best friends, during the war and before the war. They lived
around the corner, Marion and Stefan; they were twins." Marion and
Stefan had arrived some four weeks earlier, so "they could tell me everything I wanted to know." The three children were together until 1945,
"all day we played together and stayed together." Hunger was a constant of their lives, and they made up games with eating as the central
theme. As they had no props or toys, simple devices had to do. "We
were hungry and we had another game. When you spit, you wait a
minute, and then you can swallow your spittle and it's just like you have
something to eat or drink. It's a game."[74]

The deprivations of transit camp life, the confinement, waiting, and
hunger led, ineluctably, to the children's deterioration. They suffered
from feelings of shame and degradation. Their family structure weakened if it did not collapse entirely. And physically, nearly all the children
succumbed to a variety of illnesses and not a few to death. To be a prisoner, incarcerated, forced to obey orders, and subject to random insult

and assault on a daily basis without respite or refuge was a new and horrendous experience. There was a precedent for each of these abuses in their lives, but the combination and, as they now were in camps, the pervasive and ubiquitous nature of the persecution was without parallel in their history. As Marion Krieg put it, "My experiences of the camp, the *worst* experience I had was not that I was so hungry, but the humiliation of the people. We were nothing anymore. I was nothing." In such circumstances, traditional family configurations, especially those based on concepts of respect and power, quickly disintegrated. "My parents were nothing any more," Krieg continued. "As a child, normally you look up to your parents. 'Mama is right in what she is saying,' and 'Papa is right,' and you are proud, and so on. [But in Belsen] we didn't have the feeling that their word meant anything."[75] Krieg missed the comfort her parents had been able to provide, and the stability of the home life they had had. She was acutely aware of how very much on their own she and her two friends were:

> I felt very lonely, very lonely because I felt that I couldn't speak with my parents. They had their own troubles . . . normally they had to work in the worst circumstances. So I didn't tell what I was doing all day; I didn't. And we were very alone, the three of us.
>
> It was a specific world, our world; a very sad world. . . . It was awful, and it was very strange. We went everywhere we could, we have seen every spot of the camp, I think. The parents didn't do it, of course not, why should they? When they came back, they were tired. But we did.
>
> There was nothing for us. There was no one who was looking after us. It was a completely different world. [And we were] alone in the big world [of] the concentration camp. And we couldn't get out.[76]

Going to Westerbork and then to Bergen-Belsen "was the end" of her "protected" life as a child. At eight and nine years old she and her friends "were so grown-up already that we thought we couldn't worry them [their parents] and tell them all our troubles and fears and so on because they had enough for themselves."[77]

In such a situation of absolute powerlessness on the part of the camp inmates and absolute power on the part of the camp administration, it is not surprising that the children's perception of their parents changed radically. For Flip Frenkel this transformation occurred almost immediately upon his arrival at Vught. Frenkel had not had a close relationship with his father prior to their deportation. "My father was at that time forty-eight or fifty, and I was eleven, and I think it was a big difference then [in that era], much bigger than now," he explained. "I knew my father only working [so] I didn't know [him] very well." When the Frenkels arrived at Vught, Flip's mother, four sisters, and younger brother were sent to one part of the camp, while he and his father went to another. It was the first time he had been separated from his mother and was with his father alone. "It was very – strange is not the right word, but I don't know another word. . . . I knew my father until that time as a Father, a paterfamilias, and it was in that situation in Vught that he became just another person for me. He was a normal person, as any other. He wasn't anymore that big man who was my father. He was unmasked as a normal human being. He collapsed for me [and I lost] respect. I think it was because he had the haircut, and he lost his clothes, and we walked not in shoes but in wooden shoes. So he wasn't any more my father."[78] From her vantage point as a social worker at Rivesaltes, Vivette Hermann noticed the corruption of filial respect. "In that jungle they quickly adapt, the total anarchy and the freedom from all tutelage seduces them, there is no vestige of parental authority, the arbitrary is substituted for justice, the system D for discipline, and in that upside down universe the sharpest child, those most adroit in attending to daily existence put themselves before their parents."[79]

While parents may have lost their authority in the transit camp world, they did not necessarily lose their ability to provide emotional support and, through that affection, some semblance of structure. This was true especially for younger children who were not so conscious of the humiliation and debasement of their parents by the camp system. For Esther Levi and her two little sisters and one brother, the situation "remained familiar because our mother was with us. [In Bergen-Belsen] our mother took care of us the whole day and our father went to work. I believe that because our mother actually was always there, Mama was there, that we therefore missed our father a little bit less. We could see him at times. He was in another barrack. We could see him; less frequently [than at home] of course because he had to work. . . . In Bergen-Belsen he had to work during the day as he had to do at home. He left in the morning and came back in the evening, and Mother was always there. I think that was the reason [I didn't notice] that my father was there [in one barrack] and my mother here [in the barrack] with us."[80] The pattern from home was preserved. As we have seen, the case of older children was somewhat different as they recognized (and felt) their parents' powerlessness. Nevertheless, for them too, the fact that their mother (or father) or both was present was in itself of great comfort. The family structure may have changed in transit camp; the previous hierarchical patterns based on authority may have disintegrated, but the love and affection were still able to endure.

Not even parental love could prevent the children's physical deterioration, however. The overcrowded conditions, poor sanitation, and, above all, hunger and malnutrition led inexorably to debilitation and disease. Everyone weakened; everyone became ill. Ellen Levi went from one illness to the next. In Westerbork "I was very often quite sick with otitis, again with diarrhea." In Bergen-Belsen she was in the hospital again, this time too with "diarrhea or dysentery. Very often we had it." In Theresienstadt she got "an infection of severe hepatitis" and was sent to the pediatric hospital where she was treated by "an excellent physician, Dr Magda Miller, from Vienna."[81] The hepatitis was followed by diphtheria. This constant succession of infectious diseases was commonplace, as were ailments specifically attributable to malnutrition. On 19 June 1944 Helga Pollack's father reported that his daughter "complains of a painful tongue and gums. Avitaminosis." A week and a half later, she was given "two lemons and one orange as [she has] the worst case of avitaminosis in the home."[82] As time went on, conditions worsened and so did the children's health. Even those in groups as well protected as that to which Gabor Czitrom belonged could not escape the consequences of constant deprivation. By late autumn 1944 "I personally, physically, began somewhat to wear away. I had dysentery and I had some frozen spots on my hands that didn't heal. . . . Actually, dysentery meant death in those sorts of centers."[83] As Irene Hasenberg explained, life in transit camps "was just a progression of deterioration."[84]

We were hungry all the time. That was part of the condition, not being able to sleep at night, being hungry all the time, just continuously, always, thinking about food. Never seeing any way out of it. It changes people a lot. Aside from the emaciation and the malnutrition, and the health effects, it changes people tremendously. One of the perverse effects was that people talked about food all the time and women would talk about recipes all the time: how they cooked what, and when, and for whom, and what quantities. At night I'd try to sleep and there would be these conversations. It was just bizarre.

Mostly what I thought about was food; it was an obsession. I couldn't get food off my mind. I just always had an empty stomach and I always had hunger pains. I frequently got diarrhea and I got very weak and I'd try to regain my strength. It was just a life of steady deterioration, with illness, with weakness, with malnutrition. . . .

I had diarrhea at times, like everybody, but I didn't get typhoid. . . .
Everyone was going downhill. . . . Everyone, of course, was very thin
and underweight, and malnourished. Once you're so undernourished
and malnourished, you're subject to infections. A lot of people had
boils, and infections, and oedema, when fluids stay in the body. And
diarrhea and typhoid, which spread easily.[85]

Life in transit camp was, in short, a gradual acclimatization to the
abnormal. At the same time as the children continued with their studies,
made new friends, and celebrated holidays like Chanukkah, Rosh Hashanah, Yom Kippur, Shabbat, and even December 5th (St Nicholas Day)
or December 25th (Christmas Day), they lived on a daily basis with
shame and degradation, they saw their parents humiliated and abused,
they grew accustomed to hunger, waiting, and want, and they endured
incarceration, malnutrition, and disease. On one level, some echo, or
shadow, of normal life was preserved. For instance, however meager the
food, families ate together whenever it was possible to do so. Children
wore their own clothes. As time went on they outgrew what they had
brought, their shoes were too tight and their garments too small. But
what they wore belonged to them and had come from home. Then too,
most young people formed new friendships. Retaining their ability to develop relationships, their contacts with their camp companions reflected
the pattern of the life they used to lead. And even in that warped world,
children celebrated holidays, both religious and secular, as they had
done before. A woman who, as she herself said, had "taken on the task
of looking after children" in her barrack in Bergen-Belsen described one
such festivity in the diary she kept. Hanna Lévy-Hass had been born in
Yugoslavia and was deported to Belsen in the summer of 1944 from
Montenegro, where she worked as a schoolteacher. She was in the so-
called "Star Camp" (all the inmates wore Stars of David), the sub-camp
to which those Jews who were being held for possible exchange had
been sent, primarily from Salonica, Yugoslavia, Albania, France, and the
Netherlands.

Belsen 1.9.44. . . . Yesterday the Dutch Jews here celebrated their
beloved Queen's birthday. They even acted a play for the children.
However could they think of such a thing at a time like this? I can
hardly believe my eyes when I see them in their Sunday best. When
they were deported they were not stripped of everything by the Germans, as we were. . . . Anyway, our Dutchmen are very smartly
dressed as they walk around. Two youngsters catch my eye in particular, wearing fresh white collars and ties. They really are! A touching

occasion, this royal birthday – really moving.[86]

On another level, however, the children moved into the realm of the bizarre. Living in the world of the transit camp each day, the extraordinary became ordinary, the incredible ever more believable, and the unimaginable a commonplace occurrence. Like Hanna Lévy-Hass, Marion Stokvis-Krieg was also in the Star Camp. At the edge of their compound was the Imprisonment Camp to which inmates who had been working as slave laborers in armaments factories in other concentration camps were shipped. Next to the Star Camp was the Tent Camp which in the autumn of 1944 was filled with thousands of women arriving from Auschwitz. The mortality rate in the Tent and Imprisonment Camps was higher than that of the Star Camp.[87] Within a few months of Queen Wilhelmina's birthday celebration recorded by Lévy-Hass, "everything got worse in the concentration camp," Krieg recalled.

> There was no food anymore, of course. At the end of '44, parents were not going to work anymore. I don't know why, but it wasn't necessary. But we had nothing to eat anymore and we had all kinds of typhus, dirt, and so on and so on. Worst of all was all those bodies in the concentration camp on the other side. But already, of course, in our camp too, there were all those bodies lying on the ground.
>
> It was amazing. Even that was not so – it didn't frighten me; not at all. It was normal. So, he was dead, okay. Someone was lying in bed and didn't move any more. He was dead. Next item.
>
> It's very hard, but that's the way it was.[88]

As Petr Fischl, who had been deported to Terezín from Prague when he was fourteen years old, wrote, "we got used to it."

> We got used to standing in line at 7 o'clock in the morning, at 12 noon and again at seven o'clock in the evening. . . . We got used to sleeping without a bed, to saluting every uniform, not to walk on the sidewalks and then again to walk on the sidewalks. We got used to undeserved slaps, blows, and executions. . . . We got used to it that from time to time, one thousand unhappy souls would come here and that, from time to time, another thousand unhappy souls would go away.[89]

Finally, like Marion Stokvis-Krieg, Petr Fischl also "got accustomed to seeing people die in their own excrement, to seeing piled-up coffins full of corpses, to seeing the sick amidst dirt and filth and to seeing the helpless doctors."[90] It was not only adults that Krieg and Fischl saw. Death claimed children too in the transit camps. It was one of the ways in which the lives of far too many young people came to an end in Nazi-occupied Europe.

A small number of children were liberated. Irene Hasenberg was one of the 357 Jews from the Star Camp in Bergen-Belsen who was part of an exchange group, and she was released in January 1945. Gabor Czitrom was one of the 1,685 Hungarian Jews in the "Hungarian Camp" at Belsen to be released in December 1944.[91] Like Hasenberg, he too was put on a train – a passenger train – and sent to Switzerland. OSE, as we have seen earlier (in "Into Hiding"), was one of the many relief organizations dedicated to the release of children from the transit camps in France. Indeed, so many philanthropies were concerned with the situation of those interned in the French camps that two committees were established to coordinate welfare activities. The Commission Israélite des Camps was composed of representatives of the Jewish agencies (the most important of whom were the Éclaireurs Israélites de France (EIF, or Jewish Scouts), the Organization for Rehabilitation and Training (ORT), and OSE, which maintained missions in the camps. The Comité de Coordination pour l'Assistance dans les Camps (CCAC) was its non-Jewish counterpart. Founded by the head of the Protestant Church in France, the Pastor Marc Boegner, who worked ceaselessly to address the injustices suffered by the Jews in France, it coordinated the relief programs of the non-Jewish agencies involved in camp work (among whom were, as we have seen, the YMCA, Secours Suisse aux Enfants, American Friends' Service Committee, Unitarian Service Committee, and the Service Sociale d'Aide aux Émigrants).[92] United in their efforts, the two committees successfully petitioned Vichy for permission to release children under the age of fifteen from the camps in the Unoccupied Zone. Beginning in early spring 1941 the young people were allowed to leave the camps on condition that they would go to a children's home, that they were granted residence certificates from the prefect of the department to which they were to go, and that their parents would consent to their departure. Working in great haste and with enormous determination, new homes were opened (especially by OSE and the EIF, but also by non-Jewish organizations), the Préfect of the Department of the Hérault, Monsieur Benedetti, and his associates, Ernst and Frederici, provided the necessary permits and, with undoubtedly very mixed emotions, most parents gave their consent. In March, April, and May some 323 children had been released from the camps, and in June, July, and August another 145.[93] There were thousands more; according to an account prepared by the Comité de Nîmes in June 1941, 300 children were still in Argelès, 100 in Gurs, 100 in Noé, and 3,000 in Rivesaltes.[94] But the philanthropic organizations continued to work successfully, and by February 1942 there were only about 875 children in Rivesaltes.[95] A "report on the situation in the refugee centers and camps in the Unoccupied Zone" noted that "thanks to the work of the Secours Suisse and of OSE, in addition to that of the Quakers, the majority of the children have been pulled out of the camps, and at present the total number of children still interned must not be more than about a thousand."[96] Within two months, that figure had been reduced to fifty-five.[97]

The sudden and vicious dragnet operations in the north in July 1942 and the south the following month swelled the camp population. Working at fever pitch and in horrendous physical and emotional conditions, the relief agencies once again were successful in obtaining the release of hundreds of children from the Vichy transit camps. By this time, however, everyone realized that it was, literally, a question of life and death. For some time, freeing the children had been thought to be important, even urgent. After the round-up of the Vél d'Hiv (when 12,884 Jews were seized in Paris on 16–17 July), it was understood to be imperative. On 4 August Vichy agreed to the deportation of foreign Jews from both zones, and almost immediately 400 Jews were picked up and sent to the transit camp of Les Milles, just outside Aix-en-Provence. As they came into the camp, representatives of the Fédération des Sociétés Juives de France, OSE, and the Comité d'Aide aux Refugiés were there to meet them. A Federation report of 7 August described their activities of the previous few days. According to the account, 1,400 people were already interned in the camp, 400 newly admitted. The social workers had reason to believe that there were a number of categories of those who could remain in France, including parents with children under the age of five and "children five to eighteen years old . . . if their parents agreed to be separated from them." In the end, seventy children of the latter group were released to the care of OSE. They were freed – and they were separated from their parents.[98]

We witnessed the departure of the children on Monday morning. While they were made to board the coaches with their scant baggage, heart-rending scenes occurred. The young children, who could not understand the reasons for this separation, clung to their parents and cried. The older ones who knew how great their parents' anguish was, tried to control their own pain and clenched their teeth. The women clung to the doors of the buses as they left. The guards and even the police themselves could hardly control their emotions.

The feeling was even more horrible in that until then perfect calm had reigned in the camp. One read a heavy and bitter resignation on [the internees'] faces. There had been no protest; no cry of indignation or of anger was heard. It had seemed as if after so many attempts, the internees had no more energy to rebel against their fate.[99]

Later that month, the social workers of Vénissieux faced the same ordeal, as did the children and their parents. Towards the end of August 1942, 1,200 Jews were arrested in a *razzia* in Lyon and sent to the camp of Vénissieux.[100] "I managed to insinuate myself into the camp by declaring myself a representative of social welfare," Georges Garel (who went on to create the OSE network to hide children) explained. At that point Garel was not connected with OSE. An engineer working in Lyon, he came to Vénissieux that night at the request of his friend Charles Lederman, who was very much involved in OSE activities in the transit camps. Father Alexandre Glasberg of the Amitiés Chrétiennes was in Vénissieux too, as was (among others) Elisabeth Hirsch, Hélène Lévy, and Lily Taget (who married Garel not long afterwards) of OSE and Madeleine Barot of CIMADE. The camp was in a state of terrible confusion; orders and counter-orders followed each other in succession. "After midnight we learned that the children under sixteen years old could remain in France. . . . Many of the wretched mothers of these children managed themselves admirably. Giving up their children forever, they left with dignity. Other mothers were crazed and nearly lost their minds. One father that same night opened his veins and his blood splashed the cheeks of the child clasped to his chest. A mother threw herself from the window crying, 'I will not give up my child.'"[101]

Lily Garel-Taget remembered that night "as shocking, hallucinatory . . . it was truly a nightmare." She was twenty years old and she had begun to work at the Lyon OSE office that year, partly as a secretary and partly as a social worker. (It was through her director, Charles Lederman, that she met Georges Garel, and Lederman in turn became her brother-in-law by marrying Garel's sister.) "We were there night and day, it was truly haunting. I went for OSE. . . . It was there that my [future] husband began to help and, with Abbé Glasberg who was extraordinary, was able to release the first children from the camp. . . . Abbé Glasberg managed to falsify files; it was really he who managed to get the children out of the camp. The one who was able to do the most, I think, was Abbé Glasberg. I saw it."[102]

In addition to children under sixteen, adults with French nationality were to be released also. The question was, who was French and who was not? And precisely how old was each child? "Abbé Glasberg changed the files, pulling out some papers and replacing others." Lily Taget herself was very conflicted. She came "from a lawyer's family, in other words a family in which the law was the law. I had arrived in a nightmare world where people had to decide who was French and who was not, who could leave the camp and who could not. . . . I had the feeling, 'How can these people judge?' On the other hand, I saw Abbé Glasberg who did absolutely illegal things which just astounded me. I realized little by little that it had to be done, but it was not my upbringing."[103] Elisabeth Hirsch had left Gurs and, at Andrée Salomon's direction, had come to work with OSE at Lyon. "We entered the camp and we obtained [permission] on principle to release children up to sixteen years old. I was there all night. It was horrible to do that work. There were parents who wished to give up their children, and others who did not want to do so. It was terrible that night, to choose the people to save – that was awful, it was dreadful. Imagine that mass of people whom you know will be deported, just to get out so few: 108 children, that was nothing [in comparison with] the thousands of people who were to be deported."[104] Hirsch was right; 108 children and 60 adults were released. And to complete the tragedy "during the second night, about 80 people who had been freed after screening the previous night were retaken by the police and then reported."[105]

Most children in Nazi-occupied Europe left the transit camp in cattle cars bound for the east. In occupied France, the Netherlands, Belgium, and from Terezín in Czechoslovakia they were amongst those who were locked up and shipped out. After the round-up of the Vél d'Hiv, single people were sent to Drancy and families with children to Pithiviers and Beaune-la-Rolande. Initially it appeared that children under twelve would not be deported but be put under the care of the German-imposed Jewish Council, UGIF (The Union Générale Israélites de France). Within a few days their parents and the older children were forced into the deportation trains. "It is useless to describe the lacerating scenes at the moment of separation. There were numerous suicide attempts. These were cases of mothers who became mad. Mothers whose children were torn away while still nursing were deported, their breasts swollen with milk. Others, who pressed their little ones to themselves, had to be beaten to make them open their arms. A few of the thousand other cases amidst the cries of agony of these mothers from whom one tears their very skin."[106] In the end, the very children who had been separated from their parents were themselves deported not long afterwards.

Hélas, all efforts . . . have been in vain, and many departures of 500 children each have taken place; these children, aged two to twelve, first were transferred from Pithiviers and Beaune-la-Rolande to Drancy. It is from there that they left under the same conditions as adults, in sealed wagons, supervised by women who were deported also. . . . In some wagons there were just children alone. Upon leaving, each child is handed a bit of bread and a tin of condensed milk.[107]

In Drancy, as elsewhere, the rhythm of the departing trains was the pulse of transit camp life. In some camps the deportation trains ran irregularly, depending on the *razzia* activity in the surrounding area for victims. In a camp like Westerbork with a consistently large population, the train left on a weekly basis. Every Tuesday it was filled with those who could no longer obtain the much coveted postponement of the inevitable, inexorable departure. For Irene Hasenberg, as for the other inmates of Westerbork, children and adults alike, this weekly cycle was a nightmare. "The trauma of seeing your people go every week even if you weren't going" was horrendous. "You might be glad [to be spared], but you were still suffering." It became "the overwhelming impression of life in Westerbork; it revolved around the railroad track."[108] The journalist Philip Mechanicus shared Hasenberg's feelings, and he confided his excruciating relief to his diary when, by a miracle, no train was scheduled that week.

Tuesday, August 3rd: No transport this morning. Peace and quiet. The world seems kind and merciful. Children thank God that their parents have escaped the executioner for another week and parents thank Heaven because their children are safe for the time being. Every week means one more week and every week may be the last. Perhaps the war will not be over quite as soon as we hoped, but the regime in Germany may collapse just like the regime in Italy and then, at any rate, the persecution of the Jews will be over. Every week now represents a double or treble gain.[109]

Ultimately, no one was spared, of course. As late as 17 October 1944 Helga Pollack told her father in despair, "On a slip of paper a person's destiny is decided."[110] Friends had been claimed for a transport the day before, and others were scheduled to go the day after. Some children were deported to slave labor and death camps such as Auschwitz and Sobibor immediately. Others like Ellen Levi went eastward gradually; her route was from Westerbork to Bergen-Belsen to Theresienstadt. Eventually she too was locked into a cattle car and shipped to "Pitchipoi," as the children in Drancy called the mysterious "unknown destination" to which they dreaded to be sent. Her father had been deported from Terezín on 28 September 1944. "My mother by that time was assigned luckily to a kind of war industry with mica [so she was protected]. . . . On October 12 I went on transport without my mother. My mother asked me, 'Shall I join you out of my own free will?' Then I took one of the gravest decisions I ever had to take. I said, 'No; in this time you do not do anything out of your own free will. You stay here. I'll go by myself.' Then I went on the train."[111]

Chapter Five

Ghettos

Less than a fortnight before the Jewish quarter of Warsaw became a closed ghetto, Chaim Kaplan, who was an astute and intelligent observer of current events, could not imagine that such a transformation would occur. Nearly six months earlier, in May 1940, thick walls separating the designated Jewish area from the rest of the city had been built at the Germans' command and the Jewish community's expense. Gentiles living in the Jewish quarter had moved out and Jews living in now forbidden areas had taken up residence in the streets allocated to them. And the example of Łódź, where a closed ghetto had been instituted in May, was very much on his mind. Yet Kaplan did not believe that Warsaw would suffer the same fate. In his secret diary he wrote:

November 2, 1940
A Jewish ghetto in the traditional sense is impossible; certainly a closed ghetto is inconceivable. Many churches and government buildings are in the heart of the ghetto. They cannot be eliminated, they fulfill necessary functions. Besides that, it is impossible to cut off the trolley routes going from one end of the city to the other through the ghetto. For hundreds of years the great metropolis was built on general civil foundations, and the basis of race was entirely foreign to it. Neighborhoods and backyards of people of different faiths were next to each other, and in spite of all religious and moral differences between them, mutual trade and dealings developed which brought benefits to all. To differentiate citizens of one country according to race, and to erect partitions between them, is a sick pathological idea.

From its inception to its execution, it may be considered a symptom of insanity.[1]

Just two days later Kaplan noted, "The face of Warsaw has changed so that no one who knows it would recognize it. People from outside do not enter now, but if a miracle were to take place and one of its inhabitants who fled returned to the city, he would say, 'Can this be Warsaw?'" It was Jewish Warsaw, however, that was "especially changed."

Since the Jewish quarter was established, Jewish Warsaw has become a city unto itself, with characteristics quite different from those of Aryan Warsaw. Anyone passing from the Jewish district to the Aryan district gets the impression of having entered a new city with a different appearance and a different way of life and having nothing to do with its Jewish neighbor.

Jewish Warsaw has changed for the worse, in the direction of ugliness, tastelessness, and lack of beauty. . . . It is a graveyard, only here the skeletons of the dead walk about in the streets. They have gathered from all parts of the country and come to Warsaw. They came empty-handed, broken and crushed, without a penny, without food for a single meal or clothes to cover their nakedness.[2]

However closed the ghetto, however segregated and isolated its inhabitants, Jewish Warsaw and gentile Warsaw continued to exist cheek by jowl. Physically, geographically, the two cities were completely contiguous. They were so close that one stretch of one street (Chłodna Street), the segment that ran from Elektoralna on the east to Żelazna Street on the west, was divided into three parts. The houses and sidewalk on the north were assigned to the Jewish quarter, as were the houses and sidewalk on the south. The street itself, the thoroughfare, was in the gentile zone. Thus, that part of Chłodna Street had walls on both sides. This partition produced an obstacle. Chłodna Street intersected Żelazna Street, and the houses and sidewalk on the east side of Żelazna were in the Jewish quarter. A Jewish pedestrian walking down the Jewish sidewalk of Żelazna Street would have been forced to traverse the gentile thoroughfare of Chłodna. It was, as Chaim Kaplan remarked, "a new problem from the racial point of view." The division made it "inevitable for the two races to meet as they cross Żelazna Street. Consequently, the Nazis ordered the *Judenrat* to construct, at its own expense, a bridge about two stories high with steps leading up from Chłodna and down to the same street. . . . Thousands of people now go up and down like the angels on Jacob's ladder. There are fifty steps on each side of the bridge." The whole concept, and its actualization, was so bizarre that Kaplan concluded, "The children of future generations will listen to this tale of the Warsaw ghetto and exlaim: 'It's only a fairy tale! Could the Nazis really have been such idiots?'"[3]

Clearly, the situation in Warsaw (or Łódź, Vilna, Radom, Minsk, and all the other cities in which ghettos were established) was very different from the so-called "old people's ghetto" of Theresienstadt. In Poland and, later, the Baltic countries and occupied area of the Soviet Union, the ghettos were carved out of the heart of the cities and, in an extreme form, followed the medieval ghetto. The traditional ghetto had been an enclosed Jewish neighborhood with locked gates at night; its German-imposed descendant was an equally confined area, but with permanently barred exits. As a "ghetto" Theresienstadt was a novelty. There the Jewish community lived behind walls, but no gentile city bustled on the other side. Terezín had been emptied, evacuated of its indigenous gentile Czech population. The "town for the Jews" was as isolated in the Bohemian countryside as was any transit camp of western Europe. With the notable exceptions of Drancy (which was close to Paris) and Malines, or Mechelen (near to Brussels), nearly all of the transit camps were established in sparsely populated areas.[4] Westerbork, for example, was located in an exceptionally bleak corner of the Netherlands, and Gurs was in the foothills of the Pyrenees.

The isolation of these camps was a reflection of the place they occupied in the bureaucratic process of segregation. The transit camps were part of the administrative infrastructure of annihilation, and by the time Jews were deported to them they were as cut off from the body politic as were the institutions themselves. Through a slow, systematic, and sophisticated process they had been stripped of their civil rights and their worldly possessions. Forced off the civic map, they were relegated to areas as desolate as they.

The transit camps of western Europe were a bureaucratic invention designed to respond to such practical considerations as the availability of rail lines and the Germans' desire to screen deportation scenes. The city of Terezín was selected to be a transit camp for similarly pragmatic reasons. First of all, the railway lines were not far away and a spur could be laid without difficulty. Then too, as Terezín had been established to hold troops, the original barracks could be converted quickly to house large numbers of people. The fortifications of the garrison town were still intact. This made the complex easier to control and inhibited partisan attacks and escape attempts. Finally, Terezín was a town forgotten both by history and industry. It was an obscure, peripheral little city of neither national significance nor economic importance. The Czech gentile population could be relocated with impunity as no one would notice or care.

Such operative and logistical concerns were not ignored in eastern Europe; they simply were met by the extant situation. Large numbers of Jews lived in concentrated areas within the cities, and train lines, initially used to ship in Jews (and later for deportation purposes), were available. Furthermore, the Germans' attitude towards and ideology with regard to Slavic Europeans was very different from their sentiments and ideas about the west European peoples. Whereas in the west the Germans were anxious not to alienate the local population unduly, such considerations were of no consequence east of the Warthe. Unsolicitous of public opinion, they contumeliously moved thousands of Jews first into and then out of the metropolis. Indifferent to the integrity of the city, they tore it up and ripped it apart. And nonchalant about appearance or formality, the Germans did not institute the intricate legal system of extortion or the gradual process of pushing their prey out of the municipalities, into the margins, and then over the border as they had done in the west. Without scruples as to form, the invaders locked the Jews into walled ghettos and plundered their possessions at will.

From the perspective of the Jews, to be forced into a ghetto was not without precedent. Historical examples were well known to them. It was only at the beginning of the nineteenth century that Jews were no longer required to live in the ghetto of Frankfurt, and the ghetto of Rome had been opened in 1870. In cities like Vilna where there never had been a walled ghetto or locked gates, there were historic Jewish quarters, traditional Jewish neighborhoods. Thus, where there was no relation either in space or time between the inmates of transit camps and the area to which they were deported, the inhabitants of east European ghettos were connected to the history of the place in which they now were compelled to live. The physical environment, the streets, synagogues, and markets, had developed over the centuries to meet the Jewish community's needs; in the current situation it suggested that life was still possible. This was true even for the hundreds of thousands of refugee Jews evicted from their home towns within a few months of the German invasion.[5] Forced to flee to the larger cities, they arrived dazed and destitute, but they came to a place which was in one way or another familiar. The concept of a ghetto had a past in Jewish memory, and the ghettos themselves had a Jewish past. It was logical that, initially, there was hope for a Jewish future; it was presumed to be a situation one could survive. For over 600,000 Jews that proved to be an illusion.[6]

The primary focus of this chapter will be the notorious long-term ghettos like Warsaw, Łódź, and Vilna, but short-term ghettos were established also, especially in Hungary proper and the regions annexed to Hungary from Czechoslovakia and Rumania. The social, cultural, and intellectual life which flourished in the long-term ghettos did not have time to develop in ghettos which were in existence for a matter of weeks. Nor were the poverty, starvation, and disease of the permanent ghettos very much in evidence in their temporary counterparts. Yet they shared certain essential characteristics: both were places of forced residence within the city limits; people were at once at home and separated from the world they had known. In both, families still lived together and familial structures remained intact, but young people experienced a new freedom. And finally, in the short- as in the long-term ghettos, no one knew in advance how long the status quo would endure.

In the spring of 1944 Alexander Ehrmann lived in the town of Király-helmec in the northeast of Hungary; prior to its annexation from Czechoslovakia in 1938 it had been called Kralovsky Chlumec. Királyhelmec was in that part of Hungary which was the first to be subject to the German and Hungarian program of concentration, ghettoization, and deportation. According to the plan that had been developed by German and Hungarian officials, the country was divided into six geographic zones. Each zone was to be processed in turn. In each area Jews from the smaller towns, villages, and countryside were incarcerated in synagogues and other community buildings. After they were stripped of their possessions by edict, persuasion, threats, or torture, they were sent to specifically designated ghetto areas in the larger cities. In some cities the traditional Jewish quarter was selected to be the ghetto site, in others it was the gypsy neighborhoods, sugar-beet factories, or brickyards. They all had one feature in common: proximity to rail lines to facilitate and expedite deportation. The Jewish inhabitants of the larger cities were rounded up soon after their co-religionists from the countryside arrived. They too were forced into the ghetto and plundered viciously.[7]

Királyhelmec was in Zone I, which included Carpatho-Ruthenia and northeast Hungary, in other words, regions which were closest to the expected advance of the Soviet army, and which had become part of Hungary only recently. Thus the government could claim that it did not have responsibility for those Jews, as they were not really Hungarian citizens or part of traditional Hungarian culture. And perhaps too, the Jews in Old Hungary would believe that for these very reasons they would be protected, and therefore they would not create too many difficulties or disturbances. Alexander Ehrmann was not in Old Hungary, however, and he and his family had to confront the problem immediately, unaware that they had been abandoned by Horthy. "On the last day of

24   Refugees from the provinces arriving in the Warsaw ghetto. Photo taken by Joe J.
Heydecker, February 1941.

Pesach, which was a Saturday [22 April 1944], after lunch around one
o'clock, one of the officers in the local gendarmerie (who lived in
quarters which were requisitioned from one of the Jewish merchants) let
his 'landlord' know that they got orders to gather up all the Jews the
next morning. . . . Word spread around quickly. . . . Plans were made,
interfamily plans: 'as soon as it gets dark, we'll have to hide some of the
valuables and get prepared for the next day when they take us.' The reports were watered down somewhat by counter-reports that we were
not going to go to Germany, but the Hungarian Jews were going to be
treated differently, we were going to go to farms. . . . 'We are Hungarian
Jews, we'll be treated differently. Our great benefactor the Regent of
Hungary [Horthy] will protect us.'"[8]

Ehrmann belonged to a Zionist organization, the Mizrachi. "There
was also a Betar revisionist movement, but the Mizrachi was the
strongest in our town. We had clandestine meetings regularly." While
the adults made plans, "that Saturday afternoon when word got out we
[my siblings and I] went to visit some of our close friends. . . . The boy
and the girls [the children of that family] were our age, and other boys
and girls came there also. We were all involved in Mizrachi. We discussed things amongst ourselves, what we heard from the parents, what
was going on, what we were going to do. And we were going to continue

our Zionist activities . . . we were going to continue, wherever we were going, we would continue our ties with the ideology and somehow we would find a way – we were dreaming."[9]

That evening, when it got dark, the Ehrmann family prepared for their departure. They packed linens, leather stuffs, silver candelabras and some of their jewelry in wooden chests and metal milk tins and buried them in the dirt under the wooden floor. "We carried out the dirt that we scooped out when we made the holes under the floor in pots and pans and we dumped it outside in the little flower gardens. . . . We opened up the seams of the clothes we were going to go in, and we rolled up paper money and sewed it in there. We had some gold stuff, and everybody got something. Whatever happened, we knew at least we had some money." The remainder of their money was given to their neighbors, "nice people, nice farmers," who "said they understood and they were very sad about it and that they'd safekeep it." Early the next morning "there was a knock on the door."[10]

It was the gendarme. "Jews, you have fifteen minutes to get ready." Just like that: "Jews." "Everybody can take one bag. Don't take too many things with you because you won't need a lot of clothes where you arc going. Hurry up! If you are not ready in fifteen minutes you will go as you are." We were prepared. They said, "Let's go." We went.

The gendarmes (not our gendarmes, but gendarmes brought in from out of town) took us to the synagogue. About three o'clock in the afternoon they ordered us to start marching. By then they had brought in everybody not only from our town but from the surrounding villages. Everybody was gathered in there.

We started to march. We had to walk from the synagogue to the main street past the Catholic church. . . . It was a Sunday so people had just got out of church from the afternoon service. . . . We came to the main street and from there we made a right turn and we marched to the railroad station which was in the next village about five kilometers away. We were marching in the center of the street just like the cattle that every morning and every evening were herded to and from the pasture in the center of the street.

The neighbors were standing out in their gateways and watching. Some of them threw stones at us, yelled insults at us, spat on us. Some of them were standing there crying. Some of them were afraid to stand there and cry, so they chose to go back in; they were afraid the gendarmes would do something to them.

We were herded, everybody shlepping their packages, and we came to the railway station. On the way marching down, we [children] kept together with our parents, but we and the other boys and girls [of Mizrachi] kept an eye on each other so we wouldn't lose sight of each other. There was a train waiting for us, a cattle train. About eighty or ninety people got into one wagon and whoever of our friends came into the wagon we acknowledged each other, and we were comfortable with the presence of the other boys and girls.

They put us in the cattle train and we were moving.[11]

Upon their arrival in Sátoraljaújhely, a larger town about 30 miles distant, the Jews of Királyhelmec were instructed to take up residence with the Jewish familes who lived there. Fortunately, the Ehrmann family had cousins who "obviously took us in." In any case, the city was not new to Ehrmann. He was an Orthodox boy from a pious, observant family, and during the summer of 1939 through the winter of 1940 he had attended *yeshiva* [Jewish traditional secondary school] in Sátoraljaújhely. About two weeks after the Ehrmanns and their fellow Jews had come to town, all the Jews in Sátoraljaújhely were compelled to vacate their homes and move to the designated ghetto area. This included "the Orthodox synagogue campus, which consisted of three buildings. Several blocks away there was the Status Quo congregation which was also [three buildings]: the large sanctuary, a smaller chapel and a school. Then there was the Khosedic congregation, which was one school building, one synagogue and the *mikve* [ritual purification baths]. They all were converted to house Jews in the ghetto."[12] A soup kitchen staffed by volunteer women was organized in another community building. The Ehrmann family and their cousins were taken in by other cousins who lived within the ghetto confines.

While the people and the places were familiar to Ehrmann (he knew his cousins and their homes, and the Jewish community and its buildings), the circumstances certainly were not. For the first time in his life he was incarcerated. A barbed-wire fence was thrown up around the few streets where some 15,000 Jews were concentrated. He was hungry. "We didn't have much food, a piece of bread here, some food that we brought." The normal camaraderie of his adolescent life ceased. "During the time we were in the ghetto, there was not much social or organized interaction between families or between individuals." Ehrmann did not meet with his friends from Mizrachi. His activities were very much focused on his family, and their major occupations were to decipher the rumors that circulated and to determine what course of action would be best for them. Ehrmann's older brother, for instance, had been called up for *Arbeitsdienst*, or military work detail. "The dilemma was: he could stay with the family and be exempt, or he could go into the military." Should the family separate or stay together? Finally they decided that he should go; they chose "not to put all our eggs in one basket."[13] Still together as a family, they planned for the eventuality of permanent separation.

András Garzó was younger than Alexander Ehrmann when he and his father moved to the ghetto of Debrecen in June 1944. His family was unobservant while Ehrmann's was Orthodox. He was an only child, Ehrmann had five siblings. And where Garzó had been born and raised in a fair-sized city in Old Hungary, Ehrmann was from a small town in Czechoslovakia which had been annexed to Hungary. In many respects, however, from the moment Garzó and his father were compelled to leave their flat in the pediatric hospital where his father worked to take up residence in the ghetto area across town, the two boys' experiences were very similar. They were both in some sense at home in the ghettos in which they were forced to live, and yet their lives at home vanished from one day to the next. Garzó no longer went to school, Ehrmann did not go to work. Normal occupations like sports or clubs immediately became a thing of the past. Both spent their days in the ghetto with people their own age; Ehrmann with his brother and cousins, and Garzó with the other children. The family, nuclear and extended, was an essential structure in the lives of the two boys, and each family tried as best it could to assess its situation and to make appropriate decisions.

Garzó's father, a physician, was able to continue his professional work after the Germans occupied Hungary. A difficult man with "a very heavy nature," he was nevertheless esteemed both by his hospital colleagues and his private patients. The latter were "for the most part from the Christian gentry middle class. They were people who had conservative ideas, but they liked him [my father] very much." Garzó's father's patients did not leave him, and "if he had asked for protection, I am sure he would have got some help. In any case we did not need to go into the ghetto. My father had fought in the First World War and he was highly decorated. So we should not have gone. But my father did not want to be separated from his family. My grandparents were alive and he had two sisters with their families. We went with them into the ghetto."[14]

The ghetto of Debrecen was composed of two separate, enclosed parts, the "large" and the "small" ghettos, which were divided by Hatvan Street.[15] Garzó and his extended family lived in the large ghetto. His maternal grandparents were with them too, although his father's relations with his in-laws had been poor. Garzó's mother's family were intellectuals, people of some social standing. His maternal grandfather had been appointed by the Emperor Franz Joseph to be the director of a state gymnasium; later he founded the Jewish gymnasium in Debrecen. Garzó's father's family were neither so well educated nor so well off, and his mother's family were not happy with the marriage. When Garzó's mother died (of natural causes) in 1942 "the trouble between my father and my grandfather deepened, because my father would not permit a religious funeral to be held for my mother. And my grandfather, whose most loved child was this daughter (he had five children and this daughter, the youngest, he loved best), would not come to the funeral." Nevertheless, when the family went into the ghetto, they stayed together. Garzó's grandparents were elderly. "It was an automatic response in this situation; my father felt a responsibilty for them which superseded their former difficulties. . . . Also my grandfather felt it was natural that my father, who was a purposeful and powerful man, would take responsibility for the family."[16]

"In Debrecen (and this is typical for a Hungarian town) there was a part of the city where Jews lived in a greater percent. Christians had to exchange their flats in that neighborhood for those owned by Jews elsewhere. This part of town was surrounded and Jews were concentrated there. At that time about 100,000 people lived in Debrecen; 5 or 10 percent were Jews."[17] Like many other children, Garzó was not shocked by the move. He was more speculative, doubtful, and unsure of the future than apprehensive or anxious. His central question was: "'What is happening to us? First came the Jewish Laws, now the ghetto. From step to step the situation gets worse and worse.'" In many ways his own immediate world was still intact. His family was together and relations between them were more harmonious than they had been previously. They were crowded, but they lived in an apartment, a home. The old Jewish quarter was not new to him, and as he had attended the Jewish gymnasium he had become acquainted with, and had learned something about the history of, the Jewish community of Debrecen. Furthermore, a hospital was organized in the ghetto and his father was appointed director, so that rhythm of their lives remained constant. And finally, Garzó enjoyed playing with the other children. "We children were very happy in the ghetto. We had our own games."[18]

> In the house where I lived there was a very big door. We children hid behind the door. One boy stayed outside. We had taken a wallet and put it on the sidewalk; the wallet was attached to a string which the boy held. From our hiding place we saw that people passing by noticed this wallet. They looked around, and when they thought no one was looking they went to get it – but then, of course, the boy pulled it away. That was very, very funny. A very good game.[19]

Garzó's pleasure in the company of his friends in the ghetto was shared by many young people. Sherry Weiss-Rosenfeld was fifteen when she and her aunt's family (with whom she was living) were evicted from their home in Kolozsvár and taken directly to the brick factory on the edge of the city which served as the ghetto. "There was a lot of crying, and a lot of tears, and a lot of sadness. . . . There was no brighter side, but still we were young."[20]

> With all the uncertainty of our existence, as uncertain as it was, we kids met and we talked to each other. Now that we had freer access to each other, the boys and the girls, there was a little more dialogue going on. And as bleak as it was, there was still a certain togetherness that we felt, that there is still strength and unity. We are all together no matter how bad it is.[21]

Mária Ezner also remembered that "in the ghetto we children were happy." As we have seen (in "At Home"), on 16 May 1944 the Hungarian gendarmes ousted the thirteen-year-old Ezner, her eight-and-a-half-year-old sister and their mother from their home in Abádszalók on the Hungarian plain. (Their father had been arrested earlier, on 20 April.) "We could hire a peasant cart, and on those peasant carts we could go. We had to pay ourselves. And we could bring for every person a bed, for every person a chair, and one table for the family." The Jews of Abádszalók were driven to the larger town of Kunhegyes about 12 kilometers to the south, where they were incarcerated in a ghetto. The ghetto of Kunhegyes was not in a traditional Jewish quarter (as in Debrecen or Sátoraljaújhely), but in the gypsy area of town. According to Ezner, "gypsies in Hungary had their own streets. Gypsies weren't in the village among the inhabitants; there were gypsy streets. Like in the Middle Ages, there were Jewish streets. These gypsy streets were streets with little huts, and there was a little forest between the village and the gypsy street. . . . We got a little hut. . . . The ghetto was [guarded] by Hungarian gendarmes. No Germans."[22]

For Ezner, as for Garzó, Ehrmann, and other youngsters, life in the temporary ghetto was at once familiar and strange. They were with their families, but kicked out of their homes. They were in cities and towns, and under the rule of their own countrymen, yet they were segregated and abused. It was a continuation and, of course, an exacerbation of their previous experience of living as "second-class citizens,"[23] but at the same time it afforded new opportunities for a certain kind of freedom. "The ghetto was surrounded by a high wood fence. . . . No one could go in or out. . . . We had no bread. . . . We had a hunger you cannot imagine. We had nothing to eat in the ghetto. We had nothing to eat. But we were happy among us children."[24]

We didn't have to pretend any more that we were for the glory of the German army. We could take off our masks. We were Jewish children, and among ourselves we could say, "Down with Hitler!" We hoped that it would be soon [that Hitler would fall] and that the Americans would come, and a second front would come. From Sicily to Normandy the Germans would be beaten and beaten and beaten. To say such things, we now were free. . . .

We went to this little forest and we played, and spoke, and told Hitler jokes. We laughed at them.

And in the air there was a little sexual contact and awakening too. In the schools in Hungary before the Second World War, we were not coeducated. It was a new thing, boys and girls together. We went into this little forest and played our children's games we had learned in school. We talked about great ideas. And we spoke about the adults, that they are crazy, and why don't they give us clear answers [to our questions about what is happening].[25]

The children of Kunhegyes endured the hunger and enjoyed the freedom for a month. On 16 June "the gendarmes came and told us that in two hours we had to be ready to leave."[26] This was the next step. In Ezner's case, the route was from her house (in Abádszalók) to a ghetto (in Kunhegyes) and from the ghetto to a sugar factory (in Szolnok). Her family was driven from their home to a hut, still in a residential area, and from thence to an industrial property on the outskirts of town. In other words, as András Garzó, who with his family was sent out of the ghetto of Debrecen into a brick factory on the city limits, observed, "Brick was transported by train and we (no longer human beings but mere merchandise) were to be transported by train too."[27] Compelled to move ever farther from civic life, they were governed by an itinerary and time schedule that would bring them to their death. For Ezner and her relatives, the sugar factory in Szolnok was the last stop in proximity to the society in which they had lived. It was from there that they were deported.

Before they went on transport, however, the Jews in the short-term ghettos were robbed. At each stage of their removal from their former community and country, their possessions were plundered. Physically tortured and emotionally racked, the last pengő, jewelry, and other valuables were extorted from them. When the Hungarian gendarmes announced that the inhabitants of the ghetto of Kunhegyes had two hours before departure, Mária Ezner's mother, like all the other mothers and fathers, faced an impossible task. They were told that they could take whatever they could carry, but "my mother, with two little children, what could she pack? She was so nervous, because this was the second step. She couldn't know what we should bring with us. It was not important, what we could bring. We had to give it up anyway. But they did not know, and they thought it was very important to pack so carefully."[28] And then the brutal process of depredation began:

We were taken to a great empty field, and everybody had to sit with his baggage, and the gendarmes came to see what we had with us. And then we heard the first things. They took our toothbrushes from us. And my mother stood and said, "Toothbrushes we shouldn't bring?"

And the gendarme said, "You won't need it. You won't need it."

It was the first time. We couldn't understand it.

The wedding ring was pulled off, and my mother said, "In the regulations it said that we could have it."

It was in the regulations, also, that we could have a hundred pengö for each person, and that was taken too.

And my mother said, "But it said in the regulations: one hundred. . . ."

But the gendarme said, "You won't need it anymore."

We stood there, in this empty field, every family with its baggage. We stood there on the empty field, and my mother's handbag was taken. And she cried out, "Our papers, our personal papers!"

And then the gendarme opened her handbag and ripped our personal papers, and the text was, "You won't need it anymore."

And then we were beaten. A little house stood at the end of this field. We didn't understand. We didn't take notice of it. Then we heard names being called of people who had to go to this house. In this house sat several civilian men. They were "detectives," and they asked us where we had hidden our gold, silver, porcelain, and whatever. And who were our Christian friends to whom we had given our valuables. My mother was beaten on the soles of her feet with rubber truncheons; afterwards she could not walk. . . . I was slapped on my face and asked, because I was old enough, I must have helped hide the valuables. I remember this well.

It made me so hot, and I thought, "I hate you, I hate you." Only one thing: "I hate you." And I didn't give an answer. I was strong in my hatred.

Then they sent me to a midwife. That was miserable. The midwives examined women and young girls, maybe they had something in their vaginas, a gold ring or so. I had never seen such a table or such a chair. My mother had to lie on it and she was examined. Then I was examined, and my mother cried, "Take care! She is a child!" And I don't know what I thought of those women.

We left, and my mother limped with her arm around my shoulders. She said that we should send my little sister away from us, and she should say that she doesn't know her name, so that she wouldn't be beaten. And we sent her away, but she didn't understand why, and she wanted to stay with us because she understood that something very bad was happening and it was natural that she wanted to be with her nearest persons in the world. I whispered, "Go away, go away, go away!" . . .

It was the 16th of June 1944. It was a very hot day. On the great Hungarian plain it can get as hot as thirty to forty degrees (86–104F]. We were on the plain, and each one of us had on his winter coat. In our family our mother said, and in every family the mothers said, "Take your winter coat. We do not know where we will be brought, and your winter coat is very important." So we had our winter coats and we didn't dare take them off. It was forty degrees, and the whole day we sat by our little things that they allowed us to bring. We sat all day and names were called of men and women to be beaten.[29]

Late in the evening, the Jews of Kunhegyes were ordered to board the train wagons. They did not know their destination until they arrived at the sugar processing plant on the outskirts of Szolnok. Jews from the entire region were collected there, and for nearly a fortnight 4,666 people were held in the factory. There were no toilets, no drinking water, and nothing to eat. There was no room in the factory itself for such a large number of people, so many (the Ezner family among them) remained in the yard. "It began to rain, and my mother said, 'If a God exists, it is with them.' We sat down in the mud and it rained and it rained and it rained." Nevertheless, people who, because of the restrictions on travel for Jews, had not been able to see each other for some time, searched for their friends and relatives in the crowd. "It was a moving dunghill," Ezner recalled. "I remember the circulation of people," looking for each other and wanting to get news.

In Szolnok too the Jews were subject to the search for valuables. As in Kunhegyes, lists were made up and names called. In the factory the Ezners were reunited with the children's grandmother and she, a sixty-four-year-old woman, was "investigated" by the Hungarian "dectectives." "She was beaten and at the end thrown out through the door. We

found her lying with her face in the mud. She didn't know us anymore."
Ezner was outraged and bitter. A young adolescent, unencumbered by a
parent's desire to protect a family or an older person's prudence or
patience, she had no long-term goals or strategy, just rage. "'Why do we
allow this? Why don't we go with our ten nails against the guards!'" she
demanded of her mother. "And my mother said, 'Psst!' And I thought,
'The first rioter will be shot. The second will be shot. But they haven't
ammunition for five thousand people. We should go, and we children
should be first. Why do we allow this!'"[30]

The Jews in the sugar processing plant in Szolnok were deported
durig the last days of June. One transport went to Auschwitz, the other
to Strasshof, not far from Vienna. Rumors that this would happen went
the rounds of the factory, and Ezner's mother took them seriously. She
heard that the appointed Elder of the Jews in the plant had drawn up
lists for the transports, and she went to see him to try to get her family
on the train for Austria and not Poland.

> I said it was the same and she shouldn't take a step. I was a fatalist at
> that time. I am now. But if she wouldn't have taken that step, I
> wouldn't sit here. . . . She went to the Elder of our community and she
> said she had heard about a list to Austria, and if it were possible she
> would like to go to Austria; she speaks German, the children speak
> German.
>   The old man told her that this list was for the prominent people in
> the Jewish community, and we were only three-days' Jews, we were
> not leaders. My father wasn't a religious man, and we were not
> prominent in this Jewish community.
>   My mother said she had heard that the list was also for Jews who
> paid high taxes, and could he deny that we were paying a great tax in
> Abádszalók?
>   This old man said, "Na, good; but not the grandmother." . . .
>   We didn't know if [we were really on] the transport for Austria or
> for Poland, and we didn't know the difference. My mother thought
> Poland would be worse; the temperature was harder and the Poles
> antisemites. In Austria would be a better climate. Maybe, if we
> worked we could survive.[31]

András Garzó's father faced the same dilemma as Ezner's mother
when his family was to be deported from the brick factory in Debrecen.
There too transports were sent to Austria and to Poland; the first two
went to Strasshof and the third and last to Auschwitz. What they did not
know, and what they could not know, was that conditions would be less

harsh in Strasshof than in Auschwitz. Of the 21,000 Jews deported to Strasshof from Hungary, approximately 75 percent survived, including children. Lethal as was a 25 percent mortality rate, the comparable statistics for Hungarian Jews who were shipped to Auschwitz tell an even more bitter and bloody story. It was there that the vast majority were sent, and it was there that nearly all were killed. For older people and children up to the age of twelve or fourteen (Ezner, her sister, Garzó) there was practically no hope at all, and for the rest only a very slim chance. Indeed, of the nearly 435,000 Hungarian Jews deported to Auschwitz in less than eight weeks, from 15 May to 8 July 1944, 400,000 were murdered immediately.[32]

When Ezner's mother and Garzó's father made their decisions, however, they had no way of knowing what their choices meant. They had been evicted from their homes, robbed of their possessions, and beaten and abused. But they had not yet experienced murder, let alone systematic murder, and even though they had heard rumors about it, such tales, indeed such a concept, was literally incredible, not to be believed. Furthermore, they did not know and could not imagine what each destination would represent. And so it is not surprising that although it was not difficult in Debrecen to get on the list for the Austrian transports, Garzó's father chose not to do so. In Garzó's memory, "the first transport may have been organized on the basis of who wanted to go. My family was not very clever. We wanted to remain. We hoped maybe something would happen." They did not believe that the Soviet army would liberate Debrecen (which is in the east of Hungary) in time, or even that the Soviets would advance so near that the deportations would cease. Garzó's father simply thought it best for them to stay where they were as long as possible. "The hospital personnel went with the first or second transport, but my father wouldn't go with the hospital people, he wanted to remain in Debrecen. My mother's family went, and only we, my father's family, remained for the last transport. He had no real hopes. He just thought that we shouldn't move. 'Let us remain. Let us remain here.' "[33] It was a reasonable decision, as valid and logical as the decision taken by Ezner's mother. But for Ezner, "the sugar factory was the worst."[34] For Garzó, much, much worse was yet to come.

The Ezners and the Garzós were unusual in that they had the opportunity to consider which destination would be less sinister for their families; after all, only six or seven trains from Hungary were routed to Strasshof. But their situations were absolutely typical in that they, within the extraordinarily confined parameters of their existence under Nazi rule, made the best decisions they could. They were victims, they were the subject of abject cruelty, for the Germans mere grist for the murder mills. But they were not objects. They were autonomous human beings and not the merchandise the Germans supposed them to be. They made choices and took decisions. Tragically, the machinery of death worked so well that the outcome of those choices and decisions had nothing to do with their insight or perspicacity, and everything to do with fortune and luck.

By the end of the summer of 1944, nearly all the ghettos of eastern Europe had been liquidated, their inhabitants deported and dead. With the Soviet army approaching, the Germans became frantic to finish the task they had undertaken. The last of these ghettos of infamy, the Łódź ghetto, fell victim to their frenzy. The final dissolution of the ghetto in Łódź began in June 1944. At the behest of the Germans, on Friday, 16 June 1944, the Elder of the Jews of Łódź, Mordechai Chaim Rumkowski, issued a proclamation calling for "voluntary registration for labor outside the ghettos." The authors of the clandestine *Chronicle of the Łódź Ghetto*, the members of the ghetto's Department of Archives who surreptitiously compiled this record, noted that "the proclamation still speaks of voluntary registration. But . . . presumably the entire apparatus that has always operated in such situations will be set in motion immediately." They feared that "the actual goal is multiple, large-scale shipments of workers outside the ghetto."[35] They were correct. Voluntary registration was superseded by compulsory deportation. For four weeks pressure was brought to bear on workshop managers; they were required to compile lists of people who were not essential to production. In an entry of 19 June the *Chronicle* authors explained that "the factories have been ordered to make available a certain percentage of their workers." The first transport of 600 people was to leave on Wednesday the 21st, but "because the requisitioned freight cars will not be available it was rescheduled for the 23rd."[36] A pall fell over the ghetto. On 25 June the authors recorded that "twenty-five transports have been announced. Everyone knows that the situation is serious, that the existence of the ghettos is in jeopardy. . . . Nearly every ghetto dweller is affected this time. Everyone is losing a relative, a friend, a roommate, a colleague."[37] During the next three weeks some people volunteered, enticed by the prospect of leaving the misery of the ghetto or by the purchase price of their own bodies as a substitute for another on the list: "three loaves of bread, a half kilogram of margarine, one pound of sugar."[38] Many more sought desperately to avoid the fate doled out to them and cajoled those in power to delete their names. Others neither volunteered nor hid; they went when ordered to do so. In all, 7,196 people were deported from Łódź to the death camp in Chelmno. Then,

on 15 July, "toward noon, the Eldest was instructed to halt the resettlement." According to the authors of the *Chronicle*, "Never has the ghetto
been so happy. . . . People embraced in the streets, kissed in the workshops and departments: 'The resettlement's over!' "[39]

As the authors observed, "no one gave a second thought to whether
this was only a brief interruption of or a final halt to the transports."[40] It
was, in the end, merely a respite. On Wednesday, 2 August 1944 the
final deportation order, signed by Rumkowski, was posted on the walls
of the ghetto. "By the order of the *Oberbürgermeister* von Litzmannstadt [Mayor of Łódź] the ghetto must be moved to a new location," it
proclaimed. "Factory workers will travel with their families. . . . Family
members of factory workers should join in their transport. In that way
separation of families will be avoided. There will be separate notices
concerning the workshops that are to be moved in the next phase [trans-
port]. . . ."[41] Sara Grossman-Weil was twenty-five by the time she was
deported from Łódź. She had married in the ghetto, and she left with her
husband Manny, his brother, sister-in-law, and their two children, and
her mother and father-in-law.

> We were talking about *Übersiedlung* [resettlement], transports will be
> going out from the ghetto to a very large place which will be estab-
> lished as a tremendous workshop, because the Third Reich needed
> our work. We will be organized in such a way, we were told; the
> work has to be very efficient, and since we are skilled, we will do fine.
> The families will keep together, and we will work for the Third
> Reich. . . .
>   "It's just a question of *Übersiedlung*," of transporting us from one
> place to another. And we believed it. I believed it. I am sure Manny
> believed it, and so did his family. And so did my family. . . .
>   People were going, people were leaving. . . . Suddenly we heard
> rumors that they were put in a concentration camp. We didn't have
> any details, but evidently someone came back, or escaped, or heard
> that it's not as they are promising. But since we didn't have anything
> to go by, or to hold on to, and we did not have any choice, we did go
> too.
>   We went with the [tailoring] workshop which was managed by my
> brother-in-law. We did not go with my workshop or with Manny's
> because we wanted to prolong it. We wanted to put off leaving the
> ghetto because we did not want to separate from the family. . . .
>   I was in a dilemma. Should we stay, or should I go with the Gross-
> mans? . . . I didn't know what to do. I wanted to go with my husband
> and I wanted to stay with my parents. I was torn. I was angered. I

didn't want to make the decision.[42]

The decision Sara Grossman-Weil had to make illuminated the boundaries of the choices available to her. Her central concern throughout the nearly five years she had endured the ghetto was to be with her family, to keep her family together. As she said, in the ghetto "we were still in our homes. Whether it was a room two by two or twenty by two, we were in our homes and with the family."[43] It was this principle, this deeply felt sentiment, which made it impossible for her to leave for Palestine as she was supposed to have done in the summer of 1939 or, later, to accept the help of friends to pass as a gentile on the Aryan side. And so she had to choose: to part from her parents and brothers, or her husband and in-laws. For Grossman-Weil, the deportation order meant the obliteration of her construct of what would be possible to achieve, maintain, or manage. And that order had been signed, not by a German, but by a Jew, Chaim Rumkowski, the Elder of the Ghetto of Łódź. It was the last of the proclamations and orders Rumkowski issued during his five-year reign. The fiction of autonomy, the fiction of negotiating power, had come to an end. The idea that Rumkowski could negotiate with the Germans on behalf of the Jews, to protect the community, was seen at last as the illusion it always had been. Adam Czerniaków, the Elder of the Ghetto in Warsaw, had come to that realization two years earlier. When asked to sign a deportation order which included children, he understood that what he thought he had been able to do as head of the Judenrat had been mere manipulation, a convenience for the Germans. Unable to protect the children, he had no power, and no purpose anymore. He committed suicide the following day, 23 July 1942. "I am powerless, . . . I can no longer bear all this," his note explained.[44] Rumkowski assisted in the liquidation of his own community; Czerniaków preferred to kill himself.

To be powerless to save, defend, or shield the children was, for Czerniaków, unconscionable and, ultimately, unacceptable. Indeed, protection of the children was a central question which plagued the history of the Polish ghettos. There were two aspects to this infernal problem. First, there was the unbearable issue of how to respond to the Germans' demands for bodies for "resettlement." When Czerniaków was told that children were to be included in the resettlement action, he refused to sign the order and chose to commit suicide. But other Judenrat chairmen reasoned differently. For instance, both Jacob Gens, the Elder of the Vilna Ghetto, and Chaim Rumkowski, the Elder of the Łódź Ghetto, were given to understand by the Germans that the labor of the Jews could be essential to the occupying power, and they transformed their

25   The Grossman family, Łódź, early 1920s: Mr and Mrs Grossman, Beniek (the baby), Mr Grossmann's mother, Menek (seated), Adek (standing behind Menek), and Fawek. Upon arrival in Auschwitz in 1944, Mrs Grossman took her son Adek's five-year-old daughter, Mirka, in her arms and was sent with her to the left, directly to the gas chambers.

communities into urban work camps. They believed that survival of at least part of the community would be achieved through productivity. Given this policy, how were they to fill the Nazi Moloch's quotas for resettlement? In general, the Germans simply presented a figure to the Councils, and it was their lot to decide who was to go and who would be permitted to remain. (The option of refusing to participate was infrequently exercised for fear that if the Germans undertook the task themselves they would proceed with greater brutality and round up larger numbers of people.) If, as Gens and Rumkowski maintained, the ghetto population was a labor force, those unable to work were the obvious candidates for deportation: the aged and ill, and infants and children.[45]

Who was to be protected – and at the sacrifice of whom? Gens made his decision. "We shall not give the children, they are our future. We shall not give young women. . . . We shall not give [our workers], for we need them here ourselves."[46] He chose instead the elderly and ill. On 17 July 1942 an *Aktion* was carried out in Vilna; its target was one hundred aged or chronically ill people. Gens defended his course, claiming that "he had rejected a German demand to seize children, but that he had to obey their order to transfer the old and ill who were unable to look after themselves."[47] Three months later he faced a similar crisis of equal ethical and even greater numerical proportions. Many towns in the part of Belorussia adjacent to the Lithuanian border had been annexed in March 1942 to the administration of, as the Germans then called it, "Vilna-Land." The ghettos in those towns were liquidated and their inhabitants shot (as in the case of Kiemeliskes) or transferred to larger ghettos which had been established in four towns: Oszmiana, Svencionys, Mikaliskes, and Salos. In the early autumn of 1942 Gens was given orders to organize these ghettos on the Vilna model. By October 1942 some 4,000 Jews were concentrated in Oszmiana. Then, in the middle of the month, the Germans demanded that the Vilna ghetto police round up 1,500 "unproductive" ghetto inmates. In the end 406, and not 1,500, old and sick people were delivered to the Germans. At a meeting Gens convened in Vilna on 27 October to report on the Oszmiana action and his participation in it, he said:

My friends, I have invited you here today in order to tell you one of the most terrible tragedies of Jewish life – when Jews lead Jews to death. . . . A week ago Weiss [the SS officer who served as a liaison between the Gestapo and a volunteer Lithuanian extermination squad] came and ordered us on behalf of the SD [*Sicherheitsdienst*] to proceed to Oshmyany. He said that there were about 4,000 Jews in the ghetto there and that it was impossible that such a number remain there, that the ghetto must be reduced, that the people for whom the Germans had no need should be selected out and shot. First priority are the women whose husbands had been caught last year by the abductors, and their children. Second priority, families with many children. . . .

We had been ordered to select at least 1,500 people. We answered that we could not fill such a quota. We haggled, . . . The truth is that 406 elderly were collected at Oshmyany and were handed over.

When Weiss first came and demanded women and children, I told him that instead he should take old people. He replied: "The old ones will die off anyway during the winter, and we are obliged to reduce the ghetto population now." The Jewish police rescued all those who had to live. Those whose days were close to the end in any event had to go. . . .

I don't wish to dirty my hands and send my policemen to do this contemptible work. But I say to you today, it is my duty to sully my hands, as the Jewish people is passing through its most terrible period now. At the moment when five million are no more, it is incumbent upon us to save the strong and the young – not only in age but also in

26   Another attempt to save the children: healthy orphans hidden in a hospital in the ghetto of Kovno (Lithuania) under the pretext of illness.

spirit, and not to play with sentiments.[48]

A month earlier Rumkowski confronted the same horror. Łódź, like Vilna, was a work ghetto. And those who were not registered as part of the labor force, children under ten and adults over sixty-five years of age, were demanded of him. "In his speech of September 4, 1942," the *Chronicle* reported, "the Chairman announced that, by order of the authorities, about 25,000 Jews under the age of 10 and over 65 must be resettled out of the ghetto. . . . It was said that had this action encountered any difficulties or resistance, the German authorities would have stepped in."[49] Rumkowski asked the assembled crowd, "Should we comply and do it, or should we leave it for others to do?" But he had resolved his dilemma. "We all, myself and my closest associates, have come to the conclusion that despite the horrible responsibility, we have to accept the evil order. I have to perform this bloody operation myself; I simply must cut off the limbs to save the body! I have to take away the children, because otherwise others will also be taken, God forbid."[50] Some 15,000 people were deported, the children amongst them.

If the childless Rumkowski could be seen as a man who had evinced disdain or utter disregard for children, his decision could be interpreted as pure monstrosity: the abnormal reasoning of an abnormal man. But in his role as chairman of the ghetto, Rumkowski had sought to protect the Jewish children of Łódź. The authors of the *Chronicle* were extremely diffident in their treatment of Rumkowski, and their analyses of him cannot be seen as critical judgments. Yet even they would not have described the chairman's warm sentiments towards children in such detail had he not been commonly perceived as their friend. In mid-January 1942 they observed:

> Everyone in the ghetto knows that children and young people are the apple of Chairman Rumkowski's eye. His pre-war activities left him with an excellent reputation as a most sensitive patron and protector of children; that reputation is directly linked to his curent activity in the ghetto. The manifold child-care institutions that have been developed in the ghetto with a genuine sense of reverence and such talent clearly correspond to the ghetto leader's wishes; they are and they will remain monuments to his ardent love for children and young people. As for the Chairman's relation to young people, there is no doubt that he has established and maintained both an elementary and secondary school system that will stand out like golden threads in the history of the ghetto.[51]

Furthermore, during the months preceding the September 1942 order, Rumkowski had striven fervently to employ children over the age of ten. As members of the work force he would be better able to shield them from the Germans' jaws.[52]

There was, in other words, a second aspect to this wretched and terrible dilemma of child protection in the ghetto. The first question was where they stood on the list of sacrificial candidates, the second was what place they were assigned in ghetto society. The first was a decision taken in the face of external (German) demands, the second within the context of ghetto conditions. Incarcerated in tightly cramped quarters, sequestered from normal economic activity, with little or no access to the rudimentary necessities of life (food, clothing, shelter, fuel, medical care), the Jews in the long-term ghettos of eastern Europe were forced to decide how to distribute the resources they had. In Warsaw, for example, 30 percent of the city's population squeezed into 2.4 percent of its area. The ghetto covered just 425 acres of which 375 were devoted to residential use. With the influx of refugees from smaller cities and towns in the Warsaw district, the ghetto population swelled to 445,000 in March 1941, or 128,000 people per square kilometer and over nine persons per room. A mere 4 percent of the city streets were included in the ghetto (73 out of 1,800), and the majority did not run their entire length; a piece was in the ghetto while the remainder was in Aryan territory.[53] The rations the Germans allowed were similarly unequally distributed. The value of the daily food allotment was 2,613 calories for Germans, 699 for gentile Poles, and 184 for Jewish Poles. As the historian Yisrael Gutman has pointed out, "the Jews were victims of a double hardship: they were the most discriminated against under the system of rationing, and the nutritional value of the ration apportioned to them was only 15 percent of the minimum daily requirement, so that there was little chance of surviving on the official ration alone. On the other hand, the Jews were prevented from acquiring food on the free market."[54] Given these conditions it is not surprising that, as the Joint Distribution Committee reported at the end of 1940, 1.25 million people, or 57 percent of the Jewish population in Nazi-occupied Poland (that is, both the Government-General and the areas which had been incorporated into the Reich) needed social assistance.[55] The exigencies of the situation presented a dilemma to the ghetto leadership: should the money, food, clothes, and fuel they received through taxation of the ghetto inhabitants and, most importantly, from the American philanthropy, the Joint Distribution Committee (which underwrote nearly all the expenses of relief work in the ghettos), be distributed equally, or should the community choose specific target groups to support and sustain for the duration of the war?[56] With a basic food ration of 184 calories per person per day it was clear that if the relief resources were equally divided, everyone would starve to death slowly. If, however, one segment of the population were to be fed adequately, the community would survive through these representatives. In short, if the survival of the Jewish people were to be the basis for decisions on resource allocation, the most rational policy would have been to support young adults eighteen to twenty-five years old. They were self-sufficient, little afflicted by illness, already educated, fertile, and had stamina. To have chosen this course would have meant to abandon the elderly, handicapped, and ill, and to have disowned the infants and children. And to some extent this occurred, if not as a matter of clearly articulated policy, then as a result of a lack of policy to the contrary. Refugees, the destitute, and the elderly died disproportionately. To have chosen this policy, however, also would have implied the acceptance of the Nazi philosophy of race. It would have reduced the issue of survival to one of biological continuity: breeding. It would have negated the idea of a community, of a people. In the end, they held fast to the importance of protecting the young; it was essential to their sense of values, to their tradition, and to their hope for a better tomorrow.

Children were supported in a number of ways, especially in the early ghetto period before mass deportations began. One of the most important efforts to sustain child life was the institution of food services and policies for their benefit. In about half of the thirty-two communities in Eastern Upper Silesia the Jewish authorities provided two meals a day to children four to eight years old. In other towns, children were fed once a day, and elsewhere milk and other nourishing food was provided to infants.[57] In the enormous ghettos of Łódź and Warsaw the numbers of young people in need were greater, and the support measures correspondingly more comprehensive. Policy was vital in Łódź, where an extremely centralized bureaucracy subsumed nearly all social welfare work, and the importance of children was reflected in the fact that they received the same staple rations as adults. For instance, according to Proclamation No. 200 of the Eldest of the Jews, as of 24 January 1941 "every ghetto resident will receive 400 grams of bread."[58] Milk, constantly in short supply, was reserved for children under three and they were entitled to 200 centiliters a day. Butter too was for children alone. Furthermore, when unexpected nutrients came into the ghetto, it was the children to whom they were allocated. As an entry in the *Chronicle* of 3 March 1941 makes clear, pitifully little was available and it was usually of poor quality. Yet children were specially designated to receive what little there was. "The first of March brought the populace a pleasant surprise in the form of supplement food rations, vegetables being especially plentiful. Equally pleasant surprises were the denatured alcohol and the vinegar, neither of which had been available for a very long time. Moreover, the populace received sausage and meat, and the coal allotment came to 20 kilograms this time. In addition, the youngest ghetto dwellers each received one cauliflower."[59]

The political structure of the Warsaw ghetto was not so monolithic as Rumkowski's organization in Łódź, and in Warsaw a number of Jewish self-help societies were active independent of the central bureaucracy. The Jewish Organization for Social Care (ZTOS) served as an umbrella to coordinate the activities of a number of philanthropic, social welfare, and self-help enterprises. The most important of these were the already extant CENTOS (the National Society for the Care of Orphans), TOZ or OSE (the Society for the Preservation of Health), ORT (the Organization for Rehabilitation and Training), and the new grass-roots network of house committees, representatives appointed by the tenants of each apartment block in the ghetto. All of these organizations undertook special child welfare projects, but CENTOS and the house committee network were most involved with the younger inhabitants of the Jewish quarter. CENTOS, for instance (according to its director-general, Adolf

Berman), "maintained 20 day centers in which thousands of children received food and care during half of the day; 20 food kitchens, especially
for children, in which food was served to thousands of poor children
every day; and 30 day centers for children and youths in the refugee
houses."[60] The day care centers and soup kitchens served a double function: it was there that children received both food and education. In
Warsaw, as in the whole Government-General even prior to the establishment of the ghetto, Polish schools were closed to Jewish children and
Jewish schools were banned under the pretext that they would serve as a
breeding ground for infectious disease. Unlike in Łódź, which was in
that part of Poland which had been incorporated into the Reich and
where German authorities permitted a marginally normal school system,
elementary education continued to be forbidden in the Warsaw ghetto
until September 1941 and secondary schooling was prohibited entirely.[61]
Thus, the educational activities undertaken in the CENTOS centers were
clandestine. "Under the cloak of the children's kitchens and homes of
CENTOS," Emmanuel Ringelblum and Adolf Berman wrote to the Yiddish Scientific Institute (YIVO), Yiddish Pen Club, and a quartet of Jewish writers in New York from their hiding place in the Aryan district of
Warsaw on 1 March 1944, "a net of underground schools of various
ideologies was spread."[62] A spectrum of Jewish affiliations was represented: CYSHO, the secular, Yiddish-language Central Jewish School
Organization; Tarbut, the east European Hebrew educational and cultural organization; Agudat Israel, the World Organization of Orthodox
Jews; the Poalei Zion movement; and the Yavneh movement, which was
connected with the Mizrachi party.[63]

The CENTOS sites were not the only places where clandestine classes
were held. All over the ghetto, students and teachers met secretly to continue the process of education. As we have seen so often before, to go to
school, to persevere with one's studies, was a basic tenet of childhood. It
was an essential activity that embodied the principle of normality: life
would go on, there would be a future after this madness. Whether in hiding, in transit camps, or in the ghetto, many children wished to continue
to learn, and in extraordinary cicumstances did so. In her diary-memoir,
Winter in the Morning, the fourteen-year-old Janina Bauman explained
that she and a group of her friends in the Warsaw ghetto contacted some
teachers they knew and set up classes. Her ten-year-old sister Sophie also
joined a study group. In the early spring of 1941 Bauman's uncle, with
whom she, her mother, and sister lived, became ill with typhus. Everyone in the flat was forced to remain indoors during the weeks of quarantine. When he recovered and she was allowed to return to school she was
delighted.

16 April 1941, evening
Freedom, freedom at last! Everything was fun today, even sitting on this awful settee in Ala's room, squeezed between Zula and Hanka. Even the maths. I've missed quite a lot, by the way, but Hanka says she'll help me make it up in no time. They all seemed extremely pleased when I appeared out of the blue. Renata was so surprised that she kissed me, forgetting all sanitary precautions. Nina said she had rather expected me to die from typhus, the silly cow.

Lots of news. . . . Irena wanted to join our group, but eight is enough, said the girls, and flatly turned her down. So she asked the teachers to let her join the boys. They didn't mind and the boys were delighted, at least she says so. They are nine all together now. Could be nice to meet them – same teachers, same problems.[64]

Important as this was to the young people, it was equally essential to the teachers, who had no way to earn a living and faced fast approaching penury. The educator Chaim Kaplan discussed this problem in personal terms in his diary entry of 14 December 1939. It was, as he remarked, "contrary to my custom" to note his own circumstances in his journal, but they reflected a larger reality which applied to many others.

The unemployed Jewish teachers have found a way to partially save themselves from starving. They got together and organized small groups of children who come to the teacher's home to be taught for two or three hours. Hundreds of teachers support themselves in this fashion. It is possible that the ban against study also applies to such small groups, and if questions were asked they would have to be stopped. But no one asks questions. The matter is done quietly, underhandedly. There is no other solution. I too want to make a living, and I have organized three small groups from among my pupils and meet with them in my apartment. Two women teachers from my school teach them general subjects twenty hours a week, and I teach them Hebrew subjects. For this purpose I have set aside a special room and have placed in it five desks for ten pupils. From this I support myself.[65]

The ban on study did apply to such small groups. To continue to learn and to teach posed a mortal threat. Yet both pupils and teachers persevered. No one took the matter lightly; everyone was committed. Mary Berg turned fifteen a few weeks after Poland capitulated in September 1939. Her family was from Łódź, but they felt that as her mother had American citizenship they would be safer in Warsaw in the shadow

of the American embassy. Berg continued her studies there. In a diary
entry written on 12 July 1940, seven months after Kaplan's discussion of
his own situation and four months prior to the institution of the closed
ghetto, Berg described the dangers and difficulties of underground education. "There are now a great number of illegal schools," Berg reported, "and they are multiplying every day. People are studying in
attics and cellars, and every subject is included in the curriculum, even
Latin and Greek. Two such schools were discovered by the Germans
sometime in June; later we heard that the teachers were shot on the spot,
and that the pupils had been sent to a concentration camp near Lublin
[Majdanek]." Many of Berg's fellow students and teachers from her
gymnasium in Łódź had fled to Warsaw, and they resumed their classes
there. Because of her mother's American citizenship, Berg's flat was relatively safe, and twice a week her group met in her home. "We study all
the regular subjects, and have even organized a chemical and physics
laboratory using glasses and pots from our kitchen, instead of test tubes
and retorts. Special attention is paid to foreign languages, chiefly English
and Hebrew." The situation seemed to engender a special intensity and
warmth. "The teachers put their whole heart and soul into their teaching, and all the pupils study with exemplary diligence. There are no bad
pupils. The illegal character of the teaching, the danger that threatens us
every minute, fills us all with a strange earnestness. The old distance between teachers and pupils has vanished, we feel like comrades-in-arms
responsible to each other."[66]

With few textbooks, little writing paraphernalia, and many risks and
obstacles, the business of learning went on, even after the ghetto was
established. Finally, permission was granted to "train" children, presumably in a trade which could be exploited by the Germans. The ghetto
students and teachers took advantage of this opportunity. This was a development of great interest to Kaplan and he reported on it in his diary
on 15 February 1941:

> Jewish children learn in secret. In back rooms, on long benches near a
> table, little schoolchildren sit and learn what it's like to be Marranos
> [Jews who practiced their religion clandestinely]. Before the ghetto
> was created, when the Nazis were common in our streets, we trem-
> bled at the sound of every driven leaf; our hearts turned to water at
> the sound of any knock on the door. But with the creation of the
> ghetto, the situation improved somewhat. . . . In addition, to a certain
> extent we do have a semblance of permission. The Self-Aid is
> authorized to open and support "training points" for Jewish children.
> We are allowed to feed, direct, and train them; but to educate them is

forbidden. But since training is permitted, we allow ourselves education as well. In time of danger the children learn to hide their books.
Jewish children are clever – when they set off to acquire forbidden
learning they hide their books and notebooks between their trousers
and their stomachs, then button their jackets and coats. This is a
tried-and-true method, a kind of smuggling that is not readily
detected.[67]

Warsaw was not the only ghetto in which children were deprived of
schooling, of course. In Radom, for example, where a double ghetto was
instituted early in 1940, one school eventually did function. It was held
in three rooms of the Old Talmud Torah, and three shifts of children
were taught each day.[68] This obviously was insufficient, and most young
people carried on their education in private, although there too it was
prohibited. The nine-year-old Hanna Kent-Sztarkman had very informal
lessons for a brief period, but they were important to her. Sztarkman,
her mother, and older brother Heniek were refugees in Radom; like
Mary Berg they had fled from Łódź. "Since the Germans decided to
divide Poland into a protectorate [the Government-General], and part
include in the Reich, and our city, Łódź, was supposed to be part of the
Reich, my parents felt that perhaps life in the protectorate would be
easier," she explained. "The town that my mother lived in, and where
my grandmother and my aunt lived, Radom, was part of the protectorate, so we decided that we'd slowly move there. Well, Heniek left first,
then my mother and I; it was in December. My father and my sister were
supposed to follow as soon as they sold whatever they could."[69] In the
end, they did not manage to leave Łódź before the ghetto was closed and
they were unsuccessful in their attempt to smuggle themselves out, so the
two parts of the family were not, and indeed were never, reunited.

Sztarkman's mother and brother went to work in Radom; she, a nine-
year old, stayed home. "I did not go to school," she recalled. "I read any
book that I could get a hold of, but of course, we didn't have a library."
Fortunately, another family whom they knew from Łódź had also come
to Radom. "There were four daughters . . . one of [them] and my sister
had graduated from gymnasium together. The youngest, who was a
couple of years older than I am, took me and another girl and she would
teach us a little bit of mathematics and things, while you could. Later on,
even this couldn't work out. You just didn't. I read a lot, that was just
about it." This was a terrible loss to her. It was much more than simply a
way of passing the time. "Living is hoping, and I kept hoping that somehow something will happen and the war will end. One just had to be
strong enough to wait and I took each day the way it came. . . .

What worried me was: will I ever be able to catch up with my education. It is funny, but this is what I was talking to Heniek about – will I ever be able to catch up with my education!? In such a horrible situation; yet I tried to keep some normalcy, to look forward to something."[70] In far away Vilna, the fourteen-year-old Yitskhok Rudashevski agreed. To go to school provided a structure for normality; its absence meant a void and a dead end. On 19 September 1942, fifteen months after Vilna fell to the German army (24 June 1941) and a year after the institution of the ghetto (6 September 1941), Rudashevski confided his despair to his diary. "It is cold and sad. When in the world will we get back to our studies? When I used to go to my lessons, I knew how to divide the days, and the days would fly, and now they drag by for me grayly and sadly. Oh, how dreary and sad it is to sit locked up in a ghetto." A few weeks later (5 October), his gymnasium classes began and Rudashevski was delighted. "Finally I have lived to see the day. Today we go to school. The day passed quite differently. Lessons, subjects. . . . There is a happy spirit in school. . . . My own life is shaping up in quite a different way! We waste less time, the day is divided and flies by very quickly. . . . Yes, that is how it should be in the ghetto, the day should fly by and we should not waste time."[71]

Classes were not the sole mode of education in the long-term ghettos of eastern Europe. The larger ghettos, like Warsaw, Łódź, and Vilna, had a rich cultural life during the early period of Nazi occupation, and some young people were able to take advantage of the lectures and concerts which proliferated.[72] More important to the daily existence of the young, however, were the children's clubs and youth groups which played an essential role in the intellectual and social lives of many youngsters. In Vilna, for instance, elementary school aged children participated in clubs that had sections for crafts, painting, drama, literature, history, geography, and sports. Young people of gymnasium age had their own youth club, with separate circles devoted to drama, literature, philosophy, history, mathematics, and natural science. For Yitskhok Rudashevski, as for so many other ghetto children, the club was a mainstay of life. "Finally, the club too was opened," he wrote in his diary on Monday, 5 October 1942.[73] Two days later, he remarked:

Life has become a little more interesting. The club work has begun. We have groups for literature, natural science. After leaving class at 7:30 I go immediately to the club. It is gay there, we have a good time and return home evenings in a large crowd. The days are short, it is dark in the street, and our bunch leaves the club. There is a racket, a commotion. Policemen shout at us but we do not listen to them.[74]

Rudashevski and his companions became completely engrossed in the club activities. "The days pass quickly," he observed a few weeks later. "After eating I go to the club. Here we enjoy ourselves a little. . . . Our youth works and does not perish." Rudashevski was particularly interested in the history (especially the ghetto history division), nature, and literary (ghetto folklore division) circles. He frequently noted his commitment to and attendance at these groups, and he described in some detail the projects they undertook. He became absorbed in the work, and engaged emotionally as well as intellectually. The vitality of their enterprises clearly emerges from his depictions. "The second section of the history group, ghetto history, is also busy. We are investigating the history of Courtyard Shavler 4," he explained on 22 October.[75]

> For this purpose questionnaires have been distributed among the members, with questions that have to be asked of the courtyard residents. . . . The questions are divided into four parts: questions relating to the period of Polish, Soviet and German rule (up to the ghetto), and in the ghetto. The residents answer in different ways. . . . I got a taste of a historian's task. I sit at the table and ask questions and record the greatest sufferings with cold objectivity. I write, I probe into details, and I do not realize at all that I am probing into wounds, and the one who answers me – indifferent to it: two sons and a husband taken away – the sons Monday the husband Thursday. . . . And this horror, this tragedy is formulated by me in three words, coldly and dryly. I become absorbed in thought, and the words stare out of the paper crimson with blood.[76]

He reflected on the importance of this work two weeks later:

> Today we also went to Shavler 4 with the questionnaire for investigating the ghetto. We did not get a good reception. And I must sadly admit that they were right. We were reproached for having calm heads. . . . But I am not at fault either because I consider that everything should be recorded and noted down, even the most gory, because everything will be taken into account.[77]

Vilna's youth club network provided young people like Rudashevski with an antidote to the discomforts of the ghetto, and at the same time with another method of coping with its reality. On the one hand it was a way of alleviating the physical hardships: "It is cold outside, it is cold at home, so you want to run to the club where you do not feel anything. . . . With such activity you do not feel the cold."[78] On the other hand,

27   Children's choir in the Warsaw ghetto.

through their ghetto history and ghetto folklore projects the youths were more intimately involved with what was happening throughout the ghetto than they would have been had their perceptions been trained on their own lives and homes alone.

Not all youth groups had this dual function. While they provided opportunities for young people to be together and to enjoy each other's company, other clubs focused on activities that had little to do with the ghetto. In Radom, as in most other cities and towns with a Jewish population, Zionist youth organizations were very popular. (We have seen, for example, how Alexander Ehrmann and his brother and friends belonged to the Mizrachi in his small town of Királyhelmec.) These groups continued to function in the ghetto. They are best known, of course, for their support of armed insurrection against the Germans, both actualized (as in Warsaw) and abortive (as in Vilna). But they served as an inspiration for a spectrum of activities. For many young people, especially those who were just a bit too young to have been considered by the leaders as of "military" age, the Zionist groups offered camaraderie and hope. Mania Salinger-Tenenbaum, a native of Radom, joined the Masada organization when she was fourteen years old and in her first year of gymnasium. "Masada was my second home. . . . I mean, from school, I went straight to Masada. I just came home to sleep. Saturday I was in Masada. Sunday I was in Masada. So it was Masada that was my whole social and political life during my high school years." This closeness, this intensity and special warmth continued after the war had begun and throughout the time of the ghetto of Radom. As inevitably happens in an organization of several hundred people, smaller groups with personal affinities and common interests developed. "I was in a group of eight people. It was *our* group. . . . So my friendships of before the war and during the war were very strong."[79]

Indeed, they were so absorbing that they framed Tenenbaum's experience for the first year of the war. Her father, a shoe manufacturer, was robbed of his business. Tenenbaum herself was no longer permitted to attend school. But still there was Masada, and especially her own close group of friends from the organization. Together, during that early period, they lived their own war. They were fifteen and sixteen years old.

> I was very involved with my friends. . . . We would gather [in each other's homes], and we would listen to records and learn about opera. That's when my love for opera started, because my friend (who was already a professional singer) would sing along, or we would listen to the opera and he would tell us the story while the music played. . . .
>
> We were all together. And we had curfew. So there were a lot of times when we passed the curfew by listening to music or whatever, and we would stay overnight. We would sleep on the floor, and stay up, and fall asleep, and listen to music, and dance and giggle and tell stories or play cards. We were oblivious to what went on outside – and did not believe what was in store for us.[80]

While older youths, like Mania Salinger-Tenenbaum, Yitskhok Rudashevski, Janina Bauman, and Mary Berg, attended classes and participated in youth group activities, younger children went to nursery schools and elementary education classes, and enjoyed children's corners and children's clubs. As we saw earlier, in ghettos where primary education initially was forbidden (as in Warsaw) it was privately organized between pupils and teachers. In other ghettos (like Łódź) it was permitted from the beginning, and was one of the functions undertaken by the Judenrat. Esther Geizhals-Zucker was born in Łódź in October 1929. She was about to turn ten and to start the fourth grade when the war began. When Poland capitulated a few weeks later, "I started the fourth grade, and I did go to school for the whole year. But instead of our regular classes, in the ghetto we had languages, social studies, and a lot of Hebrew. They instituted a program of Hebrew and Yiddish. I finished the fourth grade and the beginning of the fifth."[81] In the midst of the ghetto misery, adults tried to create environments rem-

28   School children and their teacher, Esther Wasser, in the Łódź ghetto, 16 August 1941. The text is a greeting for the Jewish New Year, 5702.

iniscent of the normal childhood they wished for their children: schools, parks, playgrounds, even summer camps set up in the Łódź suburb of Marysin. In Warsaw, the volunteer agricultural organization, Toporol, transformed bombed ruins into green spaces, and courtyards into gardens. Writing in June 1941, Emmanuel Ringelblum was proud of the work Toporol had done, but chagrined at its economic use. "Seven hundred young people took courses sponsored by Toporol at 2 Elektoralna Street. Where the Hospital of the Holy Spirit used to stand before it was burned down, there is now a broad field sown with various vegetables. . . . Now the places where the war ruins used to be are blooming. . . . Many courtyards have been converted into gardens. Some of the courtyard gardens have been rented out as children's playgrounds. Naturally, the children of the rich can enjoy them, because the charge is 30–40 to 70 złoty a month. The poor children never see a patch of grass. Traffic in fresh air!"[82] These spaces never were apportioned equitably for use among the ghetto children but, through the house committees, nursery schools and children's clubs had access to them. Chaim Kaplan delighted in these developments in June 1942.

> The members of the ghetto, condemned to die, want to enjoy life as long as breath remains within them. . . .
>   It is now three years since we have seen grass growing and flowers in bloom. . . . We have been robbed of every tree and every flower.

When we saw that was the way it was going to be, we invented substitutes. . . . Desolate, lonely lots, surrounded by high walls at the backs of courtyards or planted in the space between the houses and the wall, have been turned into "gardens." Mothers and children fill them. For space for a baby's cradle they pay 50 złoty a month, and if any members of the family besides the mother accompanies or comes to visit the child, he must pay an additional admission charge. . . .

I have forgotten the main point.

Nursery schools bring their infant charges to the gardens, and older children have their lessons there. In short: an arrow in the Nazis' eyes! The arteries of life do not stop pulsing.[83]

Nor did children stop playing. Ignoring the death and destruction around them, ghetto children invented games with the very little there was to hand. The children's utter indifference to such a real horror as a corpse struck the educator Janusz Korczak so deeply that he mentioned it twice in his diary. "A following scene in the street: A young boy, still alive or perhaps dead already is lying across the sidewalk. Right there three boys are playing horses and drivers; their reins have gotten entangled. They try every which way to disentangle them, they grow impatient, stumble over the boy lying on the ground. Finally one of them says: 'Let's move on, he gets in the way.' They move a few steps away and continue to struggle with the reins."[84] David Wdowinski, who as a psychiatrist and the president of the Zionist-Revisionist Organization in Poland for many years was particularly concerned with the plight of the children in the ghetto, noted similar scenes. "The realities of Ghetto life became the normal existence for children who did not know of any other way of living, and so they made up songs and games where "action," blockade, sorrow, tears, hunger became the ordinary vocabulary of their make believe."[85] Other forms of play were far less appalling to the adult observer, but still they reflected the deprivation of ghetto life. As we have seen (in "Search and Research") children in Łódź used cigarette boxes as playing cards. A month after Oskar Rosenfeld, one of the Łódź *Chronicle* authors, reported on that game, he noted a new ghetto toy:

Wednesday, August 25, 1943

SKETCHES OF GHETTO LIFE: A TOY FOR CHILDREN

For several days now the streets and courtyards of the ghetto have been filled with a noise like a clatter of wooden shoes. . . . The observer soons discovers that this "clattering" is produced by boys who

29   Girl selling armbands (for which there was a constant demand, as the Germans required that they be worn at all times and that they be perfectly clean). Photo taken by Joe J. Heydecker in the Warsaw ghetto, February 1941.

have invented a new pastime, an entertainment. More precisely, the children of the ghetto have invented a new toy.

All the various amusing toys and noisemakers . . . are things our youngsters must, of course, do without. . . . And so, on their own, they invent toys to replace all the things that delight children everywhere and are unavailable here.

The ghetto toy in the summer of 1943: Two small slabs of wood – hardwood if possible! One slab is held between the forefinger and the middle finger, the other between the middle finger and the ring finger. The little finger presses against the other fingers, squeezing them so hard that the slabs are rigidly fixed in position and can thus be struck against one another by means of a skillful motion. . . . Naturally the artistic talents of the toy carver and performer can be refined to a very high level. . . .

The streets of the Litzmannstadt ghetto are filled with clicking, drumming, banging. . . . Barefoot boys scurry past you, performing their music right under your nose, with great earnestness, as though their lives depended on it. Here the musical instinct of Eastern European Jews is cultivated to the full. An area that has given the world so many musicians, chiefly violinists – just think of Hubermann, Heifetz, Elman, Milstein, Menuhin – now presents a new line of artists.[86]

While some sorts of play, education, and youth group or children's club activity did continue throughout the years of urban incarceration, inevitably the press of ghetto conditions squeezed out most normal childhood occupations. As Hanna Kent-Sztarkman said, later on her privately arranged informal lessons stopped. "Even this couldn't work out. You just didn't."[87] And Esther Geizhals-Zucker, in school in Łódź, had the same experience. "Then my schooling stopped in the ghetto. I had no more school because I had to work in order to get a ration card in order to get food. And there was no room for school."[88] The children's daily activities increasingly were dictated by the wretchedness and terror of ghetto life. The business of living: queuing, mending, cleaning, cooking, working in the ghetto workshops, and smuggling and begging finally became the business of childhood. In Łódź and Vilna where the ghettos operated on a "survival through work strategy," adults (women as well as men) took positions in the factories and workshops. This meant that the customary division of labor by gender in the home no longer operated. Both mother and father were part of the labor force and the household tasks devolved on their children. In his diary, Yitskhok Rudashevski described how this had transpired in his own family. "The Jews must live in blocks according to units where they are working. We too must move to the block. Life has gradually begun to 'return to normal.' . . . My parents work and I have become the 'mistress' in the house. I have learned to cook, to wash floors, and on this I spend my days. In the evening I go to meet my parents."[89] Like many other youths, Rudashevski did not find housekeeping easy, and while he was busy with it, he recognized the disjuncture between these very necessary mundane tasks and the constantly changing, momentous events occurring just outside his door.

> Today was a day of work. I have rarely done any cooking until now. My parents eat their dinners at work and bring me something too. Today I set out to cook a cabbage, and on the second flame meatballs with potatoes. I worked hard at it. Meanwhile the little room became messed up. It is hard to do everything at the same time. Meanwhile turmoil arose in the ghetto. We do not know what the trouble is.

People are not permitted to go outside. The Jewish policemen run like animals across the courtyards, drive the janitors into the houses in order to start cleaning up, and to inform those in the rooms to clean up quickly. Finally dinner is ready, there will be enough for tomorrow as well. As though in a fog, bewildered, I clean, I sweep, and now everything is cleaned up. I eat my meal, I breathe a sigh of relief. It turns out that they are expecting "distinguished guests." It is supposed to be a committee from Berlin.[90]

Hanna Kent-Sztarkman was somewhat younger than Rudashevski (she turned ten in October 1939), but she too was responsible for many of the household tasks her family needed performed. Having arrived in Radom without her father, older sister, or family savings and possessions, she and her mother and brother found themselves in the position of refugees, even though her mother had been born there. The family economy and its pre-war established assignment of tasks underwent a rapid transformation. As her then eighteen-year-old brother Heniek explained, "We found ourselves without means very, very quickly." Sztarkman and his mother realized they had to support the family, and they understood too how important it was, especially for people such as they who lacked money or position, to try to find secure posts. "The main work in the ghetto was to work for the *Ältestenrat* [the Jewish Council], so I got some meaningless clerical job in the health department," Sztarkman recalled. It was January 1940. "Eventually I was transferred to another department which had to do with the allocation of provisions. The whole thing was make-believe. We realized – or, we thought – that there was a degree of security in being involved with something semi-official. Everybody tried to appear in some way 'productive,' or somehow or other involved. Because if you did not, rumors were that you were more vulnerable to whatever action might come. . . . At this point, the Kafkaesque quality of our life became manifest, because at this point I began to see the stratification of the society in the ghetto. I saw already people starving in the street. Some were uprooted or sick or helpless. And at the same time, there were restaurants serving roast duck."[91] While Heniek's job gave him some small degree of security, the position Mrs Sztarkman obtained was far more valuable both immediately and in the future. It was better protected, and it provided food. She found work in an SS military camp which eventually had some eighty Jewish slave skilled laborers attached to it. "One of the fellows who worked there told [my mother] that they were looking for somebody [to cook for the Jewish workers]. None of the ladies of Radom, at this stage of the game, were forced to take such a position, because they were local while we were aleady uprooted. So [my mother] was more inclined to take such a job than they were at this stage." It was thanks to this that the family did not starve. "She brought, usually hidden on her body, lentils or potatoes or beans. We lived on that, together with the normal rations which were almost non-existent, just a few decagrams of bread."[92] It was Hanna who prepared that one "substantial meal" each day, and it was she who waited on line for those few decagrams of bread:

> My brother went to work and my mother went to work. I helped. I would scrub the floor, clean, prepare a meal. . . . Occasionally my mother would get some beans or some other kind of staple from which I could make a soup, so when everybody came, we had something to eat. . . . If I had to buy the rations of bread, I took care of all those things. I would iron. My mother would wash, and I would iron. I did household duties.
> The next year [1941] I took care during the day of a three- or four-year-old whose mother was working. I went to her house and took her for walks and so on. So I kept busy this way. It lasted until 1942.[93]

All the time, day by day, week by week, month by month, the situation worsened, conditions deteriorated, the atmosphere tensed. They were, Heniek Sztarkman said, "dancing on the rim of the volcano,"[94] and ever younger children took on the adult responsibilities of earning a living and procuring food. The harsh order of the ghetto, the reign of terror, and the ring of famine trapped everyone. There was no mercy or quarter for children and the best way for them to negotiate everyday life was to assume adult status. As we have seen, Esther Geizhals-Zucker left school early in 1942, not long after she had turned twelve, to go to work. For her, as for other ghetto children, obtaining a position in the ghetto factories meant a meal of soup at noon as well as the possibility of staving off deportation. As a member of the labor force in Łódź she sustained a tenuous hold on life, in terms of both food and protection. "I had to go to work in order to maintain my ration card. First I worked in the office in a dress factory. Then they needed young girls in the factory itself, so I delivered pieces of goods from the machine to the finishing table. I also did something horrible. We had irons and the irons we were working on weren't electric so we used to burn coal in it. And I used to have to burn the coal in the iron so it would make the iron hot. I remember getting horrible headaches from the fumes of the coal. I used to get terrible headaches, but I had to do it."[95]

Within a few months the choice Zucker had made became a matter of ghetto policy. As the population was transformed into a labor force, it became increasingly clear that the only way children would be protected from *Aussiedlung* would be if they too were able to join the ranks. This was impossible, of course; very young children simply were unsuited for such work. The ramifications of this situation were enacted by illusion when a commission of German authorities visited the ghetto on 4 June 1942. So important was the impression of the ghetto as a work camp that no children, old, weak, or ill people were to be seen on the streets. "In a word, the ghetto seemed to be a labor camp where idle people are not . . . on the streets during the day," the *Chronicle* reported. The implications were clear: "the populace knows and understands that this is not an ordinary inspection but concerns something larger, more important – the question of its very existence. The result of today's inspection is still unknown, but a positive impression could be read on the visitors' faces."[96]

Throughout that summer, illusion became reality. The commission's visit was followed by persistent rumors of resettlement. At that time approximately 100,000 people lived in Łódź ghetto and according to the official lists 70,000 were employed. This meant that nearly every family had one "idle" person, and they all feared the loss of their loved ones. "The rumors about a resumption of resettlement that began to circulate through the ghetto on Saturday afternoon [20 June], causing widespread anxiety, were probably caused by the Chairman's demand that he be presented with a list of the number of children over the age of 10 who . . . have been given jobs. . . . A second rumor sprang up at once in connection with the Chairman's having supposedly ordered that children between the ages of 8 and 10 . . . be employed."[97] While these stories were denied by the Judenrat, a "drive to employ children over the age of 10" was initiated, and by 2 July was "making vigorous progress." Yet the uneasiness persisted, and for good reason. What of those under ten? "Rumors are circulating among the populace that the Chairman is also attempting to find employment for younger children as well – those from 8 years old and up."[98]

The authorities continued to deny the rumors, and to work hectically to find positions for children ten years and older. It was an enormous undertaking. The young people had to be trained in a very short time to do skilled work, and places in workshops had to be secured. By 20 July, 13,000 children were employed "in various Community workshops as apprentices," the *Chronicle* noted. Bernard Ostrowski, one of the authors, applauded this development. "The intensity of the work done by the Reclassification Commission [of the School Department] is attested to by its succeeding in finding employment for 1,800 young people between the ages of 10 and 17 in the first 20 days of July. That is a record for the ghetto."[99] Some 2,000 children worked as apprentices in the tailoring divisions, but an apprentice did not have the status or, more important, the perceived protection of a skilled worker. The search for greater security was so urgent that a special two-month intensive course was established. It was a stratagem, or ploy. The object was to push as many children into the ranks of the skilled laborers as quickly as possible. It is not surprising that such a device was employed; what is astonishing is that non-technical lectures were part of the curriculum. "The children have to be taught their trade in record time. . . . Each course will be attended by 300 children. The course's classes run from 8 to 4 o'clock; there are 12 groups." Each day the children had two hours of lessons about machine sewing, two hours of hand sewing, and they were taught how to make technical drawings and to cut fabric. Machinery, accounting, and occupational hygiene were also included as was "a lecture in Yiddish each day" on a more general subject. "The establishment of these educational courses must be acknowledged as an event of far-reaching importance for the future of the children who reside in the ghetto," Ostrowski concluded.[100]

Still, the rumors persisted and in the end, of course, their gist turned out to be correct. Those who were employed were not marked for the 5–12 September resettlement action; it was children under the age of ten and adults over sixty-five who were deported. The sub-text of the children's employment drive had been all too well understood, if only dimly grasped in reality. One could fear, but one could not imagine, the dragnet of infants, toddlers, and elementary school children. Sara Grossman-Weil was a witness of and a participant in this action against the children:

In 1942, there was a general *Sperre*, an important selection. We were warned not to go out from our homes. Should we be found in the street, we'll be shot without questions. It was in the morning when this was proclaimed.

They were going from street to street, from house to house, not one, not two, not three, but a group of SS men, with dogs, and calling for the population of a given building to come out. When they came to our building, we all walked out. . . .

We all lined up in our backyard, the men, the women, the young, and the elderly. Some people were taken away; many of us went back to our rooms, to our homes.

All the children were taken away. We had to line them up, since there was such a cadre of the SS men. They had enough SS men to go

30   Deportation of children from the Łódź ghetto, September 1942.

into every room to see whether there is anyone hiding or anyone left behind. We had all the children out, twelve, thirteen, ten years old, eight years old. The children were taken away; thrown, literally thrown, on to the wagon. And when the mother objected, either she was taken with them, or shot. Or they tore the child away from her and let her go. And all the children, small children, little ones, five-, six-, four-, seven-year-old ones were thrown, literally thrown, into this wagon. The cries were reaching the sky, but there was no help, there was no one to turn to, to plead your case, to beg.[101]

Although the timing, differed in each ghetto, the pattern of their existence was invariable: establishment, deportation actions, final liquidation. From the moment of the institution of the ghettos to the hour of their demise, the children who lived in them participated in activities of a former world of childhood, games, groups, clubs, and classes, and they were plagued by the rampant and deadly hunger, cold, and disease of the ghetto world. As Sara Grossman-Weil said, "Life wasn't difficult; it was unbearable. Many of us wished just to be finished with it. But there was always this glimmer of hope."[102] Possibly it was this hope, or maybe just the habit of living, or perhaps basic, elemental hunger which was the ultimate impetus for children to take on such hitherto adult tasks as working in the ghetto factories, smuggling, and begging.

Starvation was a problem for (nearly) everyone in the long-term ghettos. The official ration was insufficient to maintain life. "I remember walking on the street and seeing those youths swollen with hunger," Hanna Sztarkman recalled. "People were starving. We were among the lucky few that we were not starving from hunger because of my mother's work, and my brother was working. There was always some food, there was no starvation for us. But you could see swollen children lying on the streets. It became such an everyday thing."[103] Hunger and famine were the basic elements of ghetto life. They dictated health and, to an extent that now, half a century later, is only dimly understood, they prescribed and circumscribed behavior. As Sara Grossman-Weil explained:

Children were brought into the [Łódź] ghetto who couldn't walk for lack of nourishment. They just couldn't walk. This is how rampant hunger was. This is what malnutrition did to us. We were always on the look-out for some food, for some crumbs. You wouldn't dare to leave a crumb on the table. You would put anything into your mouth.

I don't think anything hurts as much as hunger. You become wild. You're not responsible for what you say and what you do. You become an animal in the full meaning of the word. You prey on others. You will steal. This is what hunger does to us. It dehumanizes you. You're not a human being any more.

Slowly, slowly the Germans were achieving their goal. I think they let us suffer from hunger, not because there was not enough food, but because this was their method of demoralizing us, of degrading us, of torturing us. These were their methods, and they implemented these methods scrupulously.

Therefore we had very many, many deaths daily. Very many sick people for whom there was no medication, no help, no remedy. We just stayed there, and laid there, and the end was coming.

I never knew that nutrition, that food, not only is important to satisfy your hunger, but what it does to your physique. It impairs your walking, movements, sight, hearing. Every sense is not so sharp or acute as it should be. This was what was happening in the ghetto. . . .

We were so suppressed, we were so dehumanized, we were so under-the-boot, so obsessed with satisfying this terrible hunger that nothing else mattered really. There was no other topic of conversation — if there was any conversation. There was no socializing to speak of. Other than that there was nothing to live for, just some dim hope that maybe the tomorrow will be better than the today.[104]

31 Boy feeding his little sister in the Łódź ghetto.

Smuggling was a necessary fact of the ghetto world. The only way to obtain enough food to sustain oneself each day was through "illegal" transactions. (To eat enough to maintain one's life in the ghettos of eastern Europe had become an illegal activity.) In fact, the better part of the food in the Warsaw ghetto was transferred clandestinely from the Aryan side to the Jewish quarter and sold there on the black market.[105] Smuggling rings flourished. They were generally fairly large-scale enterprises, run by adults, lethally risky, and financially enormously profitable for everyone involved: seller, purveyor, and those who had to be bribed – German sentries, the Polish and Jewish police, the janitors of various apartment buildings through which the food traveled, and so on. Children engaged in petty smuggling. Theirs was not an especially lucrative business. They stole through crevices and crannies in the wall, begged or bought food for far lower prices than was available on the Jewish side, and returned to the ghetto and their families, food in hand. They were the breadwinners, and it was not an uncommon occupation. In May 1942 in the Jewish prison on Gesia Street there were 1,300 inmates, "most of them smugglers and many of them children."[106] These child smugglers represented only a fraction of the total number; they had been caught while others had not, and they had been incarcerated, while others were shot on the spot. Furthermore, the ghetto population changed much more rapidly than did that of a normal community. The influx of refugees and deportees, the high mortality rate, and the round-ups for forced labor constantly altered the population of the Jewish quarter. Figures for May 1942 reflect the situation at that time alone; the child smugglers imprisoned on Gesia Street three months earlier undoubtedly would have been another group entirely. In short, while it cannot be ascertained just how prevalent a practice it was for children to take on the task of providing food for their families and themselves by stealing through the wall and back, it is clear that at the very least a few thousand children in Warsaw alone maintained their loved ones in this way. This was child life in the long-term ghettos of eastern Europe. Mietek Eichel was nine years old when the Germans occupied Poland, and about twelve when he and his brother started to work as smugglers. "At first living was cheap [in the Warsaw ghetto]," he wrote in his testimony for the Historical Commission in Lublin, shortly after the war. "But then prices shot up, as there was no legal way of bringing in food. People were starving." Typhus became epidemic. "My father, mother and sister all got sick at the same time. There was only my brother and myself to take care of them."[107] The family tried to conceal the illness (although it was illegal to do so) because of the punitive measures they would have had to endure had it been known. Everyone with typhus was taken to a hospital, while the rest of the household was quarantined. This was a great loss, as they were not allowed to work, and bedding and clothes were disinfected in such a way as to be unusable, or simply burned. The two healthy children bought medicine secretly.

> Soon, though, our supplies were gone. With none of us going to work, we had no way to stock up. So my brother and I took our parents' last few zlotys, and sneaked out of the ghetto. It wasn't easy. Polish police and Jewish militia guarded the walls, and German sentries were posted at intervals along the way. But the prices were only half as high on the other side. . . .
> We got the food, all right, but we still had to get back into the ghetto. Two Germans, two Poles and three Jewish policemen stood guard at our gate. . . . So we fell back, and kept out of sight. A couple of hours later, some loaded trucks drove up. This was our chance. While the Germans searched the trucks we managed to scurry across. Every day, after that, we went out and came back.[108]

The desperate and imaginative children in the Warsaw ghetto (as elsewhere) found many ways to cross the wall. In his diary, the educator Abraham Lewin recorded the smuggling activities of adults and children at regular intervals. Prior to the establishment of the ghetto, Lewin had taught Hebrew, Biblical Studies, and Jewish Studies at the Yehudia School, a private, Zionist-oriented Jewish girls' school. After the ghetto had been instituted Lewin, along with the rest of the Yehudia staff, continued to teach underground. His interest in smuggling was a reflection of his wider and deeper concern for the children in the ghetto, and the realities of his own life: "the terrible hunger," [109] and the fact that he lived near a well-trafficked clandestine transfer site. "I live by the wall that divides the ghetto from Przejazd Street. A gap has appeared in the wall through which someone could quite easily crawl, or which is wide enough for a sack with 100 kg of potatoes or corn or other foodstuffs. The smuggling goes on without a break from dawn at half past five until nine in the evening." [110] This avenue was in adult hands; children's operations were far more primitive. "We can observe scores of Jewish children from the age of ten to 12 or 13 stealing over to the Aryan side to buy a few potatoes there," Lewin wrote on 22 May 1942. "These they hide in their little coats, with hems swollen so that the children look like balloons. Whole hosts of them can be seen climbing over the walls, crawling through the gaps or so-called 'targets' and passing through the official entrances where gendarmes and Polish police stand guard." [111]

The Jewish cemetery in Gesia Street extended beyond the ghetto confines, and although heavily guarded was a popular site for the petty smuggling of, in Chaim Kaplan's words, "the impoverished and pauperized youth whose occupation is to bring in a few kilos of potatoes or onions. A whole family sustains itself from this." Kaplan visited the cemetery on 7 May 1942, and recorded what he had witnessed in his diary. Children aged six or seven; "whoever sees them recognizes them immediately. Their bodies are clothed in rags and tatters – even their feet are wrapped in torn rags – and their faces attest to abysmal poverty. Besides their poverty they have another distinctive characteristic. All of them bear humps on their backs. . . . This is an artificial, manufactured hump whose inside is filled with potatoes and onions." [112] Emmanuel Ringelblum observed even younger children at work; they were so small they passed through the rainwater conduits. "Emaciated three- or four-year old children crawl through the culverts to fetch merchandise from the Other Side. Imagine what a mother must go through when her child is in momentary danger of death." [113] And of course, as Mary Berg saw, some children simply cut through the barbed wire. "Whole gangs of little children are organized, boys and girls from five to ten years of age. The smallest and most emaciated of them wrap burlap bags around their bony little bodies. Then they slink across to the 'Aryan' side through the streets that are fenced off only by barbed wire. The bigger children disentangle the wire and push the smaller ones through."[114]

Child smugglers were often the breadwinners for their families. Child beggars, by contrast, were all too frequently orphaned and, ultimately, abandoned by the ghetto administration. They were a common sight and, in a starkly visible way, an index of the misery of the community. Despite the philanthropic organizations' and Jewish Councils' attempts to cope with the problem of the poor, especially destitute and orphaned chidren, the needs overwhelmed their meager resources. Refugee shelters, orphanages, day centers, and house committee grass-roots efforts could not maintain adequately the children they helped, and there were many more who remained outside the institutional network. According to Adolf Berman, the director of CENTOS, "of the over 400,000 Jews living within the [Warsaw] ghetto walls, approximately 100,000 were children below the age of 15. At least 75 percent of these children were in need of assistance and welfare." Enormous effort and energy were expended to address this disaster, but "it soon became evident that . . . it was not possible to render aid to the thousands of children who had recently become orphans as a result of the terrible mortality rate (from starvation and plague [*sic,* typhus]) or even to alleviate the distress of the 'street urchins' and children of the refugees. It was impossible to assist the large numbers of other chidren who were in urgent need."[115] In other words, those who were not already part of the institutional framework (the newly orphaned) and those who were new to the city (having been deported to Warsaw or having come as refugees) did not receive the assistance proffered to the entrenched and the native. The community structures, and the adults who ran them, could not help these children and so they made do the best they could: they lived in the streets and made their living there. "Two little boys are begging in the street next to our gate," Janina Bauman wrote in her diary on 18 April 1941:

> I see them every time I go out. Or they might be girls, I don't know. Their heads are shaven, clothes in rags, frightfully emaciated tiny faces bring to mind birds rather than human beings. Their huge black eyes, though, are human; so full of sadness. . . . The younger one may be five or six, the older ten perhaps. They don't move, they don't speak. The little one sits on the pavement, the bigger one just stands there with his claw of a hand stretched out.[116]

The streets of Warsaw, like Radom, Vilna, Łódź, and elsewhere, were

32 A beggar child playing the violin in the Warsaw ghetto. Photo taken by Joe J. Heydecker, February 1941.

filled with beggars, and in Emmanuel Ringelblum's estimation, the majority were children. "The most painful," he found, "was the begging of three- and four-year-old children." Some beggar children did tricks or sang songs for the bread they hoped to receive. "I saw a band of four or five children who eke out an existence by playing in the street some child's game they have probably learned at school," he noted.[117] Others cried out their misery to the passers-by. "In the gutters, amidst the refuse, one can see almost naked and barefoot little children wailing pitifully," Chaim Kaplan wrote in his diary on 4 January 1942. "These are children who were orphaned when both parents died either in their wanderings or in the typhus epidemic. Yet there is no institution that will take them in and care for them as human beings."[118] The rest, like the two Janina Bauman described, too exhausted to perform or clamor aloud, persevered silently. "For the most part, the beggar children stand near the hospital on Ogrodowa Street, near the telephone building on

Leszno Street, and wait for someone to have pity and throw them a piece of bread," Ringelblum reported.[119]

Beggar children did not last long on the streets. The six-year-old boy mentioned by Ringelblum who "lay gasping all night, too weak to roll over to the piece of bread that had been thrown down to him from the balcony" was an all too common casualty of the Germans' war against the Jews. In his autobiographical memoir, *When Memory Comes*, the historian Saul Friedländer recalled a similar incident, recounted by a friend of his, a survivor of the Warsaw ghetto.

It is night. The curfew has sounded. The streets are deserted. Sitting in his room, by the light of a kerosene lamp, he [the survivor narrator] stares at a piece of bread. Should he eat it then and there or keep it for the next day? Suddenly he hears a prolonged but unintelligible cry from the deserted street. He leans out the window. The cry is repeated. At first he sees nothing, then spies a silhouette painfully making its way up the street: a child. And the child cries, more and more faintly. *A shtikl broit*, a piece of bread! Soon he is directly under the narrator's window, and the latter makes up his mind: he takes the piece of bread that had been the object of his reflections and his greed, leans out the window, calls to the child, and throws him the bread. The child is lying on the pavement, and the bread falls right next to him; the child does not budge. "Reach out your hand, to the right!" The child still does not budge. "Look, lift up your head, there's bread right next to you!" The child remains motionless. The monologue goes on for a few moments and suddenly the narrator understands: the child is dead.[120]

Starving and exposed to the elements, the street children deteriorated rapidly. They did what they could for themselves, but there was so little they could do. "There are a great number of almost naked little children, whose parents have died, and who sit in rags on the streets," Mary Berg wrote in her diary on 31 July 1941. "Their bodies are horribly emaciated; . . . Some of these children have lost their toes; they toss around and groan. . . . They no longer beg for bread, but for death."[121] In July the children died of infectious diseases and starvation; in the winter they froze. "Every morning you will see their little bodies frozen to death in the ghetto streets," Chaim Kaplan lamented in January 1942. "It has become a customary sight."[122]

In the end, begging, like smuggling and even working, was only a temporary stay in the process of extermination. Existence in the long-term

33 Two beggar children sleeping on the street in the Warsaw ghetto. Photo taken by Joe. J. Heydecker, February 1941.

ghettos of eastern Europe led to death, not life. Children, like their parents, died of infectious diseases (especially typhus), exposure, and starvation. The official mortality rates show the devastation of the population – and these figures are incomplete because they only take into account the deaths registered in hospitals and places of quarantine, and not those who died in the streets. The rates fluctuated enormously, but they were never low. The average mortality per thousand persons in Warsaw, for instance, was 10.7 throughout 1941 and 11.1 from January until August 1942. In Łódź, by contrast, the mortality rate per thousand soared from 75.9 in 1941 to 159.6 in 1942. If the number of people who died in each ghetto is considered in relation to that ghetto's average population (and an average figure is taken because while people died and were deported, others were shipped in), it is clear that all the inhabitants eventually would have succumbed to the lethal conditions of their daily lives. In Warsaw, 18 percent of the average population died between September 1939 and August 1942, and in Łódź over a third, or 34.7 percent, of the population died between May 1940 and July 1944.[123] The initially perceived stability of the physical environment of the Jewish quarter, the streets, synagogues, and markets which had developed over the centuries to meet the community's needs, had been a chimera. From its establishment to its liquidation, the ghetto had been, in fact, a slow extermination center. But "slow" was not fast enough,

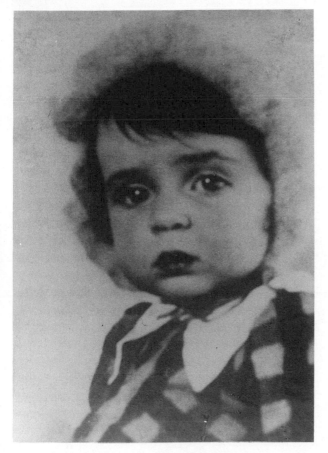

34   Mirka Grossman (aged about 2), circa 1941.

and each ghetto was emptied in turn. In Warsaw the final end came in April and May of 1943. In Łódź, it was the summer of 1944. Sara Grossman-Weil left on a transport with her husband, mother- and father-in-law, brother-in-law, his wife, Esther, their adolescent adopted daughter Regina, and their little girl, Mirka. They were herded to the train station and ordered on to the cattle cars:

> You couldn't throw a pin in, one was sitting on top of the other, with the bundles. We were in this cattle car, this wagon, and we were riding, riding, riding. There was no end to it. And the little one asked, in Polish, "Daddy, isn't it better that today it's a bad day, but tomorrow it will be better?" She was five years old. And her father said, "The today doesn't matter, the tomorrow will be much better."[124]

Their destination was Auschwitz.

Part Three

The Unrecognizable World

Chapter Six

Death and Slave Labor Camps

Esther Geizhals-Zucker was not quite fifteen years old when she and her family were deported from Łódź to Auschwitz.

I came to Auschwitz August 22, 1944. I came with my mother, my brother, my father, my aunt and uncle, and my cousin. A neighbor of ours was with us in the same wagon. He had a four-year-old child with him; he had lost his wife in the ghetto.

We got off the trains in Auschwitz and they [the Germans] separated the men right away. The women and children were on one side and the men on the other. When we got off the train and they separated the men, this little girl, the neighbor's child, was left alone. My mother (she was a saint) walked over to him and she said, "Don't worry, I will take care of the child." She took this child by the hand and she kept her, wouldn't let go of her. The child was alone and my mother wouldn't let the child stand alone.

Everything happened very rapidly. When Mengele came, he started this segregation. My aunt was with her little boy in the front and my mother with this little girl by the hand and my brother, and I was the last one. My aunt and her little boy he motioned to the left, and when he asked my mother if this was her child and she nodded yes, he sent her to the left. My brother being only twelve at the time, he sent to the left, and me he motioned to the right.

I realized my mother was on the other side and I wanted to run to my mother, I wanted to be with her. A Jewish woman who worked there caught me in the middle and said, in Polish, "Don't you dare move from here!" Because she knew that if I was on the other side I would go to the gas chamber. And she wouldn't let me move. I stood there with that woman holding me and she wouldn't let me move. This was the last time I saw my mother. She went with that neighbor's child. So when we talk about heroes, mind you, this was a hero: a woman who would not let a four-year-old child go by herself.[1]

Esther Zucker passed as an adult, and therefore survived that first selection upon entrance to Auschwitz. Her brother, just two years younger, was perceived to be a child and was condemned to death immediately. In other words, in Auschwitz and in the much smaller and far less efficiently organized Majdanek, Jewish youngsters who looked like young adults had a small chance of being sent to the right, to life.

In Chelmno and the Operation Reinhard camps, the extermination centers of Bełżec, Sobibor, and Treblinka, there was no route to life, and certainly no child life. Children were not specially singled out for slaughter; everyone, except the few slave laborers who were needed to run the murder machinery, was killed on arrival. Chelmno and the three Operation Reinhard camps (named for Reinhard Heydrich, head of the *Reichssicherheitshauptamt,* or Central Reich Security Office, and one of the most important figures in the annihilation program of the Jews) were established at the very end of 1941 and early 1942. All were in Poland, with its three million Jews (10 percent of the total population), extensive railway system, sparsely populated countryside, and thick forests. In short, in Poland there was a large concentration of Jews, an already extant infrastructure to transport them, and the possibility of secrecy. Chelmno was located approximately 50 kilometers from Łódź, within the part of Poland that was incorporated into the Reich in 1939. Its chief purpose was the extermination of the Jews of the annexed districts known as the Wartheland. Using three vans which held between eighty and a hundred people each, Jews were gassed while driven a distance of 3 kilometers from a "reception center" into the woods where they were buried in mass graves. In the summer of 1942 burning systems were added.

Bełżec, the first or pilot extermination center of the Operation Reinhard (the program to liquidate the Jews in the Government-General), was established in southeastern Poland in November 1941 in response to the addition of 500,000 Jews within the Government-General. They lived in what had been Polish East Galicia prior to 1939 and, until the summer of 1941, were under Soviet rule. In August the area was annexed to the Government-General, and the Germans proceeded ruthlessly to rid themselves of its accompanying Jews. The town of Bełżec was on the main railroad line between Lublin and Lvóv (Lemberg), and thus in the

Germans' scheme an ideal site for a killing center. Built on the outskirts of town, Bełżec began to operate in March 1942. It was the first camp to use stationary gas installations. There were no crematoria and the bodies were destroyed in open-pit fires. Sobibor, 70 kilometers southeast of Warsaw, was opened in May 1942 and also had permanent gas chambers. It was a more efficient version of Bełżec. Open-pit burning and a system of grate fires were used to destroy the bodies. The acme of the killing centers was Treblinka, where technological improvements in the murder system were implemented to make it the most effective assembly line for death. Located 120 kilometers northeast of Warsaw, Treblinka started to function in July 1942. As in Sobibor and Bełżec, gas chambers (thirteen were built by the end of its period of operation) were used to kill people by carbon monoxide poisoning. They were buried in mass graves. Later, the pits were opened and the bodies burned.[2]

No one knows precisely how many Jews were murdered in Chelmno and the three Operation Reinhard killing centers. The figures range from 150,000 to 340,000 in Chelmno; 550,000 to 600,000 in Bełżec; 200,000 to as many as 600,000 in Sobibor, and 750,000 to possibly more than a million in Treblinka.[3] Most of the Jews annihilated in these death factories were Polish but, especially in Sobibor and Treblinka, victims were shipped in from every corner of occupied Europe. The system was sordidly simple. The train of "resettlement workers" arrived, the deportees were hauled out and forced to surrender their possessions in an orderly fashion. They were killed by carbon monoxide poisoning which took between 15 and 30 minutes and their bodies were disposed of by burial or, later, cremation.

One of the few contemporary eye-witness accounts of this process was that of Kurt Gerstein. A German Protestant who had enlisted in the SS in March 1941, Gerstein used his position for resistance purposes; it was most notably through him (and, independently, through the indefatigable Polish courier Jan Karski)[4] that the Allies were informed of the extermination camps during the war. Early in 1942 Gerstein was appointed head of the Disinfection Services of the Waffen-SS, military wing of the SS. He specialized in disinfection apparatus and the purification of drinking water for soldiers. He was also considered an expert on prussic acid and toxic gases. It was for this reason that Gerstein was chosen to go to Bełżec; the extermination camp authorities and their superiors hoped he could suggest cleaner and quicker alternatives to their carbon monoxide poisoning system. The diesel engines which produced the carbon monoxide did not operate efficiently and needed much maintenance. Frequent engine problems caused delays and disturbances. Gerstein was not told where he was going. The Central Security Office

35   Women and children sent directly to the gas chambers upon arrival at Auschwitz.

simply ordered him to obtain 100 kilograms of the gas which had proved so effective in Auschwitz, Zyklon B (prussic acid), and to transport it to a place known to his driver. When Gerstein arrived at Bełżec he was given a tour of the facilities and asked to perfect the function of the gas chambers. He noted that a "small special station with two platforms was set up against a yellow sand hill, immediately to the north of the Lublin-Lvóv railway. . . . Alongside the station was a large hut marked 'Cloak Room' with a wicket inside marked 'Valuables.' Further on, a hall, designated 'Hairdresser,' containing about a hundred chairs. Then came a passage about 150 yards long, open to the wind and flanked on both sides with barbed wire and notices saying: 'To the Baths and In-halation Rooms.'" This path led to "a building of the bathhouse type; left and right, large pots of geraniums and other flowers. On the roof, a copper Star of David. The building was labeled: 'Heckenholt Founda-tion.'"[5]

Gerstein witnessed the entire process of murder from the arrival of the train to the mass burial of its 6,000 passengers. He described how, as "the train drew in, 200 Ukrainians detailed for the task tore open the doors and, laying about them with their leather whips, drove the Jews out of the cars. Instructions boomed from a loudspeaker, ordering them to remove all clothing, artificial limbs, and spectacles. Using small pieces of string handed out by a little Jewish boy, they were to tie their shoes together. All valuables and money were to be handed in at the valuables counter, but no voucher or receipt was given. Women and young girls were to have their hair cut off in the hairdresser's hut (an SS-Unterführer on duty told me: 'That's to make something special for U-boat crews').["6] The plunder of the Jews, which had begun whilst they were still at home, had reached its penultimate stage. All that was left was the gold in their teeth, which was extracted after their death. In the end, the Nazi official total value of the possessions appropriated from the Operation Reinhard victims at the three extermination sites was RM 178,745,960 and 59 pfennings.[7]

> Then the march began. On either side of them, left and right, barbed wire; behind, two dozen Ukrainians, guns in hand.
>
> They drew nearer to where . . . I [was] standing in front of the death chambers. Men, women, young girls, children, babies, cripples, all stark naked, filed by. At the corner stood a burly SS man, with a loud priestlike voice. "Nothing terrible is going to happen to you!" he told the poor wretches. "All you have to do is to breathe in deeply. That strengthens the lungs. Inhaling is a means of preventing infectious diseases. It's a good method of disinfection!" They asked what was going to happen to them. He told them: "The men will have to work building roads and houses. But the women won't be obliged to do so; they'll do housework or help in the kitchen." . . . They walked up a small flight of steps and into the death chambers, most of them without a word, thrust forward by those behind them. One Jewess of about forty, her eyes flaming like torches, cursed her murderers. Urged on by some whiplashes, . . . she disappeared into the gas chamber. . . .
>
> Inside the chambers, SS men were crushing the people together. "Fill them up well," [SS Captain Christian] Wirth had ordered, "700 to 800 of them to every 270 square feet." Now the doors were closed. Meanwhile, the rest of the people from the train stood waiting, naked. "Naked even in winter!" somebody said to me. "But they may catch their death!" "That's what they're here for!" was the reply. At that moment, I understood the reason for the inscription "Heckenholt." Heckenholt was the driver of the diesel truck whose exhaust gases were to be used to kill these unfortunates. . . . The diesel started . . . Twenty-five minutes dragged by. Many of those inside were already dead. They could be seen through the small window when an electric lamp inside went on for a few moments and lit up the chamber. After twenty-eight minutes, few were left alive. Finally, at the end of thirty-two minutes, all were dead.

Some Jewish workers on the far side opened the wooden doors. In return for this terrible service, they had been promised their lives and a small percentage of the valuables and money collected. Inside, the people were still standing erect, like pillars of basalt, since there had not been an inch of space for them to fall in or even lean. Families could still be seen holding hands, even in death. It was a tough job to separate them as the chambers were emptied to make way for the next batch. The bodies were tossed out, blue, wet with sweat and urine, the legs soiled with faeces and menstrual blood. A couple of dozen workers checked the mouths of the dead, which they tore open with iron hooks. "Gold to the left, other objects to the right!" Other workers inspected anus and genital organs in search of money, diamonds, gold, etc. Dentists moved around hammering out gold teeth, bridges and crowns. . . .

Then the bodies were flung into large trenches, each about 100 yards by 20 by 12, which had been dug close to the gas chambers.[8]

Gerstein's account is clear and correct on all points but one: the Jewish slave laborers used by the Germans to keep the assembly line moving and to deal with the possessions of the dead were not permitted to live as they had been promised. They were killed in turn.

There were individual and extraordinary exceptions to this inexorable process, the most notable being the slave laborers, because they were not murdered immediately. Most of them were young adults, but a few children also were given specific tasks to do, like "that little Jewish boy of three or four years of age who was made to hand out bits of string with which the victims had to tie their shoes together,"[9] in Bełżec, or kept as pets like the thirteen-year-old Simon Srebnik, one of the two survivors of Chelmno. Srebnik was in a work detail, but he outlived his cohorts because he was a favorite of the SS. He won jumping contests and speed races they organized for their own amusement among the worker-prisoners, and he had a fine singing voice. Finally, he was shot together with all the remaining workers two days before the Soviet army arrived, but he survived.[10] Sobibor and Treblinka had larger work crews, totaling between 700 and 1,000 people. "We were 700 prisoners in Sobibor," the then twenty-year-old Abraham Margulies testified later, "including eighty women and some children."[11] The thirteen-year-old Fishel Bialowitz and his older brother Simha were transported to Sobibor by truck at the end of April 1943. "As we got down from the lorry," Simha recounted, the SS officer "Gustav Wagner screamed, 'Doctors, dentists, pharmacists, plumbers, all forward!' Many answered his appeal, and I dragged my brother with me. The SS chose only five or six people; the others were killed on the spot." Simha was sent to work in the forest and Fishel was assigned to the clothing depot. Similarly, a thirteen-year-old girl, Rywka, was put to work digging ditches, and a thirteen-year-old boy, Max, was in charge of the camp stable. Another boy the same age, Leibl Fleisher, also worked in the camp and died in the famous 14 October 1943 uprising.[12] In Treblinka too there was a small number of young adolescents who worked for a time before they were murdered. According to the survivor Yankel Wiernik, a few thirteen- and fourteen-year-old boys were treated as favorites by the camp administration. They were given good food and warm clothes; their job was to tend geese and to do odd chores. Eventually the SS tired of these pets and the boys were killed.[13] Several youngsters were servants for the SS. They cleaned the officers' rooms, polished their boots, and brought them loot from amongst the possessions of the newly arrived victims. They too were destined to die, and few escaped that fate.[14]

These children were exceptions to the murder process described by Gerstein because they were not killed immediately. They had been awarded a temporary existence permit for the duration of which they functioned as slave laborers, or amused or entertained the SS. Other children were exceptions to the assembly-line system of death not because they lived longer, but because they were murdered by another method: shot, beaten, suffocated, smashed, or ripped apart. But for the hundreds of thousands of children who passed through these murder mills, the common pattern prevailed. Essentially, there was no child life in Chelmno or the Operation Reinhard killing centers.

Just as Jewish children were a rare phenomenon in the prisoner population of the extermination camps in Poland, they were also an infrequent presence in the original concentration camps in Germany. These camps formed the core of what became a network of terror, a world which evolved its own rules, bureaucracy, and apparatus. If Chelmno and the Operation Reinhard camps were created explicitly to kill Jews, the original German concentration camps were designed to eliminate any actual, attempted, or potential opposition to the National Socialist Party rule.[15] This system of suppression which eventually engendered hundreds of camps throughout Nazi-occupied Europe (with the parent camps and sub-camps set up near factories, mines, quarries, or any other enterprise willing to utilize slave labor) began with a nucleus of three camps strategically located throughout the country. Dachau was established in 1933 outside Munich in the south of Germany; Sachsenhausen, not far from Berlin, opened in 1936 and served the north of the country; and Buchenwald, near Weimar, began to operate in 1937 and covered the middle belt. To that triumvirate eight more camps were added in quick succession: Flossenbürg (in western Germany near the Czech border), Mauthausen (near Linz), and Ravensbrück (not far from Berlin and for women only) were established in 1938; Stutthoff (close to Danzig, or Gdansk) in 1939; Neuengamme (outside Hamburg) and Gross-Rosen (in Silesia) in 1940; Natzweiler-Struthof (in Alsace-Lorraine) in 1941; and, lastly, Dora (on the outskirts of Nordhausen) in 1943.

These camps and their hundreds of satellites were meant for political opponents and criminals. With time, however, the early separations and divisions were superseded by the Germans' pragmatic consideration of their military industrial needs and troop placement. Thus, Jewish children who entered the concentration camp system through deportation to Auschwitz or Majdanek, and who survived the first selection, may have been dispatched to any of these camps later on in the war (starting at the end of 1943) for labor purposes. Furthermore, with the advance of the Soviet army the Germans evacuated the camps in the east and force-marched the prisoners deep into Germany, to those core camps and their sub-camps, and to Bergen-Belsen. But this was a later phenomenon in the war. Originally there was no, or nearly no, Jewish child life in the Germans' concentration camp system, just as in principle there was no Jewish child life in the Operation Reinhard extermination centers.

Auschwitz and Majdanek were the gates to the concentration camp network, the unique, terrifying, and bizarre world, the *univers concentrationnaire*, as the French resister David Rousset, who survived the German camp system, called it.[16] Complete with both industrial-scale killing facilities and concentration camps where prisoners subsisted and slaved, Auschwitz and Majdanek were hybrids of the Operation Reinhard centers and the German camps. Auschwitz, in fact, was a complex of individual camps: Auschwitz I, with its old military barracks built by the Austrians, served as the headquarters for the whole operation. Auschwitz II/Birkenau was an extermination site and a concentration camp for Jewish prisoners. And Auschwitz III, 8 kilometers away in the village of Monowitz, was the site of I.G. Farben's Buna IV factory. It was there that synthetic rubber and synthetic gasoline and, by the end of 1944, all kinds of synthetic materials were manufactured. There were also satellite camps to serve other companies, most notably Krupp, the Hermann Göring Works, and Siemens-Schuckert. Children who passed through the portals of Auschwitz and survived the selection became adult slaves in one or another part of the complex. In other words, once in the camp, we are no longer in the realm of the history of Jewish child life, but in that of those rare Jewish children who labored as adults.

There were no young children and there was no child life. There were only older youths and a slave existence. And yet those Jewish youngsters who passed the selection lived until the moment they succumbed to disease or starvation, or were killed, or were liberated, and so the history of their lives is part of the history of Jewish children in Nazi-occupied Europe.

The infinite cruelty and absolute victimization which are the hall-marks of the slave labor camp world are well known to us. We, who have had the advantage of nearly half a century of memoirs, scholarship, and films have been prepared for what the young people were about to experience in a way that they could not have been. As even the term *univers concentrationnaire* indicates, the concentration camp world has taken on a mythical character for us. It reflects the idea that the slave labor camps were not specific sites of misery, but together constituted a whole universe which challenged the basic framework of all we knew and everything in which we believed. Historians, theologians, and philosophers have used this universe as a foundation for extremely important discussions about the nature of modern western civilization. But for the children who were about to enter that portal, the camp was not a "universe"; it was a lived experience of horror. This was not a world they contemplated, but a reality they endured. To understand what this meant for the children we must follow them through their daily lives and listen to what they, in their own voices, tell us about it. It is their story – that story which philosophers have told us cannot be communicated in any language – their experience, their personal history, which is our focus here. For the children, the train journeys, selections, beatings, starvation, overcrowding, harsh labor conditions, and rampant disease and death were the stunning, unimaginable, but daily realities of life.

The journey to the "unknown destination" to which young people and their families were deported was their introduction to the hell they were to experience. However horrendous their lives had been in hiding, transit camps, or ghettos, this was a new stage of misery. The cattle cars themselves formed an antechamber to Auschwitz. Locked for days on end into wagons intended for the transport of animals, with two small barred windows for light and air, little food or water, and no sanitary facilities, Jewish children and their elders were shipped to the gates of Auschwitz. Sherry Weiss-Rosenfeld had just turned fifteen when she and the aunt and uncle with whom she lived in Koloszvár were deported from the brickyards on the edge of town late in May 1944. "We were packed in until we were bursting through the slats. Everyone was standing up with packages in their hands and the gendarmes kept shoving

more people in. We were about a hundred people in that cattle car, . . .
and the only window we had was just a little square." It was a wretched,
miserable journey. "There we were, with clothing and packages, no facilities for washing, no food, no toilets. . . . The only time I ever remember having water is when we had a rain storm. The slats of the wagon
didn't interlock completely, so the water came in and it was a jubilation
from all of us because it poured in." Rosenfeld had no memory of eating
or using the bucket which sufficed for a toilet. For her, the journey was a
nightmare which she experienced by "coming in and out of a coma type
sleep. I remember that somehow we sat down and I fell in and out of
sleep." Her only other very distinct recollection was that they were told
to sew a yellow star marked with their names and addresses on every
garment they owned "so we could get them when we got off the train."
In retrospect, there was no reason for it, "it was just another form of torture really," but at the time it seemed terribly important. "Well, if chaos
– I don't even think that was an appropriate word to describe what went
on in that wagon. Imagine a hundred people rummaging through their
packages to get out their clothing and their belongings to put their name
on. For what reason? Nobody got back anything."[17]

Alexander Ehrmann was much more alert than Weiss-Rosenfeld
when he and his family were deported from the ghetto in Sátoraljaújhely. Indeed, he was extremely conscious of his physical surroundings,
both within and without the wagon. Like everyone else, the Ehrmann
family did not know their destination. Familiar with the region and the
train routes, they noted the railway station signs anxiously, trying to
guess their final terminus. As the train continued north they realized they
were moving towards the border. "They were taking us to Poland, and
we thought maybe we were going to be in a factory in Poland."[18] Ehrmann was an older adolescent who had turned eighteen about a month
earlier, and he was acutely aware of the people with whom he was incarcerated. There were two nice girls whom he knew to chat with, and
his father, whom he loved and who was deeply religious. This conflict
was made more bizarre by the situation.

> On the train there were no facilities. There were two small windows
> with iron bars. The door was locked shut. . . .
>   I sat next to my father. To my right were two girls whom I knew; I
> knew their parents. Their father was not with them because he was in
> the military. Their mother was with them. I knew them from the time
> I went to school in Sátoraljaújhely. My brother, mother, and two sis-
> ters were sitting across from us (there was no aisle) and next to them
> was another lady, a spinster from town whom I also knew. She was

one of those intellectuals that put on a robe, for instance, with an embroidered dragon on the back. "Can I get to the window?" she asked. "I'd like to enjoy the sights." I looked at her and I said to myself, "A typical Hungarian Jew. We don't know where we are going, and wherever we are going we have *tsores* [troubles], and she wants to see the sights."

As we travelled, dark came, the evening. I know that I have to go, what do we do? Somebody volunteers an empty pot. They hang up a coat to make a temporary curtain. We also had a pot. Quickly we hung up coats. Before long in several spots of the wagon they arrange for curtains and a pot comes out and people start using it.

Next to me sat these two girls my age. I was trying to keep up light conversation with them. Maybe three steps from me was this private area. Somebody was always in there using it. In the meantime, I saw my father. He was praying. And I asked myself, "Where are we going? What's going to happen? How important is it to stick to the religion? Is prayer important? Yes, it's important." My father looked at me and I started to pray too. I wanted to please him. So I started to pray and I said to myself, "What is Father thinking?" Here we are going, God only knew, maybe to our death, and I was thinking about girls, talking to girls. My next thought was: But I'm not doing anything; it's just conversation. But maybe instead I should be talking to my father and engaging in learning or praying instead of talking to girls."[19]

These sorts of dilemma knew no national or gender boundaries. Frieda Menco-Brommet had celebrated her nineteenth birthday in the transit camp of Westerbork in the Netherlands a few weeks before she and her parents were deported on 3 September 1944. It was the last transport from the Netherlands. In the wagon with Brommet was a man she had met in Westerbork. "One man (I think he was forty and I thought he was as old as Methuselah) was absolutely crazy about me and was drawing me the whole day. . . . Well, we were sitting in the wagon. And my parents were sitting together. I was also in that wagon. I was sitting with that man in the cattle train. Three days and three nights we were sitting like that, and I think it was maybe twenty years before I got rid of the guilt feeling that I hadn't sat with my father."[20] Painful as were these predicaments, for older and weaker people the anxiety, tension, and physical hardships were simply too great to bear. "There were about eighty people in one wagon on our transport from Debrecen," the then twelve-and-a-half-year-old András Garzó recalled. "Many people died or went insane. I do not know who they were, but I remember the fact that it happened very distinctly. The transport lasted five days."[21]

While the cattle cars were an introduction to the misery of Auschwitz, they were by no means a preparation for it. Nothing could have prepared the young people and their elders for that hell. Emilio Foă, born in Rivarolo Mantovano in the province of Mantua in Italy, had no idea that such a place as Auschwitz even existed prior to his arrival. The seventeen-year-old Foă and his prematurely grey-haired father had planned to join the partisans in the hills around Parma and had made their first contacts in December 1943. The following month they were arrested and imprisoned in a Jewish nursing home for the elderly in Mantua which had been transformed into what was supposed to be a detention center. It was, in fact, a transit camp; some two-thirds of the Jews incarcerated there were deported to Auschwitz.[22] On 4 April, a convoy from the main Italian concentration camp at Fossoli di Carpi passed through Mantua en route to Poland. The Germans added on another wagon, and Foă and his father were made to climb in; "they deported us to an unknown destination." They arrived in Auschwitz six days later (10 April), and still Foă did not know what the name signified. "The arrival was stunning. It was terrible to get down from the wagons and to see the SS with their cocked sub-machine guns, the wolf dogs, the prisoners in striped clothes with their hair shaved down to their skulls. It was a terrible, terrible shock."[23]

Unlike Emilio Foă, the fourteen-year-old Viennese girl Helga Kinsky-Pollack had heard rumors about Auschwitz and the extermination of the Jews. And while Foă had been imprisoned in Mantua for three months, where he "lacked freedom, but nothing else,"[24] Pollack had been in Theresienstadt for nearly two years. Nevertheless, she was fundamentally as unprepared for Auschwitz as he. "Auschwitz was completely, completely different from Theresienstadt. There was no comparison whatsoever. The distance between Auschwitz and Theresienstadt was much, much greater than the distance between Theresienstadt and normal life."[25] For Sherry Weiss-Rosenfeld, the transition was from the nightmare of the train journey to the shock of a previously unimaginable, ghastly scene. "We were commanded to get off the trains. My aunt told me to take the box with cakes. I took the box with cakes under my arm, and when we got down to the platform (it was late at night) we saw these chimneys aflame with fire. It was a terrifying sight. It was eerie, because we saw the smoke and the flames and it was like a horror picture. There were the sharp commands, '*Raus, raus, raus!*' as they pushed us out of the wagon."[26]

As the new Jewish arrivals got off the trains and stepped into that horror film, they were assaulted in every sense and every faculty. It was not the vision alone that stunned them. Sight, sound, smell, taste, and touch were abused from that first instant. "We arrived around one o'clock in the morning in an area with lights, floodlights and stench," Alexander Ehrmann recalled. They were parched and famished. "We saw flames, tall chimneys. We still did not want to accept that it was Auschwitz. We preferred to think we didn't know than to acknowledge that we were there. The train stopped. Outside we heard all kinds of noises, stench, language, commands we didn't understand. It was in German, but we didn't know what it meant. Dogs barked. The doors flung open and we saw strange uniformed men in striped clothes. They started to yell at us in the Yiddish of Polish Jews: '*Schnell! Raus!*' We started to ask them, 'Where are we?' They answered, '*Raus, raus, raus.*' Sentries and their dogs were there, and they yelled at us also as they beat us out of the wagon."[27]

This was another world, a new dimension, an unknown and unsuspected actualization of horror. "And still," Emilio Foà noted, "I never imagined what would happen next." In the center of this scene was the SS officer physician Josef Mengele, the Angel of Death, who was responsible for maintaining the camp population balance. It was his job to feed to capacity (but not overburden) the gas chambers and crematoria, to ensure a steady supply of slave laborers, and to prevent the camp from becoming so overcrowded that it would overwhelm the terrorist discipline of the guards.[28] Mengele divided the incoming Jews into two lines, Foà recalled, "one to the left and one to the right. One line was the destiny of those who went directly to the gas chambers. In the other line were those who were fated to work temporarily, for a shorter or longer period. The criteria for selection were a bit summary: nearly all the younger people went one way and the older people, or in any case those who appeared older because they had grey hair (like my father, for example, who turned grey very young, by the age of forty-five) went the other way."[29] Magda Somogyi was with her parents, two brothers, sister, and grandparents when they arrived in Auschwitz from their small town in Hungary. She saw that not only old age but youth too could be sufficient cause for the death sentence. "We were together, the whole family, but the first day when we arrived in Auschwitz we were selected. My parents, my grandmother, my grandfather, and my little brother all were selected by Mengele and sent to the crematorium. The very first hour."[30]

As we have seen, all very young children (and their mothers) were sent to the left, as were most pre-teenagers. At twelve and a half, András

36   Deportation from Westerbork to Auschwitz.

Garzó was unusual to have passed the selection, and he only just managed it:

> As we left the wagons, we were ordered to form a queue. We stood one behind the other, men separate from the women. The queue began to move and at the head facing us was Mengele himself. (I saw him later, and so I know it was he.) He was very attractive, nice-looking, and strong. A pretty man. He stood with his hands on his hips and with his thumb he directed people to the right or to the left. Just with his thumb. We were not allowed to approach closer than eight or ten meters. . . .
>
> We were beaten and kicked to keep the line moving. My father went before me, and he did not speak German very well. I do not remember, or I do not know, how he managed to tell Mengele that I was his son, and to ask him to let me go with him. Maybe he said that I was an orphan, I had no mother. I don't know. Mengele signaled me to join my father.
>
> This took place on the train station where the trains were directed

on a ramp; a railway siding. They were not passenger trains, but cattle cars. Upon our arrival, the long, long train in which we had been deported to Auschwitz/Birkenau was divided into two parts. A passage was created between these two parts. If Mengele pointed to the right, we passed through that little corridor. The road was there, and an SS man stood there, in full uniform. He had a very nice face and was laughing.

By this point we were in a five-man formation. I myself stood in the middle of our five-man line, and not on either end. I was the only one in short pants. I was not tall. But I was always strong and robust looking.

The SS man noticed me. He discovered me in the middle, and I think he presumed I had joined the line surreptitiously. He ordered us to stand still, and he went to Mengele.

I do not know, in fact, what transpired. I think he went to ask Mengele why this child (me) was in the line. We felt the situation, but we did not see anything because the train blocked our view of Mengele and in any case we were ordered to face front.

But we felt that this must have been the case. The SS officer did not stop any of the rows ahead of us. Only our row he stopped, and he looked at me. Then he went in the direction of Mengele, and then he returned. We were allowed to march on.[31]

With Mengele's permission to live for the time being, the young people (and their elders) were inducted through the rites of passage to prisoner status. As the German-born Ellen Levi, who by sixteen had been deported from Westerbork to Bergen-Belsen to Theresienstadt before she got to Auschwitz explained, it was a "ceremony" of sorts.[32] Its purpose was to obliterate the individuality and personality of the human beings who came into the system and to transform them into numbered slaves. A new kind of baptism was practiced at Auschwitz/Birkenau, and what was a sacrament of salvation in the church was a rite of perdition in the camp. For 2,000 years Christendom had tried to lure the Jews into what they proclaimed to be the Kingdom of Life. Now their self-proclaimed successors forcibly christened them into the Kingdom of Death. Stripped naked and shorn of all hair, the initiates were reduced to an infantile state which was followed by the sprinkling of water (the shower) and the presentation of a new name (a number) and new clothes (ill-fitting tatters). It was truly a new world to which these Jewish children had been brought. Hanna Kent-Sztarkman was fourteen years old when she and her mother and brother were deported to Auschwitz in the summer of 1944. All three passed the selection and Sztarkman and her

mother remained together. "We were ordered to undress, to leave everything that we had and to undress." They showered. "Then our hair was
shaved. We looked at each other and we couldn't recognize anybody.
We were thrown a dress, no underwear, nothing, just a dress and some
shoes. And then we were tattooed [with our identification number]."[33]

The procedure for men was the same. Alexander Ehrmann and his
sixteen-year-old brother were separated from their parents, their older
sister, and her two-year-old son when they reached the top of the queue
and faced Mengele. The boys were sent to the right. The older couple,
the small child, and his twenty-five-year-old mother went to the left.
"Schnell! And the sentries were there and the dogs and we had to move,
and that was the last we saw of our parents and sister and nephew."
They trudged on, prodded to move faster. "We were walking and
beyond the barbed-wire fences there were piles of rubble and branches,
pine tree branches and rubble burning, slowly burning. We were walking by, and the sentries kept on screaming, 'Lauf! Lauf!' [Run! Run!],
and I heard a baby crying. The baby was crying somewhere in the distance and I couldn't stop and look. We moved, and it smelled, a horrible
stench. I knew that things in the fire were moving, that there were babies
in the fire. And we moved on and on." They arrived at the prisoner processing barrack. "'Take off your clothes.' We were shaved and disinfected with liquid." They were told they would go to shower. "We wondered: Is it going to be a real bath, or is it going to be the famous bath
that we heard about, a gas bath? We came out of the bath, we picked up
our shoes, and we marched into camp. . . . And we were told, 'Forget
your name. From now on your number, that's all you are. Remember
that. Your name is not important.'"[34]

The effect of this unprecedented physical and moral assault was an
existential despair followed by emotional numbness and a reduction of
scope from the future to the present. It is within this context that the
young people's use of the word "survival" must be understood. It did
not signify a long-term strategy to outlive the Nazi regime, rather it
meant a more or less inchoate formulation of a number of basic precepts
to help them navigate the perils of daily existence. In the world of
Auschwitz, "to survive" meant to get through each hour of the day, not
to plan for the end of the war. This response of humiliation, despon-
dency, and a consequent specificity of focus on the quotidian was an
almost universal reaction. It did not matter if the child were a young boy
like András Garzó or an older adolescent girl like Frieda Menco-Brommet, if one came from an observant family as did Magda Somogyi and
Alexander Ehrmann, or an assimilated, little-practicing home like
Emilio Foǎ and Helga Kinsky-Pollack. Nor did previous experience or

country of origin alter the pattern. Young people who had been in hiding, transit camps, other labor camps, and ghettos, and who came from every corner of occupied Europe were affected similarly. In short, the differences of culture, class, age, gender, degree of religious observance, nationality, and individual war-time history were irrelevant. "I was cold and bewildered," Sherry Weiss-Rosenfeld recalled. "The feeling was something indescribable; it was a feeling of total despair. I never, ever in my life had the same feeling. . . . I saw the desperate situation we were in. And I said to myself, 'Even if I were to sprout wings all of a sudden I could not fly out of here – let alone walk out.' It was a terrible, terrible desperate feeling that came over me. I felt totally lost and beyond hope."[35] "I had the feeling, or I understood somehow, that this was a place where anything could happen,"András Garzó commented. "I did not know it to be true, but I understood that this was a harsh place where anything could happen."[36] It was a place with a law unto itself, where all normal social limits had ceased to exist. "When I came to Auschwitz, I had the feeling that this was a terminal destination," Helga Kinsky-Pollack remembered.[37] Emilio Foà agreed. "I had the feeling that I would never leave Auschwitz. I felt that I was a prisoner in a place from which there was no exit. There was no hope, just terrible despair."[38] Mania Salinger-Tenenbaum came to Auschwitz after she had worked for nearly two years in a slave labor camp at Pionki (near Radom) which served the ammunition factory Pulverfabrik. She was an extraordinarily cheerful person, but at that point "I lost all my optimism." Auschwitz was different. "When my head was shaved, and I had striped clothing, and my arm was tattooed, and they took my clothes and shoes away, I just did not feel like living. I turned around and went straight to the electric fence. I started running to the fence. I felt that I was going to die anyway. I was so humiliated. At that point I felt that I was not a human being anymore. My sister saw me. She started to scream and some people ran after me and grabbed me and shlepped me back. And all my optimism and all my strength just left me completely. I became a vegetable."[39]

Humiliated, in despair, and numb, the young people focused on the immediate situation. "We sort of made up our minds, my brother and I, number one: the two of us always will stick together," Alexander Ehrmann explained. This was not a calculated decision, thought through with time and careful debate. It was an atavistic response to the circumstances in which they found themselves. "Number two: we are concerned with survival, the next day and as far beyond the next day as we can go. Survive, one day after another. Don't get into danger. If you see a sentry, keep away from him because you don't know if he is going to take out his gun and shoot you or if he's going to hit you. You don't know how long you are going to last. Stay away from Kapos because Kapos beat. . . . Escape from danger, just keep out of danger."[40]

Auschwitz was the most common, but not the sole means of entering the slave labor camp system. There were young people like Mania Salinger-Tenenbaum who went from the ghetto of Radom to a farm in nearby Sola, and from there to the Pulverfabrik (an ammunition factory) in Pionki. Eventually she too was deported to Auschwitz, but not all the young people who were impressed directly into the forced labor camp network went through that central portal. Jack Rubinfeld, for instance, was born in the *shtetl* of Bircza, west of Lvóv, in Galicia. Protected by the Soviets from 1939 until they retreated in 1941, Rubinfeld and the other Jewish children in the village continued to go to school and to practice their religion. It was an Orthodox community. Within half a year of the German invasion, Rubinfeld's father was shot and his son went to a clandestine *minyan* [prayer quorum] to say Kaddish for him. In the summer of 1942, when Rubinfeld was thirteen years old, the Jewish population of Bircza was evacuated. They were driven from Bircza to Przemyśl; older people, his mother amongst them, were shot and buried on the side of the road. From Przemyśl the survivors were taken to Starachowice, where they were joined by all the Jews who had been rounded up in the region. Unknown to them, they were scheduled for deportation to Bełżec.

Rubinfeld came from a family of eight. His parents had been killed and four of the six children had dispersed. Just he, an older married sister whose husband had left with the Soviets, and her baby were together in Starachowice. As they sat and waited to see what would happen, "my sister said, 'Look, they're picking out people over there.' My first thought was that maybe that was to work here, close by, so maybe I could pick up something and help my sister. My sister said, 'Maybe you should go and get in there.' . . . They were singling out young people who seemed to be good workers." Rubinfeld was not large for his age, but he went closer to the group that had been especially chosen "and kneeled down next to them. I noticed right after that one of my close friends who I was at school with came and wanted to join that group also, and they just smashed his head in two. Just like that. I didn't realize what I was doing, I didn't know that I was doing something wrong. And I didn't realize that they were picking people to work in a motor factory for airplanes in Rzeszów. . . . Finally, they handed us over to guards from the factory who had come specially to pick us up. Well, we went, and that's how I wound up in that camp in Rzeszów."[41] The factory was the Flugzeugmotorenwerk Reichshof. Rubinfeld never saw his sister or her child again.

Like Jack Rubinfeld, Mária Ezner was thirteen years old when she was deported from the ghetto in Szolnok (Hungary) to Strasshof (Austria). She too entered the slave labor camp system directly. And they both were fortunate in that they were sent to camps where it was possible to live. Unlike Rubinfeld, however, Ezner was not alone; her mother and younger sister were with her. When they left Szolnok they did not know their destination, and their journey did not augur well.

It was hell in the wagon. It was dark, in the day too. At night it was like in a sack. People who used the pail with excrement were supposed to hold it between their legs and with their hand. It became full. We were hungry, we didn't eat, and still it became full. When the wagon moved, the excrement shot out. My mother, with two little girls, had to hold it often. And old people, who had no strength, held it.

People shouted at each other. People went mad and pulled out their hair, and screamed. There were old people, ill people. One snored, one moaned, another prayed loudly. "Don't pray so loud! I am not interested in your prayers."

A little air came in at the windows, and there was a fight for a spot near there. "Let me get to the window! I can't get any air!" Hysterical cries are in my memory. Then somebody said that we should take turns, one after the other should go to the window and breathe the air.

If the train stopped, then everyone asked, "Where are we?" and everybody wanted to get to the window. This went on for three days and three nights.[42]

Their arrival was no more auspicious than their journey had been.

On the third day, early in the morning, we came to the *Lager* [camp]. We saw barbed-wire fences and gates, and German soldiers with great German shepherd dogs. The train stopped and the doors were opened. *"Alles herunter! Alles herunter!"* Everyone out, they cried. We saw women holding whips, but they were in civilian clothes, not German uniform. They were Ukrainians. *"Alles herunter! Schneller! Schneller! Schneller!"* and the Ukrainians came with their whips and beat us out of the wagons.

We had to go through a narrow passageway in the barbed-wire fence. There were 5,000 people, and it was terribly hot. It was the

29th or 30th of June. We didn't know where we were. The queue
moved very, very slowly.

Rumors began to circulate. "Maybe they want only the first 200 or
(I don't know) 2,000 people, and they will go to work and the others
will be killed." The crowd surged forward. People from the back
wanted to go first. And then came other whispers. "Wait up. What
has happened to the people in front? Have you seen anybody come
out? Wait up! Then the crowd dropped back. We had no information, we didn't know what was happening, and we were in panic.

We were told that we had no right to sit, that we had to stand in
formation. But I couldn't stand anymore, and my sister couldn't
either. We sat on the ground and my mother said, "You mustn't!"
But in the end she saw that there was nothing to be done. Children are
not trained for such trouble; children cannot hold out. "Haven't you
sat enough in the wagon?!" she cried. But the air and the heat were
overpowering. If you had sat enough in the wagon, you couldn't
stand.[43]

There was no selection at Strasshof, and Ezner and her mother and
sister remained together. Their induction ceremony was a modified and
gentler version of the Auschwitz baptism. Forced to abandon their packages and to strip naked, they were painted under the arms and across the
pubic area with a lilac-colored disinfectant against lice. They were
weighed and measured by white-coated, German-speaking personnel
who were not unfriendly. The prisoners were neither shaven nor tattooed and when they went to shower they were given little bits of soap
which, to their disappointment, did not lather. Ultimately, they were
permitted to retrieve the clothes and shoes they had worn. "They had
been disinfected and had a horrible smell, but they were our own, and
we got back our winter coats too."[44] Six days later, the Ezners were
transferred to a *Lager* in the Stadtlau district of Vienna, and Mária and
her mother began to work in an iron and steel works, the Wagnerbüro.

Young people who entered the slave labor network, whether through
the selection at Auschwitz/Birkenau or because they were sent directly to
a forced labor camp, shed their childhood with their names. They were
robbed of their youth just as they were stripped of their packages,
clothes, and hair. From the moment they joined the slave ranks they had
no choice but to act as the adult laborers they were taken to be.[45] This
was true not only of the children's role with regard to the Germans, but
also within the personal context of a son and his father or a daughter
and her mother. The system dictated relationships. The young people
were no longer in a position to be the children of their parents, and the

adults were defeated in their attempts to protect their progeny. For Garzó and the others who had been sent to the right, the sub-text of the situation was forcibly demonstrated, if not articulated. "When we were naked, the children were separated from the adults. There were other children besides me, although all were a little older. (Perhaps a few were younger, but they may not have been, they just may have been less robust than I.) I do not remember if they said that children up to the age of eighteen were to stay to one side, or if they separated the younger people from the grown-ups by looking at us. The order was carried out by the Jewish commando, by the prisoners in the striped pyjamas. Germans stood everywhere, but the actual work was done by the Jewish commando." After the shower, hair-cut, and so on, the children were marched to one block, which they shared with German gypsies, and the adults to another some 10 meters away. "The first night the fathers came to their sons. Contact between the two barracks was prohibited, but the situation was so harsh that our fathers came to sleep with us, to try to protect us a little. The gypsy *Blockältester* came with German soldiers and began to scream that everybody should stand up. Our fathers had to bare their bottoms and to bend over the brick heating tunnel which ran down the center of the room. They were beaten by the gypsy *Blockältester* and his Hungarian Jewish deputies so that they wouldn't come again. And they didn't come again."[46]

Young people learned that they were no longer children very quickly, whether they were alone, with a sibling, or, as in Garzó's case, with an adult. Jack Rubinfeld had no family with him when he was taken to the airplane motor factory in Rzeszów. In camp, "I had to grit my teeth and bear it, and try to show that I was tough, that I was just like the adults. I could take it just as an adult. I *was* an adult."[47] Magda Somogyi, Sherry Weiss-Rosenfeld, and Hanna Kent-Sztarkman shared the same experience, but they manifested their new role differently. They took on the care of others. The sixteen-year-old Magda Somogyi was with her seventeen-year-old sister after the selection in Auschwitz/Birkenau. As they resembled each other very closely they were thought to be twins, and about a month after their arrival they were sent to a special barracks for the twins on whom Mengele experimented. Somogyi and her sister had been on a road building detail before the transfer, so in physical terms the twins' barrack was "the beginning of my child life in Auschwitz," as she called it. On an emotional level, however, it was a shock into maturity.

Life there was relatively better than in the other block. But for me, it was an awful life because I knew what was happening to me and to the other children. I cannot begin to express, or describe, how awful these experiments were. One twin was terribly fat, and the other terribly thin. One of them was very sad and melancholy, and the other awfully gay and happy.

The first word little children who could not yet speak learned was "*Nachtwache,*" which means "night watchman." Not "mama." None of the little children knew the words "mama" or "papa"; only "*Nachtwache.*" This was because in the night they had to go to the toilet, and if they couldn't call for the *Nachtwache* or say, "I need to go to the toilet," they lived no more. If they urinated in their bed they would be sent to the crematorium. That is why children one year old, one-and-a-half years old, could say: "*Nachtwache*, I need to make pee-pee."[48]

Somogyi, her sister, and the other older girls felt responsible for the little ones. It was not simply a matter of helping them to get dressed, or to eat their food.

The little children had little parents in the block. For example, I was a little mama for twins, two girls named Evichka and Hanka. They were Czech. My sister was the mother for Hanka and I was the mother for Evichka. . . . The life was relatively better because Evichka had a mother and Hanka had a mother. We were together and we spoke about our lives. I was curious, and I asked the twins where they came from, and what their life had been like, and so on. Evichka told me that she had a mother and a father, but that they had gone away on transport. The twins were four years old.

I said to her, "I will be your mother."

She said, "But you are only sixteen years old; it doesn't matter?"

I said, "No it doesn't matter because it is more important that we are together and that we are not alone. You have a mother and I have a daughter."

For my sister too it was so. She had a daughter and Hanka had a mother. We lived like that together. Evichka cried often in the night. I always said, "Don't cry Evichka. I am with you; you are not alone."

One day she asked me, "What will happen when the war is over?"

And I answered, "I don't know exactly, but we will remain together, I promise you."

But we couldn't remain together, because on January 18th the whole *Lager* was evacuated. All the older children went by foot into Germany, and the little children stayed in the block. My sister and I were selected to go, and from that time I did not hear anything of

Evichka and Hanka.[49]

Sherry Weiss-Rosenfeld and Hanna Kent-Sztarkman also accepted the responsibility of looking after someone else, only in their case it was an older person and a member of their own family. Rosenfeld had been deported to Auschwitz/Birkenau with her aunt, and both passed the selection. "In concentration camp, I became the adult, and my aunt became the younger of the two in my eyes. I felt that since I was the younger, maybe I was the stronger, and I needed to protect her."[50] Sztarkman had a similar experience. By the time she and her mother were deported to Auschwitz, "my mother was deteriorating." They had worked as cooks for the Jewish laborers in an SS camp (SS Truppenwirtschaftslager) in Radom, and the ordeal of the years in the ghetto and then in the *Lager* had taken a great toll on the older woman especially. Soon after they arrived in Birkenau, Sztarkman asked the *Blockälteste* to allow her to get the coffee in the morning so that she could give some to her mother while it was still hot. She hoped it would give her the strength to stand the long hours of *Appell*. "Instead of waiting for the coffee until after the *Appell* when it was cold, the people who went for it got it before. I was determined to go so that I should have something warm for my mother. The *Blockälteste* let me. It meant that I woke up at four in the morning, but I got the hot coffee for my mother." After five months, Sztarkman and her mother were evacuated by forced march and then cattle car transport to Bergen-Belsen. There, in the course of the normal hazards of camp life, Mrs Sztarkman was kicked in the groin. "It seems like with that, she went down. I don't know if it got infected, but I know she was very weak. She could not stand at *Appell*. . . . So she became the child and I became the mother. That was in the beginning of 1945. I was fifteen years old."[51]

Life, or (more accurately) mere existence, in the slave labor camps was fraught with perils. The initial selection at Auschwitz was just the first of the daily hazards and assaults the prisoners endured. Like Mrs Sztarkman, most people eventually perished from the constant and persistent abuse. In her case, the heavy-booted kick she received from the Ukrainian guard was more than her emaciated and fatigued constitution could withstand. But the predicament was ubiquitous, and their common plight multi-faceted. Starvation, exposure, overcrowding, the lack of hygiene and sanitary facilities, and the strain of the work itself, all contributed to the ravaging physical decay of the camp inmates. Many of the then-young prisoners have said that food was the first problem, because if they had been well nourished, they would have been better able to do the work, withstand the cold, and fight disease. But food was not to be had. "The food they gave us [in Auschwitz] was such that I only had bread in my mouth for six months," Sherry Weiss-Rosenfeld recalled. "The 'soup' was grass and dirt cooked together. I don't know what it was. . . . I couldn't get myself to eat it, I just couldn't."[52] András Garzó, who did eat it, saw more than she. "Once we found a mouse in it . . . and another time the foot of a horse with the metal horseshoe still attached."[53] There were, as Rosenfeld said, "people who used to die for it and kill for it, because it was some kind of nourishment, some kind of something to sustain them,"[54] but it provided few calories and had even less nutritional value.

The food in the forced labor camps initially was marginally better both in quality and quantity than that in Auschwitz, but in the last year of the war when the Reich was overflowing with human resources in the form of slaves, and pressed for material resources such as food, even less was allocated to the camp inmates. Helga Kinsky-Pollack was in Auschwitz for only four days before she was sent on to a sub-camp of Flossenbürg in Oederan (near Chemnitz), where she worked in an ammunition factory. "At the beginning we were all quite well-fed, better fed than in Theresienstadt [where she had been for two years], because they had a real cook from the town of Oederan. She thought she was supposed to feed us. . . . But soon, of course, it was less and less and less because they didn't have anything in Germany. Then we started losing weight. . . . I lost a lot of weight."[55] Like Pollack, Ellen Levi was in Auschwitz for just a short time before she went on transport to a sub-camp of Mauthausen in Lenzing, near Linz (Austria). She was placed in a factory which produced artificial wool. "It was awful work. We were bending over this sulphur dioxide which smells awful. The other people, the non-Jewish prisoners got milk for it, but we did not." Not only was milk withheld, the inmates got little of anything else to eat either. "We were fed very badly and very, very little. We had terrible hunger; absolutely awful. I remember a terrible, terrible hunger. It was the autumn and winter of 1944–5. We were hungry all the time."[56]

Pollack and Levi worked with inedible objects, and so they did not have the opportunity to pilfer food. When Garzó and his father were deported from Auschwitz to Mühldorf, a satellite camp of Dachau, he was detailed to a potato-peeling group. He had raw potatoes in his hands all the time and had access to carrots too. Furthermore, the SS officer in charge of the food storehouse took a liking to Garzó and told the boy that he could go to him every day to get extra food. "That was such an exceptional situation that I did not dare go to him *every* day, but I did go from time to time." Nevertheless, by 1945 there was "starvation in the camp." Even though "I was in a better situation because I could eat raw potatoes or raw carrots, and I could go to the SS officer to ask for something to eat and get a piece of bread with ersatz honey or jam," he too could not escape the great hunger that clutched the camp.[57]

Emaciation and malnutrition exacerbated the effects of exposure to the weather. Clad in scant and ill-fitting clothes, the prisoners were completely unprotected from the elements or the extreme temperatures of central Europe. Many young people spent hours out of doors each day on work sites (building roads, quarrying stone, on construction or demolition crews, and so on). And all the prisoners were forced to stand *Zahlappell*, the ritual counting of the inmates each day. "The first thing" they had to do every morning, Hanna Kent-Sztarkman reported, was "to stand *Appell* for a few hours. The SS men would walk by and count us."[58] The process could take any amount of time. According to Garzó, it usually took "more than an hour, but sometimes they couldn't reckon properly, and then we had to stay there until the figures tallied."[59] In those instances, the prisoners were forced to stand for as long as eight hours without respite. "When we stood *Zahlappell*," Sherry Weiss-Rosenfeld reported, "if they miscalculated, or sometimes it happened that a guard was drunk and he didn't count properly, or if somebody was sick and couldn't get out to *Zahlappell*, or had died for that matter; for whatever reason, until they found the exact number, we were standing *Zahlappell*. At one time we were at *Zahlappell* for eight hours. As a punishment we had to kneel for having them go through all that. Kneeling for eight hours because they couldn't find a person. Ultimately they found someone dead in her bunk."[60]

The physical strain of remaining in one position for so many hours was exceedingly wearing, but the harsh weather made the ordeal nearly unmanageable. Like Rosenfeld, Frieda Menco-Brommet also remembered "standing there for eight hours a day," but it was the bitter temperature that she felt most acutely. "It was very, very cold. It was 20 degrees below zero, centigrade. This was October, and it was already very, very, very cold."[61] Rosenfeld recollected that it was cold in the summer too, because *Zahlappell* began in the middle of the night. "We were constantly on *Zahlappell*. At two o'clock in the morning they woke us up for *Zahlappell* and we were shivering in that one little rag we had to wear. Then by the time the sun came up it was so hot we fainted."[62] Not only were the prisoners' clothes insufficient, their shoes provided little protection or support, and bore no relation to their foot size. Esther Geizhals-Zucker had been thrown "shoes with high heels, and they were about three sizes too big. I couldn't wear those shoes because we had to walk fast and I couldn't walk in those shoes. So I used to go barefoot. I remember that one morning my feet froze to the ground." It was Sep-

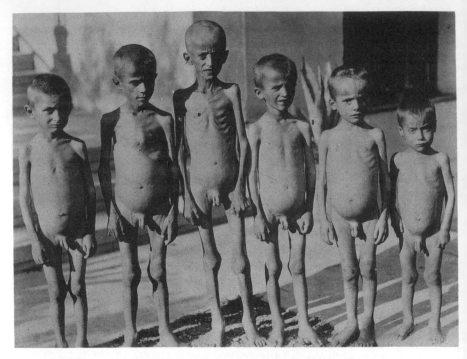

37   Young boys in a Yugoslav concentration camp run by local fascists.

tember 1944, and "in Poland, September is already cool, with frosty nights. I remember standing in Auschwitz in the *Zahlappell* in the morning ... and I couldn't walk, I just couldn't. My feet stuck to the ground."[63]

Just as the harsh camp administration (the physically abusive treatment, the lack of food, the long hours of *Zahlappell*, the absence of shoes or clothing worthy of the name) debilitated and weakened the prisoners, the structure of Birkenau itself, the material conditions in which the inmates existed, also posed a daily hazard to their lives. Birkenau was divided into a number of separate camps. Each of these camps, or *Lagers*, was enclosed by a barbed-wire fence and contained about thirty-eight barracks, or blocks. The camps were given alphabetical designations and had specific functions. Thus, for example, C camp was the women's *Lager*, D camp was for the men, the gypsies were held in E camp and the prison hospital was in F camp.[64]

There was little variation in the architecture of, or the conditions in, the blocks of the different camps. The most common barracks in Birkenau had no windows; a skylight under the roof eaves was the sole source of light and air. Three-tiered bunks were built into the side walls of the barracks, and a brick heating tunnel about a meter high with a stove on either end ran the median of the block. There were neither toilets nor taps in the sleeping barracks.[65] András Garzó was in E camp, and the latrine and washroom barracks in his *Lager* were typical of the facilities at Birkenau. "The washroom had three long troughs that ran the length of the block. Above it there was a pipe with holes, and the water dripped through the holes. The whole apparatus was at least 50 or even 80 meters long. The WC was structured similarly. There were three rows of cement platforms, again between 50 and 80 meters long, with circles cut out at the top, and we sat on those. Five hundred people used the facility at once." Use of the latrine and washing barracks was strictly controlled. "We were awakened about six o'clock in the morning. We had to line up in formation, five people to a line, and then we marched to the washing and WC barracks. We were told how much time we would have; I don't remember how long it was, but it wasn't much. We were counted as we entered and as we left, so no one could remain in there."[66]

Many young people recalled the structure of the Birkenau barracks with great specificity. As Garzó said, "The impression they made went so deep that such things remain. One remembers these details. The difference between that life and my former life was like hell and heaven."[67] They also had very clear and extremely precise recollections of the population congestion in camp. The barracks in Birkenau were so overcrowded that prisoners slept cheek by jowl. If one person turned over, the rest of the bunk occupants had to move too. There were so many people packed into one block (usually 4–500, or twice the originally estimated possible capacity) that if one wanted to relieve oneself during the night, one had no choice but to walk on one's fellow inmates to get to the piss pots at the back of the barrack. In Sherry Rosenfeld's memory, as in that of very many others, it was quite simply "hell inside of the barracks." There were hundreds of people in a small space, and their physical needs were great and the goods available few.

> One evening I decided to save my bread so that when I would get my ration the next morning I could eat both together and have a little bit the feeling of being satisfied. It was hell inside of the barracks because someone stole my bread. It was hell in the barracks because they stole my blanket. . . . It was hell in the barracks because every night there was screaming and nightmarish things going on, people waking up screaming and crying and yelling for their children. And self-recriminations: "Why didn't I go with my child? Why didn't I go with my mother? Why did I let somebody take my child out of my hands!" The nights were troubled and the days were troubled."[68]

The barracks and sanitary facilities in the labor camps were, initially,

more habitable than those of Birkenau. In the barracks of the Flugzeugmotorenwerk Reichshof in Rzeszów, for instance, the slave workers got
clothes (plundered from the Jews in the ghetto of Rzeszów) which were
laundered in the camp by Jewish women, and they themselves took cold
showers every day. "It was cold," Jack Rubinfeld reported, "and we'd
go in the wintertime when it was freezing, but we would have a shower
every day. . . . We didn't have lice there." Unlike Birkenau, it was a camp
where existence was possible. "Nobody would die from starvation in
that camp. We had soups, something like that, and bread. It was enough
to survive. It wasn't a good diet, but it was enough to survive."[69] Alexander Ehrmann's experience in a work camp in Warsaw was very similar. He and the other inmates had been brought in to tear down the
houses in the (now defunct) ghetto, salvaging reusable parts such as
bricks, plumbing pipes, and beams as they did so. "The food was relatively good. . . . But what was really good about Warsaw were the sanitary conditions. . . . I remember the bath barracks very well. They were
artificial marble shower-tubs, open showers in a circle like a fountain.
Water was spouting all the time and we could go there and wash ourselves from the waist up. They encouraged us to wash every morning
and every evening and even lunchtime, if you had the time. . . . The
latrines were also tiled. The barracks were spotlessly clean. The bed
bunks were new. We had straw. There were no lice whatsoever."[70]

While the food and sanitation in the work camps initially may have
been "sufficient to survive," the problem was that these camps, like the
work details in Auschwitz, demanded labor of the inmates. Often this
required greater strength or more concentration than the workers' nutritional state could engender, and sometimes the task itself was directly
hazardous. Thus, for instance, Magda Somogyi found the road-building
commando in Birkenau wearing in the extreme. "We built roads. We
carried heavy stones from the mountains to the road. We were always
hungry and thirsty. . . . Once I dropped a great big stone because it was
so heavy. I couldn't carry it, and it fell down. The SS officer came to me
and whipped me. From that time, every day he whipped me before I
began to work. And he said to me, 'You understand: you will learn that
you do not need to drop the stones.' He was right; I didn't drop any
more stones. I could carry them."[71] "I was chosen for heavy labor,"
Emilio Foà explained, "to unload train cars full of war materiel, just at
the exit of Auschwitz. . . . I worked there for many months, and
although it was really hard work, I managed to pass another two selections and was still considered fit for work. . . . I lacked food, naturally,
vitamins, and so on, and so boils and eczema broke out over my body,
however the body itself was healthy, and my youth still helped me to

resist well."[72] Mária Ezner worked a lathe and a drill in the Wagner plant in Vienna, which she initially found rather interesting. After some months, however, her malnutrition was so advanced and she was so exhausted that "in the end, I was very weak. I wanted only to sleep. . . . And my mother whispered, 'Don't sleep! Don't sleep!' But I couldn't stop myself. At thirteen years old you need more vitamins and more to eat." Ezner risked more than the consequences of detection. Eventually, "I just existed, and I slept during the day. I worked a drill, and one time, I think I was asleep, I had an accident. My clothes were torn in two parts – but my arm wasn't. But my poor mother was beside herself because she understood that I was asleep at the machine and there was nothing she could do to help me."[73]

Alexander Ehrmann's experience in the slave labor camps to which he was sent was typical of the pattern of most young people, until they no longer had the strength to pass the selections or survive the rampant illnesses and infectious diseases. His history clearly illustrates the progressive deterioration due both to the strain of work and to the continual decline in the camp conditions in the last year of the war. Ehrmann and his brother were in the demolition and salvage camp in Warsaw for about four months before the Soviets got so close to the city that the Germans were forced to evacuate the *Lager*. At the end of July 1944, just before the Warsaw uprising began (1 August), the slave laborers were force-marched and then sent by train to Dachau. From there they went to the satellite camp of Mühldorf where Ehrmann's brother was selected for the potato-peeling commando. (András Garzó joined him a month later.) Ehrmann himself was detailed to the central task of the camp, which was to build an underground aircraft factory:

The main work was cement mixing. . . . Everything else was auxiliary. . . . I told them I was an electrician, hoping to get into the electrician commando. . . . [After a few days] I was grabbed and put into a cement detail. . . . By then we'd found out that people were falling like flies from the cement; it settled in their lungs. Nobody lasted more than two, three weeks in that commando. They just dried up, visibly dried up as it settled on their lungs. Whether they contracted tuberculosis, or it had the effect of tuberculosis, in any case their noses started running, they developed gangrene in their feet, infection set in. Literally, there were some people falling off the gangplank with their bag of cement, and falling dead. There was a death wagon especially to haul away people who died at work. . . .

We were getting into the fall, and weather started to be a factor also. . . . When we came to that camp, the food was relatively good. It wasn't plentiful, but it was just enough to get by. Where we had problems was that the water was not good. And lice, we had a *lot* of lice by then. . . . We had typhus already. . . .

There was a bath barrack which consisted of one plumbing pipe running over a wooden trough. Water dripped, and you could wash. But all day the cement settled on our bodies and we had no soap or wash rags or anything. How could we wash it off?

There was a latrine barrack, but it was an open latrine. We never cleaned it. Excrement just piled up. There were a lot of sick people and their excrement was infected and the latrine system spread the infection even more. . . .

Regularly, about every second week, sometimes every week, people would go into the *Revier* [infirmary block]. A typical thing that would happen to people is that they would develop boils on their legs and on their arms. . . . They would start to ooze pus and there was nothing they could do. It was running and infected. Pretty soon, theirs was a hopeless case.[74]

Wherever the young people were, whether in Auschwitz/Birkenau or the slave labor camps, it was merely a matter of time before their temporary stay of execution ran out. Death from starvation, disease (especially typhus and dysentery), and traumatic injury (both willfully inflicted and accidentally sustained) was always commonplace, but as time went on it became the rule. In Auschwitz, where Mengele kept the gas chambers filled to capacity, selections were conducted regularly, not only on the newly arrived prisoners, but on the inmate population as well. It was another risk the young people ran each day; a lottery which depended on their luck and Mengele's whim. Everyone who experienced such a selection, and survived, can recall it with great clarity. As we have seen, Emilio Foà survived two such determinations for death. "The selection would happen like this: Suddenly in the evening, or night, or even at midnight, a bell would ring to awaken us. We did not know if this was a summons for urgent work or a selection. We always imagined that it would be a selection and in fact twice, chilled to the bone, I and the others in my block went to Block 1 where two SS officers sat at a table and watched the naked deportees file past." From the selections they made, Foà deduced that the officers focused on emaciation, which in men was very evident in their buttocks. "If they saw anyone who was particularly thin or emaciated, especially if they saw violet, hollow buttocks they took note. Evidently, for the physicians it was a symptom of rapid physical decline; in camp jargon we called such people 'Mussulmen.' (I don't know why.) In such cases they took the number, they wrote it on a register, and the following day or that same evening the group of all those whose numbers had been noted was sent back to Birkenau where the gas chambers were."[75] Sherry Weiss-Rosenfeld remembered a very similar process, but her experience was that it did not matter how thin the women's buttocks were, breast size was the determining factor. "Mengele used to come in at random and just select us. If you were young and well-endowed, even if you were very young, he let you live. But if you were flat-chested, that was the end of you. It happened several times. I looked like a twelve-year-old. I was emaciated looking. But I had breasts, and that's why I always remained among the working group, the surviving group, for the time being."[76]

It is not surprising that the inmates should have found a logical explanation for the behavior they witnessed. They presumed a rational basis for their experience. In fact, it was an arbitrary proceeding. Foǎ feared emaciation. Rosenfeld was emaciated, and dreaded the loss of her breasts. Hanna Kent-Sztarkman was flat-chested, and survived. Her older sister Miriam, who was in Auschwitz when Hanna and their mother arrived (they found each other in camp) had an ample bosom. Indeed, her lack of a bra was so bothersome to her that, with their bread rations, her mother and sister bought one for her from another prisoner. It was Miriam's tragic ill-luck (as discussed in "Search and Research") to have boils. "She complained to us on Rosh Hashanah that she had boils, and that she was very annoyed with her *Blockälteste* who was also the nurse for the block. She [the *Blockälteste*] was a religious Hungarian and she told my sister that she could not help her because it was Rosh Hashanah. Then we didn't see her anymore. I assume she didn't make it through the selection because of the boils." But Foǎ had boils, and he passed. Finally, at the very end of October 1944, Mrs Sztarkman was selected. Hanna did not want to be parted from her mother. "I said, 'I want to go with my mother.' So Mengele said, 'All right, let her go with her mother. . . . I assumed that if I went with my mother I would go to my death. I didn't *know* anything, but I assumed that. But I wanted to be with my mother."[77] While they were awaiting their turn to be gassed, the policy on the "special treatment" of the Jews changed. On 2 November 1944, Reichsführer-SS (head of the SS) Heinrich Himmler, the chief of the camp system, ordered the selection and gassing of the Jews to cease. A few weeks later, on 26 November, he commanded the camp administration in Auschwitz to destroy the gas chambers and crematoria. The Soviet army was approaching and Auschwitz would have to be evacuated. It was essential to eliminate evidence of the mass murders. Hanna Kent-Sztarkman and her mother were saved, only to participate in the forced march to Bergen-Belsen and Mrs Sztarkman's death there.

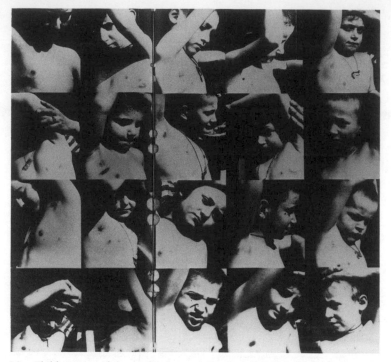

38 Child victims of the medical experiments of the Nazi physician Kurt Heissmeyer, at the Neuengamme concentration camp just outside Hamburg.

No reprieve in the camp system was secure.

The death march and the conditions in the camps to which the prisoners were sent ravaged the inmates. Magda Somogyi and her sister were evacuated from Auschwitz on 18 January when the camp was liquidated. They marched for eight days and then rode in open cattle cars, without warm clothing, coats of any sort, or food or water. They went to Ravensbrück where "the whole day we were in the block. We lay on the floor, and we were so sick, so weak, and covered with lice and boils on our skin. Every day, early in the morning, we stood *Zahlappell* and afterwards the SS whipped us back into our bunk." This existence continued until April, when they were marched to Neustadt. "My sister had typhus. Her face was covered with spots but there was no mirror and she didn't see, and I didn't tell her. Her hair began to turn white. She said she was going to die. . . . She weighed about 25 kilos and I weighed 30 kilos, which meant that I was stronger than she. One day, she told me, 'Magda, I will die.' I told her, 'Don't do it. You need not. No. No. No. No.' She said, 'I can't live anymore.' Two weeks before we were liberated she died."[78]

It is hard to imagine that under conditions such as these people continued to make choices. The circumstances were so narrowly constructed and so harshly imposed that it is difficult to conceive of any room for maneuver. And yet, everyone took decisions and made choices. They did not have the information they needed to make informed decisions and they were not at all certain what fate their choices would bring them. Nevertheless, they persevered, and they did the best they could. When Mária Ezner and her mother and sister came to Strasshof they found that the camp administration "searched for factory workers, seamstresses, agricultural workers, miners," and so on. They had no technical skills, and they had to choose some line of work. Farm laborers were requested first. "My mother thought that agricultural work would be very hard and that neither she nor I could take it. She said we should wait a little. Then, they looked for people to work in a factory." By that time, the Ezners had been in Strasshof only five or six days but the food was so meager that "my mother thought we should go. If we remained there much longer she feared we would be so emaciated that we couldn't work. She reasoned that in a factory there are so many types of work that we could find work too. I was thirteen years old, but I could work." Furthermore, Mrs Ezner was concerned about her younger daughter who was not of an age to be employed. "My mother thought that if two of a family of three people were working, maybe they could save the third one, my sister. She was right in her logic"; the people who disappeared were those who had no working family members. "But she was not right that we should go to a factory. Because in a factory you can't eat iron nails, and in agriculture they could find a potato in the earth. We went to a factory, and that was hunger itself."[79]

András Garzó and his father faced a similar dilemma in Birkenau. Frequently, people were selected, or were asked to volunteer, for industrial work in Germany – or so it was rumored. "I remember that sometimes I was angry with my father because we had different ideas about what to do. I do not remember who took which position, but one of us thought we should leave Birkenau as quickly as possible, while the other thought we should remain; we could not know where we would be transported and maybe it would be a much worse place than where we were." It was a logical deduction. Each place they had been was more brutal than the last. "I really do not remember who wanted to stay and who wanted to go. Perhaps I wanted to go, so that something would happen, and my father had wanted to remain in the brick factory, that is for sure. But there is no reason why we should have been consistent in our ideas, so I really do not know. In any case, it happened that once one of us was chosen to go, but not both. Whichever of us it was drew back from the group. These quarrels were not so deep that we wanted to be separated. Eventually, after about ten weeks, we both were selected to go to work in Germany."[80]

The question of whether to volunteer for anything at all (a task, a commando, a transport) was a serious issue. Was it possible to do something to ameliorate one's situation, or were there too many unknown factors to hazard such a step? With varying degrees of self-consciousness, each young person made that decision. Jack Rubinfeld, for example, presumed that it would be best for his sister, her child, and himself if he could join the group that appeared to be selected for work. He managed to mingle in, and he went to a factory where the inmates did not die either from starvation or lack of sanitation. His friend also tried to insert himself among those who had been specially selected, and the Germans cracked his head open for his pains. Other people in the compound with Rubinfeld and his friend and sister chose not to try and they were deported to Bełżec. There was just no way to know what action would be deleterious, and what beneficial. Sherry Weiss-Rosenfeld's decision "to try to keep a low profile and never to volunteer for anything"[81] was as rational and logical as Rubinfeld's more active stance. The young inmates could not know until the choice was made that (as we have seen) the outcome of their decisions was dependent on luck and chance, rather than insight or perspicacity, and so they continued to choose.

Each young person made individual decisions as to how best to negotiate camp life: in which work detail should one try to obtain a position? Should one put oneself forward or keep in the background? Should one eat one's soup or trade it for a bread ration? What articles were worth their purchase with a food ration, and so on. Nearly all the young inmates, however, chose to remain together with their family or friends, or lacking such intimate ties, to form new companionships. For the great majority of Jewish youths in the slave labor camps of Nazi-occupied Europe, close relationships were extremely important. We have seen, for instance, how Alexander Ehrmann and his brother decided, "number one: the two of us always will stay together."[82] Despite their quarrels and differing opinions, András Garzó and his father made sure to be chosen for the same transport. Magda Somogyi and her sister mothered the two little four-year-old twins, Hanka and Evichka, and, like the Ehrmanns and the Garzós, they too stayed together. Only death stepped between them. Hanna Kent-Sztarkman defied even that division. When Mengele selected her mother for the gas chambers, Hanna joined her.

These relationships were important for two central reasons. First, they were the last remaining shard of their lives as free human beings, a remnant of their existence before they were numbered slaves. Through these intimate human bonds they maintained an interior self which cared for something beyond bread. If it is true, as the Talmud teaches, that he who saves one life saves as it were the whole world, then it is also true that she who continues to love, care for, look after another human being preserves that gift for herself and for humanity. The second reason why these relationships were so essential to the lives of the young inmates is because, in purely practical terms, they added to their resources to cope with the situation. When the Ehrmann brothers were in Mühldorf, Alexander contracted spotted typhus. By that time there were so many sick people that part of the camp was partitioned off to form a quarantine section. No one wanted to go there, as the conditions amongst the ill were even worse than in the rest of the camp. "I managed to stay in my bunk, I remember, three, four days, five days maybe. Then they transferred me to the sick area. . . . My brother would come [there to see me]. They didn't let prisoners come into that area but somehow he got in. He brought me coffee and aspirins. How he got hold of aspirins I don't know, he never told me. I'd always ask him and he never told. 'I organized it,' was all he'd say. And he kept me alive."[83] In Auschwitz, Frieda Menco-Brommet's mother helped her in very much the same way. Menco-Brommet was sick with one illness after another: scarlet fever, spotted typhus, dysentery, and three bouts of pleurisy. "The strange thing was," she said, "before the war my mother was a very luxurious woman. She always had some sickness, and I was never sick. [In Auschwitz], she was never sick and I was always sick. And we owe it to each other and to ourselves that we are alive because she was physically much stronger than I was. . . . But I was mentally much stronger than she. So we helped each other."[84]

Caring, helpful, and supportive relationships were not maintained solely with family members. As Frieda Menco-Brommet, among many others, emphasized, in addition to the horror and misery "there was also friendship around me." Just one example of this generosity of spirit, time, and physical energy, Brommet remembered, was in January 1945 shortly before the liquidation of Auschwitz. "I didn't see [my mother] for ten days, so I thought she was on transport. There were French girls [in the barrack] who were older than I was. By that time I had typhus, and they told me, 'Don't worry, we'll take you back to Paris with us. From now on, we'll take care of you.' There was another woman who put very, very tiny pieces of bread in my mouth and a little bit of water."[85] Ellen Levi was deported from Terezín to Auschwitz alone, as she had urged her mother not to accompany her. In Birkenau she met two of her companions from Terezín. Hella was one of the girls in her room in the children's home, and Judith was their *Betreuerin*, the head of the room. They went on transport to Lenzing together. "We were to-

gether all the time." While all three were close, the relationship between
the two younger girls (who were sixteen at that time) was especially so.

Hella and I were inseparable. We slept in one bed in order to stay
warmer. I think the relationship with Hella and me was always closer
than with Judith. She was a bit outside, not a real protector, not really
taking care of us, but concerned about us. Concerned, yes. She was
concerned. But with Hella it was very clear. We always managed to
work together and be very close together. . . . Every bit of bread we
shared, really shared. . . . It was very important to have somebody
close, if not a sister then a friend or whatever. I think it was an absolutely human feeling. [It was a relationship] I'm quite sure, of real
friendship [which was] absolutely precious and, yes, *essential.*[86]

Given the circumstances of the inmates' lives it is not surprising that
these relationships did not endure to the end. Occasionally, the situation
changed people. Much more frequently, however, it was death that
ripped them apart. This loss was tragic. It represented the demise of
what they had preserved, of all that had come before, and it brought
total isolation and loneliness. What is astonishing is that those who remained summoned the emotional resources to form new friendships.
When Helga Kinsky-Pollack was deported from Theresienstadt to
Auschwitz she, like Ellen Levi, went alone. She too had urged her father
to remain in the transit camp. However, the head *Betreuerin* from her
room in the children's home, Ella (whom the girls called "Tella"), was in
the transport to Auschwitz with her and both were then sent on to Oederan. The two stayed together "but we had no contact anymore. We
were in the same room but the changed conditions made different people
out of us and it [the relationship] changed. Tella broke down somehow,
inside. She was a wreck; and she was no longer my *Betreuerin,* not even
my friend. Nothing. She was as if I had never been in her room." This
was devastating for the fourteen-year-old Pollack. "At the beginning I
still thought I had a hold on somebody in this queer situation. But soon I
noticed that I didn't have a hold on anybody." She felt abandoned and
forlorn. "I was very much alone, but I had the luck to meet a girl one
year older than I who came from a big family with lots of sisters and
brothers. She was the eldest [in her family], and she looked after me. It
helped me very much. We shared one bed (we always slept two together
there, in the bunks). . . . And she also needed somebody." This relationship had practical as well as emotional benefits. "For instance,
when I got my food, I ate it up immediately. I did not organize keeping a
piece of bread so that I would always have something to eat. She started

to organize it, that I must eat only so much for breakfast and so on. And then, which was wonderful of her, towards the end of our stay there when our hair began to grow, the Jewish head cook recognized her as being from her village. She told her to come to the kitchen when everybody already had got her food, and to fetch another plate of soup. That was the rest in the pot, where there was a lot in it. And she never would eat it alone. She always shared."[87]

Pollack's contact with Tella was severed as a result of their altered circumstances. For most young people, death claimed their closest companions. As we have seen, Esther Geizhals-Zucker arrived in Auschwitz with her mother. Mengele, the Angel of Death, separated the two at the initial selection when he sent the older woman to the left and Esther to the right. "The pain was so great . . . I realized this is the end, I'll never see her again. Somehow I just had the feeling that I would not see my mother again. I was all alone." She began life in Birkenau without a single friend and stunned by the loss of her mother. "There were two young sisters in the same barrack where I was, a girl of maybe twenty, a lovely, lovely girl, and a younger sister who was about my age, and she [the elder] took care of that sister. When she saw that I was alone, she took me under her wing. . . . She knew I was alone and she was very good to me . . . as if I were her younger sister too."[88]

Zucker was bereft of family and close friends within a few hours of her arrival at Auschwitz. Sztarkman was with her mother and Somogyi with her sister almost until the end of the war, when death claimed both. Sztarkman was fifteen, Somogyi a year older. Sztarkman was from Poland, Somogyi from Hungary. The former had lived in a large city, the latter in a small town. Both were devastated by their loss. In Bergen-Belsen Sztarkman tried desperately to keep her mother alive by bartering a portion of her bread for whatever the older woman fancied to eat: sugar, onions, and so on.

One day I came by her bed at the window and she didn't recognize me. Her eyes were still open, she was breathing, but she couldn't see me. Of course, I had seen a lot of dead people, but I didn't see people in the process of dying. The death that I had seen was already final. But I'd never seen a normal person die. I ran into the hospital and I tried to give her some coffee and she couldn't swallow anymore. That was February 1945. When the nurse came in, she threw me out of the room. She took my mother out of the bed and I never saw my mother again. I assume she was one of those dead people in the pile I was passing by each day, and eventually she was buried in a common grave. . . .

At that point I was completely alone. . . . I was just existing like this. [I was walking around] . . . seeing mountains of dead people and I knew that my mother was lying among them, and yet I walked around, eating and sort of living, if you call it living.[89]

Soon after, Sztarkman ran into a woman who recognized her and directed her to *mishpokhe* [extended family] of hers, a woman "who was related through relations of ours, cousins of cousins." That woman was a *Blockälteste*, and Sztarkman stayed in her block. "In that barrack occasionally I got extra soup. She made me what they called a 'runner,' [or messenger]. This is where I stayed the last few weeks until the war ended."[90]

Sztarkman's mother died two months before liberation, Magda Somogyi's sister a fortnight before they were freed. Prior to her sister's death, Somogyi had not experienced any emotion for a long time, "but this tragedy was so deep for me that I began to cry."[91]

For a day I could cry. It was a great emotion for me that I could cry, that I could feel sadness about my sister's death. But always I was thinking these very phrases: "I am alone. I am alone. I am alone. What shall I do alone in the world? So alone."

I did not want to live anymore. I was thinking about my death and I was thinking that it would be better if I died too. After my sister, I could not live anymore.

But in the block there were two Dutch girls. They told me the same words I told Evichka. "You are not alone because we are with you, and we will stay together." You see, there was no difference between us: Hungarians, Dutch, or Polish or Czech; there was no difference. We felt we must be together and from then on I was always with those two Dutch girls. From the time my sister died, I was together with the two Dutch girls. One of them was about twenty-two years old, and the other about twenty. They were older than I, and that is why the elder, the twenty-two-year-old, told me that she would be my mother.[92]

Despite the emotional support and material advantages personal relationships provided, the young inmates were profoundly and fundamentally affected by the system in which they were trapped. Companionship and caring, essential as they were, simply could not protect the young people from the overwhelming, elemental evil they witnessed and the constant, violent abuse they sustained. They deteriorated physically, and they languished spiritually. Foǎ described life in camp as a process of annihilation. "The fact of being incarcerated, of becoming a number, of not having a name anymore" worked to obliterate character, individuality, emotions, and will. "The first thing that happened was that the Germans sought to nullify our personalities. We became numbers. We became automatons, we obeyed orders not even out of fear, but because we became accustomed to doing so, because our will was quashed, first attenuated and then eradicated." There was no positive readjustment, no regrouping of resolution. Time brought progressive degeneration. "Our personalities, our will, our interests were obliterated. We hardly thought about our homes. We did not have either the time (so oppressed were we by the severity of daily life) or the desire to think about our dear ones who remained in my case in Italy, in other cases in other countries." In short, "we vegetated, surviving. . . . Our consciousness was dimmed. [From time to time] there was a glimmer of interest, but then we plunged back to our prosaic life, to a life of absolute robots, of slaves – slaves in the true meaning of the word."[93]

Life was too harsh, and the young people were too busy coping with it, to have the time or space to react emotionally. They very soon became numb and apathetic. "The first days" after she arrived in Auschwitz, "I cried," Magda Somogyi remembered. "After a month I did not cry anymore. I did not cry. I did not laugh. I wasn't sad, nothing, nothing."[94] The day Ellen Levi arrived in Auschwitz she met Judith, her room leader from Terezín, who had been deported from the transit camp a week earlier. "Then I asked a very important question. I said, '*Judith, wo ist deine Mutter?* Where is your mother?' Then Judith told me what happened. That was my first realization of what really happened. Then I realized that my father [who had been sent on transport earlier] was not there anymore, that he was gone. I did not mourn him then, absolutely not. I had to put that away; there was no time."[95]

To suppress emotions, to cease to think, was the only way to get through the day. Living became a matter of quotidian demands and difficulties. As Jack Rubinfeld explained, "after a few weeks I quit thinking about my family. I figured they were dead, and that's it. I kept a back hope, but that was all. I couldn't dwell on it. I couldn't spend much time on it. I was busy surviving the day, busy between working, and how to get food, and how to do this and how to get that." As we have seen, the inmates' focus became increasingly narrow and specific. To negotiate each day was the sole goal, everything else was peripheral. This was what was meant by "survival." It was not a question of "having the luxury of figuring will I survive until after the war," Rubinfeld emphasized. "No, I didn't think that far. I was just thinking of surviving from day to day. I wasn't even thinking. I was just surviving, just staying alive,

39   An American soldier views a child and an infant in an open grave in Nordhausen
concentration camp upon liberation in 1945.

getting some food into myself somehow or other. The best way to pass
the day and night, that's about as far as I thought. I didn't think of anything long-range, or what will be a month from now."[96]

It was not only a question of not having enough time. Many young
people, Alexander Ehrmann among them, pointed out that in the Kingdom of Death there was too much anguish, evil, and malignity to think
about anything other than the day's needs. They did not want to be conscious and they tried to avoid involvement:

> I suspended myself over what was happening. I did not want to be in-
> volved emotionally with what was going on. When I realized that
> Auschwitz was real, all that I heard and didn't understand, or didn't
> want to believe, I dismissed as impossible – suddenly it was real.
> When I heard the babies crying, I said to myself, "Get away from it."
> At the same time I couldn't get away from it. So I said to myself, "Just

. keep your eyes open and try to find the best avenue, whatever is best to escape and survive."[97]

Ellen Levi put it slightly differently. "I think I suppressed all emotions, otherwise I could not survive. I saw people dying, I saw the furnace of the crematorium. And I suppressed feelings; I had to. I think even earlier, even already in Westerbork I suppressed feelings about the trains. I did not want to think about where they were going. I knew fear, but I really didn't know, and I preferred not to know. And this suppression of feelings continued afterwards, it continues, yes, for a long, long time. It continues."[98]

This physical degeneration and emotional atrophy marked the last phase of the history of Jewish children in Nazi-occupied Europe. Baptized into the Kingdom of Death, the young inmates continued to make choices and to maintain relationships. But they had no control over the system. The machinery of death worked too well and ground too fine. Despite the young people's efforts to find a way to navigate the perils of camp life, the support and care they gave to and received from their closest companions, they were doomed. The circumstances of their lives conduced to deterioration, not amelioration. Most young people eked out an existence each day until their ordeal ended in death by selection, starvation, or disease. Liberation saved all too few.[99]

Part Four

Conclusion and Epilogue

Chapter Seven

My War Began in 1945

For nearly half a century after the demise of Nazi Europe, historians have pondered many aspects of those twelve years of terror. They have researched and analyzed the development of National Socialism, the institution of a political system of suppression based on violence, the military campaigns, occupation, collaboration, and national resistance movements, economic growth and exploitation of human resources, the euthanasia program (the destruction of "unworthy life"), and the persecution of minorities, especially homosexuals, gypsies, and Jews. The Judeocide has commanded an especially inspired historiographical literature. The machinery of destruction, the economics of persecution, the social and political history of the ghettos, the role of the Jewish Councils, the issue of Jewish resistance, the system of concentration camps, and the suffering of the victims have been the subject of myriad works of scholarship. The literature is as rich as it is vast, and this book could not have been written without it.

The focus of all these histories, however, is adults. Children are conspicuously, glaringly, and screamingly silently absent. It is not surprising that this should be so. When we think of "society" we understand this to mean the world of adults. Our dominant paradigm is that society consists of productive, or voting, or participatory members. The only place children have in that scheme is as future participants, the citizens of tomorrow. Given this conceptual framework, it is hard even for those who are concerned with the history of childhood to argue why that history is not marginal. Indeed, the usual theme of children's history has been child-rearing practices and education, in other words, how adults develop the next generation of adults.

While it is not surprising that the history of children should be, and has been, seen as a peripheral concern, this perception is neither correct nor appropriate. If we accept that the *Shoah* [annihilation] is the most radical challenge our society has experienced, and if we accept that the heart of that catastrophe was the murder of one and a half million children because they were without question or discussion totally innocent (the notion of a two-year-old as a participant in the great Zionist conspiracy is ludicrous), then it becomes clear that our relationship to children is the core of our civilization, and that it is now impossible to write our history without recognition of the children's central place. With an understanding of the *Shoah* stripped bare of all rationalizations, explanations, or justifications, in other words, with an apperception of the quintessence of this evil – the persecution of children – we must acknowledge that a history of our society which does not accord a focal role to children fails to provide us with a proper or useful analysis.

One of the most obvious examples of the practical application of the dominant paradigm as reflected in historiography is the dearth of scholarship about the resistance networks that helped Jewish children. While the subject of national resistance movements has received a great deal of attention, the sorts of activities included in these discussions are those which traditionally have been considered to be public and political: armed defiance, sabotage of industry and transport, underground publications, lightning attacks to destroy records or steal documents, and so on. Such missions have defined, until recently, the term "resistance." The result of this conceptual framework is that it reserved the honor of being a resister primarily to men. It also fostered and supported an ideology of courage and heroism that was framed in (what Carol Gilligan has shown us to be) a conventional and quintessentially male construct: the pursuit of an abstract concept of justice.[1] The objective of caring, of saving and preserving lives, of another sort of justice in fact, was relegated to the realm not of history but of charity: to do good works. These resistance activities were consigned to the world of the private and personal, and the (predominantly) women who dedicated themselves to such rescue efforts were not the subject of the historians' curiosity. In this regard, it is interesting to note that the history of women who took on what was considered to be men's work, both legal and underground, such as factory positions, the Maquis [guerrilla resistance], or the clandestine press, has a place in recorded history. In other words, when women moved into "society," into the world of men, they became legitimate subjects of scholarship. Those who remained within the traditional domain of women and devoted themselves to succor, save, and sustain others, especially children, were overlooked, even though the protection and defense of their young charges imperiled their own lives. Danger, dedication to a humanitarian cause, and steadfast resistance to the Nazi program clearly were not, by themselves, the criteria for publicly acclaimed or analytically researched heroism.

The dominant paradigm of society obscured our vision and narrowed our scope of inquiry. If we accept a view of society that is limited to the adult public realm, we lose the richness of the lives of the majority of the population and the world they inhabit: the homely, the private, and the personal, in short, the "marginal." And so a number of central issues of the *Shoah* received little or no attention, such as what human beings did for each other to safeguard their neighbors and how the ideology of the stranger, the other, was brought to bear on the most vulnerable members of the community, those Jewish children without power or resources.

In a similar way, the whole question of Jewish resistance has been framed by the same traditional concepts of armed action.[2] Thus, the Warsaw Ghetto uprising has been the focus of much interest and is remembered each year in the commemoration of Yom Hashoah (a day dedicated to reflection on the *Shoah*). By contrast, the efforts of Jewish underground networks (such as the Oeuvre de Secours aux Enfants – OSE in France, TOZ in Poland – or the Éclaireurs Israélite de France, the French Jewish Scouts) and, indeed, the actions of a number of Jewish councils towards the relief and rescue of the community's children have received much less consideration and are never celebrated. I do not wish to minimize or denigrate armed defiance. The Warsaw Ghetto uprising was a spectacular, awe-inspiring, and monumentally courageous campaign. My point is that there are other forms of courage and other genres of resistance. The policy, for example, of Czerniaków in Warsaw and Gens in Vilna to educate, feed, and protect children out of proportion to their ghettos' resources was another way in which Jews opposed the press of Nazism and held fast to their principles and responsibilities. The activities of Jewish networks throughout Nazi-occupied Europe to save the children is also too frequently forgotten. And, most poignant, the decisions taken by the children's parents on behalf of their daughters and sons is an overwhelmingly painful form of courage and resistance. It cannot be stressed too fervently that it was the parents who took the first and most terrifying step in the protection of their children, as it was they who had to determine whether it was best to send them into hiding, to try to smuggle them out of the country, or to keep them at their side.

The history of children in Nazi-occupied Europe challenges the boundaries of traditional historiography in a multitude of ways. As the literature amply demonstrates, historians have been able to deal with the question of the persecution of adults, or of an entire people, but they have not been able to face the even more harrowing subject of the persecution of children. This is a problem distinct from the issue of who are acceptable or appropriate subjects for historical inquiry, and has to do with sensibilities and sentiment. The historians' unwillingness to accept the murder of children is emotionally different from their incomprehension of the genocide of adults, and so, like everyone else, they have been loath to pursue the subject. While there are a number of reasons for this special sensitivity, the most important is that whereas adults are never seen as totally helpless, children are (and are expected to be) utterly defenseless and dependent. Our understanding of an adult, our archetypal image, is of a person who can make choices and take decisions. Our concept of a child is someone who must be cared for, looked after. To research and analyze the systematic destruction of adults is, consequently, subjectively different from investigating the same program as it applied to children. In the former instance, the historian has the option to lament that the adults did not do more, but in the case of children one can only mourn their fate.

A corollary of these points was raised in "Search and Research": in discussions of the genocide of the Jews the question, "why did you allow this to happen to you?" is often raised. How could those whom we perceive as "adults" – people with power, resources, connections, education, insight, and experience of the world – have done so little to help themselves? If, however, we recognize that children are central to the *Shoah*, that their experience is the heart of that horror and evil laid bare of rationalizations and stereotyped conceptions, then it is clear how inconsequent or, better, how irrelevant such a question is. It is obvious that the only meaningful question is not "why did you allow this to happen to you?" but "why was this allowed to happen?" The treatment of the innocent and the protection of the powerless are, after all, key issues through which we can understand and judge a society. The central conundrum is not why did the *Jews* allow this to happen, but where were the *gentiles*? It is the collusion of the gentile world, their responsibility in the oppression of children and their failure to defend their young neighbors, which emerges as the principal dilemma.

There is a further twist to this discussion. Those who have never confronted the history of the children have deduced from the mortality statistics that the Jews permitted themselves to be handled like the inanimate merchandise (or, alternatively, animate vermin) the Germans supposed them to be. In our history, however, we have seen over and over again that people took decisions and made choices. Adults did so on behalf of children, and as the press of Nazism squeezed harder and

children took on what formerly had been seen as adult tasks and responsibilities, they too decided and chose what to do. While still at
home, parents had to decide whether to try to emigrate as a family, to
send their children to safety in another country, or to attempt to hide,
either all together or separately. If they had no personal contacts who
could help, but had been put in touch with a resistance network that
undertook to find homes, should they relinquish their child to absolute
strangers? The children too made decisions. Older children could not be
forced to hide; should they leave their parents? The then twelve-year-old
Irene Butter-Hasenberg and her elder brother Werner, for instance, had
resolved not to part from their parents even if the latter were successful
in finding a hiding place for their children. As we saw in Chapter 2, "To
Hide," Marianne Marco-Braun shared the young Hasenbergs' feelings.
When her friends Jacob and Gerard Musch found addresses for her
brother and her, she was adamant that she could not, and would not,
hide herself knowing her parents had nowhere to go. "I said, 'But we
can't go without our parents. What about our parents?' They felt it was
more important to take us, being young. I couldn't take that. I said, 'No,
we can't go unless you find something also for my parents.'"[3]

Both the parents and the children were faced with what the scholar
Lawrence Langer has called "choiceless choices,"[4] but as autonomous
human beings (and not ciphers or vermin) they faced those choices and
made decisions. This continued to hold true even after families were
forced to leave their homes and applied to major as well as minor mat-
ters. For example, the gravest and most oppressive decision parents and
children had to make in the transit camps was whether to accompany
family members who were called to go on transport first. As we know,
Ellen Levi insisted that her mother, and Helga Kinsky-Pollack that her
father, remain in Theresienstadt when they were deported to Auschwitz.
Theirs were but two cases of the dilemma thousands of families were
forced to resolve. The issue of choices was a constant everywhere and in
every situation. Just a few instances will serve as a reminder: in the
ghetto, children chose to go over the wall to obtain food, and parents
attempted to ascertain which "resettlement" transport would be best for
their family; in the slave labor camps, young people tried to determine
which work detail would be the most secure, came to their own conclusions about the advisability of volunteering, and chose (even in the
face of death itself) to remain together with their loved ones. These decisions may have availed them little, but they were the acts of thinking
human beings. The young people were not simply numbers.

To make choices does not mean to have a "survival strategy" however. Indeed, the only point at which a long-term survival strategy was

conceivable, let alone feasible, was when the children were still at home. There, they had their whole lives in front of them. The future as yet belonged to them and so did their past. At home they were in a position to make plans which they presumed would hold for the duration of the war. At each successive stage, more of the past and more of the future collapsed, and the scope of their designs for survival increasingly focused on the present. Most children who went into hiding or lived in ghettos were removed from their own homes and neighborhoods, but in the former instance they were with their gentile countrymen, who participated in the outside world, and in the latter they were in an enforced Jewish community in cities and towns they knew. Thus, while they were separated from their personal past, their lives still had some connection to history. Plans for the future in hiding and in ghettos were framed by the conditions of the war: can we remain here until the war is over? If the war ends soon, we will manage.

Such a concept evaporated into a dream in the transit camps. Removed from community and society, isolated from and forgotten by their fellow citizens, children in transit camps literally were distanced from their past, and their future revolved around the *Aussiedlung* transport schedules. Schemes for survival focused on how to elude the list of persons designated for the next train. Everyone in camp, children included, lived according to the rhythm of deportation. That was the end point, and they could not imagine beyond it. And when they arrived in the slave labor camps, the scope of their plans collapsed to a single day. There the young people had no past, no history. They had been baptized into a new world, the Kingdom of Death. There were no long-term plans, just quotidian demands. Their project was daily existence.

Notwithstanding the plans the young people and their parents devised, the choices they made, and the decisions they took, the dominant factors in the determination of their lives were the omnipresent, ubiquitous program for destruction and luck. In the end, the actions people took of their own volition were as likely to work to their detriment as to their benefit. They simply did not have enough information to calculate knowledgeably. The situation they faced was so alien, so different from anything they had experienced personally or had learned through education that they could not apply their knowledge to it. Caught as they were in the net of Nazism, luck and chance ultimately transpired to be the major variables in their lives. In every pattern or phase of life (in hiding, transit camps, the ghettos, and the slave labor camps), fortune and accident were the primary determinants of how the young people negotiated the machinery of death. Thus, for example, Judith Belinfante and Georges Waysand were taken into homes in neighborhoods where everyone knew or surmised their identity but no one betrayed them. Others, like Sara Spier's parents, were betrayed by neighbors who argued with the host family over clothes pins. "They got into a quarrel, and then the neighbor said, 'Well, now I go to the police and tell you have Jews.' They didn't believe he would, but he did."[5]

Irene Butter-Hasenberg has attributed her survival to three miracles.

One of them was that when we were still in Amsterdam, my father met a friend one day who had gotten a South American passport through a man in Sweden. He had written to that man, and he'd gotten these passports. These passports would put you on a list, and being on any list meant that you weren't going to go to Auschwitz. What would happen to you, you didn't know, but it meant protection from going to Auschwitz.

This friend of my father had just gotten these passports, and he gave my father the name of the man in Sweden and said: "Write to him." So my father did that. He sent a little note as if he were an old friend, and he said, "I know you haven't heard from us for a long time, and you're probably curious about how we're all doing. I'm enclosing some pictures so you can see how much the children have grown." And that was that.

When we were in Westerbork, these [Ecuadorian] passports came from Sweden. They were sent to our home address and they were forwarded in the mail. One day my parents got the mail, and there were the passports. I have never been able to understand this; very little mail was forwarded, and how did they [the passports] manage to get through?[6]

The Hasenbergs' passports were forwarded, they passed the controls, and they were not stolen. That was decidedly good luck, and it saved the family from Auschwitz. They were deported to Bergen-Belsen.

Alexander Ehrmann and his family were not so fortunate. They very nearly were saved from deportation through the intervention of an uncle of his. This relative was involved with the Jewish leadership in Hungary and he became a courier who carried money to buy off specific people. Through this work he had contact with a Hungarian officer whom he persuaded to go to the ghetto in Sátoraljaújhely. "On the eve when they took us to the synagogue in the ghetto for the third transport, somebody came in. There was some kind of military officer looking for the Ehrmann family. Supposedly, he was sent by an uncle. We tried to get out but we couldn't because the doors were sealed. A sentry was posted outside. It was a rumor anyway. After the war my uncle confirmed that he really had sent the officer to look for us, but it was too late. The next morning we boarded the train."[7]

Within the construct of the Nazi system of destruction, the role of chance occurrence, of accidental action or timing in the life of each victim cannot be overestimated – both for good and for ill. Hanna Kent-Sztarkman and her mother were miraculously lucky on two separate occasions, once in the ghetto of Radom, and once in Auschwitz.

> One night [in Radom in 1942] we heard shooting. . . . We looked out the window and we saw people running and German soldiers shooting. We got dressed and then a couple minutes later we heard German soldiers in the building yelling, "*Raus! Raus! Raus!*" meaning "Out! Out! Out!"
>
> We all went out and there were masses of people on the street. You could go either to the right or to the left into the middle of the street. We turned to the left. We stood there for about half an hour, and then they told us to go back into the apartment house. We didn't know what happened.
>
> Then we found out: Radom had two ghettos, a small ghetto on one side of town and the bigger ghetto, where we were, in another part of the town. They [the Germans] sent out everybody from the small ghetto to Treblinka that night. They had a few cattle cars left, so they needed some more people. They got all the people from the big ghetto out on the street, and they counted how many people they needed. Some of our neighbors who, when they left the apartment, went to the right were sent to Treblinka. And we, because we turned to the left, were not sent. The luck of the draw.
>
> When my brother and my neighbor's son came home from work, my neighbor's son didn't find his mother and sister. My brother found us. It was just one of those things.[8]

The second time Sztarkman and her mother cheated death was discussed in the last chapter. It occurred in Auschwitz in the autumn of 1944. When Mrs Sztarkman was selected by Mengele for the gas chambers in late October, her daughter chose to go with her. While they awaited their turn, Himmler ordered the camp administration to cease the extermination by gas and to dismantle the crematoria. Chance overrode choice.

In this life of evil and horror that was determined by the ubiquitous murder machinery and luck, children still had their own place, a space that was theirs alone. It was the arena of childhood, and it was within those boundaries, protected by the adults who cared for them, that education, play, and relationships continued. In all the patterns of life that we have discussed, except the slave labor camps, children lived on two levels simultaneously. They adapted to the increasingly alien and bizarre world they were forced to inhabit, and they struggled to maintain a certain normality, to safeguard basic structures of their pre-war existence: school, the activities of youth, family life, and friendships. As their lives moved away from home towards the final destination, less and less space was allowed to this realm until it disappeared entirely in the camps. Yet the children struggled to preserve it.

We have seen that whilst still at home, children were subjected to the Nazi-imposed persecution of segregation (separation from their former gentile companions and the larger communities in which they lived), isolation (banishment from their former world of schools, parks, playgrounds, candy stores, and so on), and differentiation (being marked with a star). The children accommodated to these conditions. They made friends amongst their Jewish peers, and they attended established and newly instituted Jewish schools. They shopped when permitted, and they played only in their own courtyards, gardens, and homes. They learned to wear their stars as a matter of course. And they were in their own homes, with their parents, brothers and sisters, and relatives. They were still all together. Their familial world was still intact.

Evicted from their homes, their situation changed radically. Living a clandestine existence in hiding, most children were bereft of family relationships. Some formed warm attachments to their hosts, most did not. Still, a few basic tenets of childhood remained. The children tried to continue with their education and took up activities and hobbies appropriate to their age: model building, creative writing, knitting, sewing, drawing. Those who were in hiding but lived openly had greater possibilities of maintaining a (superficially) normal childhood. They played with other youngsters, developed relationships with their foster families and, if old enough, sometimes even went to school.

In the ghetto too, at least initially, many children were able to continue with certain aspects of their former lives. They went to school or attended clandestine classes. They maintained friendships. The younger children played games in the streets, the adolescents developed an interest in each other. They went to children's circles and youth clubs, and their Zionist organization activities did not stop. Furthermore, while most young people no longer were in their own homes, the immediate family remained together.

In the transit camps and after the first months of life in the ghettos, these structures crumbled under the pressure of Nazi oppression. In the camps females and males were separated and families were divided. Everyone lived institutionally, in barracks. In the ghettos, *razzias*, forced labor round-ups, and random violence tore families apart. Educational activities in the transit camps and, after some time, in the ghettos too ceased for the most part. The pastimes of children and youths came to an end. Deportation neared. When it finally came and the young people entered the concentration camp world, their lives as children ended. As we have seen, only those old enough to pass as adults, or as bodies capable of adult labor, were allowed to live. The remainder was killed within hours. Those who passed the selection took on the responsibilities of their elders. Often, they felt as if they had become the grown-ups, and their adult relatives were the children for whom they had to care. As the two generations moved through the system of destruction the family structure was shattered, the last vestiges of pre-war parental power and authority were lost, but love and affection endured.

For those Jewish children who were old enough to remember, the memory alone of family life was a source of strength and solace. Children who were separated from their parents when they went into hiding or through the hazards of deportation, daughters who lost contact with their fathers and brothers through the separation of sexes in the camps or because the latter had been picked up in the streets for a forced labor detail, sons who no longer saw their mothers and sisters, and siblings who were not able to remain together remembered each other as they were at the time of parting. Throughout the war they preserved the hope or dream that some day the family would be reunited. In a vague, inchoate way, they presumed that when the war was over they would resume their former life, and the old structures and certainties would be restored. Even those who had seen family members killed, or who had been told that such a fate had befallen them, held out hope for the rest. This was not a clearly formulated or articulated principle, but a fundamental assumption, an interior conviction that carried a certain stability.

Maurits Cohen was eight years old when he went into hiding; his older brothers who also hid were ten and eleven. Neither of the latter survived. One was picked up by the Germans when he and a grandson of the farmer Boogaard (who, it may be remembered, with his family saved over 300 Jews and others hunted by the regime) had bicycled into the nearby village. The other was hiding with a family and attended the local school; he had been told to say that he was an evacuee from Rotterdam. One day, German soldiers entered his classroom and asked which children came from Rotterdam. The little boy said he was, and he was caught. Maurits Cohen was not told of these tragedies at the time. "I learned of everything after the war," he explained.

During the war, I was a child and I was engaged with everyday living. The very impact of the consequences of the war I experienced after the war ended. My war began in 1945, and not in 1940. When I learned that my father and mother would not come back, and my brothers, then the war started. It took me years to get used to the idea, to find my own place, an only child, of course. We had had a very big family, so as a child I had to carry the whole weight of survival.[9]

The children discovered after the war that their dreams had been fantasies, their hopes, illusions. Very few nuclear families were reunited after the war in their entirety, and no extended family escaped without losses. The survivors returned to their homes to find that their loved ones would never join them and that the Jewish community itself had been destroyed. Pre-war society had changed and the life they had known, the habits, manners, tenets, and beliefs had vanished. Indeed, the very shards of their lives had disappeared. Nothing that had been left in their homes was to be found and little that had been entrusted to friends and neighbors was recovered. The plunder of their possessions was permanent. The Germans had done their work thoroughly and, in spiritual collusion with them, the victims' neighbors looted whatever was left. The survivors returned to naught.

When the war ended, Mária Ezner was convinced that her father, who had been arrested before the rest of the family was deported, would survive. Her mother and sister shared her belief, and together they walked and jumped trains from Strasshof to Budapest. The roads and rail lines overflowed with people as the Soviet Army moved west and those who were liberated streamed east. The Ezners were debilitated and exhausted but they continued, driven by the urgent expectation of their reunion with their father and husband. As they trudged on, they saw "Cossacks on their horses. And we saw Tartars [Mongolians], like the great, great Plague of Europe, the Tartars in 1241, the same people. We saw elite troops coming, and Russian soldiers – women – who with two flags organized the traffic at the bridges, and so on." They slept in abandoned homes and ate the food they found in the larders. And then Ezner's mother fell horribly ill with dysentery. "One day she fell, and she thought she couldn't get up. We stood and cried that she should stand up, and then she got the strength and she stood up and we went on and on. If she had known that our father wouldn't come back, maybe she wouldn't have managed. But she said she had the feeling that she had to lead her two children home." Finally they arrived in Budapest, where they stayed with friends of relatives who had not yet returned. They checked the lists of survivors posted by the Joint Distribution Com-

mittee, but "the name of my father never showed up on the list." A few
days later, "somebody said he had met a peasant from our community
and this peasant had said, 'Oh, the lawyer Ezner is at home!' And then
my mother said, 'We'll go home.'"[10] They organized transport with a
peasant who brought a laden cart to the market-place in Pest and returned with it empty. Leaving in the early morning, they arrived in
Abádszalók the following morning.

> The house was empty. Not only was Father not there, the whole
> house was totally empty. No bed, no table, not a chair, nothing. Only
> one thing remained: my mother's piano was brought into the garden.
> Maybe it was too heavy. The people who had robbed everything had
> just left it. That one thing was in the garden. My mother still had her
> blanket with the SS stamp with her and we laid down on the floor and
> went to sleep. That was our homecoming.
>   If I had known that my father would not come back, maybe I
> would have told my mother that we should go to Vienna and not re-
> turn. I adored my father more than anybody. I have never met a man
> such as he. So there was no question as to whether we would return to
> Hungary, because we hoped that Father was working under similar
> conditions to ours. . . . We didn't know that Auschwitz existed. . . .
>   We came back because we didn't know that our father wouldn't
> come back. And we were there; Mother on the ruins of her life. We
> imagined that when we returned we would come back to our old
> lives. The old life never came back. . . . And we had nothing.[11]

A couple of their former friends returned bits of their furniture. "Some
of our neighbors came and denounced other people who had our things.
We went to them, and there were people who said, 'Surely, surely we'll
bring it back.' But there were others who said, 'We?' and we knew that it
was hidden in the attic or cellar." Ezner, her mother, and her sister were
devastated, depressed, and impoverished. "We had no money. We had
nothing."[12]

The Ezners' homecoming was a common occurrence throughout
Europe. Older and younger children, from the cities and the villages, of
all social classes, degrees of religious observance, and nationalities experienced the same return to a void.[13] Mária Ezner had recently turned
fourteen when she, the child of a lawyer, went back to the small village
where she had lived an assimilated, Jewishly unobservant life before the
war. Gerry Mok, by contrast, was just eight years old when the Netherlands was liberated. His father had owned a small fruit shop in the Jewish neighborhood in east Amsterdam where they lived, and they had had

a very Jewish life. Yet, essentially they confronted the same reality. "My personal Auschwitz came after 1945, not before," Mok explained. "I didn't really lose anyone during the war. People left, and I knew that was a disaster, supposedly a disaster, that anything might happen to them. But more or less, I expected them to come back, reasonable or not, and even notwithstanding the fact that people told me that probably my parents were dead. Do you think I believed them? . . . I thought I knew better. I was wrong." He waited and waited. "I expected my parents to come back. I expected everyone to come back. And no one came." It was a loss from which, in a certain sense, he never recovered. Since that time, "I have been missing my parents, I have been missing my grandparents and I have been missing my neighborhood. And I still do."[14]

No one from his enormous extended family returned, and few of his family possessions were given back to him. The day Mok left his parents in February 1942, his father confided their valuables to a gentile man with whom he did business from time to time; "they bought fruits together, things like that." This business associate "came before I left and was asked to take care of all the things that belonged to my parents and my grandparents. He got a big iron box with all the jewels and things of my grandmother, who had a lot of such pieces. He took the box and put it on the back of his car." Mok remembered it well, because it was a sure sign that his parents intended to join him in his hiding home, as they told him they would. "I knew that they would follow me because they gave those valuable things to this man. I knew if my parents did that, they really were planning also to come." When the war was over, and Mok came to the painful realization that his parents would not return and he would not go back to his home, he recalled that some of his parents' things would have been saved, and he would have something that had belonged to them and to his grandparents. "I remembered who had taken the box, and I remembered the man's address because I had been there a thousand times. [My step-parents and I] went there, and oh yes, the man lived at that address and, oh yes, he knew I had lived there, and how fine that little Gerry survived. And I got fruit from him, and he was very nice, but 'the child must be completely mistaken because I never got anything.'" It was frustrating and infuriating, and especially so for Mok whose claim had no authority precisely because he was a child. "I remembered his name, I remembered his address, I remembered his car, I remembered the place he put it on his car, I remembered that he came, I remembered the fuss that was made about it. And then I went there, he recognized me, yes he knew my father, yes he knew my grandfather's wagon driver, he knew everybody. And everything was true except, coincidentally, strangely enough, what I told about valuables. So: 'The child must be wrong; how nice that a child can imagine a thing like that.'"[15]

The extent of the neighborly theft and the degree to which these ordinary people had justified their gains to themselves ranged from the astounding to the bizarre. Many children who survived and returned to their home towns after the war have related that, when they went to visit neighbors, friends of their parents, they were nicely treated and amiably received. They even were invited to come in, to sit down, and to eat. But the same people denied having received jewelry, china, linen, or silverware from the deported family. And there the child sat, eating off her mother's own dishes. In rural areas, where land and livestock were the valuables a family owned, children returned to villagers who denied that they or their families had ever existed. In some cases their reception was benign: the children simply never had lived there. In other instances, people who had the temerity to return were murdered.[16] Wealth so easily obtained was not so easily renounced. In many places, Jews who survived were an unwanted encumbrance, an intolerable presence. Moishe Kobylanski and his family were hidden by several people in and around their village of Gruszwica in the Ukraine, some of them Ukrainian and some Czech. The last family to take them in were Czech farmers who lived very near to the Kobylanskis' own home. From late 1943 until the beginning of February 1944 the Kobylanski family hid in a six by six by four foot pit which had been dug out under the pigsty. The wooden floor of the pigsty was their roof. "When the Russians came in, February 2nd of 1944, we were about two blocks away from our house. The Russians came one day, and early the next morning, before dawn we got out of the hole. We didn't wait to have breakfast with these people. We didn't want to compromise them. We left the hiding place in the pigsty and we went to our house. That way, no one knew where we came from, no one would know where we had been. The people who hid us would be safe and no one would know that they had hidden Jews, because some people might take retribution against them." The Kobylanskis returned to their home only briefly. They did not stay. They were no longer members of that community. "There was no question. We left the house. Everything was very casual. There was no sense of belonging and no sense of things belonging to us. The term 'my house' had no meaning. I think that's how I felt at that time. The house was just another encumbrance. We couldn't carry it with us, we couldn't sell it. So the hell with it."[17] To wait until they could sell it was out of the question. It was too dangerous. Once again, they left their home for safety elsewhere.

Returning children received little sympathy from their neighbors, and they encountered indifference from their national governments. In the

immediate post-war period (from 1945 to 1950) politicians were preoccupied with the business of rebuilding their countries, and the plight
of Jewish children did not figure prominently in that agenda. The cities
had been bombed, the infrastructure shattered, and the financial system
was in ruins. The population, which had been united under a national
flag before the war, had been riven apart by Nazism, Fascism, and the
occupation. Resisters and collaborators had fought against each other
for years while the great majority of people simply had endured the
hardships of war. There was no solidarity between these three factions;
they had not experienced the war in the same way and there was no sympathy between them. It was the politicians' job to stitch their citizenry
together. This was the predominant national project, and the issue of the
Jews, the iniquities that had been perpetrated against them during the
war, their current plight, and their uncertain future, was a low-priority
problem.[18]

Surviving Jews were, after all, perceived to be marginal to society.
They were few in number and, as the local conditions were so inhospit-
able, a considerable proportion emigrated shortly after they had returned. Stripped of power and resources, and severely debilitated by
their years of hardship, the Jews – especially Jewish children – were not
part of the mainstream. Furthermore, the enormity of the Judeocide was
not fathomed. The Jews were seen as just another group of victims; their
special history and predicament was neither recognized nor understood.
This obtuseness was exacerbated by the ideology of the newly elected
Social Democratic governments in the west and the instituted socialist
regimes in the east. These governments eschewed the nationalist and
racist designations of Nazism and Fascism, and as part of their political
theory demanded that all citizens were the same and were to be treated
equally. In so doing they failed to acknowledge and indeed denied the
unique situation of the Jews during the war.[19]

In short, because of the pragmatic considerations of reuniting the
country, the apparent marginality of the Jews, and the contemporary
political ideology, the national goal throughout Europe was a ritualistic
purification rather than a serious attempt to redress wrongs or to
address the dilemma of accountability.[20] Justice (abstract or concrete)
was not the order of the day. After popular rage was spent during the
first few days following liberation, and after a public condemnation of
all those (and their families) who had been members of collaborationist
organizations, attention was diverted from the ordinary sympathizers to
the extraordinary villains.[21] In each country a few major figures were
tried, but in general their crime was high treason, not genocide. Those
who had benefited from their fellow countrymen's misfortunes, who had

betrayed their neighbors, who had been involved in the expropriation of property; the bureaucrats who had maintained the national train systems and who had demanded payment for the Jews who were shipped on their lines, and the industrialists who had used Jews as slave laborers, were rarely brought to trial. That what had happened to the Jews was of no consequence becomes all too clear in an examination of the one comprehensive attempt to screen a whole nation: the de-Nazification process in occupied Germany. The *Fragebogen*, or questionnaire, which had to be answered by everyone whom the Allied Military Government suspected of having been associated with the National Socialist regime, focused on nine distinct topics. These included personal data (name, address, nationality, religion, etc.), education, profession or trade, employment and military service, membership in and service for organizations, writings and speeches, income and assets, and travel or residence abroad. The Final Solution was never mentioned, and the systematic destruction of the Jews was alluded to in only four of the 131 questions (numbers 121–4). Under the heading "Income and Assets" the respondent was asked whether he or she "had acquired property which had been seized from others," and whether "you ever acted as an administrator or trustee of Jewish property in furtherance of Aryanisation decrees or of ordinances?"[22] Possessions, not persons, were of interest. No one was asked what he did when he saw a two-year-old taken away.

The result of this project (which, it must be emphasized, was shared by all the governments in Europe), was that the singular responsibility of each country towards its Jewish citizens was disregarded and the survivors' sensibilities dismissed. They were neither defended nor avenged. And there was no national policy to integrate them into society, to provide the special economic, social, and psychological assistance they required. Children who returned had lost years of education and normal socialization as well as family, friends, home, and community. Little effort was expended and few programs were instituted to help them normalize their lives, rejoin their gentile peers.[23] To the contrary, they were left to deal with their difficulties alone. Indeed most children did not even have the company of other young people in the same predicament to provide support. When Mária Ezner and her mother and sister returned to their empty home in Abádszalók, they had no money and nothing to sell. Mrs Ezner was a broken woman, and it was the fifteen-year-old Mária's responsibility to provide food for her family. Education, gymnasium and university studies, was out of the question. "It was the negation of my personality that I would not go on to study. That was a problem I myself confronted alone. There was no community, no mass of people, like in the deportation. There were no children with whom I could speak, like in the ghetto. I stood alone. And the whole misery of our situation fell on my head then."[24] Sara Spier had no home to which to go, and although she waited for them, her parents and her little brother did not return from deportation. She and her sister found that they had to fend for themselves. Like Mária Ezner's, her pre-war assumptions about her future were absolutely impracticable in the post-war world. She was fifteen when she went into hiding and eighteen when she re-entered society. "When the war was over, I had had two years of gymnasium. I couldn't go to university. I would have loved to. I had thought to study Dutch or medicine. And there I was, I had only two years of high school, I had no parents, and I could see that I was not going to be looked after. I had to look after myself from the very moment the war was over." The couple who had helped her to hide, Cor and Trijntje van Stam, got her a position in a hospital where she could study to be a nurse. At that time, there was no school for nursing in the Netherlands. Both the theoretical and the practical education were conducted in the hospital, and the young women trainees received pocket money, room, and board. Three weeks after the war ended, Spier moved to the hospital. She had no home, no money, and no profession. The nursing course offered all three. In its own way, it was another choice-less choice and, as she said, "I was very, very lonely after the war." She completed the course and took her examinations, and "then I thought, 'I'd like to study medicine; I'll go to school in the evening.' During the day I was a nurse and in the evening, I did my high school course. So I only worked and I ate and I slept. So, really, another piece of my youth was completely gone. Ultimately, I succeeded and got my gymnasium diploma. I was twenty-eight years old, and I was so tired by that time that I did not go to do university studies."[25]

The sub-text of the lack of policy to provide Jewish children with the help they needed, of the emphasis on the project of national rebuilding and unity rather than responsibility and accountability was: "We, as a nation, must forget about the past and look to the future. And you, Jewish children, must forget what happened to you, and go on with your lives." There was a sub-text to that message too, and it read: "We do not want to know. We do not want to hear about it." Thus, the European enthusiasm for the establishment of the state of Israel was because it provided a country for the Jews to build. The survivors too could work towards the future of their nation. Israel was a convenient counterpart to their own agenda and, by the way, an expedient national home – not for the Jews as individuals, but for people whose very presence remained a challenge to the Europeans' carefully constructed national histories of the war years and the national self-perception of heroism and Christian charity.

On a personal level, the sub-text was clearly articulated. Sara Spier's experience with the head nurse of the hospital where she had obtained a training position is a typical example of the imposed conditions for readmission into society. The head nurse had done many wonderful things during the war. She had helped Jews and others who had had to hide, and she had hidden people in the hospital itself. "But when I went just to make her acquaintance, she said, 'Well, you can come here, you can work like everybody else, but the war is over now, so no word about the war. You may come, you come to work and you come to learn to be a nurse, and we won't speak about the war and you don't speak about your Jewish background. No stories.'"[26]

The children could not forget their histories, of course, and just because they were forbidden to speak did not mean that they would not remember. Within each Jewish child who survived the war, the past remained intact and undigested. It became an unspoken and unintegrated personal history; an unopened internal package. The silence continued. Now adults, most child survivors have not recounted their histories to their spouses or children. I was grateful that so many agreed to share their past with me, and I asked why they were willing to do so. In every European language, the same answer was given: "Because you asked."

Notes

For the convenience of the reader, all books which have been translated into English will be cited in the English version. The original language edition will be noted in brackets if it was used. (The quality of the translation varies greatly.) All other translations (of texts, interviews, and archive documents) have been done by the author. The names of the child survivors as they appear in the text are as they were at the time, with the insertion of women's married names, if used. The corresponding names in the notes are those in current use. Thus, for example, Hanna Kent-Sztarkman was born Hanna Sztarkman. Kent is her married name. The current spelling of her name is Hannah Kent-Starkman, and this is how it appears in the notes.

Please note that page numbers have been given for the interview transcripts, even though neither the tapes nor texts are held in a public repository. It is my hope that eventually they will be made available and I have provided specific citations with that end in mind.

The following abbreviations have been used:
CDEC   Centro di Documentazione Ebraica Contemporanea (Milan)
CDJC   Centre de Documentation Juive Contemporaine (Paris)
PRO   Public Records Office (London)
RIOD   Rijksinstituut voor Oorlogsdocumentatie (Amsterdam)
YIVO   Jewish Scientific Research Institute (New York)

Introduction: Search and Research

1   For a description and analysis of the Yad Vashem Martyrs' and Heroes' Memorial Authority in Jerusalem, see James E. Young, *Writing and Rewriting the Holocaust: Narrative and the Consequences of Interpretation* (Bloomington: Indiana University Press, 1988), pp.186–7.
2   There is a substantial discussion in the historical literature on the role of

language in the Nazi machinery. See, inter alia: Hannah Arendt, *Eichmann in Jerusalem* (New York: Penguin, 1984), pp.52, 83–6, 105–11, 135–50; C.C. Aronsfeld, *The Text of the Holocaust* (Marblehead, MA: Micah Publications, 1985), esp. the introduction and pp.1–59; Randall Bytwerk, *Julius Streicher* (New York: Stein and Day, 1983), Chapter 7 and pp. 143–59; Gerald Fleming, *Hitler and the Final Solution* (Berkeley and Los Angeles: University of California Press, 1984), pp.17–31; Henry Friedlander, *The Holocaust* (Millwood, NY: Kraus International Publishing, 1980), pp.103–13; Saul Friedländer, *Reflections on Nazism* (New York: Avon Books, 1986); Sara Gordon, *Hitler, Germans, and the "Jewish Question"* (Princeton: Princeton University Press, 1984), pp.91–118.

3   The cynicism of this transformation was not lost on contemporaries. Its first official use by the National Socialists as a mark of shame and segregation was in the anti-Jewish boycott of 1 April 1933. In response, on 4 April the well-respected Berlin Zionist periodical, *Jüdische Rundschau*, published an editorial, "Wear the Yellow Badge With Pride," by its editor-in-chief, Robert Weltsch. See: Robert Weltsch, "Wear the Yellow Badge With Pride," in *Out of the Whirlwind*, ed. Albert Friedlander (New York: Schocken, 1976), pp.119–23. Weltsch's article is well known and frequently mentioned in the historical literature. See, for example, Lucy Dawidowicz, *The War Against the Jews, 1933–1945* (New York: Bantam, 1986), p.176; or Yehuda Bauer, *A History of the Holocaust* (N.Y.: Franklin Watts, 1982), pp.114–45. Private diaries also noted the transmutation of armbands of "honor" to armbands of "shame." See Chaim A. Kaplan, *Scroll of Agony: The Warsaw Diary of Chaim A. Kaplan*, edited by Abraham I. Katsh (New York: Collier, 1973), pp.78, 81. See also the general discussion of Jewish reaction to the star in Philip Friedman's "The Jewish Badge and the Yellow Star," in Philip Friedman, *Roads to Extinction* (New York: The Jewish Publication Society, 1980), pp.11–33; Raul Hilberg, *The Destruction of the European Jews* (New York: Holmes and Meier, 1985), pp.753–54; Léon Poliakov, *L'étoile jaune* (Paris: Éditions du Centre, 1949), pp.43–48; Jacob Presser, *The Destruction of the Dutch Jews* (New York: Dutton, 1969), pp.118–27 [*Ondergang* (The Hague: Staatsuitgeverij, 1965)].

4   For a summary of the antisemitic policies of Germany's European axis allies see: Nora Levin, *The Holocaust* (New York: Schocken, 1973), pp.459–68, 527–618. For a more detailed discussion, see: Hilberg, *Destruction of the European Jews*, 2 vols., pp.660–79, 718–860. Recommended individual monographs on the history of the Jews in each of these countries during this period include: Rumania: Julius S. Fisher, *Transnistria: The Forgotten Cemetery* (New York: Thomas Yoseloff, 1969); Hungary: Randolph L. Braham, *The Politics of Genocide* (New York: Columbia University Press, 1981), 2 vols.; Nathaniel Katzburg, *Hungary and the Jews: Policy and Legislation, 1920–1943* (Ramat Gan: Bar-Ilan University Press, 1981); Italy: Renzo De Felice, *La storia degli ebrei sotto il fascismo* (Turin: Einaudi, 1961); Meir Michaelis, *Mussolini and the Jews: German-Italian Relations and the Jewish Question in Italy, 1922–1945* (Oxford:

Oxford University Press, 1978); Bulgaria: Frederick B. Chary, *The Bulgarian Jews and the Final Solution* (Pittsburgh: University of Pittsburgh Press, 1972).

5   Claude Levy and Paul Tillard, *Betrayal at the Vél d'Hiv* (New York: Hill and Wang, 1969), pp.158–59 [*La Grande Rafle du Vél d'Hiv* (Paris: Robert Laffont, 1967)].

6   Alexander Donat, *The Holocaust Kingdom* (New York: Holocaust Library, 1978), p.89.

7   Ibid., p.91.

8   See the testimony of Rudolf Vrba in Claude Lanzmann, *Shoah* (New York: Pantheon, 1985), p.152. See also Robert J. Lifton, *The Nazi Doctors* (New York: Basic Books, 1986), pp.147, 149, 176. Pregnant women who managed to pass through the initial selection were in constant danger of detection and, of course, subsequent death. Jewish prisoner physicians and midwives were called upon to perform abortions or, if the child was born, to murder it immediately so as to make it appear to have been a stillbirth. See: Olga Lengyel, *Five Chimneys – Story of Auschwitz*, esp. chapter 15, "Accursed Births" (Chicago: Ziff Davis, 1947), pp.99–103; Lifton, *Nazi Doctors*, pp.149, 183, 224–5; Giselle Perl, *I Was a Doctor in Auschwitz* (New York: International Universities Press, 1948), and an article about Perl, "Out of Death, a Zest for Life," *The New York Times*, 15 November 1982.

9   Sara Grossman-Weil, interview with author, Malverne, NY, 29 and 30 April 1987, transcript p.28. Not surprisingly, the immediate selection of mothers and children for death is recorded over and over again in the camp survivor literature. See, inter alia, the testimonies of Marika Frank Abrams, Lydia Brown, and Sally Grubman in *Voices from the Holocaust*, ed. Sylvia Rothchild (New York: New American Library, 1981), pp.188, 280, 244–5; Donat, *Holocaust Kingdom*, p.164; Thomas Geve, *Guns and Barbed Wire* (Chicago: Academy Chicago Publishers, 1987), pp.35–6; Livia E. Bitton Jackson, *Elli: Coming of Age in the Holocaust* (New York: Times Books, 1983) pp.66, 74–5; Isabella Leitner, *Fragments of Isabella* (New York: Dell, 1978), p.31; Primo Levi, *Survival in Auschwitz* (New York: Collier, 1961), p.16 [*Se questo é un uomo* (Turin: Einaudi, 1985)].

10   Ida Groenewegen van Wyck-Roose, Cor Grootendorst, and Truus Grootendorst-Vermeer, interview with author, Nieuw Vennep, The Netherlands, 1 July 1986, transcript pp.13–4.

11   Primo Levi, *Moments of Reprieve* (New York: Summit Books, 1985), pp.30–32 [*Lilit e altri raconti* (Milan: Einaudi, 1986)].

12   Berthe Jeanne (Bertje) Bloch-van Rhijn interview with the author and Robert Jan van Pelt, Doetinchem, The Netherlands, 21 June 1984.

13   Interview with Groenewegen, Grootendorst, and Grootendorst-Vermeer, p.13.

14   For more information, see Lucjan Dobroszycki's nearly 60-page scholarly introduction to the *Chronicle*. Lucjan Dobroszycki, ed., *The Chronicle of the Łódź Ghetto* (New Haven: Yale University Press, 1984).

15   Dobroszycki, *Chronicle*, pp.16, 61.

16 Ibid., pp.360–1.
17 Emmanuel Ringelblum, Notes from the Warsaw Ghetto, edited by Jacob
    Sloan (New York: Schocken, 1974), pp.295–6.
18 Ibid., p.140.
19 Ibid., pp.204–5.
20 Ibid., pp.223, 233–4.
21 Kaplan, Scroll of Agony, pp.25, 27, 30, 57–8, 400.
22 Philip Mechanicus, Waiting for Death (London: Calder and Boyers, 1968),
    p.16.
23 Kaplan, Scroll of Agony, pp.81, 220.
24 Mechanicus, Waiting for Death, p.100.
25 Ibid., p.179.
26 There is a large literature on oral history, including a number of extremely
    helpful general studies and several journals which reflect the continuing de-
    velopment in the field. See: E. Culpepper Clark et al., "Communicating in
    the Oral History Interview: Investigating Problems of Interpreting Oral
    Data," International Journal of Oral History 1 (February 1980): 28–40;
    George Ewart Evans, Where Beards Wag All: The Relevance of the Oral
    Tradition (London: Faber, 1970); David Henige, Oral Historiography
    (New York: Longman, 1982); Paul Thompson, The Voice of the Past
    (Oxford: Oxford University Press, 1978); Jan Vansina, Oral Tradition
    (Chicago: Aldine, 1965) [De la tradition orale, in Annales du Musée Royal
    de L'Afrique Centrale, Sciences Humaines, 36 (Tervuren, Belgium, 1961)].
    Suggested journals for further reading: International Journal of Oral
    History; Oral History; Oral History Review. Articles about oral history
    projects in other communities, but which deal with problems apposite to
    this study: Sherna Gluck, "What's So Special About Women: Women's
    Oral History," and Tamara Hareven, "The Search for Generational
    Memory," in Oral History: An Interdisciplinary Anthology (Nashville,
    TN: American Association for State and Local History, 1984), pp.221–37,
    248–63; Kenneth Kann, "Reconstructing the History of a Community,"
    International Journal of Oral History 2 (February 1981):4–12.
27 CDJC Document XCIV-2. Jacques Bloch, "Jewish Child-Care, Its Organ-
    isation and Problems" (A report presented at the Geneva Council of the
    International Save the Children Union) in When Winter Comes . . . Special
    Issue of the Information Bulletin of the OSE Union (Geneva, December
    1946) p.12. The precise figures adduced by Bloch were: pre-war population
    of 1.6 million Jews under 16 years old living in what became the theater of
    war; post-war population of 175,000; "This figure includes 30,000 chil-
    dren repatriated from the Soviet Union to Poland and Romania." CDJC
    Document XCIV-3. Z.H. Wachsman, The Rehabilitation of Jewish Chil-
    dren by the 'OSE' (New York: American Committee of OSE Inc., NY,
    1947), p.3. According to Wachsman, at the time of liberation in 1945, only
    6–7 percent of the original number of Jewish children had survived the
    war. Later, with repatriates from the Soviet Union, the numbers increased
    to an estimated pre-war child population of 1.5 million and post-war figure
    of 170,000. The percentage of child survivors was not uniform across

Europe, of course. According to Lucjan Dobroszycki, there were close to a million Polish Jewish children aged fourteen or under in 1939. After the war there were approximately 5,000, or half a percent. This figure does not include children who survived in the Soviet Union and were repatriated later, nor, *nota bene*, those aged fifteen and sixteen. Nevertheless, it is clear that the survival rate for children in Poland was lower than elsewhere, as was the survival rate (10 percent) for Polish Jews in general. Lucjan Dobroszycki, "Redemption of the Children" in Alizah Zinberg, Barbara Martin, and Roger Kohn, *An Inventory to the Rescue of Children, Inc. Collection, 1946–1985* (New York: Yeshiva University Archives, 1986), p.6. Kiryt Sosnowski has adduced the same figure of 5,000 children in his book, *The Tragedy of Children Under Nazi Rule* (Poznań: Western Press Agency, 1962), p.73.

28 Interview with Sara Grossman-Weil, conversation preceding taped recording.

29 Not surprisingly, this belief is often mentioned also in the survivor memoir literature written by women. See, for example, Jackson, *Elli*, p.95.

30 Henry Starkman, interview with author, Bloomfield Hills, MI, 8 December 1984 and 19 January 1985, transcript pp.24–5.

31 Hannah Kent-Starkman, interview with author, Stamford, CT, 13 December 1985, transcript p.24. See also the specific mention of boils as a reason for being sent to death in Lifton's chapter, "Selections in the Camp," in *Nazi Doctors*, p.181.

32 The issue of narrative structure has usually been discussed from the perspective of the professional historian, but obviously it is applicable to the history recounted by what I call the "participant/historian," i.e. child survivor or adult resistance worker. See: Lionel Gossman, "History and Literature," Louis O. Mink, "Narrative Form as a Cognitive Instrument," and Hayden White, "The Historical Text as Literary Artifact," in *The Writing of History: Literary Form and Historical Understanding*, ed. Robert H. Canary and Henry Kozicki (Madison: University of Wisconsin Press, 1978), pp.3–40, 129–50, 41–62. See also the first three chapters in Hayden White, *The Content of Form* (Baltimore: Johns Hopkins University Press, 1987), 1–82. David Faris has applied some of White's ideas to oral history: David Faris, "Narrative Form and Oral History: Some Problems and Possibilities," *International Journal of Oral History* 1 (November 1980): 159–80.

33 Hayden White, *Metahistory: The Historical Imagination in Nineteenth-Century Europe* (Baltimore: Johns Hopkins University Press, 1973), pp.7–9.

34 I use the term "boys' adventure tale" advisedly. This form was never used by women. Interestingly, in his article on Ruhr miners under Nazi oppression, the historian Detlev Peukert noted that "Men tend to recall the heroic, while women resuscitate the dull grey of everyday." I would put it otherwise, and certainly the reason Peukert adduces for the gender differences ("the division of roles between the sexes") is not sufficient to explain the gender-specific differences in narrative styles among the resistance workers

with whom I spoke, yet our experience was the same. Detlev Peukert, "Ruhr Miners Under Nazi Oppression," *International Journal of Oral History* 1 (June 1980): 118.

35 Alice Hoffman, "Reliability and Validity in Oral History," in *Oral History*, ed. David K. Dunaway and Willa K. Baum (Nashville, TN: American Association for State and Local History, 1984), p.69. See also Trevor Lummis, "Structure and Validity in Oral Evidence," *International Journal of Oral History* 2 (June 1981): 109–20.

36 Levi, *Moments of Reprieve*, pp.10–11. As Levi was born in 1919 and the Italian racial laws were passed in 1938, he was nineteen years old when Fascism first affected his life in a significantly negative way.

37 Halina Birenbaum, *Hope Is the Last to Die* (New York: Twayne Publishers, 1971), p.244.

38 Leitner, *Fragments of Isabella*, pp.102, 105.

39 The charges of passivity, cooperation, and indeed collusion occur over and over again in the historical literature in various guises and with regard to many aspects of life under Nazi rule. The Jewish leadership, of course, is the most frequent target of these criticisms. For a small sampling of this sort of debate, see: Raul Hilberg's "Reflections," in which he has observed that "the Jewish victims, caught in the straitjacket of their history, plunged themselves physically and psychologically into the catastrophe." *The Destruction of the European Jews* (New York: Holmes and Meier, 1985), pp.1030–44; Hannah Arendt, *Eichmann in Jerusalem: A Report on the Banality of Evil* (New York: Penguin, 1984), pp.117–26; Jacob Robinson's response to Arendt, *And the Crooked Shall be Made Straight: The Eichmann Trial, the Jewish Catastrophe, and Hannah Arendt's Narrative* (Philadelphia: Jewish Publication Society of America, 1965), especially Chapter 4, "Jewish Behavior in the Face of Disaster," and Chapter 5, "The Fate of Jews in Specific Areas and Periods." For more recent discussions of similar issues focused on western Europe rather than the Judenräte of central and eastern Europe, see: Jacques Adler, *The Jews of Paris and the Final Solution: Communal Response and Internal Conflicts, 1940–1944* (New York: Oxford University Press, 1987) [*Face à la persécution: les organizations juives à Paris 1940 à 1944* (Paris: Calmann-Lévy, 1985)]. Note in particular Adler's analysis of the role of the Union Générale des Israélites de France (UGIF) with regard to children and the children's homes they ran, pp.123–8, 158–61. Hans Knoop, *De Joodsche Raad* (Amsterdam: Elsevier, 1983); and Maurice Rajsfus, *Des juifs dans la collaboration: l'UGIF, 1940–1944* (Paris: Études et Documentation Internationale, 1980) and *Sois juif et tais-toi: 1930–1940, les français "israélites" face au nazisme* (Paris: Études et Documentation Internationale, 1981).

Chapter One: At Home

1 Hilma Geffen-Ludomer, interview with author, Ann Arbor, MI, 29 November 1984, transcript pp.1, 2.

2 Philip Gerrit Mok, interview with author, Amsterdam, The Netherlands, 11

June 1986, transcript p.1.

3   Ibid., pp.1–4.

4   Martin Koby, interview with author, Ann Arbor, MI, 11 and 25 November 1987, transcript pp.1–2.

5   Ibid., pp.2–5, 12–3, 15.

6   Mania Salinger-Tenenbaum, interview with author, Bloomfield, MI, 10 and 29 January, and 7 March 1987, transcript p.2.

7   Ibid., pp.2–3, 5–7.

8   Frieda Menco-Brommet, interview with author, Amsterdam, The Netherlands, June 1986, transcript p.1.

9   Ibid., pp.1–2.

10   Ibid., p.4.

11   There is a vast literature on the machinery of genocide. See first: Raul Hilberg, *The Destruction of the European Jews*, revised and definitive edition, 3 vols. (New York: Holmes and Meier, 1985). Then, inter alia, Christopher Browning, *Fateful Months: Essays on the Emergence of the Final Solution* (New York: Holmes and Meier, 1985); Lucy Dawidowicz, *The War Against the Jews* (New York: Bantam, 1986); Gerald Fleming, *Hitler and the Final Solution* (Berkeley: University of California Press, 1984); Martin Gilbert, *The Holocaust: A History of the Jews of Europe during the Second World War* (New York: Holt, Rinehart and Winston, 1985); Gerhard Hirschfeld, ed., *The Policies of Genocide: Jews and Soviet Prisoners of War in Nazi Germany* (Boston: Allen and Unwin, 1986); Ian Kershaw, *The Nazi Dictatorship: Problems and Perspectives of Interpretation* (London: Edward Arnold, 1985); Claude Lanzmann's film, *Shoah*; Nora Levin, *The Holocaust: The Destruction of European Jewry, 1933–1945* (New York: Schocken, 1973); Michael Marrus's clear and informative bibliographic essay on this subject, "The Final Solution," in Marrus, *The Holocaust in History* (Toronto: Lester and Orpen Dennys, 1987); Arno J. Mayer, *Why Did The Heavens Not Darken? The "Final Solution" in History* (New York: Pantheon, 1990); George Mosse, *Toward the Final Solution: A History of European Racism* (New York: H. Fertig, 1978); Karl Schleunes, *The Twisted Road to Auschwitz: Nazi Policy Towards the Jews, 1933–1939* (Urbana: University of Illinois Press, 1970).

12   Reprinted in: Raul Hilberg, *Documents of Destruction: Germany and Jewry, 1933–1945* (Chicago: Quadrangle Books, 1971), pp.20–1.

13   Reprinted in: Renzo De Felice, *Storia degli ebrei italiani sotto il fascismo* (Turin: Einaudi, 1972), p.563.

14   Reprinted in Yitzhak Arad, Yisrael Gutman, and Abraham Margaliot, eds, *Documents on the Holocaust* (Jerusalem: Yad Vashem, 1981), p.214.

15   For a discussion of this process see Hilberg, *The Destruction of the European Jews*, pp.94–134.

16   Israel Cohen, "The Jews in Hungary," *Contemporary Review*, November 1939, pp.571–79; Nathaniel Katzburg, *Hungary and the Jews: Policy and Legislation, 1920–1943* (Ramat Gan: Bar-Ilan University Press, 1981), pp.94–157; Levin, *The Holocaust*, pp.600, 603–4; Gyorgy Szaraz, "The Jewish Question in Hungary: A Historical Perspective," in Randolph L.

Braham and Bela Vago, eds., *The Holocaust in Hungary: Forty Years Later* (New York: Columbia University Press, 1985), p.21.

17 Michael Marrus and Robert Paxton, *Vichy France and the Jews* (New York: Schocken, 1983), p.3.

18 Jacqueline Kami-Cohen, interview with author, Baltimore, MD, 17 May 1984, transcript p.5.

19 Ralph Montrose, interview with author, Cardiff, Wales, 22 July 1985, transcript pp.2, 8. N.B.: building floors are counted according to the European system; add one to arrive at the corresponding figure in the United States. Thus, the Montroses lived on the first floor (European); this would be considered the second floor in the United States.

20 Ibid., pp.2, 3, 11.

21 Ibid., pp.11, 15.

22 Alexander Ehrmann, interview with author, West Bloomfield, MI, 15 November and 13 December 1986 and 24 January 1987, transcript pp.5–6.

23 Reprinted in Arad, Gutman, and Margaliot, eds., *Documents on the Holocaust*, 85. See also: Rudolph Stahl, "Vocational Retraining of Jews in Nazi Germany, 1933–1938," *Jewish Social Studies 1* (1939): 169–94.

24 Mirjam Levi, interview with author, Voorschoten, The Netherlands, 26 June 1986, transcript p.10.

25 Mariella Milano-Piperno, interview with author, Rome, Italy, 6 June 1985, transcript p.2.

26 According to De Felice, the establishment and maintenance of academic facilities was one of the two major activities of the Union of Jewish Communities, or l'Unione delle Communità, from 1940 on. See his discussion of this question, De Felice, *Storia degli ebrei*, pp.415–6.

27 Interview with Mariella Milano-Piperno, p.3. In 1849 the ghetto rules had been reapplied, and all Jews who lived outside its former walls were forced to return to the confined area. The ghetto of Rome was without doors or gates, but nevertheless bounded by strict lines of demarcation. See: Sam Waagenaar, *The Pope's Jews* (London: Alcove Press, 1974), pp.270–4.

28 Interview with Mariella Milano-Piperno, transcript pp.3–5. The extent to which the people I interviewed throughout Europe agreed about the importance of the broad Jewish education they received as children, the excellence of their teachers, and the singularly deep and enduring friendships they formed at the Jewish School was astonishing. With regard to Italy, see also the published memoirs: Fabio Della Seta, *L'incendio del Tevere* (Trapani: Editore Celebes, 1969); Giorgio Piperno, "Fermenti di vita giovanile ebraica a Roma durante il periodo delle leggi razziali e dopo la liberazione della città," in Daniel Carpi, Attilio Milano, Umberto Nahon, eds., *Scritti in memoria di Enzo Sereni: Saggi sull'ebraismo romano* (Milan: Editrice Fondazione Sally Mayer, 1970), 293–313; and the report of the fiftieth anniversary of the founding of the Scuola Media Ebraica (Jewish middle school) in Trieste: Jane Boutwell, "Letter from Trieste," *The New Yorker* 26 December 1988, pp.76–80.

29 Jacob Presser, *Destruction of the Dutch Jews* (New York: Dutton, 1969), pp.76–80 [*Ondergang* (The Hague: Staatsuitgeverij 1965)].

30 Salvador Bloemgarten, interview with author, Amsterdam, The Netherlands, 18 June 1986, transcript p.6. See also the description of the shadow of deportations which hovered over the Jewish Lyceum in: Presser, *Destruction of the Dutch Jews*, pp.142–3.

31 As Presser noted, the absentees "were not quite the ordinary absentees, as for the usual reasons some were never seen again. Thus, class 2B which, in the autumn of 1942, counted twenty-eight pupils was reduced to four in May 1943. The writer will never forget the look on his pupils' faces when names were called from the register and there was once again no voice to answer." Ibid., p.258.

32 Ibid., pp.258–9.

33 Interview with Salvador Bloemgarten, pp.6–7. Jozeph Michman, to whom Bloemgarten referred, now lives in Israel and is an active scholar. Presser is the historian Jacob Presser, who devoted his professional life after the war to investigating and analyzing the tragedy of the Dutch Jews during the Second World War.

34 Interview with Mirjam Levi, pp.11–3.

35 Szaraz, "The Jewish Question," and Nathaniel Katzburg, "The Tradition of Anti-Semitism in Hungary," in Braham and Vago, eds., *The Holocaust in Hungary*, pp.21, 5.

36 Sherry Weiss-Rosenfeld, interview with author, Southfield, MI, 26 January 1987, transcript p.2.

37 Gabor Czitrom, interview with author, Paris, France, 30 June and 1 July 1987, transcript pp.4, 5, 7.

38 In Germany the chronological order was different, as a quota on Jewish pupils was introduced in 1933 and the Nuremburg Laws were not passed until 1935. The general pattern of social ostracism (which I have characterized as a three-stage assault) imposed on the Jewish population throughout Nazi and Axis Europe is discussed in greater or lesser detail in the very rich historical literature on this period. A selected sample is noted here. See, inter alia, Jacques Adler, *The Jews of Paris and the Final Solution* (New York: Oxford University Press, 1987), pp. 32–50 [*Face à la persécution* (Paris: Calmann-Lévy, 1985)]; Frederick Chary, *The Bulgarian Jews and the Final Solution* (Pittsburgh: University of Pittsburgh Press, 1972), pp.35–68; Dawidowicz, *The War Against the Jews*, pp.359–401; De Felice, *Storia degli ebrei*, pp.335–71; Hilberg *The Destruction of the European Jews*, pp.149–54, 166–80; Levin, *The Holocaust*, pp.389–618; Marrus and Paxton, *Vichy France*, pp.234–40; Presser, *Destruction of the Dutch Jews*, pp.82–94, 118–27; Georges Wellers, *L'étoile jaune à l'heure de Vichy* (Paris: Fayard, 1973), pp.65–71; Susan Zuccotti, *The Italians and the Holocaust* (New York: Basic Books, 1987), pp.36–51.

39 The actual time interval varied, of course. For example, expulsion from schools began in Germany in 1933 while the star was introduced in 1941. In Belgium, Jewish children were expelled as of 31 December 1941 and the star was instituted in June 1942. And in Hungary, the *numerus clausus* was restored in May 1939, while the star decree was effective as of 29 March 1944, and antisemitic edicts and regulations followed in rapid succession

thereafter.

40 Lydia Gasman-Csato, interview with author, Charlottesville, VA, spring 1986, transcript pp.1–2, 4, 6, 3–4.

41 Interview with Alexander Ehrmann, p.4.

42 Interview with Frieda Menco-Brommet, p.4.

43 Interview with Hilma Geffen-Ludomer, p.2.

44 Lore Gang-Saalheimer, interview with author, Cardiff, Wales, 22 July 1985, transcript pp.3, 9, 3.

45 Martin Buber, "A Proposal for a Jewish Education Office," reprinted in Lucy S. Dawidowicz, *A Holocaust Reader* (New York: Behrman House Publishers, 1976), pp.159–62; Solomon Colodner, *Jewish Education in Germany under the Nazis* (New York: Jewish Education Committee Press, 1964); Dawidowicz, *The War Against the Jews*, pp.169–96; Herbert Freeden, "A Jewish Theater under the Swastika," *Leo Baeck Institute Year Book* 1 (1956): 142–62; Fritz Friedlander, "Trials and Tribulations of Jewish Education in Nazi Germany," *Leo Baeck Institute Year Book* 3 (1958): 187–201; Richard Fuchs, "The 'Hochschule für die Wissenschaft des Judentums' in the Period of Nazi Rule," *Leo Baeck Institute Year Book* 12 (1967): 3–31; Hans Gaertner, "Problems of Jewish Schools in Germany during the Hitler Regime," *Leo Baeck Institute Year Book* 1 (1956): 123–41; Max Gruenewald, "Education and Culture of the German Jews under Nazi Rule," *Jewish Review* 5 (1948); Abraham Margaliot, "The Struggle for Survival of the Jewish Community in Germany in the Face of Oppression," and Joseph Walk, "Jewish Education Under the Nazis – An Example of Resistance to the Totalitarian Regime," in *Jewish Resistance During the Holocaust, Proceedings of the Conference on Manifestations of Jewish Resistance* (Jerusalem: Yad Vashem, 1971), pp.100–111, 123–31.

46 The events of *Kristallnacht* are covered in some detail in many of the histories of this era. For a single work on this pogrom see: Rita Thalmann and Emmanuel Feinermann, *Crystal Night* (New York: Holocaust Library, 1974) [*La nuit de cristal: 9–10 Novembre 1938* (Paris: Robert Laffont, 1972)]. It is not surprising that *Kristallnacht* is also mentioned in a good deal of the memoir literature based in Germany. Yitzhak Herz's "Kristallnacht at the Dinslaken Orphanage," is unique as it was written in 1940 and based on daily notes taken by the author in 1938. It is also of particular interest because, while it is a memoir, its central subject (the orphans of Dinslaken) is especially relevant to our study. *Yad Vashem Studies* 2 (1976): 344–68.

47 Interview with Lore Gang-Saalheimer, pp.8–10.

48 Peter Levi, interview with author, London, England, 14 May 1987, transcript p.3.

49 Interview with Philip Gerrit Mok, p.12.

50 Interview with Gabor Czitrom, pp.8–9, 12.

51 Bertje Bloch-van Rhijn, unpublished diary, entries of 1 and 8 May 1942, pp.11–12.

52 Irene Butter-Hasenberg, interview with author, Ann Arbor, MI, 10 October and 7 November 1986, and 5 March and 16 April 1987, transcript

pp.24–5. N.B.: There is no doubt but that many gentile Dutch people were sympathetic to the plight of the Jews, and manifested their solidarity with their compatriots on the issue of the star. It is questionable, however, as to how many actually wore a star themselves. My research indicates that this was a contemporary myth which has not been revised. Thus, it is very likely that large numbers of Dutch gentiles went out of their way to express supportive sentiments, but not so clear that such a great number actually took to the streets with a badge on their clothes.

53 Interview with Jacqueline Kami-Cohen, pp.3, 4.
54 Hilde Cohen-Rosenthal, interview with author, Cardiff, Wales, 21 July 1985, transcript pp.3, 5.
55 Mária Ember, interview with author, Paris, France, 28 and 31 May 1987, transcript p.3.
56 Isabelle Silberg-Riff, interview with author, London, England, transcript p.1.
57 Interview with Irene Butter-Hasenberg, pp.45–8.

Chapter Two: Into Hiding

1 Ivan Shaw, interview with author, London, England, 7 May 1987, transcript p.4.
2 Anne Frank, *The Diary of Anne Frank: The Critical Edition,* edited by David Barnouw and Gerrold van der Stroom (New York: Doubleday, 1989) [*De Dagboeken van Anne Frank* (The Hague: Staatsvitgeverij, 1986)]; idem, *Tales from the Secret Annex* (New York: Washington Square Press, 1983); Miep Gies, *Anne Frank Remembered* (New York: Simon and Schuster, 1987).
3 Jerzy Kosinski, *The Painted Bird* (New York: Bantam, 1978); Jack Kuper, *Child of the Holocaust* (New York: New American Library, 1980).
4 Margaret Ascher-Frydman, interview with author, Paris, France, 5 June 1987, transcript p.2. The Congregation of Franciscan Sisters of the Family of Mary was specially committed to helping Jewish children. According to Władyslaw Bartoszewski, the Family of Mary "concealed several hundred Jewish children in their homes throughout the country [Poland]." Bartoszewski, "On Both Sides of the Wall," in Bartoszewski and Levin (eds) *Righteous Among Nations: How the Poles Helped the Jews, 1939–1945* (London, Earlscourt, 1969), pp.lxxxii–iii. See also the testimonies of Irena Sendler and Władyslaw Smolski, *ibid.,* pp.51 and 347–52. Philip Friedman mentions the Sisters in *Their Brothers' Keepers* (New York: Holocaust Library, 1978), p.124. In Ewa Kurek-Lesik's study of "The Conditions of Admittance and the Social Background of Jewish Children Saved by Women's Religious Orders in Poland from 1939–1945" (*Polin,* 3 (1988): 244–75), she found that "two-thirds of the 74 female religious communities in Poland took part in helping Jewish children and adults" (p.246) the Family of Mary amongst them. Kurek-Lesik has estimated that at least 1,500 children were saved in this way. According to Kurek-Lesik, the sisters of the Family of Mary and the sisters of the Grey Ursulines were encourag-

ed to participate in such rescue activities by their superiors. In other orders, the decision to help was taken on a local basis by each individual convent. Kurek-Lesik's research on the social background of the children who came to the convent and the means by which the contact was made coincides with my own. She has found that although the children who were taken in were, by and large, from professional and educated families, finances were by no means the determining factor: "a decided majority of Jewish children were taken in with no provision for their keep" (p.268). Rather, it was a question of contacts with the gentile world, access to the community outside the ghetto, fluency in the national language, and chance. "The condition governing the admission of the Jewish child into the house of a female religious community in Poland during 1939–1945 was its fortuitous arrival at the convent gates," Kurek-Lesik has concluded (p.272).

5   Roberto Milano, interview with author, Rome, Italy, 6 June 1985, transcript p.3.

6   Eline Veldhuyzen-Heimans, interview with author and Robert Jan van Pelt, Culemborg, The Netherlands, 13 June 1986, transcript pp.2–4.

7   Georges Waysand, interview with author, Paris, France, 30 May 1987, transcript pp.1–3, 5–6.

8   Maurits Cohen, interview with author, The Hague, The Netherlands, 9 June 1986, transcript p.3. Cohen claims the Boogaard family organization helped to save 324 people.

9   Antoinette Sara Spier, interview with author, Amsterdam, The Netherlands, 27 June 1986, transcript pp.1–2. Also interview of 20 June 1984, transcript pp.3–5.

10 Paul Mogendorff, interview with author, Zevenaar, The Netherlands, 20 June 1986, transcript pp.2, 5.

11 There is very little published literature on the Boogaard family. See: Cor van Stam, *Wacht Binnen de Dijken* (Haarlem: Uitgeverij de Toorts, 1986) pp.67–95, and the article by the investigative reporters Anita van Ommeren and Ageeth Scherphuis, "De Onderduikers in de Haarlemmermeer," *Vrij Nederland*, 16 March 1985, pp.1–25 and a follow-up in the letters section of *Vrij Nederland*, 30 March 1985.

12 Interview with Maurits Cohen, transcript pp.1–2.

13 The issue of the motivation to help is a fascinating topic and there is a developing psychological and sociological literature which focuses on this question. See, for example, Eva Fogelman and V.L. Wiener, "The Few, the Brave, and the Noble," *Psychology Today* 19 no.8 (August 1985): 60–65; Samuel P. and Pearl M. Oliner, *The Altruistic Personality* (New York: The Free Press, 1988); Nechama Tec, *When Light Pierced the Darkness* (New York: Oxford University Press, 1986).

14 Irena Sendler, "People Who Helped Jews," in Bartoszewski and Lewin (eds.), *Righteous Among Nations*, pp.41–2.

15 Władysław Bartoszewski, "On Both Sides of the Wall," and Sendler, "People who Helped Jews," in Bartoszewski and Lewin, eds., *Righteous Among Nations*, pp.xliv–lii and 41–62 (see also the section, "Under the Wings of 'Żegota,'" pp.41–108); Friedman, *Their Brothers' Keepers*,

118–21; Yisrael Gutman and Shmuel Krakowski, *Unequal Victims: Poles and Jews During World War II* (New York: Holocaust Library, 1986), pp.252–99; Yisrael Gutman, "The Attitude of the Poles to the Mass Deportations of Jews from the Warsaw Ghetto in the Summer of 1942," and Joseph Kermish, "The Activities of the Council for the Aid to Jews ('Żegota') in Occupied Poland," in Yisrael Gutman and Efraim Zuroff, eds., *Rescue Attempts During the Holocaust*, Proceedings of the Second Yad Vashem International Historical Conference (Jerusalem: Yad Vashem, 1977), pp.413–4, 367–98 (see also the debate, pp.451–63); Kazimierz Iranek-Osmecki, *He Who Saves One Life* (New York: Crown Publishers, 1971), pp.139–51, 224–6, 234–7, 315–6; Teresa Prekerowa, "The Relief Council for Jews in Poland, 1942–1945," in Chimen Abramsky, Maciej Jachimczyk, and Antony Polonsky, eds., *The Jews in Poland* (London: Basil Blackwell, 1986), pp.161–76; *Saving Jews in War-Torn Poland* (Melbourne: Polish Weekly, 1969), pp.22–3, 40–1.

16 Written testimony of Rebecca van Delft to author, Graft-de Rijp, The Netherlands, 16 June 1986, pp.5–6.

17 Jooske Koppen-de Neve, interview with author, Amerongen, The Netherlands, 7 August 1987, transcript pp.24, 4.

18 Anon., interview with author, Amsterdam, The Netherlands, 19 June 1986, transcript p.22.

19 Marianne Marco-Braun, interview with author, London, England, 9 May 1987, transcript pp.8, 10–2.

20 Ida Groenewegen van Wyck-Roose, Cor Grootendorst, and Truus Grootendorst-Vermeer, interview with author, Nieuw Vennep, The Netherlands, 1 July 1986, transcript p.3.

21 Ibid., p.4.

22 Interview with anon., transcript pp.1–2; Anita van Ommeren and Ageeth Scherphuis, "De Crèche, 1942–1943," *Vrij Nederland*, 18 January 1986, pp.2–21; Jacob Presser, *The Destruction of the Dutch Jews* (New York: Dutton, 1969) [*Ondergang* (The Hague: Staatsuitgeverij, 1965)], pp.281–82.

23 Interview with Groenewegen, Grootendorst, and Grootendorst, transcript p.8; Semmy Riekerk-Glasoog, interview with author, Amsterdam, The Netherlands, 4 July 1986, transcript p.19.

24 Interview with Semmy Riekerk-Glasoog, transcript p.20. Of the five people at that original meeting, only Semmy Riekerk-Glasoog is still living. Jaap Musch was caught by the Germans on 7 September 1944 and shot on the spot for his underground activities. Theo Woortman was arrested on 19 July 1944 in Amsterdam and sent to Amersfoort. On 4 September he was deported to Bergen-Belsen where he died on 12 March 1945. Gerard Musch and Dick Groenewegen were arrested in Amsterdam's central railway station on 9 May 1944. Both were deported, Dick to Burscheid (via Amersfoort) and Gerard to Sachsenhausen (via Vught). Both survived and died of natural causes much later (Musch in 1979 and Groenewegen in 1985). For a history of the NV, see the journalist Max Arian's personal and historical account, "Het grote kinderspel," in *De Groene Amsterdammer*, 4 May

1983, pp.5–7, 9; and his interview with Semmy Riekerk in the same issue, pp.10–12. See also the master's thesis of Bert-Jan Flim at Groningen University, *De NV en Haar Kinderen, 1942–1945*, May 1987; and a series of articles by Jan van Lieshout in the *Limburgs Dagblad*: "Joop Woortman: 'Breng ze maar naar Limburg'" (25 May 1977); "De ongehuwde vaders en moeders van Brunssum" (26 May 1977); "Elke dreumes was een drama" (27 May 1977); "De vliegende non van het pompstation" (28 May 1977).

25 Statement by van Delft, p.7.

26 Ibid., p.4.

27 Interview with Jooske Koppen-de Neve, transcript p.9.

28 Ibid., pp.3–4.

29 Interview with anon., transcript pp.2–3.

30 Interview with Groenewegen, Grootendorst, and Grootendorst, transcript p.9.

31 Ibid., p.9.

32 Piet Meerburg, interview with author, Amsterdam, The Netherlands, 27 June 1986, transcript pp.5, 13.

33 Interviews with Groenewegen, Grootendorst, and Grootendorst, transcript p.12; and Meerburg transcript p.12.

34 Interview with Meerburg, transcript pp.3–4.

35 Ibid., p.5.

36 Ibid., p.6; see also Nico Dohmen, interview with author, Baarn, The Netherlands, 30 June 1986, transcript p.23. There is, if anything, even less printed material on the Meerburg group than on the NV. See the series of short articles by Jan van Lieshout in the *Limburgs Dagblad*: "Het grote gezin van 'Tante Hanna' en 'Oom Nico'" (4 May 1977); "Het verraad van Tienray" (5 May 1977); "Duitser verleid: Hanna bevrijd" (6 May 1977); "Rietje het vergeet – mij – nietje," (10 May 1977); and the master's thesis of Paul J.M. Dolfsma, *Uit de illegaliteit naar de studie. De ontstaansgeschiedenis van de stichting Onderlinge Studenten Steun en haar bioscoop Kriterion*, Amsterdam, 1985, chapter 3: "Verzet van studenten," pp.50–84.

37 It is not clear whether the figures adduced by Meerburg and Dohmen are incompatible. According to Meerburg, one third of the 3–400 children hidden by his network came from the crèche. (p.11.) Nico Dohmen estimated that 80 percent of the 132 children hidden in the Tienray area were rescued from the crèche. Perhaps the majority of the children smuggled out of the crèche and passed to the Meerburg group were sent to Nico Dohmen and Hanna van der Voorst.

38 Meerburg, transcript pp.10–1.

39 Interviews with Meerburg, transcript p.17; also Dohmen, transcript p.8, and Groenewegen, Grootendorst, and Grootendorst, transcript pp.4–5.

40 Interview with Groenewegen, Grootendorst, and Grootendorst, transcript p.5.

41 Ibid., p.5, and interview with Dohmen, transcript p.8.

42 Interview with Dohmen, transcript p.15.

43 Ibid., p.15; also interviews with Meerburg, transcript pp.4, 6, and Marco-

Braun, transcript p.18.
44 Interview with Groenewegen, Grootendorst, and Grootendorst, transcript p.15.
45 Ibid., p.15; also interview with Meerburg, transcript p.16. The comparative willingness of poorer people to open their homes to Jews in contrast to the hesitancy of those who were financially better off was well recognized at the time. It is not clear whether this was a popular (and perhaps populist) myth, but a common saying was: "The poor offer you shelter, the rich someone else's address." My own research tends to support this contention.
46 Interview with Dohmen, transcript pp.7, 23–4.
47 Interview with Meerburg, transcript pp.10, 25–6.
48 There is a fair amount of published literature on OSE and a wealth of archival documentation. See first, inter alia: *The American OSE Review*; Centre de Documentation Juive Contemporaine (CDJC), *L'activité des organisations juives en France sous l'Occupation* (Paris: Centre de Documentation Juive Contemporaine, 1983 reissue of 1947 text), pp.117–79; Hillel J. Kieval, "Legality and Resistance in Vichy France: The Rescue of Jewish Children," *Proceedings of the American Philosophical Society*, 124, no.5 (October 1980): 339–66; Serge Klarsfeld, *The Children of Izieu* (New York: Abrams, Inc., 1985) [*Les enfants d'Izieu: Une tragedie juive* (Paris: Publiée par Serge Klarsfeld, 1984)]; Anny Latour, *The Jewish Resistance in France* (New York: Holocaust Library, 1981) [*La résistance juive en France* (Paris: Stock, 1970)]; Lucien Lazare, *La résistance juive en France* (Paris: Stock, 1987); Ernst Papanek and Edward Linn, *Out of the Fire* (New York: William Morrow, 1975), especially pp.34–5; Zosa Szakowski, *Analytical Franco-Jewish Gazetteer, 1939–1945* (New York: Frydman, 1966), pp.73–5 and *passim*. See also Jacques Adler, *The Jews of Paris and the Final Solution* (New York: Oxford University Press, 1987), pp.167, 226–27 [*Face à la persécution: les organisations juives à Paris de 1940 à 1944* (Paris: Calmann-Lévy, 1985)]; Yehuda Bauer, *A History of the Holocaust* (New York: Franklin Watts, 1982), pp.291–3; David Diamant, *Les juifs dans la Résistance française, 1940–44* (Paris: Le Pavillon, 1971), pp.56–9; Dorothy Macardle, *The Children of Europe* (London: Victor Gollancz, 1949), pp.184–8; Sabine Zeitoun, *Ces enfants qu'il fallait sauver* (Paris: Albin Michel, 1989), pp.145–70. The major archival collections are in the Centre de Documentation Juive Contemporaine and the OSE institution itself in Paris and in the YIVO in New York.
49 CDJC, *L'activité des organisations juives*, pp.118–22.
50 There is a plethora of documents in the archives which describe the activities undertaken by OSE. See, for example, CDJC doc.CCCLXVI–11 "Rapport sur l'activité de l'Union OSE pour les mois Juin, Juillet, et Août 1941." OSE was engaged in a number of concerns, but the children commanded their primary interest. The report noted that 1,201 children were under their sole care, which was about 100 more than in the previous trimester. "The series of tragic cases encountered during the last trimester continues and often we are obliged to admit immediately to our homes children who,

in the majority of cases, have nearly been picked up [by the police]; they remain alone in the world without support and it is impossible for us not to
take them." (p.4.)

51 Michael Marrus and Robert Paxton, *Vichy France and the Jews* (New
York: Schocken, 1983), pp.64–5, 165–6; Joseph Weill, *Contribution à
l'histoire des camps d'internement dans l'Anti-France* (Paris: Éditions du
Centre, 1946) pp.9–15, 21–2.

52 The Unitarian Service Committee, YMCA, Caritas, American Friends' Service Committee, Secours Suisse aux Enfants, Service Social d'Aide aux Emigrants, and CIMADE were very active.

53 CDJC, *L'activité des organisations juives*, p.129.

54 Vivette Samuel-Hermann, interview with author, Paris, France, transcript
p.8.

55 CDJC doc. CCXIII–86, "Rapport sur les conditions de vie à Drancy."

56 CDJC doc. CCCLXVI–11, p.9.

57 Klarsfeld, *The Children of Izieu*, pp.18–9; CDJC doc. CCLXVI–13 "OSE."

58 Diamant, *Les juifs dans la Résistance française*, pp.119–20; Claude Levy
and Paul Tillard, *Betrayal at the Vél d'Hiv* (New York: Hill and Wang,
1969 [*La Grande Rafle du Vél d'Hiv* (Paris: Laffont, 1967)]; Marrus and
Paxton, *Vichy France and the Jews*, pp.250–2; Georges Wellers, *L'étoile
jaune à l'heure de Vichy* (Paris: Fayard, 1973), pp.83–5; CDJC doc.
CCXIV–74, "Situation au 25 Août 1942," pp.1–3.

59 CDJC, *L'activité des organisations juives*, pp.141–2; CDJC docs.
CCXVI–12a, "Exposé sur le circuit Garel," p.2; CCXVIII–104, "Travail
clandestin de l'OSE. Témoignage de M. Georges Garel," pp.8–9;
CCLXVI–13; CCLXVI–16, "La situation actuelle du judaisme en France,"
July 1941, p.25. According to this report, 1,000 to 1,200 children were
evacuated by OSE-Nord from the Occupied Zone to the south.

60 CDJC doc. CCXVII–12a, p.1.

61 Late in August 1942, some 1,200 Jews were arrrested in a sudden dragnet
operation in Lyon and sent to the Vénissieux internment camp. Shortly
thereafter Garel, who was a resister but not a member of OSE, managed to
enter Vénissieux in an official capacity to help liberate the children who
were legally entitled to their freedom, as well as a number who were
decreed prey: 108 in all. Garel, Charles Lederman, Elisabeth Hirsch, and
Hélène Lévy from OSE, the director of the interconfessional philanthropic
group Les Amitiés Chrétiennes, l'Abbé Glasberg, Madeleine Barot, the
general secretary of the Protestant Comité Inter-Mouvements auprès des
Evacués (CIMADE), the Jesuit priest Pierre Chaillet, and others worked
furiously to free children under sixteen years of age who were not tech-
nically under arrest. Within a few days the policy with regard to the children had been changed, but by that time they had "disappeared." See, inter
alia, Bauer, *A History of the Holocaust*, p.292; Diamant, *Les juifs dans la
Résistance française*, p.58; Lazare, *La résistance juive*, pp.208–11; René
Nodot, *Les enfants ne partiront pas!* (Lyon: Nouvelle Lyonnaise, 1970);
Weill, *Camps d'internement dans l'Anti-France*, pp.206–9; CDJC doc.
CCXVIII–104, pp.1–3. Lily Garel-Taget, interview with author, Paris,

France, 19 June 1987, transcript pp.4–6; and Elisabeth Hirsch, interview with author, Neuilly-sur-Seine, France, transcript pp.22, 24.

62 CDJC doc. CCXVIII–104, p.3.

63 Diamant, *Les juifs dans la Résistance française*, p.132; Lazare, *La résistance juive*, pp.179–81; Marrus and Paxton, *Vichy France*, pp.206, 271.

64 CDJC, *L'activité des organisations juives en France*, pp.157–60; CDJC doc. CCXVIII–104, pp.3–5.

65 CDJC doc. CCXVII–12a, pp.1–2. According to a statement by the American Joint Distribution Committee, OSE was responsible for smuggling 2,000 children into Switzerland. CDJC doc. CCCLXVI–14, "American Joint Distribution Committee," p.5. Bruno-Georges Loinger, interview with author, Paris, France, 25 June 1987, transcript pp.1–10.

66 CDJC docs. CCXVII–12a, pp.1–2; CCXVIII–104, pp.3–8.

67 OSE was merely one already extant institution to develop networks to protect and save Jewish children. In France alone such work was undertaken by a spectrum of organizations: public, private, Catholic, Protestant, communist, and socialist. Indeed, within just the Jewish community a plethora of associations formed special child welfare services. The Young Zionists (Jeunesses Sionistes), Jewish Scouts (Éclaireurs Israélites de France), Committee for Refugee Assistance (Comité d'Assistance aux Réfugiés), Rehabilitation and Training Organization (ORT), and Zionist socialist groups like Hashomer Hatzair, Dror, and Gordonia were committed to the protection of young people. There were also numerous newly created groups, of course.

68 Unpublished statement of Madeleine Dreyfus, in possession of author, pp.2–3.

69 Lucien Steinberg, "Jewish Rescue Activities in Belgium and France," in Yisrael Gutman and Efraim Zuroff, eds., *Rescue Attempts During the Holocaust* (Jerusalem: Yad Vashem, 1977), pp.608–9.

70 In his book, *Le Comité de défense des Juifs en Belgique, 1942–1944* (Brussels: Éditions de l'Université de Bruxelles, 1973), Lucien Steinberg has argued that Jewish mothers gave up their children to be saved by strangers out of an instinctual sense of "collective preservation, we can say even an instinctual sense of national preservation." He has argued further that "the Jewish mothers felt that the preservation of the Jewish people would occur through their separation from their children. . . . One could not contend that there was never any hesitation. To the contrary, they often hesitated, sometimes for a long time. But the fact that they did accept, en masse, to entrust their children is the proof, in our view, of the intervention of an instinct of collective preservation that is aroused when the group is threatened" (p.88). My own research flatly contradicts Steinberg's hypothesis. Parents, mothers and fathers, gave up their children because they came to accept, or believe, that they themselves could not protect their youngsters, that the risks and dangers of the Nazi system were too great and that they, as parents, had neither power nor control. This decision was in no way structured within the context of collective or national preservation. The sole goal, or in any case the overwhelmingly urgent goal, was to pro-

tect their children precisely and specifically because those young people were *their children*. For an informative discussion of the networks involved in saving children in Belgium (note the role of women in that work), see Steinberg pp.89–109; and Shlomo Kless, "The Rescue of Jewish Children in Belgium During the Holocaust," *Holocaust and Genocide Studies* 3 no.3 (1988): 275–87.

Chapter Three: In Secret

1   Marco Anav, interview with author, 16 June 1985, Rome, Italy, transcript p.9.
2   Martin Koby, interview with author, Ann Arbor, MI, 11 and 25 November 1987, transcript p.49.
3   Judith Ehrmann-Denes, interview with author, Ann Arbor, MI, 28 January, 2 March, and 16 April 1987, transcript p.3.
4   Salvador Bloemgarten, interview with author and Robert Jan van Pelt, Amsterdam, The Netherlands, 18 June 1986, transcript p.11.
5   Interview with Judith Ehrmann-Denes, pp.2, 6.
6   Herta Montrose-Heymans, interview with author, Cardiff, Wales, 21 July 1985, transcript pp.11, 14.
7   Ibid., pp.11, 14, 12.
8   Bertje Bloch-van Rhijn, interview with author and Robert Jan van Pelt, Doetinchem, The Netherlands, 21 June, 1984, transcript pp.18, 21–2.
9   Philip Maas, interview with author and Robert Jan van Pelt, Hilversum, The Netherlands, 23 June 1986, transcript p.12.
10 Interview with Herta Montrose-Heymans, transcript pp.7–8.
11 Selma Goldstein, interview with author and Robert Jan van Pelt, Doetinchem, The Netherlands, 22 June 1984, transcript pp.9–10.
12 Interview with Philip Maas, transcript pp.10, 16.
13 Interview with Selma Goldstein, transcript pp.5–6.
14 Interview with Philip Maas, transcript p.12.
15 Interview with Martin Koby, transcript pp.45, 47–8, 49.
16 Interview with Sara Spier of 27 June 1986, transcript pp.5–6.
17 Frieda Menco-Brommet, interview with author, 18 June 1986, transcript p.8.
18 Interview with Sara Spier of 20 June 1984, p.4.
19 Interview with Frieda Menco-Brommet, pp.7–8.
20 Interview with Bertje Bloch-van Rhijn, pp.20, 24.
21 Interview with Sara Spier of 20 June 1984, p.5.
22 Interview with Sara Spier of 27 June 1986, pp.18–9.
23 Interview with Salvador Bloemgarten, p.12.
24 Max Gosschalk, interview with author, Deventer, The Netherlands, 1 August 1987, transcript pp.16–17. Foster care in normal life is not the same as the foster care situation of Jewish children in hiding from the Nazis and their allies, but certain aspects of foster care research can help us to understand the complexities of the problem. With regard, for instance, to the issues of adaptation and of age, see, inter alia: David Fanshael and Eugene

B. Shinn, *Children in Foster Care: A Longitudinal Investigation* (New York: Columbia University Press, 1978); and Trudy Festinger, *No One Ever Asked Us ... A Postscript to Foster Care* (New York: Columbia University Press, 1983).

25 Interview with Sara Spier of 27 June 1986, pp.24–5.

26 Eugenie (Jenny) Lee-Poretzky, interview with author, London, England, 15 May 1987, transcript pp.4–5.

27 Peter Levi, interview with author, London, England, 14 May 1987, transcript p.4.

28 Jacqueline Kami-Cohen, interview with author, Baltimore, MD, 17 May 1984, transcript p.16.

29 Romano Dell'Ariccia, interview with author, Rome, Italy, 7 June 1984, transcript pp.4–5.

30 Interview with Peter Levi, p.3.

31 Zippora Soetendorp-van Yssel, interview with author, The Hague, The Netherlands, 19 June 1986, transcript pp.2–3.

32 Mirjam Levi, interview with author, Voorschoten, The Netherlands, 26 June 1986, transcript pp.25, 28–9, 35, 37–8.

33 Georges Waysand, interview with author, Paris, France, 30 May 1987, transcript pp.8, 9.

34 Dolly Hamery-Przybysz, interview with author, Paris, France, 27 May 1987, transcript pp.2–3. Dolly Hamery-Przybysz's history had yet another bizarre twist. On 29 February 1944, the CGQJ (Commissariat Général aux Questions Juives, the French office which dealt with "the Jewish question") wrote to the UGIF (Union Générale des Israélites de France, the French equivalent to the Jewish Council) demanding "that the child Prysbsz [sic] Dolly be returned to Paris." (She was then living with her adoptive parents in the département d'Ille-et-Vilaine.) A few days later (2 March 1944), UGIF answered: "Given that the child is now placed with Aryans, and that there are no more Israelites authorised to live in the department Ille-et-Vilaine, we have asked [the regional] préfect if he would be so kind as to have the child brought to Paris by a social worker, so that she can be housed in an UGIF center. We have informed him that UGIF will take care of the expenses necessary for [her] return." (CDJC doc.CDXXIII–29) Evidently, the prefect or the social worker (and not UGIF) foiled the Germans' allies' plans. Dolly Hamery-Przybysz was not removed from her foster parents, and she was never turned over to the care of UGIF. Had she been, she probably would not have survived. Unlike OSE, UGIF did not disperse the children from its homes soon enough, and many were deported.

35 Nico Dohmen, interview with author, Baarn, The Netherlands, 30 June 1986, transcript pp.22–3.

36 Alfred van der Poorten, interview with author, Paris, France, 19 May 1987, transcript p.7.

37 Max Arian, interview with author, Amsterdam, The Netherlands, 11 and 14 June 1986, transcript pp.31, 34, 35.

38 Judith Belinfante, interview with author, Amsterdam, The Netherlands, 24 June 1986, transcript p.1.

39 Ibid., pp.12, 6.
40 Philip Gerrit Mok, interview with author, Amsterdam, The Netherlands, 11 June 1986, transcript pp.26, 25, 27.
41 Ibid., p.28.
42 Interview with Jenny Lee-Poretzky, p.2.
43 Ibid., pp.7–8.
44 Giacometta Cantatore-Limentani, interview with author, Rome, Italy, 12 June 1985, transcript pp.4, 6.
45 There is no parallel in normal life to the situation of being in hiding or concealed secretly but research on the isolation of the elderly, and the social, emotional, and intellectual deprivation it engenders provides valuable insights into the general problem of enforced solitude and its sequelae. See, inter alia: Lee H. Bowker, *Humanizing Institutions for the Aged* (Lexington, MA: Lexington Books, 1982); Sylvester Kohut, Jeraldine J. Kohut, and Joseph J. Fleishman, *Reality Orientation for the Elderly* (Oradell, NJ: Medical Examine Books, 1987), Eloise Rathbone-McCuan and Joan Hashimi, *Isolated Elders: Health and Social Intervention* (Rockville, MD: Aspen Publications, 1987).
46 Jana Levi, interview with author, London, England, 7, 11, and 12 July 1985, pp.42, 45.
47 Ibid., pp.46–8.
48 Ibid., pp.50–1. Throughout her conversations with me about her war years, Jana Levi gave her age as she would have been as Janina Lesiak, i.e., one year younger than her chronological age.
49 Ibid., p.54.
50 Ibid., p.42.
51 Ibid., pp.55–6, 60–1.
52 Hilma Geffen-Ludomer, interview with author, Ann Arbor, MI, 29 November 1984, transcript p.28.
53 Ibid., p.32.
54 Ibid., p.36.
55 Ibid., p.41.
56 Interview with Philip Gerrit Mok, p.32.
57 Interview with Max Arian, pp.29, 32.
58 Interview with Philip Gerrit Mok, p.40.
59 Andrew Nagy, interview with author, Ann Arbor, MI, 7 February 1986, transcript pp.39–40, 48. With regard to the rescue work undertaken in Budapest in 1944, see: Per Anger, *With Raoul Wallenberg in Budapest* (New York: Holocaust Library, 1981); Arieh Ben-Tov, *Facing the Holocaust in Budapest: The International Committee of the Red Cross and the Jews in Hungary, 1943–1945* (Dordrecht: Martinus Nijhoff Publishers, 1988), esp. pp.237–41 (ICRC protected houses), 288–322 (children's homes), 292–3, 307–8 (letters of protection issued by ICRC), 357–62 (care of children); John Bierman, *Righteous Gentile: The Story of Raoul Wallenberg, Missing Hero of the Holocaust* (New York: Viking Press, 1981); Jacques Derogy, *Le cas Wallenberg* (Paris: Éditions Ramsay, 1980); Elenore Lester, *Wallenberg: The Man in the Iron Web* (Englewood Cliffs, NJ:

Prentice-Hall, 1982); Elenore Lester, "Raoul Wallenberg: The Righteous Gentile From Sweden," in Randolph Braham and Bela Vago (eds), *The Holocaust in Hungary Forty Years Later* (New York: Columbia University Press, 1985), pp.147–60; Jenö (Eugene) Levai, *Black Book on the Martyrdom of Hungarian Jewry* (Zurich: Central European Times, 1948), pp.381–2, 405–17 (Wallenberg), 386 (children protected by the Red Cross); Kati Marton, *Wallenberg* (New York: Random House, 1982); Robert Rozett, "Child Rescue in Budapest," *Holocaust and Genocide Studies*, 2 no.1 (1987): 49–59; Frederick Werbell and Thurston Clarke, *Lost Hero: The Mystery of Raoul Wallenberg* (New York: McGraw-Hill, 1982).

60 The remarkable story of that extraordinary village has been reconstructed and analyzed by Philip Hallie in his book, *Lest Innocent Blood be Shed* (New York: Harper and Row, 1980), and (the child survivor) Pierre Sauvage in his documentary film, "Weapons of the Spirit" (1989). See also Philippe Boegner, *"Ici on a aimé les juifs"* (Paris: J.-C. Lattès, 1982); Marc Donadille, "Le Coteau Fleuri at le Chambon-sur-Lignon," in Jeanne Merle d'Aubigné and Vilette Mouchons, *God's Underground* (St. Louis, MO: Bethany Press, 1970) [*Les clandestins de Dieu* (Paris: Arthème Fayard, 1968)]; Carol Rittner and Sondra Myers, *The Courage to Care* (New York: New York University Press, 1986), pp.97–119; Pierre Sauvage, "A Most Persistent Haven: Le Chambon-Sur-Lignon," *Moment*, October 1983; Sabine Zeitoun, *Ces enfants qu'il fallait sauver* (Paris: Albin Michel, 1989), chapter 5: "Le Chambon-sur-Lignon ou 'l'autre France,'" pp.211–244.

61 Naomi Levi, interview with author, Paris, France, 22 May 1987, transcript pp.5–6.

62 Ibid., pp.7, 5–6.

63 Cirlène Libermen-Zinger, interview with author, Paris, France, 23 May 1987, transcript pp.4–5.

64 The extent to which the Catholic institutions in Rome and the Vatican proper helped Jews during the occupation of that city has been the subject of some disagreement. In many respects it is simply one issue in the debate over the silence of Pope Pius XII (for which I can accept neither excuse·nor justification, and which I interpret as the canonical example of collusion and collaboration). The specific question of the shelter and aid offered to the Jews of Rome during the nine-month occupation is its own historical (and historiographical) chapter, however. In 1961 the Jesuit priest Robert Leiber (who was a close associate of Pius XII) published the same article, "Pio XII e gli Ebrei di Roma," in *La civilitá cattolica* and *Stimmen der Zeit*. He adduced certain claims that reflected a great deal of help from the Church and her institutions. He maintained, for example, that over 4,000 Jews were harbored by the Church during the occupation and that huge amounts of Vatican money were spent saving Jews. These distorted figures were subsequently repeated by excellent historians such as Guenter Lewy in his book, *The Catholic Church and Nazi Germany* (New York: McGraw-Hill, 1965) p.301, and Renzo De Felice, *Storia degli ebrei italiani sotto il fascismo* (Turin: Einaudi, 1972), pp.466–7. Indeed, the latter work in-

cludes a short list from Leiber to provide an institutional breakdown of his earlier claim of some 4,000. In his book, *The Pope's Jews*, Sam Waagenaar (London: Alcove Press, 1974) challenged Leiber. On the basis of my own research, I find Waagenaar's refutation both convincing and compelling.

With regard to the history of the Jews of Rome during the German occupation see especially Giacomo Debenedetti, *16 ottobre 1943* (Rome: OET, 1945), and Robert Katz, *Black Sabbath* (New York: Macmillan, 1969). See also: R.P. Capano, *La resistenza in Roma* (Naples: Gaetano Macchiaroli Editore, 1963); Alberto Giovannetti, *Roma città aperta* (Milano: Editrice Ancora, 1962); Pinchas Lapide, *Three Popes and the Jews* (New York: Hawthorn Books, 1967).

For a discussion of the role of the Catholic Church in general, and Pius XII in particular, see inter alia: Daniel Carpi, "The Catholic Church and Italian Jewry Under Fascists," *Yad Vashem Studies*, 4 (1960); Carlo Falconi, *Il silenzio di Pio XII* (Milan: Sugar Editore, 1965); Saul Friedländer, *Pius XII and the Third Reich* (New York: Knopf, 1966); Rolf Hochhuth, *The Deputy* (New York: Grove Press, 1964); Leo Herbert Lehmann, *Vatican Policy in the Second World War* (New York: Agora, 1946); Meir Michaelis, *Mussolini and the Jews: German-Italian Relations and the Jewish Question in Italy* (Oxford: Oxford University Press, 1978); John F. Morley, *Vatican Diplomacy and the Jews during the Holocaust, 1939–1943* (New York: Ktav Publishing House, 1980); and Léon Poliakov, "The Vatican and the 'Jewish Question,'" *Commentary*, November 1950.

In evaluating the question of the role of the Church in Nazi-occupied Europe, I would urge the reader to distinguish between what the French call "la grande église," or the church hierarchy emanating from the Holy See, and "la petite église," the local religious institutions. I found the latter far more responsive. For examples of this sort of grass-roots help, see (with regard to France): Denise Hervichon, "J'étais une enfant juive à Massip," *Rencontre Chrétiens et Juifs*, 61 (1979): 162–65; and (with regard to Poland): Ewa Kurek-Lesik, "The Conditions of Admittance and the Social Background of Jewish Children Saved by Women's Religious Orders in Poland from 1939–1945," *Polin*, 3 (1988): 244–75.

65 Emma Fiorentino-Alatri, interview with author, Rome, Italy, 2 June 1985, transcript pp.5, 7.

66 Sergio Tagliacozzo, interview with author, Rome, Italy, June 1985, transcript p.7.

67 Interview with Judith Belinfante, p.13.

68 Interview with Romano Dell'Ariccia, p.5.

69 Isabelle Silberg-Riff, interview with author, London, England, 13 May 1987, transcript pp.14–5.

70 Vivette Samuel, "Camoufler son nom et/ou assumer son identité: Quelques remarques concernant la signification du changement de nom des enfants juifs durant l'Occupation," unpublished paper, OSE archives, Paris. See also Vivette Samuel-Hermann, interview with author and Tolya Barsky, Paris, France, 3 June 1987, transcript pp.24–5, 27–8.

71 Ibid., p.4. Claude Berri's film, "Le vieil homme et l'enfant" ["The Two of

Us"] (1968), is a lovely rendition of the life of a little boy in hiding on a farm in occupied France and the dilemmas he faces. The eight-year-old child in the film is the (now grown) son of Claudine Cohen, the director of the memorial and library at CDJC. Madame Cohen had been an OSE child during the war. Prior to the deportation of her parents they had consigned her to OSE's care.

72 Interview with Jana Levi, pp.59–60.

73 For a discussion of the issues of baptism and conversion in just a few countries, see (inter alia): Louis Allen, "Jews and Catholics," in Roderick Kedward and Roger Austin, eds., *Vichy France and the Resistance* (Totowa, NJ: Barnes and Noble, 1985), pp.73–87; Roger Braun, "Les enfants juifs à la libération en France," *Rencontre Chrétiens et Juifs*, 65 (1980): 88–94; Shlomo Kless, "The Rescue of Jewish Children in Belgium during the Holocaust," *Holocaust and Genocide Studies*, 3, no.3, pp.283–5; and with regard to a foster couple's thoughtful care to reintroducing their hiding child to Judaism after the war: Werner Weinberg, "A Dutch Couple," *The Christian Century* (22–29 June 1983): 611–15.

74 Interview with Cirlène Libermen-Zinger, p.6.

75 Interview with Jana Levi, pp.56–7.

76 Interview with Sara Spier of 1984, pp.8–9. See also interview of 1986, p.19.

77 Interview with Mirjam Levi, pp.28, 30, 28–9. See also the discussion of the influence of hiding in a Catholic convent or monastery school on self-perception and identity in Janina David, *A Square of Sky/A Touch of Earth* (London: Penguin Books, 1981); Saul Friedländer, *When Memory Comes* (New York: Avon, 1980) [*Quand vient la souvenir* (Paris: Éditions du Seuil, 1978)]; Frida Scheps Weinstein, *A Hidden Childhood* (New York: Hill and Wang, 1985) [*J'habitais rue des Jardins Saint-Paul* (Paris: Balland, 1983)].

78 Raul Hilberg, *The Destruction of the European Jews* (New York: Holmes and Meier, 1985), p.9.

Chapter Four: Transit Camps

1   Frieda Menco-Brommet, interview with author, Amsterdam, The Netherlands, 18 June 1986, transcript pp.8–9.

2   Ibid., p.9.

3   Esther Levi, interview with author and Robert Jan van Pelt, Hilversum, The Netherlands, 12 June 1986, transcript pp.1–2.

4   Ibid., pp.6–7.

5   Irene Butter-Hasenberg, interview with author, Ann Arbor, MI, 10 October and 7 November 1986; and 5 March and 16 April 1987, transcript p.32.

6   Ibid., pp.32–3.

7   Ivan Shaw, interview with author, London, England, 7 May 1987, transcript pp.2–4.

8   CDJC doc. CCXX–7, "Programme d'aide aux enfants" (n.d.), p.6; Martin Gilbert, *Atlas of the Holocaust* (New York: Da Capo, 1984), pp.48–9; Michael R. Marrus and Robert O. Paxton, *Vichy France and the Jews*

(New York: Schocken, 1983), pp.172–3, 176; Georges Wellers, *L'étoile jaune à l'heure de Vichy* (Paris: Fayard, 1973), p.100.

9   CDJC doc. CCXX–8, "Situation à Gurs" (n.d.).

10 CDJC doc. CCXIII–101, "Visite du 19 Juin à la Permanence des Assistantes Sociales à Pithiviers," p.2.

11 Jacob Presser, *The Destruction of the Dutch Jews* (New York: Dutton, 1969), p.446 [*Ondergang* (The Hague: Staatsuitgeverij, 1965)].

12 Interview with Esther Levi, p.10.

13 Simon Philip Frenkel, interview with author and Robert Jan van Pelt, Rotterdam, The Netherlands, 13 June 1986, transcript p.13.

14 Interview with Irene Butter-Hasenberg, pp.37, 50.

15 Philip Mechanicus, *Waiting for Death* (London: Calder and Boyars, 1968) [*In Depot* (Amsterdam: Polak and van Gennep, 1964)] p.179; see also Presser, *The Destruction of the Dutch Jews*, p.446. These problems were not unique to Westerbork, of course. In his book on Drancy, Georges Wellers noted that the school at that camp had as many as 400 pupils at a time, but that the student population dropped to thirty or forty after each transport to the east. Wellers, *De Drancy à Auschwitz* (Paris: Éditions du Centre, 1946), pp.67–8.

16 These included people with double nationality, South American passports, top Jewish administrators or cultural figures, and people with Palestine certificates who could be exchanged for Germans living in Palestine.

17 Céline Joosten-Mogendorff, interview with author, Arnhem, The Netherlands, 30 July 1987, transcript pp.5, 6.

18 Gabor Czitrom, interview with author, Paris, France, 30 June and 1 July 1987, transcript p.17.

19 The 640 inmates at Barneveld were protected, for unknown reasons, by K.J. Fredericks, the Secretary-General of the Department of the Interior, and Professor van Dam, the Secretary-General for Education, Science and Culture. If the motivation of Fredericks and van Dam who were neither Nazis nor antisemites is unclear, that of the German authorities, Schmidt and Seyss-Inquart, who permitted the establishment of the special camp is even more ambiguous. It has been argued that selection for this special camp was made entirely by social class and was meant to ensure the survival of the Dutch Jewish haute bourgeosie. According to Presser, however, skilled workers were sent to Barneveld also. It seems clear that social class and profession were requisite but insufficient cause to be among the elect. As we have seen, Frenkel's father was a physician and his mother was a dentist. It is also noteworthy that one of his brothers worked for a time for the Jewish Council. However, there were many Jewish physicians and dentists who were not chosen to go to Barneveld, and his brother certainly did not have a powerful position at the Council. The Frenkels were very lucky, but there is no compelling explanation for their good fortune. Frenkel himself believes that a third factor may have been the determinant: Fredericks was from Zeeland, as was Frenkel's mother. At that time, the people from Zeeland were proud of their non-industrialized culture of farmers and seafarers, which had remained intact; indeed the local people still wore tradi-

tional costume. According to Frenkel, "Many people on that list were Zeeuwen, born there. My mother was also born in Zeeland. It was a crazy society in that time. That was a reason to keep you alive, or to come on a list and to be protected." Interview with Simon Philip Frenkel, p.18. See also Mechanicus, *Waiting for Death*, p.168. (Quotes in text from the interview with Simon Philip Frenkel, pp.15–6, 12, 15–6.)

20 Ibid., pp.14, 16–7. See also Mechanicus, *Waiting for Death*, pp.168–9.
21 See, inter alia, Raul Hilberg, *The Destruction of the European Jews* (New York: Holmes and Meier, 1985), pp.430–9, and Zdenek Lederer, *Ghetto Theresienstadt* (London: Goldston and Son, 1953), pp.8–14.
22 H.G. Adler, *Theresienstadt, 1941–1945: Das Antlitz einer Zwangsgemeinschaft* (Tübingen: J.C.B. Mohr/Paul Siebeck, 1960), pp. 47–8. See also Adler's extended discussion of the statistics adduced on pp.37–60.

There is some confusion in the literature with regard to the statistics pertaining to children. Thus, for example, in the epilogue to the very lovely ...*I Never Saw Another Butterfly* ... (New York: Schocken, 1978), Jiri Weil has noted that "there were 15,000 of them [children] and 100 came back." (p.61.) An entire page (p.81) is devoted to the presentation of this statistic. Above a child's drawing of a flower and a butterfly the following information appears: "A total of around 15,000 children under the age of 15 passed through Terezín. Of these, around 100 came back." From these sentences it would be logical to assume that approximately 15,000 children were deported to Theresienstadt, and only 100 survived. Many writers have made that deduction, and these figures are adduced quite commonly. For instance, in Inge Auerbacher's autobiographical memoir, *I Am A Star* (New York: Prentice-Hall, 1986), she explained, "Of fifteen thousand children imprisoned in Terezín between 1941 and 1945, about 100 survived. I am one of them." (p.1.) The introduction to *Terezín*, published by the Council of Jewish Communities in the Czech Lands (Prague, 1965) offered a variation on these figures. "The transports [out of Terezín, to the east] included also 15,000 children, of whom less than 150 returned." (p.5.)

This interpretation made no sense to me, as I have had contact with at least eight child survivors of Theresienstadt (I do not include Auerbacher), which would mean that I, making no special effort to find them, would have heard the histories of somewhere in the neighborhood of 10 percent of the child survivors of Terezín. In his book on Theresienstadt, Adler presented a different set of figures which, coincidently, help to explain the source of the original error. According to Adler, 6,588 children were transported *out of* Theresienstadt and of those only 100 lived to see liberation; Adler believed that all of the survivors were between fourteen and sixteen years old. However, 7,407 children under the age of fifteen were transported *into* Theresienstadt. Furthermore, a certain number (probably quite small) were born in the transit center. An entire transport of children from Bialystock mysteriously arrived in Theresienstadt and not so mysteriously disappeared again (it is presumed that these children were killed, but this has not been proved definitively). Adler figured that the Bialystock children brought the total number to about 10,000 children. To this, he added 2,000 to account for the fifteen-

and sixteen-year-olds. In other words, according to Adler, there were 12,000 children in Theresienstadt at one time or another. At the end of October 1944, there were 819 children still in Terezín; more arrived thereafter. When Terezín was liberated, there were 1,633 children under fifteen years old (pp.572–3). See also Lederer, *Ghetto Theresienstadt*, p.263.

23 Ellen Levi, interview with author, Amsterdam, The Netherlands, 3 August 1987, transcript p.23.

24 Interview with Simon Philip Frenkel, pp.20–1.

25 Adler, *Theresienstadt, 1941–1945*, pp.547–8, 560, 562; Council of Jewish Communities, *Terezín*, pp.78, 93; Lederer, *Ghetto Theresienstadt*, pp.41, 47, 97, 132–3, 137. The well-known rabbi Leo Baeck was the last head of the Jugendfürsorge.

26 Unpublished diary of Otto Pollack, in the possession of his daughter, Helga Kinsky-Pollack, entry for 23 January 1943.

27 Helga Kinsky-Pollack, interview with author, Vienna, Austria, 15 August 1989, transcript p.31.

28 Ibid., p.9.

29 Ibid., p.9.

30 Ibid., p.14. See also Council of Jewish Communities, *Terezín*, p.80.

31 Ibid., pp.32, 25–6, 19. Three of Helga Kinsky-Pollack's paintings are on exhibit at the Jewish Museum in Prague (under the surname of Pollackova). For a discussion of the Czech boys' home, L417, see: Adler, *Theresienstadt, 1941–1945*, pp.552–6.

32 Lederer, *Ghetto Theresienstadt*, p.52.

33 Ibid., pp.125–7; Council of Jewish Communities, *Terezín*, pp.207–62.

34 Interview of Helga Kinsky-Pollack, pp.25, 19.

35 Elisabeth Hirsch, interview with author, Neuilly-sur-Seine, 25 June 1987, transcript p.14.

36 Privately produced volume in honor of Ruth Lambert, by the Kibbutz Schluchot, doc. no.10.

37 CDJC doc. CCXX–13, "Camp de Gurs, Noël 1940."

38 Interview with Esther Levi, p.9. See also the autobiographical memoir: Jona Oberski, *Childhood* (New York: Signet, 1984), pp.32–5.

39 Interview with Irene Butter-Hasenberg, p.48.

40 Hilberg, *Destruction of the European Jews*, p.844; Jenö Levai, *Black Book on the Martyrdom of Hungarian Jewry* (Zurich: Central European Times, 1948), pp.270–3.

41 Interview with Gabor Czitrom, p.17.

42 Interview with Ellen Levi, pp.18, 23.

43 Interview with Frieda Menco-Brommet, p.11.

44 Interview with Esther Levi, p.18.

45 Interview with Irene Butter-Hasenberg, pp.40, 38, 50.

46 Joseph Weill, *Contribution à l'histoire des camps d'internement dans l'Anti-France* (Paris: Éditions du Centre, 1946), pp.112–3.
    The population of the Vichy transit camps was neither stable nor, in most cases, homogeneous. Everyone whom the authorities wished to incarcerate was ordered into the camps. Thus, in the autumn of 1940

Spaniards and Poles as well as stateless, foreign-born, or (as in the case of Grindel and her sisters) French-born Jews were in Agde. At that time Gurs was primarily a camp for Jews, especially those from the upper Rhineland, but Spanish refugees were there also. With time, an increasing proportion of the camp population was Jewish. In the occupied zone, Beaune-la-Rolande, Pithiviers, and Drancy were camps primarily for Jews.

47 Marie Claus-Grindel, interview with author, Paris, France, 2 June 1987, transcript pp.1–2. Grindel's fears were not irrational. For a discussion of excremental assault see: Terrence Des Pres, *The Survivor* (New York: Oxford University Press, 1976), pp.53–71.

48 Interview with Ivan Shaw, p.4.

49 Kibbutz Schluchot, volume in honor of Ruth Lambert, letter by Lambert of 17 October 1984.

50 Weill, *Camps d'internement*, pp.32–3.

51 Interview with Irene Butter-Hasenberg, p.37.

52 Ibid., pp.52, 44. Hannelie Goslar is known in the literature as Lies Gossens. Her married surname is Pick.

53 Interview with Ellen Levi, p.25.

54 Ibid., p.25.

55 Interview with Esther Levi, p.18.

56 Interview with Gabor Czitrom, p.17.

57 Interview with Irene Butter-Hasenberg, pp.44–5.

58 Interview with Ellen Levi, pp.20–1.

59 Weill, *Camps d'internement*, pp.37–41.

60 CDJC doc. CCLXVI–2, "Reunion de la commission des enfants du 22 Mai 1941 à Nîmes," from: Joseph Weill, Union OSE Terrasson (Dordogne) to: L. Miller, Union OSE, Montpellier, date: 36 [26?] May 1941, pp.1–2.

61 CDJC doc. CCXIII–85, "Le Camp de Drancy. Du 20 Août au debut de Novembre 1941 d'après les témoignages de quelques libérés," n.d., p.2.

62 CDJC doc. CCXIV–74, "Situation au 25 Août 1942," pp.1, 4.

63 Interview with Marie Claus-Grindel, p.1.

64 CDJC doc. CCXIX–68, "Union O.S.E.," Montpellier, November 1941, p.1. With regard to Gurs, see also the letter of Ruth Lambert to Father Gross of 26 February 1944 in the volume in her honor published by the Kibbutz Schluchot.

65 Vivette Samuel, "Une internée volontaire," *Évidences*, 14 (Nov. 1950): 7. See also Vivette Samuel, interview with author, Paris, France, 3 June 1987, transcript p.9.

66 Ibid., p.11; see also interview with Vivette Samuel, p.14.

67 Interview with Simon Philip Frenkel, pp.11, 16, 18, 22.

68 Diary of Otto Pollack, entry of 10 April 1943.

69 Unpublished diary of Helga Kinsky-Pollack, entry of 16 March 1943. In possession of author. Excerpts from this diary are published in English translation in: Council of Jewish Communities, *Terezín*, pp.103–5.

70 "Excerpts from the Diary of Fourteen-Year-Old Charlotte Veresova of Prague," in: Council of Jewish Communities, *Terezín*, p.110.

71 Auerbacher, *I Am A Star*, pp.47–8.

72   Interview with Gabor Czitrom, p.16.
73   Ibid., p.16.
74   Marion Stokvis-Krieg, interview with author, Amsterdam, The Nether-
     lands, 30 June 1986, transcript pp.8–9.
75   Ibid., p.13.
76   Ibid., pp.9–10.
77   Ibid., p.10.
78   Interview with Simon Philip Frenkel, pp.9–10.
79   Samuel, "Internée," *Évidences*, p.12.
80   Interview with Esther Levi, pp.15–6.
81   Interview with Ellen Levi, pp.17, 18, 22, 23.
82   Unpublished diary of Otto Pollack, entries of 19 and 30 June 1944.
83   Interview with Gabor Czitrom, p.20.
84   Interview with Irene Butter-Hasenberg, p.47.
85   Ibid., p.46.
86   Hanna Lévy-Hass, *Inside Belsen* (Brighton: Harvester Press, 1982), p.15
     [*Vielleicht war das alles erst der Anfang* (Berlin: Rotbuch Verlag, 1979)].
     See also the last chapter of the book which is a concise and very clear
     description of the camp, "The Concentration Camp at Belsen," pp.128–34;
     the German edition includes a brief discussion of references, "Das KZ Ber-
     gen-Belsen," pp.105–10.
87   Ibid., pp.130–1.
88   Interview with Marion Stokvis-Krieg, p.9.
89   Weil, . . . *I Never Saw Another Butterfly* . . . , p.14.
90   Ibid., p.14.
91   Lévy-Hass, *Inside Belsen*, pp.129, 131.
92   The Comité de Coordination pour l'Assistance dans les Camps (CCAC) be-
     came a sort of umbrella committee, subsuming also the Commission Israé-
     lite des Camps. The committee met at least once a month in Nîmes, from
     which the name by which it was commonly known, le Comité de Nîmes,
     was derived. In Joseph Weill's opinion, "the activity of the CCAC was a
     particularly important page in the history of mutual aid and in the history
     of occupied France. Side by side, in an atmosphere of equality and mutual
     trust, the most diverse organizations, with differing goals, formed a unique
     front of moral and material resistance." Weill, *Camps d'internement*,
     p.109. The Comité de Nîmes was in operation from October 1940 until
     March 1943 when it became impossible to carry on legal work. A full list of
     the organizations which participated in the committee is in Weill's *Camps
     d'internement*, pp.110–1.
93   CDJC doc. CCCLXVI–11, "Rapport sur l'activité de l'Union OSE pour les
     mois Juin, Juillet, et Août 1941," p.9.
94   Weill, *Camps d'internement*, p.53.
95   Ibid., p.134.
96   CDJC doc. CCXIII–88, "Rapport sur la situation des centres d'héberge-
     ment et des camps en zone non occupée" (n.d.), p.6.
97   Hillel J. Kieval, "Legality and Resistance in Vichy France: The Rescue of
     Jewish Children," *Proceedings of the American Philosophical Society*, 124,

no.5 (Oct. 1980) 351.
98 CDJC doc. CCXII–60, To: The Fédération des Sociétés Juives en France; From: Representatives at Camp des Milles; Date: 7 Aout 1942, p.1.
99 Ibid., p.2.
100 See "Into Hiding," note 61; see also Hillel Kieval, "Vichy France and Jewish Children," pp.355, 358–9; Joseph Weill, *Camps d'internement* pp.206–9. There is a disagreement in the sources as to the precise date. Weill, *Camps d'internement*; René Nodot, *Les enfants ne partiront pas!* (Lyon: Nouvelle Lyonnaise, 1970); and CDJC, *L'Activité des organisations juives en France* (Paris: Éditions du Centre, 1947), cite 20 August. Anny Latour, *The Jewish Resistance in France* (New York: Holocaust Library, 1981) [*La Résistance juive en France, 1940–1944* (Paris: Stock, 1970)], and Georges Garel, CDJC doc. CCXVIII–104, "Travail clandestin de l'OSE. Témoignage de M. Georges Garel, Directeur-Général de l'Union O.S.E. à Paris," n.d., cite the 26th. Relying on these sources, subsequent authors note either the one or the other.
101 CDJC doc. CCXVIII–104, "Travail clandestin de l'OSE," pp.1–2.
102 Lily Garel-Taget, interview with author, Paris, France, 19 June 1987, transcript p.4.
103 Ibid., p.4.
104 Interview with Elisabeth Hirsch, p.24.
105 CDJC doc. CCXVIII–104, "Travail clandestin de l'OSE," p.2.
106 CDJC doc. CCXIV–74, "Situation au 25 Août 1942," p.6.
107 Ibid., p.7. See also Martin Gilbert, *Final Journey* (New York: Mayflower Books, 1979), chapter 12: "The Children's Convoys," pp.143–8; Joseph Weill, *Camps d'internement*, pp.217–8; and Georges Wellers, *De Drancy à Auschwitz*, pp.55–8.
108 Interview with Irene Butter-Hasenberg, p.35.
109 Philip Mechanicus, *Waiting for Death*, p.111.
110 Diary of Otto Pollack, entry of 17 October 1944.
111 Interview with Ellen Levi, p.26.

Chapter Five: Ghettos

1   Chaim A. Kaplan, *Scroll of Agony: The Warsaw Diary of Chaim A. Kaplan*, trans. and ed. by Abraham I. Katsh (New York: Collier Books, 1973), pp.218–9.
2   Ibid., pp.219–20.
3   Ibid., p.298.
4   That Malines (or, in Flemish, Mechelen) was in a populated area was such an exception that Lucien Steinberg specifically noted it was "contrary to the Nazi custom." Lucien Steinberg, *Le Comité de défénse des juifs en Belgique, 1942–1944* (Brussels: Éditions de l'Université de Bruxelles, 1973), p.161.
5   According to Lucy Dawidowicz, approximately 330,000 Jews, or one-tenth of the Jewish population in Poland, became refugees. Lucy Dawidowicz, *The War Against the Jews, 1933–1945* (New York: Bantam, 1986),

pp.199–200.
6 Raul Hilberg, *The Destruction of the European Jews* (New York: Holmes and Meier, 1985), p.1219.
7 Randolph L. Braham, *The Politics of Genocide*, vol.1 (New York: Columbia University Press, 1981), pp.528–37.
8 Alexander Ehrmann, interview with author, West Bloomfield, MI, 15 November, 13 December, 1986, and 24 January 1987, transcript p.25.
9 Ibid., p.27.
10 Ibid., pp.25, 26.
11 Ibid., pp.26–9.
12 Ibid., p.29. At that time, Hungarian Jewry had three different types of congregations. The Orthodox adhered strictly to traditional practices and rituals; the Orthodox congregations in the east of Hungary tended to be Hasidic. The Neolog, or Reform or Congressional Jews, adopted more modern (and more assimilationist) rites. Finally, the Status Quo Ante (usually known simply as Status Quo) congregations, few in number, rejected the positions of the other two, and sought a third, center alternative. American Jewish Committee, *The Jewish Communities of Nazi-Occupied Europe* (New York: Howard Fertig, 1982), section on "The Jews of Hungary," p.3. (The book is not numbered consecutively throughout.)
13 Interview with Alexander Ehrmann, pp.32, 31.
14 András Garzó, interview with author and Mária Ember, who translated Hungarian – English – Hungarian, Budapest, Hungary, 16 and 18 July 1987, transcript pp.3, 9–10.
15 Braham, *Politics of Genocide*, vol.2, p.646.
16 Interview with András Garzó, pp.2, 17–8.
17 Ibid., p.12. In this interview, as in nearly all the oral histories recorded for this study, the degree of accuracy and clarity on the part of the participant is quite stunning. Garzó stressed the fact that his figures were only approximate, and that he was relying entirely on his by then forty-three-year-old memory of the demography of Debrecen. He was astonishingly correct, however. According to Braham, the Jewish population of Debrecen was 9,142 in 1942, or about 7.3 percent of the city's total. See: Braham, *Politics of Genocide*, vol.2, p.661.
18 Ibid., p.14.
19 Ibid., p.14.
20 Sherry Weiss-Rosenfeld, interview with author, Southfield, MI, 26 January 1987, transcript pp.17, 18.
21 Ibid., p.18.
22 Mária Ember, interview with author, Paris, France, 28 May 1987, transcript pp.4, 3, 3–4.
23 Ibid., p.1.
24 Ibid., p.4.
25 Ibid., p.4.
26 Ibid., p.5.
27 Interview with András Garzó, p.15.
28 Interview with Mária Ember, p.5.

29 Ibid., pp.5–6. See also the discussion of the torture of Jews to compel them to surrender their valuables in: Braham, *Politics of Genocide*, vol.1, pp.535, 572, 581–2; and Janö Levai, *Black Book on the Martyrdom of Hungarian Jewry* (Zurich: Central European Times Publishing Co., 1948), p.144.

30 Interview with Mária Ember, pp.6, 7.

31 Ibid., pp.7–8.

32 Braham, *Politics of Genocide*, vol.2, pp.652, 674–6.

33 Interview with András Garzó, pp.20–1.

34 Interview with Mária Ember, p.9.

35 Lucjan Dobroszycki, ed., *Chronicle of the Łódź Ghetto, 1941–1944* (New Haven: Yale University Press, 1984), p.504.

36 Ibid., p.509.

37 Ibid., p.515.

38 Ibid., p.516.

39 Ibid., p.526.

40 Ibid., p.526.

41 Ibid., p.lxiv.

42 Sara Grossman-Weil, interview with author, Malverne, NY, 29 and 30 April 1987, transcript pp.26–7.

43 Ibid., p.20.

44 *The Warsaw Diary of Adam Czerniaków*, eds. Raul Hilberg, Stanislaw Staron, Josef Kermisz (New York: Stein and Day, 1982), p.23. For a discussion of Czerniaków's attitude towards children and his suicide, see the introduction to his diary by Josef Kermisz, p.23; and the introduction by Hilberg and Staron, pp.59, 70. See also Yisrael Gutman, "Adam Czerniaków – The Man and His Diary," in Yisrael Gutman and Livia Rothkirchen, eds., *The Catastrophe of European Jewry* (Jerusalem: Yad Vashem, 1976), pp.464, 484–6.

45 For a discussion of the survival through work strategy, see inter alia, Yitzhak Arad, *Ghetto in Flames: The Struggle and Destruction of the Jews in Vilna in the Holocaust* (New York: Holocaust Library, 1982), pp.333–8; Isaiah Trunk, *Judenrat: The Jewish Councils in Eastern Europe Under Nazi Occupation* (New York: Macmillan, 1972), pp.xxix, 75–99, 400–13.

46 Trunk, *Judenrat*, p.421.

47 Arad, *Ghetto in Flames*, p.340.

48 Ibid., pp.342–4. According to Trunk, the date is uncertain; it may have been either 25 or 27 October. Trunk, *Judenrat*, p.421.

49 Dobroszycki, *Chronicle*, pp.250–1.

50 Trunk, *Judenrat*, p.423.

51 Dobroszycki, *Chronicle*, p.122.

52 Faced with the Germans' implacable demands, Rumkowski sought to negotiate within the context and construct they had dictated. Thus, he pressed them to allow nine- and ten-year-olds to join the labor force, but to no avail. See: Dobroszycki, *Chronicle*, pp.211, 218; and Josef Zelkowicz, "Days of Nightmare," in Lucy Dawidowicz, ed., *A Holocaust Reader* (New York: Behrman House, 1976), p.307.

53 Yisrael Gutman, *The Jews of Warsaw, 1939–1943* (Bloomington: Indiana University Press, 1982), pp.60, 62–3. See also Trunk, *Judenrat*, p.130.
54 Gutman, *Jews of Warsaw*, pp.66–7; Trunk, *Judenrat*, pp.99–105. Kirył Sosnowski has cited contemporary estimates that "the actual [ration] allowance covered, at the most, 10 per cent of basic requirements." *The Tragedy of Children Under Nazi Rule* (Poznań: Western Press Agency, 1962), p.113.
55 Trunk, *Judenrat*, p.135.
56 For a general discussion of the finances of the Jewish councils, see Trunk, *Judenrat*, pp.230–58; on taxation: pp.236–43. On the JDC see idem, p.116, and for a detailed discussion of the role of the JDC in Warsaw see Yehuda Bauer, *American Jewry and the Holocaust* (Detroit: Wayne State University Press, 1981), pp.322–34.
57 Trunk, *Judenrat*, pp.124–5.
58 Dobroszycki, *Chronicle*, p.13. See also Bendet Hershkovitch, "The Ghetto in Litzmannstadt (Łódź), *YIVO Annual of Jewish Social Science*, 5 (1950): 102.
59 Dobroszycki, *Chronicle*, p.26.
60 Adolf Berman, "The Fate of the Children in the Warsaw Ghetto," in Gutman and Rothkirchen, eds., *Catastrophe of European Jewry*, p.404. For a discussion of the organization of the house committees, see Michel Mazor, "The House Committees in the Warsaw Ghetto," in Yehuda Bauer and Nathan Rotenstreich, eds., *The Holocaust as Historical Experience* (New York: Holmes and Meier, 1981), pp.95–108.
61 In his diary entry for 5 September 1941, Czerniaków wrote, "At last permission was given today for opening the elementary schools." *The Warsaw Diary*, Hilberg, Staron, Kermisz, eds., p.277.
62 Philip Friedman, ed., *Martyrs and Fighters: The Epic of the Warsaw Ghetto* (New York: Praeger, 1954), p.113.
63 Berman, "Children in the Warsaw Ghetto," in Gutman and Rothkirchen, eds., *Catastrophe of European Jewry*, p.405; Gutman, *The Jews of Warsaw*, p.102; Kaplan, *Scroll of Agony*, pp.71, 193–6, 273; Trunk, *Judenrat*, pp.196–215.
64 Janina Bauman, *Winter in the Morning: A Young Girl's Life in the Warsaw Ghetto and Beyond, 1939–1945* (London: Virago, 1986), p.41.
65 Kaplan, *Scroll of Agony*, p.86.
66 Mary Berg, *Warsaw Ghetto* (New York: L.B. Fischer, 1945), pp.32–3.
67 Kaplan, *Scroll of Agony*, p.242.
68 Trunk, *Judenrat*, p.204.
69 Hannah Kent-Starkman, interview with author, Stamford, CT, 13 December 1985, transcript p.4.
70 Ibid., pp.7, 11.
71 Yitskhok Rudashevski, *The Diary of the Vilna Ghetto, June 1941–April 1943* (Israel: Ghetto Fighters' House and Kibbutz: Hameuchad Publishing House, 1973), pp.56, 65.
72 See, inter alia, Arad, *Ghetto in Flames*, pp.320–3; Friedman, *Martyrs and Fighters*, pp.123–9; Zelig Kalmanovitch, "A Diary of the Nazi Ghetto in

Vilna," *YIVO*, 8 (1953): 47–54.

73 Rudashevski, *Diary*, p.65.

74 Ibid., p.66.

75 Ibid., pp.72–3, 96, 73.

76 Ibid., p.73.

77 Ibid., p.84.

78 Ibid., p.91.

79 Mania Salinger-Tenenbaum, interview with author, Bloomfield, MI, 10 and 29 January and 7 March 1987, transcript pp.7–8. For a discussion of the role of the youth movements in the underground resistance, see: Reuben Ainsztein, *The Warsaw Ghetto Revolt* (New York: Holocaust Library, 1979), esp. chapter 1, "The Road to Resistance," pp.1–54; Lester Eckman and Chaim Lazar, *The Jewish Resistance: The History of the Jewish Partisans in Lithuania and White Russia during the Nazi Occupation, 1940–1945* (New York: Shengold Publishers, 1977), pp.62–9; Yisrael Gutman, "Essay: The Youth Movements in Eastern Europe as an Alternative Leadership," *Genocide and Holocaust Studies*, 3 no.1 (1988): 69–74; idem, "Youth Movements in the Underground and Ghetto Revolts," in *Jewish Resistance During the Holocaust* (Jerusalem: Yad Vashem, 1971), pp.260–84. Some children did participate in the underground, of course, primarily as couriers. For a short report of three such children, see Jacob Greenstein, "Children – Couriers in the Ghetto of Minsk," in Yuri Suhl, ed., *They Fought Back: The Story of the Jewish Resistance in Nazi Europe* (New York: Crown Publishers, 1967), pp.241–5.

80 Interview with Mania Salinger-Tenenbaum, p.11.

81 Esther Geizhals-Zucker, interview with author, Bloomfield Hills, MI, 9 November 1985, transcript pp.1–2. See also Hershkovitch, "The Ghetto in Litzmannstadt," *YIVO*, 5 (1950): 98–100; Trunk, *Judenrat*, pp.207–9.

82 Emmanuel Ringelblum, *Notes from the Warsaw Ghetto*, ed. and trans. by Jacob Sloan (New York: Schocken, 1974), pp.187–8.

83 Kaplan, *Scroll of Agony*, pp.353–4.

84 Janusz Korczak, *Ghetto Diary* (New York: Holocaust Library, 1978), pp.129–30; also p.121. Korczak himself is a fascinating figure. For more information about him, see: Joseph Arnon, "The Passion of Janusz Korczak," *Midstream*, May 1973, pp.32–53; and Betty Jean Lifton, *The King of Children: A Biography of Janusz Korczak* (New York: Farrar, Straus and Giroux, 1988).

85 David Wdowinski, *And We Are Not Saved* (New York: Philosophical Library, 1963), p.49.

86 Dobroszcki, *Chronicle*, pp.373–4. For a detailed discussion of children's games in the ghettos and camps, see: George Eisen, *Children and Play in the Holocaust: Games among the Shadows* (Amherst: University of Massachusetts Press, 1988).

87 Interview with Hannah Kent-Starkman, p.7.

88 Interview with Esther Geizhals-Zucker, p.2.

89 Rudashevski, *Diary*, p.47.

90 Ibid., pp.77–8.

91 Henry Starkman, interview with author, Bloomfield Hills, MI, 8 December 1984 and 19 January 1985, transcript pp. 20, 17, 18.
92 Ibid., pp.31–2, 21.
93 Interview with Hannah Kent-Starkman, pp.7–8.
94 Interview with Henry Starkman, p.19.
95 Interview with Esther Geizhals-Zucker, p.3.
96 Dobroszycki, *Chronicle*, p.199.
97 Ibid., p.211.
98 Ibid., p.218.
99 Ibid., p.226.
100 Ibid., p.228.
101 Interview with Sara Grossman-Weil, p.21. See also the description by Josef Zelkowicz, "Days of Nightmare," in Dawidowicz, *A Holocaust Reader*, pp. 298–316. Note the difference in tone between this account and his entry on the same subject in the *Chronicle*, 14 September 1942, pp.250–5.
102 Ibid., p.25.
103 Interview with Hannah Kent-Starkman, p.11.
104 Interview with Sara Grossman-Weil, pp.22, 25. Hunger and starvation were so prevalent in the ghettos that a group of physicians in Warsaw decided to record their clinical findings. They studied the pathological anatomy of starvation, and undertook clinical and biochemical investigations, especially on the circulatory system, the blood, and on the ophthalmological complications of long-term starvation. Three of the researchers, A. Braude-Heller, J. Rotbalsam, and R. Elbinger, studied starvation in children. They noted, for instance, that nursing babies were the first children to be brought to the clinic, and that had begun as early as the end of 1939, within four months of the invasion of Poland. Longitudinal research revealed an arrest of growth especially in those aged two to five and seven to nine. Emil Apfelbaum, *Maladie de famine* (Warsaw: American Joint Distribution Committee, 1946), esp. pp.173–87.
105 Gutman, *The Jews of Warsaw*, p.67. The details of this situation were known to the outside world. See: Poland, Ministry of Foreign Affairs, *Mass Extermination of Jews in German Occupied Poland. Note Addressed to the Governments of the United Nations on December 10th, 1942, and other documents.* (New York: Roy Publishers, 1942), p.5.
106 Abraham Lewin, *A Cup of Tears: A Diary of the Warsaw Ghetto*, ed. Antony Polonsky (New York: Basil Blackwell, 1989), introduction by Polonsky, p.18. According to the Polish government report, food prices in the Warsaw ghetto were ten times higher than on the Aryan side. Poland, Ministry of Foreign Affairs, *Mass Extermination*, p.5.
107 Mietek Eichel, "Warsaw and After," in *The Root and the Bough: The Epic of an Enduring People*, ed. Leo W. Schwarz (New York: Rinehart and Co., 1949), p.284.
108 Ibid., p.285.
109 Lewin, *Cup of Tears*, p.152.
110 Ibid., p.77.
111 Ibid., p.89.

112 Kaplan, *Scroll of Agony*, pp.327–8.
113 Ringelblum, *Notes*, p.172.
114 Berg, *Warsaw Ghetto*, pp.72–3.
115 Berman, "Children in the Warsaw Ghetto," in Gutman and Rothkirchen, eds., *Catastrophe of European Jewry*, p.403.
116 Bauman, *Winter in the Morning*, p.41.
117 Ringelblum, *Notes*, p133, 202.
118 Kaplan, *Scroll of Agony*, p.290.
119 Ringelblum, *Notes*, p.204.
120 Ibid., pp.204–5; Saul Friedländer, *When Memory Comes* (New York: Avon, 1980) [*Quand vient le souvenir . . .* (Paris: Éditions du Seuil, 1978)], pp.75–76.
121 Berg, *Warsaw Ghetto*, p.87.
122 Kaplan, *Scroll of Agony*, p.290.
123 Trunk, *Judenrat*, pp.151–2, 154.
124 Interview with Sara Grossman-Weill, p.27.

Chapter Six: Death and Slave Labor Camps

1   Esther Geizhals-Zucker, interview with author, Bloomfield Hills, MI, 9 November 1985, transcript pp.5–6. In Kiryl Sosnowski's book on *The Tragedy of Children Under Nazi Rule* (Posnań: Western Press Agency, 1962), he noted that "Jewish children as an 'unproductive element' were, as a rule, the first to be killed." This was a matter of policy. According to the testimony of Rudolf Höss, the Commandant of Auschwitz, "'. . . Children of tender years were invariably exterminated since by reason of their youth they were unable to work . . .'" A contemporary camp report explained that women were killed "'because most of them had children.'" (Quoted by Sosnowski, pp.70–1).

2   Konnilyn G. Feig, *Hitler's Death Camps: The Sanity of Madness* (New York: Holmes and Meier, 1981), pp.266–312. See also Gitta Sereny's study of Sobibor and Treblinka through her remarkable examination of Franz Stangl, the Commandant of Treblinka. Sereny, *Into That Darkness: An Examination of Conscience* (New York: Vintage Books, 1983).

3   The higher estimates are from Feig, *Hitler's Death Camps*, pp.266, 277, 285, 296. The lower figures are given by Hilberg, *The Destruction of the European Jews* (New York: Holmes and Meier, 1985), p.1219.

4   Jan Karski, *The Story of a Secret State* (Boston: Houghton Mifflin Co., 1944), pp.339–52. The industrialist Eduard Schulte also tried, valiantly and repeatedly, to inform the Allies of Hitler's plan to exterminate the Jews. He was not an eyewitness, as were Gerstein and Karski, and had obtained his information through his own contacts and sources. Walter Laqueur and Richard Breitman, *Breaking the Silence* (New York: Simon and Schuster, 1986).

5   Saul Friedländer, *Kurt Gerstein: The Ambiguity of Good* (New York: Alfred Knopf, 1969), p.106 [*Kurt Gerstein ou l'ambiguité du bien* (Paris: Casterman, 1967)]. See also Pierre Joffroy's study of Gerstein: Joffroy, *A*

Spy for God: The Ordeal of Kurt Gerstein (London: Collins, 1971) [*L'espion de Dieu* (Paris: Éditions Bernard Grasset, 1969)].

6   Friedländer, *Kurt Gerstein*, p.107.
7   Yitzhak Arad, *Bełżec, Sobibor, Treblinka: The Operation Reinhard Death Camps* (Bloomington: Indiana University Press, 1987), p.161.
8   Friedländer, *Kurt Gerstein*, pp.107–11.
9   Ibid., p.113.
10 Claude Lanzmann, *Shoah* (New York: Pantheon Books, 1985), pp.3–4.
11 Testimony of Abraham Margulies, "From Warsaw to Sobibor," in Miriam Novitch, ed., *Sobibor: Martyrdom and Revolt* (New York: Holocaust Library, 1980), p.64.
12 Testimony of Simha Bialowitz, "From Izbica to Sobibor"; testimony of Eda Lichtman, "From Mielec to Sobibor," in Novitch, *Sobibor*, pp.67, 59–60. See also Gitta Sereny's interview with the then fourteen-year-old Stanislaw Szmajzner, one of the thirty-two survivors of the breakout from Sobibor. Sereny, *Into That Darkness*, pp.119–31.
13 Alexander Donat, *The Death Camp Treblinka: A Documentary* (New York: Holocaust Library, 1979), p.176.
14 Samuel Willenberg, *Surviving Treblinka* (Oxford: Basil Blackwell, 1989), p.137.
15 See the discussion of this issue in: Eugen Kogon, *The Theory and Practice of Hell: The German Concentration Camps and the System Behind Them* (New York: Octagon Books, 1976), p.30.
16 David Rousset, *L'univers concentrationnaire* (Paris: Éditions de Minuit, 1965; re-edition of 1945).
17 Sherry Weiss-Rosenfeld, interview with author, Southfield, MI, 26 January 1987, transcript pp.18–9.
18 Alexander Ehrmann, interview with author, West Bloomfield, MI, 15 November and 13 December 1986 and 24 January 1987, transcript p.34.
19 Ibid., pp.35–6.
20 Frieda Menco-Brommet, interview with author, Amsterdam, The Netherlands, 18 June 1986, transcript pp.11–2.
21 András Garzó, interview with author and Mária Ember who translated Hungarian – English – Hungarian, Budapest, Hungary, 16 and 18 July 1987, transcript p.22.
22 According to De Felice, thirty-nine people were deported and one returned. (Renzo De Felice, *Storia degli ebrei italiani sotto il fascismo* [Turin: Einaudi, 1972], p.453.) Giuseppe Mayda's figures are slightly different, with sixty-three imprisoned in Mantua and forty-two deported. He also, however, notes one return. (Giuseppe Mayda, *Ebrei sotto Salò* [Milan: Feltrinelli, 1978], pp.209–11.) That one person was the youth Emilio Foá.
23 Emilio Foá, interview with author, Rome, Italy, 4 and 6 June 1985, transcript p.1.
24 Ibid., p.9.
25 Helga Kinsky-Pollack, interview with author, Vienna, Austria, 15 August 1989, transcript p.34.
26 Interview with Sherry Weiss-Rosenfeld, p.19.

27 Interview with Alexander Ehrmann, p.34.
28 For a discussion of the practical purpose of the selections, see Robert Jan van Pelt, "After the Walls Have Fallen Down," *Queen's Quarterly*, 96 (Autumn 1989): 641–60, and chapter 9 ("Apocalyptic Abjection") of his book (with C.W. Westfall), *Architectural Principles in the Age of Historicism* (New Haven: Yale University Press, 1991).
29 Interview with Emilio Foá, pp.1–2.
30 Magda Somogyi, interview with author, Budapest, Hungary, 19 July 1987, transcript p.1.
31 Interview with András Garzó, pp.25–30.
32 Ellen Levi, interview with author, Amsterdam, The Netherlands, 3 August 1987, transcript p.26.
33 Hannah Kent-Starkman, interview with author, Stamford, CT, 13 December 1985, transcript p.22.
34 Interview with Alexander Ehrmann, pp.34, 35–6.
35 Interview with Sherry Weiss-Rosenfeld, p.20.
36 Interview with András Garzó, p.26.
37 Interview with Helga Kinsky-Pollack, p.34.
38 Interview with Emilio Foá, p.10.
39 Mania Salinger-Tenenbaum, interview with author, Bloomfield MI, 10 and 21 January 1987 and 7 March 1987, transcript pp.33–4.
40 Interview with Alexander Ehrmann, pp.37, 53. See also Terrence Des Pres's discussion of the reduction of scope to the immediate in his book, *The Survivor: An Anatomy of Life in the Death Camps* (New York: Oxford University Press, 1976), pp.181–8.
41 Jack Rubinfeld, interview with author, Ann Arbor, MI, 9 and 23 November 1987, transcript pp.20–1.
42 Mária Ember, interview with author, Paris, France, 28 and 31 May 1987, transcript p.9.
43 Ibid., pp.9–10.
44 Ibid., p.11.
45 There were rare exceptions to this rule. At Strasshof, for instance, there was no selection, and dependents remained alive so long as others in the family worked. Thus, Mária Ezner's younger sister did not have a position in the factory where her mother and Ezner herself worked. She remained in the barracks all day. Elderly people who could not work also remained in the camp, but if they were alone, unaccompanied by a productive member of the family, they "disappeared" after some time.
46 Interview with András Garzó, pp.33–4, 45 and also 55.
47 Interview with Jack Rubinfeld, p.27.
48 Interview with Magda Somogyi, pp.3–4. Experiments were conducted on children at Auschwitz and at Neuengamme. For a report on the latter, see: Günther Schwarberg, *The Murders at Bullenhuser Damm: The SS Doctor and the Children* (Bloomington: University of Indiana Press, 1984) [*Der SS-Arzt und die Kinder: Bericht über den Mord vom Bullenhuser Damm* (Stern Bücher im Verlag Gruner & Jahr AG & Co., 1980.)]
49 Interview with Magda Somogyi, pp.4–5.

50 Interview with Sherry Weiss-Rosenfeld, p.17.
51 Interview with Hannah Kent-Starkman, pp.22–3, 33.
52 Interview with Sherry Weiss-Rosenfeld, p.21.
53 Interview with András Garzó, pp.47–8.
54 Interview with Sherry Weiss-Rosenfeld, p.21.
55 Interview with Helga Kinsky-Pollack, pp.40, 37.
56 Interview with Ellen Levi, p.30.
57 Interview with András Garzó, pp.78, 93.
58 Interview with Hannah Kent-Starkman, p.22.
59 Interview with András Garzó, p.61.
60 Interview with Sherry Weiss-Rosenfeld, p.22.
61 Interview with Frieda Menco-Brommet, p.13.
62 Interview with Sherry Weiss-Rosenfeld, p.21.
63 Interview with Esther Geizhals-Zucker, p.8.
64 See the plan of Auschwitz II-Birkenau extermination camp in Filip Müller,
    Eyewitness Auschwitz: Three Years in the Gas Chambers (New York: Stein
    and Day, 1979), p.175.
65 Feig, *Hitler's Death Camps*, pp.344–5. See also for a general description of
    Auschwitz: Roger Manvel and Heinrich Fraenkel, *The Incomparable
    Crime* (New York: G.P. Putnam, 1967), chapter 5: "Communities of
    Death," pp.130–85; and Ber Mark, *The Scrolls of Auschwitz* (Tel Aviv:
    Am Oved Publishers, 1985).
66 Interview with András Garzó, pp.56–7.
67 Ibid., pp.62–3.
68 Interview with Sherry Weiss-Rosenfeld, p.23.
69 Interview with Jack Rubinfeld, pp.23–4.
70 Interview with Alexander Ehrmann, p.40.
71 Interview with Magda Somogyi, pp.2, 9.
72 Interview with Emilio Foá, pp.2–3.
73 Interview with Mária Ember, pp.14, 22.
74 Interview with Alexander Ehrmann, pp.45–8.
75 Interview with Emilio Foá, p.3.
76 Interview with Sherry Weiss-Rosenfeld, p.21.
77 Interview with Hannah Kent-Starkman, pp.24, 30–1.
78 Interview with Magda Somogyi, pp.9, 10, 6.
79 Interview with Mária Ember, p.11.
80 Interview with András Garzó, pp.64, 66, 67.
81 Interview with Sherry Weiss-Rosenfeld, p.23.
82 Interview with Alexander Ehrmann, p.37. For a discussion of human re-
    lationships in the camps, see Des Pres, *The Survivor*, pp.97–9, 132–42.
83 Ibid., p.50.
84 Interview with Frieda Menco-Brommet, p.14.
85 Ibid., pp.15, 14.
86 Interview with Ellen Levi, pp.28, 50–1.
87 Interview with Helga Kinsky-Pollack, pp.36–7.
88 Interview with Esther Geizhals-Zucker, p.6.
89 Interview with Hannah Kent-Starkman, pp.35–6, 40.

90 Ibid., p.36.
91 Interview with Magda Somogyi, p.10.
92 Ibid., pp.10–11.
93 Interview with Emilio Foá, p.12.
94 Interview with Magda Somogyi, p.8.
95 Interview with Ellen Levi, pp.26–7.
96 Interview with Jack Rubinfeld, p.28.
97 Interview with Alexander Ehrmann, p.53.
98 Interview with Ellen Levi, p.63.
99 According to Kiryl Sosnowski, 180 children under the age of fourteen were found alive at the liberation of Auschwitz, about 500 in Bergen-Belsen, 500 in Ravensbrück and 1,000 in Buchenwald. *The Tragedy of Children*, p.99.

Chapter Seven: My War Began in 1945

1 Carol Gilligan, *In a Different Voice: Psychological Theory and Women's Development* (Cambridge, MA: Harvard University Press, 1982).
2 Reuben Ainsztein's book, *Jewish Resistance in Nazi-Occupied Eastern Europe* (New York: Barnes and Noble, 1974), is an example of this ideology. Throughout the nearly one thousand pages of his study, Ainsztein has focused on "the fighter and soldier," Jewish partisans, "the fighting city-ghettoes," and the revolts of the Warsaw ghetto and in the death camps.
3 Marianne Marco-Braun, interview with author, London, England, 9 May 1987, transcript p.10.
4 Lawrence Langer, "The Dilemma of Choice in the Death Camps," in Alan Rosenberg and Gerald Myers, eds., *Echoes from the Holocaust: Philosophical Reflections on a Dark Time* (Philadelphia: Temple University Press, 1988), pp.118–27.
5 Sara Spier, interview with author, Amsterdam, The Netherlands, 27 June 1986, transcript p.4.
6 Irene Butter-Hasenberg, interview with author, Ann Arbor, MI, 10 October and 7 November 1986, and 5 March and 16 April 1987, transcript pp.33–4.
7 Alexander Ehrmann, interview with author, West Bloomfield, MI, 15 November and 13 December 1986, and 24 January 1987, transcript pp.33–4.
8 Hannah Kent-Starkman, interview with author, Stamford, CT, 13 December 1985, pp.8–9.
9 Maurits Cohen, interview with author, The Hague, The Netherlands, 9 June 1986, transcript p.4.
10 Mária Ember, interview with author, Paris, France, 28 and 31 May 1987, transcript pp.24, 27.
11 Ibid., p.27.
12 Ibid., p.28.
13 More attention has been paid to this phenomenon recently than forty-five years ago. See, for example, Jos Gerards, "Joden kregen niet thuis in '45," *Algemeen Dagblad*, 8 April 1989, p.53.

14   Philip Gerrit Mok, interview with author, Amsterdam, The Netherlands, 11
     June 1986, transcript pp.29, 31, 30.
15   Ibid., pp.17–8, 44.
16   See, for instance, Malcolm J. Proudfoot, *European Refugees, 1939–1952: A
     Study in Forced Population Movement* (Evanston: Northwestern Universi-
     ty Press, 1956), esp. pp.318–68. Note, for example, the pogrom in Kielce
     (Poland) on 4 July 1946 (p.341); and Péter Várdy, "The Unfinished Past –
     Jewish Realities in Postwar Hungary," in Randolph L. Braham, ed., *The
     Tragedy of Hungarian Jewry: Essays, Documents, Depositions* (New
     York: Columbia University Press, 1986), again note the 1946 pogroms in
     the Hungarian provinces, pp.148–9.
17   Martin Koby, interview with author, Ann Arbor, MI, 11 and 25 November
     1987, transcript pp.71, 74.
18   For a discussion of the kinds of problems post-war European governments
     faced see, for example, Victor Gollancz, *In Darkest Germany* (London:
     Victor Gollancz, 1947). With regard to the situation of the post-war Euro-
     pean Jewish population, see: Louis de Jong, *Het Koninkrijk der Nederlan-
     den in de Tweede Wereldoorlog* (Leiden: Martinus Nijhof, 1969–1988),
     vol. 12 (1988), esp. pp.55, 676–705; Joel S. Fishman, "The European Jew-
     ish Communities After the Holocaust," in Alex Grobman and Daniel
     Landes, eds., *Genocide: Critical Issues of the Holocaust* (Los Angeles: The
     Simon Wiesenthal Center, 1983), pp.338–47; Karen Gershon, *Postscript: A
     Collective Account of the Lives of Jews in West Germany Since the Second
     World War* (London: Victor Gollancz, 1969); Albert A. Hutler, with Mar-
     vin J. Folkertsma, Jr., *Agony of Survival* (Macomb, IL: Glenbridge Publish-
     ing Co., 1989), chapters 3, 5, 6, and the epilogue; Peter Meyer, Bernard D.
     Weinryb, Eugene Duschinsky, and Nicolas Sylvain, *The Jews in the Soviet
     Satellites* (Syracuse: Syracuse University Press, 1953); A.J. van Schie, "A
     Restitution of Economic Rights after 1945," in Jozeph Michman and Tirt-
     sha Levie, eds., *Dutch Jewish History: Proceedings of the Symposium on
     the History of the Jews in the Netherlands* (Jerusalem: Institute for Re-
     search on Dutch Jewry, 1984); Zorach Warhaftig, *Uprooted: Jewish
     Refugees and Displaced Persons after Liberation* (New York: Institute of
     Jewish Affairs of the American Jewish Congress, 1946).
19   This ideology was manifested in a number of ways. For example, through-
     out Europe, national monuments to the suffering of the civilian population
     during the war do not note that Jews were specially marked. Thus, the
     monument on the Isle de la Cité in Paris is to French citizens who were
     deported, and the monument on the Dam in Amsterdam which is meant to
     represent the agony of the people not only fails to mention the unique,
     tragic fate of the Jewish population, but the design itself is a variation of a
     crucifixion scene. The central suffering figure is in cruciform position.
     Monuments throughout central and eastern Europe, especially in the anni-
     hilation and slave labor camps, which were specifically designed to remem-
     ber those who were murdered, also are silent on the particular issue of the
     Judeocide. See in this context, James E. Young, *Writing and Rewriting the
     Holocaust*, chapter 10, "The Texture of Memory: Holocaust Memorials

and Meaning," (Bloomington: Indiana University Press, 1988), pp.172–89. The special history of the Jews has been ignored also in the historiographical literature in the east of Europe. See Lucy S. Dawidowicz, *The Holocaust and the Historians* (Cambridge, MA: Harvard University Press, 1981), esp. pp.68–124; William Korey, "In History's 'Memory Hole': The Soviet Treatment of the Holocaust," in Randolph Braham, ed., *Contemporary Views on the Holocaust* (Dordrecht, The Netherlands: Kluwer-Nijhoff, 1983), pp.145-·56; Péter Várdy, "The Unfinished Past," in Randolph Braham, ed., *The Tragedy of Hungarian Jewry*, pp.141–4. Finally, one of the long-term effects of the European governments' project, the problem of memory and history, has received much attention recently. See, for example, Charles S. Maier, *The Unmasterable Past: History, Holocaust, and German National Identity* (Cambridge, MA: Harvard University Press, 1988), perhaps especially chapters 1 and 5, and the epilogue; Judith Miller, *One, by One, by One: Facing the Holocaust* (New York: Simon and Schuster, 1990); Ted Morgan, *An Uncertain Hour: The French, the Germans, the Jews, the Klaus Barbie Trial, and the City of Lyon, 1940–1945* (New York: Arbor House, 1990), chapter 1, "Lyon '87."

20 See, for example, Benjamin J. Ferencz, *Less Than Slaves: Jewish Forced Labor and the Quest for Compensation* (Cambridge, MA: Harvard University Press, 1979).

21 Adalbert Rückerl, *The Investigation of Nazi Crimes, 1945–1978: A Documentation* (Hamden, CT: Archon Books, 1980).

22 Ernst von Salomon, *Fragebogen* [*The Questionnaire*] (New York: Doubleday and Co., 1955), p.351.

23 Women who worked with child survivors after the war wrote about the children's difficulties, and their own problems maintaining programs to help them. See, inter alia, Judith Hemmendinger, *Survivors: Children of the Holocaust* (Bethesda, MD: National Press, 1986) [*Les enfants de Buchenwald* (Paris: Éditions Favre and Star Agency, 1984)]; Lena Küchler-Silberman, *My Hundred Children* (New York: Dell, 1987); Ursula Torday (psn. Charity Blackstock), *Wednesday's Children* (London: Hutchinson & Co., 1966), esp. pp.149–52.

24 Interview with Mária Ember, p.29.

25 Sara Spier, interview with author, Amsterdam, The Netherlands, 20 June 1984, transcript pp.20–2.

26 Idem., interview of 27 June 1986, p.31.

Bibliography

N.B.: The dates refer to the edition I used. Original language editions are cited only for those books which were used in the original. Translations of Hebrew or Polish texts, for example, are cited only in the English, French, or German translation.

Please note also that documentary films have not been listed here. Such films as Aviva Kempner and Joshua Waletzky's *The Partisans of Vilna*, Claude Lanzmann's *Shoah*, Marcel Ophuls's *Hotel Terminus*, and Pierre Sauvage's *Weapons of the Spirit* (to mention a mere handful) are excellent critical works, and contribute enormously to the study of the Judeocide.

Abella, Irving and Troper, Harold, *None Is Too Many: Canada and the Jews of Europe, 1933–1948*, New York: Random House, 1982.

Abramsky, Chimen, Jachimczyk, Maciej and Polonsky, Antony, eds., *The Jews in Poland*, New York: Basil Blackwell, 1986.

Adelman, Yehuda, *Heroes Without Medals*, New York: Vantage Press, 1983.

Adelson, Alan and Lapides, Robert, *Łódź Ghetto: Inside a Community Under Siege*, New York: Viking Penguin, 1989.

Adler, H.G., *Theresienstadt, 1941–1945: Das Antlitz Einer Zwangsgemeinschaft*, Tübingen: J.C.B. Mohr (Paul Siebeck), 1960.

Adler, Jacques, *Face à la persécution: les organisations juives à Paris de 1940 à 1944*, Paris: Calmann-Lévy, 1985. English edition: *The Jews of Paris and the Final Solution: Communal Response and Internal Conflicts, 1940–1944*, New York: Oxford University Press, 1987.

Adolphs, Lotte, *Kinder in Ketten: Kinderschicksale in Ghettos und Konzentrationslagern*, Duisburg: Walter Braun Verlag, 1984.

Agnon, S.Y., *The Bridal Canopy*, New York: Schocken Books, 1968.

Ainsztein, Reuben, *Jewish Resistance in Nazi-Occupied Eastern Europe*, New York: Barnes and Noble, 1974.

Ainsztein, Reuben, *The Warsaw Ghetto Revolt*, New York: Holocaust Library, 1979.

Aliav, Ruth and Mann, Peggy, *The Last Escape*, London: Victor Gollancz, 1974.

Allainmat, Henry, *Auschwitz en France: La vérité sur le seul camp d'extermination Nazi en France, Le Struthof*, Paris: Presses de la Cité, 1974.

Allen, Louis, "Jews and Catholics," in *Vichy France and the Resistance*, R. Kedward, and R. Austin, eds., Totowa, New Jersey: Barnes and Noble Books, 1985.

Allen, William Sheridan, *The Nazi Seizure of Power: The Experience of a Single German Town, 1922–1945*, New York: Franklin Watts, 1984.

American Jewish Committee, *The Jewish Communities of Nazi-Occupied Europe*. New York: Howard Fertig, 1982.

Anderson, John R. and Bower, Gordon H., *Human Associative Memory: A Brief Edition*, Hillsdale, New Jersey: Lawrence Erlbaum Associates, 1980.

Anger, Per, *With Raoul Wallenberg in Budapest*, New York: Holocaust Library, 1981.

Anne Frank Stichting, *Die Welt der Anne Frank, 1929–1945*, Amsterdam: Uitgeverij Bert Bakker, 1985. English edition: *Anne Frank in the World*, published in the same volume.

Anstadt, Sera, *Een eigen plek: Verhalen van een opgejaagde jeugd*, The Hague: Uitgeverij BZZTOH, 1985.

Apfelbaum, Emil, *Maladie de famine: Récherches cliniques sur la famine exécutées dans le ghetto de Varsovie en 1942*, Warsaw: American Joint Distribution Committee, 1946.

Apolito, Arnaldo, "Psychoanalysis and Religion," *American Journal of Psychoanalysis*, 30 (1970): 115–26.

Appelfeld, Aharon, *The Age of Wonders*, Boston: David R. Godine, 1981.

Appleman-Jurman, Alicia, *My Story*, New York: Bantam Books, 1990.

Arad, Yitzhak, *Bełżec, Sobibor, Treblinka: The Operation Reinhard Camps*, Bloomington: Indiana University Press, 1987.

Arad, Yitzhak, *Ghetto in Flames: The Struggle and Destruction of the Jews in Vilna in the Holocaust*, New York: Holocaust Library, 1982.

Arendt, Hannah, *Eichmann in Jerusalem: A Report on the Banality of Evil*, New York: Penguin Books, 1984.

Arian, Max, "Het grote kinderspel," *De Groene Amsterdammer*, 4 May 1987, pp.5–7, 9.

Arian, Max, "Een gesprek met Semmy Riekerk," *De Groene Amsterdammer*, 4 May 1987, pp.10–12.

Arieti, Silvano, *The Parnas*, New York: Basic Books, 1979.

Arnon, Joseph, "The Passion of Janusz Korczak," *Midstream* (May 1973): 32–53.

Arnould, Fernand, "L'Abbé Joseph André," *Rencontre Chrétiens et Juifs*, 65 (1980): 97–100.

Asscher-Pinkhof, Clara, *Star Children*, Detroit: Wayne State University Press, 1986.

Auerbacher, Inge, *I Am A Star: Child of the Holocaust*, New York: Prentice-Hall, 1986.

Baddeley, Alan D., *The Psychology of Memory*, New York: Basic Books, 1976.

Bartoszewski, Władyslaw and Lewin, Zofia, eds., *Righteous Among Nations: How Poles Helped the Jews, 1939–1945*, London: Earlscourt Publications, 1969.

Bauer, Yehuda, *American Jewry and the Holocaust: The American Jewish Joint Distribution Committee, 1939–1945*, Detroit: Wayne State University Press, 1982.

Bauer, Yehuda, *A History of the Holocaust*, New York: Franklin Watts, 1982.

Bauer, Yehuda and Rotenstreich, Nathan, eds., *The Holocaust as Historical Experience*, New York: Holmes and Meier, 1981.

Bauman, Janina, *Winter in the Morning: A Young Girl's Life in the Warsaw Ghetto and Beyond*, London: Virago Press, 1986.

Baumann, Denise, *Une famille comme les autres*, Paris: Albin Michel, 1985.

Ben-Tov, Arieh, *Facing the Holocaust in Budapest: The International Committee of the Red Cross and the Jews in Hungary, 1943–1945*, Dordrecht: Martinus Nijhoff Publishers, 1988.

Berg, Mary, *Warsaw Ghetto*, New York: L.B. Fischer, 1945.

Bergmann, Martin S. and Jucovy, Milton E., eds., *Generations of the Holocaust*, New York: Basic Books, 1982.

Berkley, George E., *Vienna and Its Jews: The Tragedy of Success, 1880s–1980s*, Cambridge, MA: Abt Books, 1988.

Berkowitz, Sarah Bick, *Where Are My Brothers? From the Ghetto to the Gas Chamber*, New York: Helios Books, 1965.

Bermant, Chaim, *The Cousinhood: The Anglo-Jewish Gentry*, London: Eyre & Spottiswoode, 1971.

Bernadac, Christian, *Le train de la mort*, Paris: Éditions France-Empire, 1970.

Bierman, John, *Righteous Gentile: The Story of Raoul Wallenberg, Missing Hero of the Holocaust*, New York: Viking Press, 1981.

Birenbaum, Halina, *Hope Is the Last to Die*, New York: Twayne Publishers, 1971.

Biss, André, *A Million Jews to Save: Check to the Final Solution*, London: Hutchinson, 1973.

Blatter, Janet and Milton, Sybil, *Art of the Holocaust*, London: Orbis Publishing, 1982.

Boegner, Philippe, *"Ici on a aimé les Juifs,"* Paris: J.C. Lattès, 1982.

Bolkosky, Sidney, "Listening for the Silences," *Witness*, 1, no.1 (Spring 1987): 66–75.

Bolles, Edmund B., *Remembering and Forgetting: An Inquiry into the Nature of Memory*, New York: Walker and Company, 1988.

Bor, Josef, *The Terezín Requiem*, London: Heinemann, 1963.

Borowski, Tadeusz, *This Way for the Gas, Ladies and Gentlemen*, New York: Penguin, 1988.

Boutwell, Jane, "Letter from Trieste," *The New Yorker*, 26 December 1988, pp.76–80.

Bowker, Lee H., *Humanizing Institutions for the Aged*, Lexington, MA: Lexington Books, 1982.

Braham, Randolph L., ed., *Contemporary Views on the Holocaust*, Dordrecht, The Netherlands: Kluwer-Nijhoff Publishing, 1983.

Braham, Randolph L., *The Destruction of Hungarian Jewry: A Documentary Account*, New York: Pro Arte, 1963.

Braham, Randolph L., ed., *The Tragedy of Hungarian Jewry: Essays, Documents, Depositions*, New York: Columbia University Press, 1986.

Braham, Randolph L. and Bela Vago, eds., *The Holocaust in Hungary: Forty Years Later*, New York: Columbia University Press, 1985.

Braun, Roger, "Les enfants juifs à la libération en France," *Rencontre Chrétiens et Juifs*, 65 (1980): 88–94.

Brett, Elizabeth A. and Ostroff, Robert, "Imagery and Posttraumatic Stress Disorder: An overview," *The American Journal of Psychiatry*, 124, no.4 (April 1985): 417–24.

Bronson, David, "Children of the Holocaust," *Midstream*, 27 (1981): 50–6.

Browning, Christopher R., *The Final Solution and the German Foreign Office: A Study of Referat D III of Abteilung Deutschland 1940–43*, New York: Holmes and Meier, 1978.

Buber, Martin, *I and Thou*, New York: Scribner, 1970.

Bujak, Adam, *Oswiecim-Brzezinka*, Auschwitz: The Auschwitz Museum.

Bullock, Alan, *Hitler: A Study of Tyranny*, New York: Harper and Row, 1964.

Calvocoressi, Peter and Wint, Guy, *Total War: Causes and Courses of the Second World War*, New York: Penguin, 1979.

Camp de Concentration: Natzwieller Struthof, Comité National pour l'Érection et la Conservation d'un Memorial de la Déportation au Struthof, 1976.

Capano, R.P., *La resistenza in Roma*, Naples: Gaetano Macciaroli Editore, 1963.

Caracciola, Nicola, *Gli ebrei e l'Italia durante la guerra 1940–1945*, Rome: Bonacci, 1986.

Cargas, Harry James, ed., *When God and Man Failed: Non-Jewish Views of the Holocaust*, New York: Macmillan, 1981.

Carmel, Herman, *Black Days, White Nights*, New York: Hippocrene Books, 1984.

Carpi, Daniel, "The Catholic Church and Italian Jewry Under the Fascists," *Yad Vashem Studies*, 4, 1960.

Centre de Documentation Juive Contemporaine, *Activité des organisations juives en France sous l'Occupation* (2nd ed.), Paris: Centre de Documentation Juive Contemporaine, 1983.

Centro di Documentazione Ebraica Contemporanea, *Ebrei in Italia: Deportazione, Resistenza*, Florence: Tipografia Giuntina, 1975.

Chary, Frederick B., *The Bulgarian Jews and the Final Solution, 1940–1944,* Pittsburgh: University of Pittsburgh Press, 1972.

Chciuk, Andrzej, ed., *Saving Jews in War-torn Poland: 1939–1945,* Clayton, Victoria: Wilke and Company, 1969.

Chodoff, Paul, "Survivors of the Nazi Holocaust," *Children Today,* 10 (Sept.–Oct. 1981): 2–5.

Clare, George, *Last Waltz in Vienna: This Rise and Destruction of a Family, 1842–1942,* New York: Holt, Rinehart and Winston, 1982.

Clark, Tim, "The Righteous Gentile," *Yankee,* 50 (1986): 104–9, 155–7.

Cohen, Elie A., *Human Behavior in the Concentration Camp,* New York: Grosset and Dunlap, 1953.

Concentration Camp Dachau, 1933–1945, Brussels: Comité International de Dachau, 1978.

Council of Jewish Communities in the Czech Lands, *Terezín,* Prague: Council of Jewish Communities in the Czech Lands, 1965.

Czerniaków, Adam, *The Warsaw Diary of Adam Czerniaków,* edited by Hilberg, Raul; Staron, Stanislaw; and Kermisz, Josef, New York: Stein and Day, 1979.

Darton, Lawrence, *An Account of the Work of the Friends' Committee for Refugees and Aliens, First Known as the Germany Emergency Committee of the Society of Friends, 1933–1950,* London: Friends' Committee for Refugees and Aliens, 1954.

D'Aubigné, Jeanne Merle and Mouchon, Violette, *Les clandestins de Dieu,* Paris: Fayard, 1968. English edition: *God's Underground.* St. Louis: Bethany Press, 1970.

David, Janina, *A Square of Sky/A Touch of Earth: A Wartime Childhood in Poland,* New York: Penguin, 1981.

Dawidowicz, Lucy S. *The Holocaust and the Historians,* Cambridge, MA: Harvard University Press, 1981.

Dawidowicz, Lucy S., ed., *A Holocaust Reader,* New York: Behrman House, 1976.

Dawidowicz, Lucy S., *The War Against the Jews, 1933–1945,* New York: Bantam, 1975.

Debenedetti, Giacomo, *16 Ottobre 1943,* Rome: O.E.T., 1945.

De Felice, Renzo, *Storia degli ebrei italiani sotto il fascismo,* Turin: Einaudi, 1972.

de Jong, Louis, *De Jodenvervolging I,* Amsterdam: Rijksinstituut voor Oorlogsdocumentatie, 1978.

de Jong, Louis, *De Jodenvervolging II,* Amsterdam: Rijksinstituut voor Oorlogsdocumentatie, 1978.

de Jong, Louis, *Het Koninkrijk der Nederlanden in de Tweede Wereldoorlog,* 12 vols., Leiden: Martinus Nijhoff, 1969–1988.

Della Seta, Fabio, *L'incendia del Tevere,* Trapani: Editore Celebes, 1969.

Demetz, Hana, *The House on Prague Street,* New York: Bantam, 1983.

Derogy, Jacques, *Le cas Wallenberg,* Paris: Éditions Ramsay, 1980.

Derogy, Jacques, *100,000 Juifs à la mer*, Paris: Éditions Stock, 1973.

Des Pres, Terrence, *The Survivor*, New York: Oxford University Press, 1976.

Deutsch, Harold C., *The Conspiracy Against Hitler in the Twilight War*, Minneapolis: University of Minnesota Press, 1968.

Diamant, David, *Les juifs dans la Résistance française, 1940–1944 (Avec armes ou sans armes)*, Paris: Le Pavillon, 1971.

Distel, Barbara and Jakusch, Ruth, eds., *Concentration Camp Dachau, 1933–1945*, Brussels: Comité International de Dachau, 1978.

Dobroszycki, Lucjan, ed., *The Chronicle of the Łódź Ghetto, 1941–1944*, New Haven: Yale University Press, 1984.

Documents of the Persecution of the Dutch Jews, 1940–1945, Amsterdam: Polak & Van Gennep, 1979.

Dolfsma, Paul J.M., *Uit de illegaliteit naar de studie: De ontstaansgeschiedenis van de Stichting Onderlinge Steun en haar bioscoop Kriterion*, Amsterdam: Dolfsma, 1985.

Donat, Alexander, ed., *The Death Camp Treblinka: A Documentary*, New York: Holocaust Library, 1979.

Donat, Alexander, *The Holocaust Kingdom: A Memoir*, New York: Holocaust Library, 1978.

Dribben, Judith Strick, *A Girl Called Judith Strick*, New York: Cowles Book Company, 1970.

Druks, Herbert, *Jewish Resistance During the Holocaust*, New York: Irvington Publishers, 1983.

Druks, Herbert, *The Failure to Rescue*, New York: Robert Speller & Sons, 1977.

Eckman, Lester and Lazar, Chaim, *The Jewish Resistance: the History of The Jewish Partisans in Lithuania and White Russia during the Nazi Occupation 1940–1945*, New York: Shengold Publishers, 1977.

Eisen, George, *Children and Play in the Holocaust: Games Among the Shadows*, Amherst, MA: University of Massachusetts Press, 1988.

Eisenberg, Azriel, ed., *The Lost Generation: Children in the Holocaust*, New York: Pilgrim Books, 1982.

Eisenberg, Azriel, ed., *Witness to the Holocaust*, New York: Pilgrim Press, 1981.

Eisner, Jack, *The Survivor*, New York: Bantam, 1982.

Eliach, Yaffa, *Hasidic Tales of the Holocaust*, New York: Vintage, 1988.

Eliach, Yaffa and Gurewitsch, Brana, *The Liberators: Eyewitness Accounts of the Liberation of Concentration Camps*, 1, Brooklyn, NY: Center for Holocaust Studies, Documentation and Research, 1981.

Elkins, Michael, *Forged in Fury*, New York: Ballantine, 1971.

Ember, Mária, *100 Kép*, Budapest: Magveto Kiado, 1984.

L'Entraide Temporaire, *Sauvetage d'enfants juifs sous l'occupation*, Privately published, but available from M. Robert Frank, 19 Rue Leriche, 75015 Paris.

Eschwege, Helmut, "Resistance of German Jews against the Nazi Regime," *Leo Baeck Institute Year Book*, 15 (1970): 143–80.

Ettinger, Elżbieta, *Kindergarten*, Boston: G.K. Hall, 1986.

Fackenheim, Emil L., *From Bergen-Belsen to Jerusalem: Contemporary Implications of the Holocaust*, Jerusalem: The Hebrew University of Jerusalem, 1975.

Fackenheim, Emil L., *The Human Condition After Auschwitz: A Jewish Testimony A Generation After*, The B.G. Rudolph Lectures in Judaic Studies, April 1971.

Falconi, Carlo, *Il silenzio de Pio XII*, Milan: Sugar Editore, 1965.

Fanshel, David, and Shinn, Eugene B., *Children in Foster Care: A Longitudinal Investigation*, New York: Columbia University Press, 1978.

Feig, Konnilyn G., *Hitler's Death Camps: The Sanity of Madness*, London: Holmes and Meier, 1981.

Fein, Helen, *Accounting for Genocide: Natinal Responses and Jewish Victimization during the Holocaust*, New York: Free Press, 1979.

Fenelon, Fania, *Playing for Time*, New York: Berkeley, 1983.

Ferderber-Salz, Bertha, *And the Sun Kept Shining . . .* , New York: Holocaust Library, 1980.

Ferencz, Benjamin B., *Less Than Slaves: Jewish Forced Labor and the Quest for Compensation*, Cambridge, MA: Harvard University Press, 1979.

Festinger, Trudy, *No One Ever Asked Us . . . A Postscript to Foster Care*, New York: Columbia University Press, 1983.

Fink, Ida, *A Scrap of Time*, New York: Schocken, 1987.

Fisher, Julius S. *Transnistria: The Forgotten Cemetary*, New York: Thomas Yoseloff, 1969.

Fleming, Gerald, *Hitler und die Endlösung: "Es ist des Führer's Wunsch . . . "*, Wiesbaden: Sprache Limes Verlag Niedermayer und Schluter, 1982. English edition: *Hitler and the Final Solution*, Berkeley: University of California Press, 1982.

Flender, Harold, *Rescue in Denmark*, New York: Holocaust Library, 1963.

Flim, Bert Jan, *De NV en haar kinderen, 1942–1945*, master's thesis, Groningen University, May 1987.

Flinker, Moshe, *Young Moshe's Diary: The Spiritual Torment of a Jewish Boy in Nazi Europe*, Jerusalem: Yad Vashem, 1965.

Fodor, Renee, "The Impact of the Nazi Occupation of Poland on the Jewish Mother-Child Relationship." *YIVO Annual of Jewish Social Science*, 11 (1956–7).

Fogelman, Eva, and Wiener, Valerie L., "The Few, the Brave, the Noble," *Psychology Today*, 19 (August 1985): 61–65.

Formiggini, Gina, *Stella d'Italia, Stella di David: Gli ebrei dal risorgimento alla Resistenza*, Milan: U. Mursia, 1970.

Frank, Anne, *De Dagboeken van Anne Frank*, The Hague: Staatsuitgeverij, 1986. English edition: *Anne Frank: The Diary of a Young Girl: The Critical Edition*, New York: Doubleday, 1989.

Frank, Anne, *Anne Frank's Tales from the Secret Annex*, New York: Washington Square Press, 1983.

Freier, Recha, *Let the Children Come: The Early History of Youth Aliyah*, London: Weidenfeld and Nicolson, 1961.

Friedenson, Joseph and Kranzler, David, *Heroine of Rescue*, Brooklyn, NY: Mesorah Publications, 1984.

Friedlander, Albert H., ed., *Out of the Whirlwind: A Reader of Holocaust Literature*, New York: Schocken Books, 1976.

Friedländer, Saul, *Kurt Gerstein ou l'ambiguité du bien*, Paris: Casterman, 1967. English edition: *Kurt Gerstein: The Ambiguity of Good*, New York: Knopf, 1969.

Friedländer, Saul, *Pius XII and the Third Reich*, New York: Knopf, 1966.

Friedländer, Saul, *Quant vient le souvenir . . .* , Paris: Éditions du Seuil, 1978. English edition: *When Memory Comes*, New York: Avon Books, 1980.

Friedman, Philip, *Martyrs and Fighters: The Epic of the Warsaw Ghetto*, New York: Praeger, 1954.

Friedman, Philip, *Roads to Extinction: Essays on the Holocaust*, New York: The Jewish Publication Society of America, 1980.

Friedman, Philip, *Their Brothers' Keepers*, New York: Holocaust Library, 1978.

Fubini, Guido, *La condizione giuridica dell'ebraismo italiano: Del periodo Napoleonico alla Repubblica*, Florence: La Nuova Italia Editrice, 1974.

Garel, Georges, "Le sort des enfants juifs pendant la guerre," *Le Monde juif* (Jan.–Mar. 1978): 20–5.

Garfinkels, Betty, *Les Belges face à la persecution raciale 1940–1944*, Brussels: Éditions de l'Institut de Sociologie de l'Université Libre de Bruxelles, 1965.

Gehrig, Berig, *"Bist 'ne Jüdische? Haste den Stern?"* Berlin: Dirk Nishen Verlag in Kreuzberg, 1985.

Gerards, Jos, "Joden kregen niet thuis in '45," *Algemeen Dagblad*, 8 April 1989, p.53.

Gershon, Karen, *Postscript: A Collective Account of the Lives of Jews in West Germany Since the Second World War*, London: Gollancz, 1969.

Gershon, Karen, ed., *We Came As Children: A Collective Autobiography*, New York: Harcourt, Brace, 1966.

Geve, Thomas, *Guns and Barbed Wire: A Child Survives the Holocaust*, Chicago: Academy Publishers, 1987.

Gies, Miep, *Anne Frank Remembered: The Story of the Woman Who Helped to Hide the Frank Family*, New York: Simon and Schuster, 1987.

Gilbert, Martin, *Final Journey: The Fate of the Jews in Nazi Europe*, Boston: George Allen & Unwin, 1979.

Gilbert, Martin, *The Holocaust: Maps and Photographs*, New York: Hill and Wang, 1978.

Gilbert, Martin, *The Holocaust: A History of the Jews of Europe during the Second World War*, New York: Holt, Rinehart and Winston, 1985.

Gilbert, Martin, *The Macmillan Atlas of the Holocaust*, New York: Da Capo Press, 1982.

Gilligan, Carol, *In a Different Voice: Psychological Theory and Women's De-*

velopment, Cambridge, MA: Harvard University Press, 1982.

Ginzel, Günther B., *Jüdischer Alltag in Deutschland, 1933–1945*, Düsseldorf: Droste Verlag, 1984.

Gionannetti, Alberto, *Roma, cittá aperta*, Milan: Editrice Ancora, 1962.

Gollancz, Victor, *In Darkest Germany*, London: Gollancz, 1947.

Gray, Martin, *For Those I Loved*, Boston: Little, Brown, 1972.

Grobman, Alex and Daniel Landes, eds., *Genocide: Critical Issues of the Holocaust*, Los Angeles: The Simon Wiesenthal Center and Rossel Books, 1983.

Gross, Leonard, *The Last Jews in Berlin*, New York: Bantam, 1983.

Grossman, Mendel, *With a Camera in the Ghetto*, edited by Zvi Szner and Alexander Sened, New York: Schocken, 1977.

Gruber, Ruth, *Haven: The Unknown Story of 1000 World War II Refugees*, New York: New American Library, 1984.

Gutman, Yisrael, *The Jews of Warsaw, 1939–1943: Ghetto, Underground, Revolt*, Bloomington: Indiana University Press, 1982.

Gutman, Yisrael, "Essay: The Youth Movements in Eastern Europe as an Alternative Leadership," *Genocide and Holocaust Studies*, 3, no.1 (1968): 69–74.

Gutman, Yisrael and Krakowski, Shmuel, *Unequal Victims: Poles and Jews During World War II*, New York: Holocaust Library, 1986.

Gutman, Yisrael and Rothkirchen, Livia, eds., *The Catastrophe of European Jewry: Antecedents, History, Reflections*, Jerusalem: Yad Vashem, 1976.

Gutman, Yisrael and Zuroff, Efraim, eds., *Rescue Attempts During the Holocaust*, Proceedings of the second Yad Vashem International Historical Conference, Jerusalem: Yad Vashem, 1977.

Hallie, Philip, *Lest Innocent Blood Be Shed: The Story of the Village of Le Chambon and How Goodness Happened There*, New York: Harper Colophon, 1980.

Handler, Andrew, ed., *The Holocaust in Hungary: An Anthology of Jewish Response*, University, AL: University of Alabama Press, 1982.

Hautzig, Esther, *The Endless Steppe: A Girl in Exile*, New York: Scholastic Book Services, 1968.

Heifetz, Julie, *Too Young to Remember*, Detroit: Wayne State University Press, 1989.

Heller, Celia S., *On the Edge of Destruction: Jews of Poland Between the Two World Wars*, New York: Schocken Books, 1980.

Hellman, Peter, *Avenue of the Righteous*, New York: Atheneum, 1980.

Hemmendinger, Judith, *Les enfants de Buchenwald*, Paris: Éditions Favre, 1984. English edition: *Survivors: Children of the Holocaust*, Bethesda, MD: National Press, 1986.

Henry, Frances, *Victims and Neighbors: A Small Town in Nazi Germany Remembered*, South Hadley, MA: Bergin & Garvey, 1984.

Hersh, Gizelle and Mann, Peggy, *"Gizelle, Save the Children,"* New York: Everest House, 1980.

Hershkovitch, Bendet, "The Ghetto in Litzmannstadt," *YIVO Annual of Jewish*

Social Science, 5 (1950): 85–122.

Hervichon, Denise, "J'étais une enfant juive à Massip," *Rencontre Chrétiens et Juifs*, 61 (1979): 162–5.

Herz, Yitzhak S. "Kristallnacht at the Dinslaken Orphanage," *Yad Vashem Studies*, 11, 1976, pp.344–368.

Heydecker, Joe J., *Das Warschauer Getto: Foto-Dokumente eines deutschen Soldaten aus dem Jahr 1941*, Munich: Deutscher Taschenbuch Verlag, 1983.

Heyman, Éva, *The Diary of Éva Heyman*, New York: Shapolsky Publishers, 1988.

Hilberg, Raul, *The Destruction of the European Jews*, 3 volumes, New York: Holmes and Meier, 1985.

Hilberg, Raul, ed., *Documents of Destruction: Germany and Jewry, 1933–1945*, Chicago: Quadrangle Books, 1971.

Hillesum, Etty, *Het verstoorde leven: Dagboek van Etty Hillesum, 1941–1943*, Bussum: De Haan/Unieboek, 1981. English edition: *An Interrupted Life: The Diaries of Etty Hillesum, 1941–1943*, New York: Pantheon, 1983.

Hillesum, Etty, *Het denkende hart van de barak*. Bussum: De Haan/Unieboek, 1982. English edition: *Letters from Westerbork*. New York: Pantheon, 1986.

Hochhuth, Rolf, *The Deputy*, New York: Grove Press, 1964.

Hoess, Rudolph, *Commandant of Auschwitz*, Cleveland: World Publishing Company, 1959.

Hughes, Henry Stuart, *Prisoners of Hope: The Silver Age of the Italian Jews 1924–1974*, Cambridge, MA: Harvard University Press, 1983.

Hutler, Albert A. with Folkertsma, Marvin J., Jr., *Agony of Survival*, Macomb, IL: Glenbridge Publishing, 1989.

Imposed Jewish Governing Bodies Under Nazi Rule, YIVO Colloquium December 2–5 1967, New York: YIVO Institute for Jewish Research, 1972.

. . . I Never Saw Another Butterfly . . . : Children's Drawings and Poems from Terezín Concentration Camp, 1942–1944, New York: Schocken Books, 1978.

Iranek-Osmecki, Kazimierz, *He Who Saves One Life*, New York: Crown, 1971.

Israël Gérard, *Heureux comme Dieu en France, 1940–1944*, Paris: Éditions Robert Laffont, 1975.

Jackson, Livia E. Bitton, *Elli: Coming of Age in the Holocaust*, New York: Times Books, 1983.

Jaffe, Ruth, "Dissociative Phenomena in Former Concentration Camp Inmates," *International Journal of Psycho-Analysis*, 49 (1968): 310–2.

Jewish Communities of Nazi-Occupied Europe, The, New York: Howard Fertig, 1982.

Jewish Resistance During the Holocaust, Proceedings of the Conference on Manifestations of Jewish Resistance, Jerusalem, April 7–11, 1968, Jerusalem: Yad Vashem, 1971.

Joffo, Joseph, *A Bag of Marbles*, New York: Bantam, 1977.

Joffroy, Pierre, *L'espion de Dieu*, Paris: Bernard Grasset, 1969. English edition:

A Spy for God: The Ordeal of Kurt Gerstein, London: Collins, 1970.

Kalmanovitch, Zelig, "A Diary of the Nazi Ghetto in Vilna," *YIVO Annual of Jewish Social Science*, 8 (1953): 9–81.

Kaplan, Chaim A., *Scroll of Agony: The Warsaw Diary of Chaim A. Kaplan*, edited by Katsh, Abraham I., New York: Collier, 1973.

Karski, Jan, *Story of a Secret State*, Boston: Houghton Mifflin, 1944.

Katz, Josef, *One Who Came Back: The Diary of a Jewish Survivor*, New York: Herzl Press and Bergen-Belsen Memorial Press, 1973.

Katz, Robert, *Black Sabbath: A Journey Through a Crime Against Humanity*, Toronto: Macmillan, 1969.

Katzburg, Nathaniel, *Hungary and the Jews: Policy and Legislation, 1920–1943*, Ramat-Gan, Israel: Bar-Ilan University Press, 1981.

Kedward, Roderick and Austin, Roger, eds., *Vichy France and the Resistance: Culture and Ideology*, Totowa, NJ: Barnes & Noble, 1985.

Keilson, Hans, *Sequentielle Traumatisierung bei Kindern*, Stuttgart: Ferdinand Enke Verlag, 1979.

Kenworthy, Leonard S., *An American Quaker Inside Nazi Germany: Another Dimension of the Holocaust*, Kennett Square, PA: Quaker Publications, 1982.

Kerr, Judith, *When Hitler Stole Pink Rabbit*, London: Lions, 1983.

Kestenberg, Judith, "Child Survivors of the Holocaust – 40 Years Later: Reflections and Commentary," *Journal of the American Academy of Child Psychiatry*, 24 (July 1985): 408–12.

Kestenberg, Milton, "Legal Aspects of Child Persecution During the Holocaust," *Journal of American Academy of Child Psychiatry*, 24 (July 1985): 381–4.

Kieval, Hillel, "Legality and Resistance in Vichy France: The Rescue of Jewish Children," *Proceedings of the American Philosophical Society*, 124, no.5 (1980): 339–66.

Kimble, Daniel P. *The Anatomy of Memory*, Vol. 1 of *Proceedings of the First Conference on Learning, Remembering and Forgetting*, Palo Alto: Science and Behavior Books, 1965.

Klarsfeld, Serge, *Les enfants d'Izieu: Une tragédie juive*, Documentation réunie et publiée par Serge Klarsfeld, Paris: Éditions AZ Repro, 1984. English edition: *The Children of Izieu*, New York: Abrams, 1985.

Klarsfeld, Serge, *Memorial to the Jews Deported from France, 1942–1944: Documentation of the Deportation of the Victims of the Final Solution in France*, New York: The Beate Klarsfeld Foundation, 1983.

Klein, Gerda Weissmann, *All But My Life*, New York: Noonday Press, 1988.

Kless, Shlomo. "The Rescue of Jewish Children in Belgium during the Holocaust," *Holocaust and Genocide Studies*, 3, no.3 (1988): 275–87.

Knoop, Hans, *De Joodsche Raad*, Amsterdam: Elsevier, 1983.

Knoop, Hans, *De zaak Menten*, Amsterdam: H.J.W. Becht's Uitgevermaatschappij, 1977. English edition: *The Menten Affair*, New York: Macmillan, 1978.

Kogon, Eugen, *The Theory and Practice of Hell*, New York: Farrar, Straus and Cudahy, 1950.

Kohn, Nahum and Roiter, Howard, *A Voice from the Forest: Memoirs of a Jewish Partisan*, New York: Holocaust Library, 1980.

Kohner, Hanna and Walter, *Hannah & Walter: A Love Story*, New York: Random House, 1984.

Kohut, Sylvester Jr., Kohut, Jeraldine J., and Fleishman, Joseph J., *Reality Orientation for the Elderly*, Oradell, NJ: Medical Examine Books, 1987.

Kok, Bert, *Aan het goede adres*, Utrecht: Sjaloom, 1985.

Kolb, Eberhard, *Bergen-Belsen*, Hannover: Verlag für Literatur und Zeitgeschehen, 1962.

Korczak, Janusz, *Ghetto Diary*, New York: Holocaust Library, 1978.

Kosinski, Jerzy, *The Painted Bird*, New York: Bantam, 1981.

Kovaly, Heda Margolius, *Under a Cruel Star: A Life in Prague, 1941–1968*, Cambridge, MA: Plunkett Lake Press, 1986.

Kraus, H., *International Relief in Action, 1914–1943*, Philadelphia: American Friends' Service Committee, 1944.

Krystal, Henry, ed., *Massive Psychic Trauma*, New York: International Universities Press, 1968.

Krystal, Henry, "Trauma and Affects," *The Psychoanalytic Study of the Child*, 33 (1978): 81–116.

Krystal, Henry and Niederland, William G., eds., *Psychic Traumatization: Aftereffects in Individuals and Communities*, vol. 8, no, 1. Boston: Little, Brown, 1971.

Kuechler-Silberman, Lena, *My Hundred Children*, New York: Laurel-Leaf Books, 1987.

Kuper, Jack, *Child of the Holocaust*, New York: New American Library, 1980.

Kurek-Lesik, Ewa, "The Conditions of Admittance and the Social Background of Jewish Children Saved by Women's Religious Orders in Poland from 1939–1945," *Polin*, 3 (1988): 244–75.

Kwinta, Chava, *I'm Still Living*, Toronto: Simon & Pierre, 1974.

Laloum, Jean, "L'U.G.I.F. et ses maisons d'enfants: le centre de Montreuil-sous-Bois," *Le monde juif*, no.116 (Oct.–Dec. 1984): 153–71.

Langer, Lawrence L. *The Holocaust and the Literary Imagination*, New Haven: Yale University Press, 1975.

Lanzmann, Claude, *Shoah: An Oral History of the Holocaust*, New York: Pantheon, 1985.

Lapide, Pinchas, *Three Popes and the Jews*, New York: Hawthorne Books, 1967.

Laqueur, Walter, *The Terrible Secret: Suppression of the Truth about Hitler's "Final Solution,"* New York: Penguin, 1980.

Laqueur, Walter and Breitman, Richard, *Breaking the Silence*, New York: Simon and Schuster, 1986.

Laska, Vera, ed., *Women in the Resistance and in the Holocaust: The Voices of*

Eyewitnesses, Westport, CT: Greenwood Press, 1983.

Latour, Anny, *La Résistance juive en France (1940–1944)*, Paris: Éditions Stock, 1970. English edition: *The Jewish Resistance in France*, New York: Holocaust Library, 1981.

Lazare, Lucien, *La Résistance juive en France*, Paris: Éditions Stock, 1987.

Leboucher, Fernande, *Incredible Mission*, Garden City, NY: Doubleday, 1969.

Lederer, Zdenek, *Ghetto Theresienstadt*, London: Edward Goldston, 1953.

Lehmann, Leo Herbert, *Vatican Policy in the Second World War*, New York: Agora, 1946.

Leitner, Isabella, *Fragments of Isabella: A Memoir of Auschwitz*, New York: Laurel Books, 1978.

Leitner, Isabella, *Saving the Fragments: From Auschwitz to New York*, New York: New American Library, 1985.

Lengyel, Olga, *Five Chimneys: The Story of Auschwitz*, New York: Howard Fertig, 1983.

Lester, Elenore, *Wallenberg: The Man in the Iron Web*, Englewood Cliffs, NJ: Prentice-Hall, 1982.

Levai, Jenö, *Black Book on the Martyrdom of Hungarian Jewry*, Zurich: Central European Times Publishing Co., 1948.

Levi, Primo, *La chiave a stella*, Turin: Einaudi, 1978. English edition: *The Monkey's Wrench*, New York: Penguin, 1987.

Levi, Primo, *Lilit e altri racconti*, Turin: Einaudi, 1981. English edition, with additional stories included: *Moments of Reprieve*, New York: Summit, 1986.

Levi, Primo, *Se non ora, quando?* Turin: Einaudi, 1982. English edition: *If Not Now, When?* New York: Penguin, 1985.

Levi, Primo, *Se questo é un uomo*, Turin: Einaudi, 1958. English edition: *Survival in Auschwitz*, New York: Collier, 1961.

Levi, Primo, *Il sistema periodico*, Turin: Einaudi, 1975. English edition: *The Periodic Table*, New York: Schocken Books, 1984.

Levi, Primo, *I sommersi e i salvati*, Turin: Einaudi, 1986. English edition: *The Drowned and the Saved*, New York: Summit, 1988.

Levi, Primo, *La tregua*, Turin: Einaudi, 1963. English edition: *The Reawakening*, New York: Collier, 1965.

Levin, Meyer, *Eva: A Novel of the Holocaust*, New York: Behrman House, 1979.

Levin, Nora, *The Holocaust: The Destruction of European Jewry, 1933–1945*, New York: Schocken Books, 1973.

Levy, Claude and Tillard, Paul, *La Grand Rafle du Vél d'Hiv*, Paris: Robert Laffont, 1967. English edition: *Betrayal at the Vél d'Hiv*. New York: Hill and Wang, 1969.

Lévy-Hass, Hanna, *Vielleicht war das alles erst der Anfang: Tagebuch aus dem KZ Bergen-Belsen, 1944–1945*, Berlin: Rotbuch Verlag, 1979. English edition: *Inside Belsen*, Sussex: Harvester Press, 1982.

Lewin, Abraham, *A Cup of Tears: A Diary of the Warsaw Ghetto*, edited by Antony Polonsky, New York: Basil Blackwell, 1989.

Lewis, Charles N., "Memory Adaptation to Psychological Trauma," *The American Journal of Psychoanalysis*, 40, no.4 (1980): 319–23.

Lewy, Guenter, *The Catholic Church and Nazi Germany*, New York: McGraw-Hill, 1964.

Lieberman, J. Nina, "Kindertransport Reunion: Searching for Memories and Survivors," *Outlook*, 60, no.2 (Winter 1989): 8–10.

Lifton, Betty Jean, *The King of the Children: A Biography of Janusz Korczak*, New York: Farrar, Straus and Giroux, 1988.

Lifton, Robert Jay, *The Nazi Doctors: Medical Killing and the Psychology of Genocide*, New York: Basic Books, 1986.

Lusky, Irena, *La traversée de la nuit*, Geneva: Livre Metropolis, 1988.

Lustig, Arnost, *Darkness Casts No Shadow*, New York: Avon, 1978.

Lustig, Arnost, *A Prayer for Katerina Horovitzova*, New York: Avon, 1975.

Mack, John E. with Rogers, Rita S., *The Alchemy of Survival: One Woman's Journey*, New York: Addison Wesley, 1988.

Maier, Charles S., *The Unmasterable Past: History, Holocaust, and German National Identity*, Cambridge MA: Harvard University Press, 1988.

Manvell, Roger and Fraenkel, Heinrich, *The Incomparable Crime*, New York: Putnam, 1967.

Mark, Ber, *The Scrolls of Auschwitz*, Tel Aviv: Am Oved Publishing House, 1985.

Marrus, Michael R., *The Holocaust in History*, Toronto: Lester & Orpen Dennys, 1987.

Marrus, Michael R., "Vichy et les enfants juifs," *L'histoire*, no.22 (April 1980): 6–15.

Marrus, Michael R. and Paxton, Robert O., *Vichy France and the Jews*, New York: Schocken Books, 1983.

Maršálek, Hans, *Die Geschichte des Konzentrationslagers Mauthausen*, Vienna: Oesterreichische Lagergemeinschaft Mauthausen, 1974.

Marton, Kati, *Wallenberg*, New York: Random House, 1982.

Masters, Anthony, *The Summer That Bled: The Biography of Hannah Senesh*, New York: Washington Square Press, 1974.

Mayda, Giuseppe, *Ebrei sotto Saló: La persecuzione antisemita, 1943–1945*, Milan: Feltrinelli Editore, 1978.

Mayer, Anita, *One Who Came Back*, Canada: Oberon Press, 1981.

Mayer, Arno J., *Why Did The Heavens Not Darken? The "Final Solution" in History*, New York: Pantheon, 1990.

Mechanicus, Philip, *Waiting for Death: A Diary*, London: Calder and Boyars, 1968.

Meed, Vladka, *On Both Sides of the Wall: Memoirs from the Warsaw Ghetto*, New York: Holocaust Library, 1979.

Meltzer, Milton, *Never to Forget: The Jews of the Holocaust*, New York: Harper and Row, 1976.

Mendelsohn, John, ed., *The Holocaust: Relief and Rescue of Jews from Nazi*

Oppression, 14, New York: Garland, 1982.

Mendelsohn, John, ed., *The Holocaust: Relief in Hungary and the Failure of the Joel Brand Mission*, 15, New York: Garland Publishing, 1982.

Merin, Yehuda with Porter, Jack Nusan, "Three Jewish Family-Camps in the Forests of Volyn, Ukraine, during the Holocaust," *Jewish Social Studies*, 46 (1984): 83–91.

Mermelstein, Mel, *By Bread Alone: The Story of A-4685*, Huntington Beach, CA: Auschwitz Study Foundation, 1979.

Meyer, Peter, Weinryb, Bernard D., Duschinsky, Eugene, and Sylvain, Nicholas, *The Jews in the Soviet Satellites*, Syracuse: Syracuse University Press, 1953.

Michaelis, Meir, *Mussolini and the Jews: German-Italian Relations and the Jewish Question in Italy, 1922–1945*, Oxford: Oxford University Press, 1978.

Micheels, Louis J., *Doctor 117641: A Holocaust Memoir*, New Haven: Yale University Press, 1989.

Michel, Alain, *Les Éclaireurs israélites de France pendant la Seconde Guerre mondiale*, Paris: Édition des E.I.F., 1984.

Michman, Jozeph and Levie, Tirtsha, eds., *Dutch Jewish History: Proceedings of the Symposium on the History of the Jews in the Netherlands*, Jerusalem: Institute for Research on Dutch Jewry, 1984.

Miller, Judith, *One, by One, by One: Facing the Holocaust*, New York: Simon and Schuster, 1990.

Milton, Sybil, ed., *The Art of Jewish Children: Germany, 1936–1941*, New York: Allied Books, 1989.

Milton, Sybil, "Non-Jewish Children in the Camps," *Simon Wiesenthal Center Annual*, 5 (1988): 49–57.

Minc, Rachel, "Le comportement de l'enfant juif face au danger Nazi," *Revue d'histoire de la médecine hebraique*, no. 59 (March 1963): 25–33.

Minco, Marga, *De Glazen Brug*, CPNB, 1986.

Monchieri, Lino, *Ragazzi del lager*, Brescia: Editrice La Scuola, 1982.

Moore, Bob, *Refugees from Nazi Germany in the Netherlands, 1933–1940*, Dordrecht: Martinus Nijhoff Publishers, 1986.

Morgan, Ted, *An Uncertain Hour: The French, the Germans, the Jews, the Klaus Barbie Trial, and the City of Lyon, 1940–1945*, New York: William Morrow, 1990.

Morley, John F., *Vatican Policy and the Jews during the Holocaust, 1939–1943*, New York: Ktav Publishing House, 1980.

Moskin, Marietta D., *I Am Rosemarie*, New York: Scholastic Book Services, 1972.

Moskovitz, Sarah, *Love Despite Hate: Child Survivors of the Holocaust and Their Adult Lives*, New York: Schocken Books, 1983.

Müller, Filip, *Eyewitness Auschwitz: Three Years in the Gas Chambers*, New York: Stein and Day, 1979.

Murphy, H.B.M., *Flight and Resettlement*, Paris: UNESCO, 1955.

Niederland, William G., "Clinical Observations on the 'Survivor Syndrome,'" *International Journal of Psycho-Analysis*, 49 (1968): 313–5.

Niederland, William G., "The Survivor Syndrome: Further Observations and Dimensions," *Journal of the American Psychoanalytic Association*, 29 (1981): 413–25.

Nirenstein, Albert, *A Tower from the Enemy*, New York: Orion Press, 1959.

Nodot, René, *Les enfants ne partiront pas! Témoignages sur la déportation des Juifs, Lyon et Région, 1942–1943*, Lyon: Nouvelle Lyonnaise, 1970.

Novitch, Miriam, *Sobibor: Martyrdom and Revolt*, New York: Holocaust Library, 1980.

Oberski, Jona, *Childhood*, New York: New American Library, 1983.

Odijk, Sjaloom, *Kind van de rekening*, Nijmegen: Carel Kuitenbrouwer, 1977.

Oliner, Samuel P. and Oliner, Pearl M., *The Altruistic Personality: Rescuers of Jews in Nazi Europe*, New York: Free Press, 1988.

Olson, Harry A., ed., *Early Recollections: Their Use in Diagnosis and Psychotherapy*, Springfield, IL: Charles C. Thomas, 1979.

Orenstein, Henry, *I Shall Live: Surviving Against All Odds, 1939– 1945*, New York: Touchstone Books, 1989.

Pätzold, Kurt, *Verfolgung, Vertreibung, Vernichtung: Dokumente des faschistischen Antisemitismus 1933 bis 1942*, Leipzig (GDR): Verlag Philipp, Reclam, 1987.

Papanek, Ernst with Linn, Edward, *Out of the Fire*, New York: William and Morrow, 1975.

Pascal, Julia, "The Last Trains to Freedom," *Weekend Guardian*, 6–7 May 1989, pp.1–5.

Perl, Gisella, *I Was a Doctor in Auschwitz*, New York: Arno Press, 1979.

Pinkus, Oscar, *The House of Ashes*, Cleveland: World Publishing Company, 1964.

Pisar, Samuel, *Of Blood and Hope*, London: Cassell, 1980.

Poland: Ministry of Foreign Affairs, *The Mass Extermination of Jews in German Occupied Poland*, Note Addressed to the Governments of the United Nations on 10 December 1942, and other documents, New York: Roy Publishers, 1942.

Poliakov, Léon, *L'auberge des musiciens*, Paris: Éditions Mazarine, 1981.

Poliakov, Léon, *La condition des juifs en France sous l'occupation italienne*, Paris: Éditions du Centre, 1946.

Poliakov, Léon, *Harvest of Hate: The Nazi Program for the Destruction of the Jews of Europe*, New York: Holocaust Library, 1979.

Poliakov, Léon, "The Vatican and the 'Jewish Question'," *Commentary*, November 1950.

Poteranski, Waclaw, *The Warsaw Ghetto*, Warsaw: Interpress Publishers, 1968.

Poznanski, Stanislaw, *Struggle, Death, Memory, 1939–1945*, Warsaw: Council for the Preservation of the Monuments of Struggle and Martyrdom, 1963.

Presland, John, *A Great Adventure: The Story of the Refugee Children's Movement*, London: Refugee Children's Movement, 1944.

Presser, Jacob, *Ondergang*, The Hague: Staatsuitgeverij, 1965. English version: *The Destruction of the Dutch Jews*, New York: Dutton, 1969.

Proudfoot, Malcolm J., *European Refugees: 1939–52, A Study in Forced Population Movement*, Evanston, IL: Northwestern University Press, 1956.

Radax-Ziegler, Senta, *Sie kamen durch: Das Schicksal zehn jüdischer Kinder und Jugendlicher, die 1938/39 aus Österreich flüchten mussten*, Vienna: Ueberreuter, 1988.

Rajsfus, Maurice, *L'an prochain, la révolution*, Paris: Éditions Mazarine, 1985.

Rajsfus, Maurice, *Des juifs dans la Collaboration: l'UGIF (1941–1944)*, Paris: Études et Documentation Internationales, 1980.

Rajsfus, Maurice, *Sois juifs et tais-toi: 1930–1940, les français "israélites" face au nazisme*, Paris: Études et Documentation Internationales, 1981.

Rapaport, David, *Emotions and Memory*, New York: International Universities Press, 1971.

Rathbone-McCuan, Eloise and Hashimi, Joan. *Isolated Elders: Health and Social Intervention*, Rockville, MD: Aspen Publications, 1987.

Ravine, Jacques, *La Résistance organisée des juifs en France (1940–1944)*, Paris: Julliard, 1973.

Rees, Katharine, "The Child's Understanding of His Past," *The Psychoanalytic Study of the Child*, 33 (1978): 237–59.

Reiss, Johanna, *The Upstairs Room*, New York: Bantam, 1980.

Ribière, Germaine, "Les enfants juifs dans la tourmente," *Rencontre Chrétiens et Juifs*, no. 65 (1980): 82–7.

Ringelblum, Emmanuel, *Notes from the Warsaw Ghetto: The Journal of Emmanuel Ringelblum*, ed. by Jacob Sloan, New York: Schocken Books, 1974.

Rittner, Carol and Myers, Sondra, *The Courage to Care: Rescuers of Jews During the Holocaust*, New York: New York University Press, 1986.

Robinson, Jacob, *And the Crooked Shall Be Made Straight: The Eichmann Trial, The Jewish Catatrophe, and Hannah Arendt's Narrative*, Philadelphia: The Jewish Publication Society of America, 1965.

Rohtbart, Markus, *I Wanted to Live to Tell a Story*, New York: Vantage Press, 1980.

Rose, Leesha, *The Tulips Are Red*, Jerusalem: Yad Vashem, 1988.

Rosenberg, Alan and Myers, Gerald, eds., *Echoes from the Holocaust: Philosophical Reflections on a Dark Time*, Philadelphia: Temple University Press, 1988.

Rossiter, Margaret L., *Women in the Resistance*, New York: Praeger, 1986.

Roth, John K., and Berenbaum, Michael, eds., *Holocaust: Religious and Philosophical Implications*, New York: Paragon House, 1989.

Rothchild, Sylvia, ed., *Voices from the Holocaust*, New York: New American Library, 1981.

Rousset, David, *L'univers concentrationnaire*, Paris: Éditions de Minuit, 1965 (reissue of 1945 edition); English edition: *The Other Kingdom*, New York: Reynal and Hitchcock, 1947.

Rozett, Robert, "Child Rescue in Budapest, 1944–5," *Holocaust and Genocide Studies*, 2, no.1 (1987): 49–59.

Rubinowicz, Dawid, *The Diary of Dawid Rubinowicz*, Edmonds, WA: Creative Options Publishing, 1982.

Rubinstein, Erna F., *The Survivor in Us All: A Memoir of the Holocaust*, Hamden, CT: Archon Books, 1983.

Rudashevski, Yitskhok, *The Diary of the Vilna Ghetto*, Israel: Ghetto Fighter's House and Hakibbutz Hameuchad Publishing House, 1973.

Rückerl, Adalbert, *The Investigation of Nazi Crimes, 1945–1978*, Hamden, CT: Archon Books, 1980.

Rutkowski, Adam, ed., *La lutte des juifs en France a l'époque de l'Occupation (1940–1944)*, Paris: Centre de Documentation Juive Contemporaine, 1975.

Safrian, Hans and Witek, Hans, *Und Keiner War Dabei: Dokumente des alltäglichen Antisemitismus in Wien, 1938*, Vienna: Picus Verlag, 1988.

Salomon, Charlotte, *Charlotte: Life or Theater*, New York: Viking Press, 1981.

Salomon, Ernst von, *Der Fragebogen*, Rowohlt Verlag, 1951. English edition: *Fragebogen [The Questionnaire]*, Garden City, NY: Doubleday, 1955.

Samuel, Vivette, "Journal d'une internée volontaire," *Évidences*, no.14 (Nov. 1950): 7–12.

Sauvage, Pierre, "A Most Persistent Haven: Le-Chambon-sur-Lignon," *Moment*, October 1983.

Saving Jews in War-Torn Poland, 1939–1945, Melbourne: Polish Weekly, 1969.

Schramm, Hanna, *Menschen in Gurs: Erinnerungen an ein französisches Internierungslager (1940–1941)*, Worms: Verlag Georg Heintz, 1977.

Schwarberg, Gunther, *Der SS-Arzt und die Kinder: Bericht über den Mord vom Bullenhuser Damm*, Stern Bücher im Verlag Gruner & Jahr AG & Co., 1980. English edition: *The Murders at Bullenhuser Damm: The SS Doctor and the Children*, Bloomington: Indiana University Press, 1984.

Schwarz, Leo W., ed., *The Root and the Bough: The Epic of an Enduring People*, New York: Rinehart & Company, 1949.

Schwertfeger, Ruth, *Women of Theresienstadt: Voices from a Concentration Camp*, Oxford: Berg, 1989.

Segal, Nancy L., "Holocaust Twins: Their Special Bond," *Psychology Today*, 19 (1985): 52–65.

Seidel, Gill, *The Holocaust Denial: Antisemitism, Racism, and the New Right*, London: Beyond the Pale Collective, 1986.

Sereny, Gitta, *Into That Darkness: An Examination of Conscience*, New York: Vintage, 1974.

Shechtman, Joseph B., "The Transnistria Reservation," *YIVO Annual of Jewish Social Science*, 8 (1953): 178–96.

Shepherd, Naomi, *A Refuge from Darkness: Wilfrid Israel and the Rescue of the Jews*, New York: Pantheon, 1984.

Sherman, A.J., *Island Refuge: Britain and Refugees from the Third Reich*,

1933–1939, London: Paul Elek, 1973.

Shulman, Abraham, *The Case of the Hotel Polski*, New York: Holocaust Library, 1982.

Siegel, Aranka, *Grace in the Wilderness: After the Liberation, 1945–1948*, New York: Farrar, Straus and Giroux, 1985.

Siegel, Aranka, *Upon the Head of the Goat: A Childhood in Hungary, 1939–1944*, London: Dent, 1982.

Sosnowski, Kiryl, *The Tragedy of Children Under Nazi Rule*, Poznań: Western Press Agency, 1962.

Spiegelman, Art, *Maus: A Survivor's Tale*, New York: Pantheon, 1986.

Spiritual Resistance: Art from Concentration Camps, 1940–1945, New York: Union of American Hebrew Congregations, 1978.

Starkopf, Adam, *There Is Always Time to Die*, New York: Holocaust Library, 1981.

Steckel, Charles W., *Destruction and Survival*, Los Angeles: Delmar Publishing Company, 1973.

Stein, André, *Quiet Heroes: True Stories of the Rescue of Jews by Christians in Nazi-Occupied Holland*, Toronto: Lester & Orpen Dennys, 1988.

Steinberg, Lucien, *Le Comité de défense des juifs en Belgique, 1942– 1944*, Bruxelles: Éditions de l'Université de Bruxelles, 1973.

Steinberg, Lucien, *La révolte des justes: Les juifs contre Hitler, 1933–1945*, Paris: Fayard, 1970. English edition: *The Jews against Hitler (Not as a Lamb)*, New York: Gordon & Cremonesi, 1974.

Steiner, Jean-François, *Treblinka*, Paris: Fayard, 1966. English edition: *Treblinka*, New York: New American Library, 1979.

Steiner-Aviezer, Miriam, *The Soldier with the Golden Buttons*, Jerusalem: Yad Vashem, 1987.

Stern, J.P., *Hitler: The Führer and the People*, Glasgow: Fontana, 1975.

Stiffel, Frank, *The Tale of the Ring: A Kaddish*, New York: Pushcart Press, 1984.

Struggle, Death, Memory, 1939–1945, Council for the Preservation of the Monuments of Struggle and Martyrdom, 1963.

Suhl, Yuri, ed., *They Fought Back: The Story of Jewish Resistance in Nazi Europe*, New York: Crown, 1967.

Sutzkever, Abraham, *Burnt Pearls: Ghetto Poems*, Ontario: Mosaic Press/Valley Editions, 1981.

Syrkin, Marie, *Blessed Is the Match: The Story of Jewish Resistance*, London: Gollancz, 1948.

Szajkowski, Zosa, *Analytical Franco-Jewish Gazetteer, 1939–1945*, New York: S. Frydman, 1966.

Taylor, Fred, ed., *The Göbbels Diaries, 1939–1941*, New York: Penguin, 1982.

Tec, Nechama, *Dry Tears*, New York: Oxford University Press, 1984.

Tec, Nechama, *When Light Pierced the Darkness: Christian Rescue of Jews in Nazi-Occupied Poland*, New York: Oxford University Press, 1986.

Thalmann, Rita and Feinermann, Emmanuel, *La nuit de cristal: 9–10 Novembre 1938*, Paris: Laffont, 1972. English edition: *Crystal Night*, New York: Holocaust Library, 1972.

Torday, Ursula (psn. Blackstock, Charity), *Wednesday's Children*, London: Hutchinson, 1966.

Tory, Avraham, *Surviving the Holocaust: The Kovno Ghetto Diary*, Cambridge, MA: Harvard University Press, 1990.

Travers, Pamela L., *I Go by Sea, I Go by Land*, New York: Norton, 1964.

Trees, W. and van Soeren, R., *Nederland Bevrijd: Van Limburg tot de Lauwerszee*, Utrecht: Kadmos, 1985.

Trunk, Isiah, "Epidemics and Mortality in the Warsaw Ghetto, 1939–1942," *YIVO Annual of Jewish Social Science*, 8 (1953): 82–122.

Trunk, Isiah, *Jewish Responses to Nazi Persecution: Collective and Individual Behavior in Extremis*, New York: Stein and Day, 1979.

Trunk, Isiah, *Judenrat: The Jewish Councils in Eastern Europe under Nazi Occupation*, New York: Macmillan, 1972.

Trunk, Isiah, "Religious, Educational and Cultural Problems in the Eastern European Ghettos under German Occupation," *YIVO Annual of Jewish Social Science*, 14 (1969).

Tuteur, Werner, "One Hundred Concentration Camp Survivors Twenty Years Later," *The Israel Annals of Psychiatry and Related Disciplines*, 4, no.1 (Spring 1966): 78–90.

Uris, Leon, *Mila 18*, New York: Bantam, 1968.

Vago, Bela and Mosse, George L., eds., *Jews and Non-Jews in Eastern Europe 1918–1945*, New York: John Wiley, 1974.

Van Lieshout, Jan, Two series of articles in the *Limburgs Dagblad* in May 1977: "Het grote gezin van 'Tante Hanna' en 'Oom Nico'" (4 May); "Het verraad van Tienray" (5 May); "Duitser verleid: Hanna bevrijd" (6 May); "Rietje het vergeet – mij – nietje" (10 May); and "Joop Woortman: 'Breng ze maar naar Limburg'" (25 May); "De ongehuwde vaders en moeders van Brunssum" (26 May); "Elke dreumes was een drama" (27 May); "De vliegende non van het pompstation" (28 May).

Van Ommeren, Anita and Scherphuis, Ageeth, "De crèche, 1942–1943," *Vrij Nederland*, 18 January 1986, pp.2–21.

Van Ommeren, Anita and Scherphuis, Ageeth, "De onderduikers in de Haarlemmermeer," *Vrij Nederland*, 16 March 1985, pp.2–25.

Van Pelt, Robert Jan, "After the Walls Have Fallen Down," *Queen's Quarterly*, 96 (Autumn 1989): 641–60.

Van Pelt, Robert Jan, and Westfall, Carroll William, *Architectural Principles in the Age of Historicism*, New Haven: Yale University Press, 1991.

Van Stam, Cor, *Wacht binnen de dijken: Verzet in en om de Haarlemmermeer*, Haarlem: Uitgeverij de Toorts, 1986.

Vegh, Claudine, *Je ne lui ai pas dit au revoir*, Paris: Gallimard, 1979. English edition: *I Didn't Say Goodbye*, London: Caliban Books, 1979.

Von Staden, Wendelgard, *Darkness Over the Valley*, New York: Penguin, 1982.

Waagenaar, Sam, *The Pope's Jews*, London: Alcove Press, 1974.

Warhaftig, Zorach, *Uprooted: Jewish Refugees and Displaced Persons after Liberation*, New York: Institute of Jewish Affairs of the American Jewish Congress, 1946.

Washington Post, *The Obligation to Remember*, Washington, DC: Washington Post, 1983.

Wasserstein, Bernard, *Britain and the Jews of Europe, 1939–1945*, Oxford: Clarendon Press, 1979.

Wdowinski, David, *And We Are Not Saved*, New York: Philosophical Library, 1963.

Weill, Joseph, *Contribution a l'histoire des camps d'internement dans l'Anti-France*, Paris: Éditions du Centre, 1946.

Weinberg, David H., *A Community on Trial: The Jews of Paris in the 1930s*, Chicago: University of Chicago Press, 1977.

Weinberg, Joseph, *Une larme, une prière*, Paris: Éditions Actualites, 1985.

Weinberg, Joseph, *Les morts ne versent pas de larmes . . .*, Paris: Sedimo, 1964.

Weinberg, Joseph, *Le printemps des cendres*, Paris: Sedimo, 1966.

Weinberg, Werner, "A Dutch Couple," *The Christian Century*, June 22–29, 1983, pp.611–15.

Weinstein, Frida Scheps, *J'habitais rue des Jardins Saint-Paul*, Paris: Balland, 1983. English edition: *A Hidden Childhood*, New York: Hill and Wang, 1986.

Weinzierl, Erika, *Zu wenig Gerechte: Österreicher und Judenverfolgung, 1938–1945*, Graz: Verlag Styria, 1986.

Wellers, Georges, *De Drancy à Auschwitz*, Paris: Éditions du Centre, 1946.

Wellers, Georges, *L'étoile jaune à l'heure de Vichy: De Drancy à Auschwitz*, Paris: Fayard, 1973. A great deal of Wellers's earlier work, *De Drancy à Auschwitz*, has been repeated here in part three, chapter four: "Le camp de Drancy."

Wells, Leon Weliczker, *The Death Brigade*, New York: Holocaust Library, 1978.

Werbell, Frederick E. and Clarke, Thurston, *Lost Hero: The Mystery of Raoul Wallenberg*, New York: McGraw-Hill, 1982.

Wiesel, Elie, *The Night Trilogy*, New York: Hill and Wang, 1985.

Wiesenthal, Simon, *Max and Helen*, New York: Morrow, 1982.

Wiesenthal, Simon, *The Sunflower*, New York: Schocken Books, 1976.

Wijsmuller-Meijer, Truus, *Geen tijd voor tranen*, Amsterdam: Salamander, 1963.

Willenberg, Samuel, *Surviving Treblinka*, Oxford: Basil Blackwell, 1989.

Winnik, H.Z., "Contribution to Symposium on Psychic Traumatization through Social Catatrophe," *International Journal of Psycho-Analysis*, 49 (1968): 298–301.

Wolf, Christa, *Patterns of Childhood*, New York: Farrar, Straus and Giroux, 1984.

Wolf, Jacqueline, *"Take Care of Josette"*: *A Memoir in Defense of Occupied France*, New York: Franklin Watts, 1981.

Wright, Gordon, *The Ordeal of Total War, 1933–1945*, New York: Harper and Row, 1968.

Wyman, David S., *The Abandonment of the Jews: America and the Holocaust, 1941–1945*, New York: Pantheon, 1984.

Yad Vashem Bulletin: The entire run of the *Yad Vashem Bulletin* (which is published in Jerusalem by the Yad Vashem Martyrs' and Heroes' Remembrance Authority) is extremely useful as it covers a spectrum of articles relevant to the subject.

Yahil, Leni, *The Rescue of Danish Jewry: Test of a Democracy*, Philadelphia: Jewish Publication Society of America, 1969.

Young, James E., *Writing and Rewriting the Holocaust: Narrative and the Consequences of Interpretation*, Bloomington: Indiana University Press, 1988.

Youth Amidst the Ruins: A Chronicle of Jewish Youth in the War, Hashomer Hatzair Organization, New York: Scopus Publishing Company, 1941.

Zeitoun, Sabine, *Ces enfants qu'il fallait sauver*, Paris: Albin Michel, 1989.

Ziemian, Joseph, *The Cigarette Sellers of Three Crosses Square*, New York: Avon, 1975.

Zinberg, Alizah, Martin, Barbara and Kohn, Roger, *An Inventory to the Rescue Children, Inc. Collection, 1946–1985*, New York: Yeshiva University Archives, 1986.

Zuccotti, Susan, *The Italians and the Holocaust: Persecution, Rescue, Survival*, New York: Basic Books, 1987.

Zyskind, Sara, *Stolen Years*, New York: New American Library, 1983.

Glossary

Älteste	Elder or chairman
Ältestenrat	German-imposed council of Elders or Jewish council
Aktion	a liquidation operation
Appell/Zahlappell	roll call
Arbeitsdienst	forced labor detail
Assistante-chef	assistant head
Aussiedlung	evacuation
Betreuerinnen/Betreueren	child care workers, female/male
Blockältester	head prisoner of a concentration camp block
Camps d'internement/ camps de concentration	internment camps/concentration camps
Challah	traditional braided or twisted white bread
Chanukkah	Festival of Lights; a holiday to celebrate the victory of Judah Maccabee and his resistance fighters over Syrian forces in 186 BCE.
Circuit	circle
Crèche	day nursery
Gendarme	police
Goy	gentile
Gymnasium	university track secondary school
Hasid	(see *Khosed*)
Interne volontaire	volunteer resident
Jüdenrat/Joodsche Raad	German-imposed Jewish council (German/Dutch)
Khosed	adherent of a Jewish religious movement founded in eighteenth century eastern Europe; the followers are members of groups devoted to particular rabbis; in general, extreme orthodoxy,

	pious devotion; and ecstasy are stressed more than learning
Khumesh (*Khumeshim*, pl.)	the five books of Moses, or Pentateuch
Kosher/Kashruth	traditional Jewish dietary laws
Lager	camp
Maisons d'enfants	children's homes
Makhezer (*Makhzoyrim*, pl.)	holiday prayer book
Maquis	guerrilla resistance
Marranos	name used in medieval Spain for Christianized Jews who practiced Judaism clandestinely
Mikve	ritual purification bath
Minyan	quorum of ten required to hold public prayers
Mishpokhe	extended family
Oneg Shabbat	celebration of the beginning of the Sabbath
Passover/Pesach	holiday celebrating the liberation of ancient Hebrews from Egyptian bondage
Peyes	earlocks
Rafle	round-up or dragnet operation
Razzia	round-up or raid
Reseau	network
Rosh Hashanah	Jewish New Year
Schutzpass	safepass
Seder	ritual meal and home service of the first two nights of Passover
Sefer Torah	Torah scroll
Shabbat	the Sabbath, which begins on Friday evening and ends on Saturday evening
Shaytel	wig worn by traditional Jewish women
Shlep	to haul or drag
Shmuezing	chatting
Shoah	annihilation, total devastation or ruin
Shtetl	village or small town
Shul	synagogue
Sidur (*Sidurim*, pl.)	daily prayer book for private and congregational use
Sperre	blockade and curfew imposed to facilitate actions or *razzias*
Torah	five Books of Moses
Tsores	troubles, problems
Übersiedlung	resettlement
Yiddish	common language of Ashkenazi Jews before World War II
Yom Kippur	Day of Atonement
Zahlappell/Appell	roll call

Europe 1942: Index

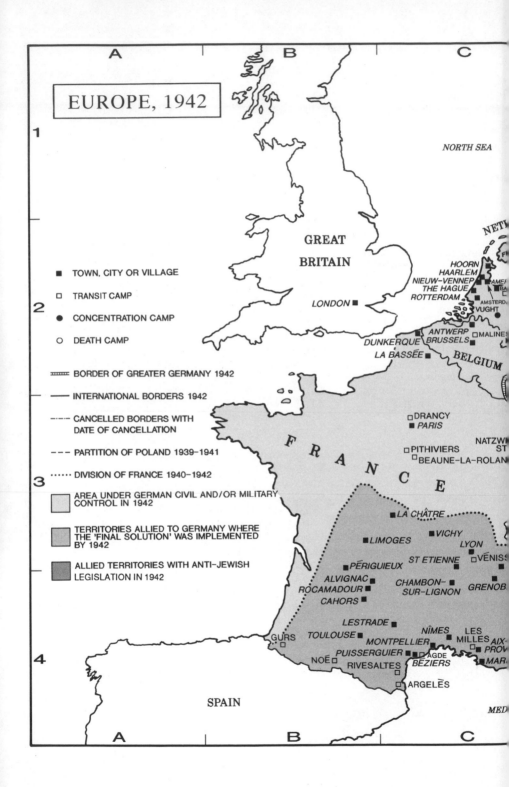

EUROPE, 1942

TOWN, CITY OR VILLAGE ■

TRANSIT CAMP □

CONCENTRATION CAMP ●

DEATH CAMP ○

▨▨▨ BORDER OF GREATER GERMANY 1942

—— INTERNATIONAL BORDERS 1942

----- CANCELLED BORDERS WITH
DATE OF CANCELLATION

- - - PARTITION OF POLAND 1939–1941

······ DIVISION OF FRANCE 1940–1942

AREA UNDER GERMAN CIVIL AND/OR MILITARY
CONTROL IN 1942

TERRITORIES ALLIED TO GERMANY WHERE
THE 'FINAL SOLUTION' WAS IMPLEMENTED
BY 1942

ALLIED TERRITORIES WITH ANTI-JEWISH
LEGISLATION IN 1942

NORTH SEA

GREAT
BRITAIN

LONDON ■

NET

HOORN
HAARLEM
NIEUW-VENNEP
THE HAGUE
ROTTERDAM
VUGHT
AMSTERD
BA
AMER
F

ANTWERP
DUNKERQUE BRUSSELS ■ ☐ MALINE
LA BASSÉE ■ BELGIUM

F R A N C E

☐ DRANCY
■ PARIS

☐ PITHIVIERS
☐ BEAUNE-LA-ROLAN

NATZW
ST

■ LA CHÂTRE ············

■ VICHY
LYON
■ LIMOGES

ST ETIENNE ☐ VÉNISS

■ PÉRIGUIEUX CHAMBON-
ALVIGNAC ■ SUR-LIGNON GRENOB
ROCAMADOUR ■
CAHORS ■

LESTRADE ■

NÎMES LES
TOULOUSE ■ MILLES
MONTPELLIER ■ ■ AIX-
GURS PUISSERGUIER ■ ■ PROV
☐ NOÉ ☐ ☐ AGDE MAR
RIVESALTES BÉZIERS
☐ ARGELÈS

SPAIN

MED

Index

The names of child survivors are entered in the index as they were at the time; girls who subsequently married are thus indexed under their maiden names. So, for example, the woman born Hanna Sztarkman, later Starkman, now Hannah Kent, is indexed as "Sztarkman, Hanna (Hannah Starkman) Kent-".